Slavery, the Civil Law, and the Supreme Court of Louisiana

Judith Kelleher Schafer

Slavery, the Civil Law, and the Supreme Court of Louisiana

Louisiana State University Press
Baton Rouge and London

Manufactured in the United States of America
Louisiana Paperback Edition, 1997
06 05 04 03 02 01 00 99 98 97 5 4 3 2 1

Designer: Laura Roubique Gleason
Typeface: Bembo
Typesetter: G&S Typesetters, Inc.
Printer and binder: Thomson–Shore, Inc.

Library of Congress Cataloging-in-Publication Data

Schafer, Judith Kelleher, 1942–
Slavery, the civil law, and the Supreme Court of Louisiana / Judith Kelleher Schafer.
p. cm.
Includes bibliographical references and index.
ISBN 0-8071-1845-1 (cloth) ISBN 0-8071-2165-7 (pbk.)
1. Slavery—Law and legislation—Louisiana—History—19th century. 2. Louisiana. Supreme Court—History—19th century. I. Title.
KFL401.6.S55S33 1994
342.763'087—dc20
[347.630287] 94-11801
CIP

The paper in this book meets the guidelines for permanence and durability of the Committee on Production Guidelines for Book Longevity of the Council on Library Resources. ♾

For Tim

CONTENTS

ILLUSTRATIONS

Maps

Other illustrations

PREFACE

SLAVES IN ANTEBELLUM LOUISIANA HAD SEVERELY CIRcumscribed legal rights. They could appear in court as plaintiffs only to claim their freedom; they appeared as defendants only if accused of a crime. Occasionally they could testify for or against a fellow slave, but never against a white or a free black. However, these limitations did not prevent slaves from being involved in thousands of lawsuits at the parish or district level and approximately 1,200 appeals to the Supreme Court of Louisiana. In the overwhelming majority of these actions the slave was neither the plaintiff nor the defendant, but the *object,* primary or incidental, of the lawsuit.

In antebellum Louisiana lawsuits began at the parish (county) or district level, determined mainly by geographical location. In rural areas the parish courthouse could be more than a hundred miles away from a litigant's residence, and a district court even further. Although the legislature created new parishes and districts (and new courts to serve them) as the population grew, the need for them often existed for some time before the legislature acted. New Orleans, however, had both a parish (in modern terms, small-claims) court and a district court; by the end of the antebellum period, rural parishes also had both parish and district courts. To qualify for a hearing in a district court, a lawsuit had to involve more than fifty dollars.[1]

Any party in a lawsuit who was unhappy with a parish or district court judgment could appeal to the state's supreme court, which was

1. Benjamin Wall Dart, ed., *Constitutions of the State of Louisiana and Selected Federal Laws* (Indianapolis, 1932), Art IV, Secs. 1–12, p. 503; Tit. IV, Arts. 62–83, pp. 513–15; Tit. IV, Arts. 61–84, pp. 528–30.

obliged to hear the case, no matter how many similar cases it had previously decided or how frivolous the appeal appeared. The modern United States Supreme Court and the highest courts in most states can, in effect, rule on a case by refusing to hear it, and thus the judgment of the lower court becomes final. The antebellum Supreme Court of Louisiana enjoyed no right of refusal. The only state constitutional requirement for an appeal to be heard by the state's highest court was that it must involve more than $300. The Constitution of 1845 expanded the court's jurisdiction to include criminal appeals of felony convictions whenever the sentence of the lower court was death or hard labor.[2] Since the supreme court lacked the right of refusal, cases before it were not exclusively landmark cases, but were somewhat more representative of typical parish and district court cases. However, the delay caused by the appeal process (often as much as two or three years), the financial requirement, increased attorney's fees, and court costs probably often restricted litigants to the wealthy. Also, since travel in antebellum Louisiana was difficult, costly, and time-consuming, the majority of state supreme court cases originated in New Orleans, not just because it was the center of the state's population, but because the court was convenient to more people; more attorneys lived in the city than in rural areas. Each year the court met at New Orleans from January through July. Ordinarily the court recessed for August and spent September and October in Louisiana towns such as Opelousas, Baton Rouge, Monroe, Alexandria, or Shreveport before returning to New Orleans for November and December terms.

This book is about slave law in Louisiana from the time of the Louisiana Purchase in 1803 to the adjournment of the Supreme Court of Louisiana on April 25, 1862, when Mayor John T. Monroe surrendered the city of New Orleans to a Federal flotilla.[3] It is not a social history of Louisiana slaves and their owners, although the legal sources teach us much about both. Its chief focus is on the decisions of the Supreme Court of Louisiana in some 1,200 appeals that involved slaves who happened to be plaintiffs, defendants, or objects of lawsuits or criminal actions in the only mixed jurisdiction in the United States.

2. *Ibid.*, Art. IV, Sec. 2, p. 503; Tit. IV, Art. 63, p. 514; Tit. IV, Art. 62, p. 528.

3. The late Joe Gray Taylor's *Negro Slavery in Louisiana* (Baton Rouge, 1963) is still the classic work on bondage in the Pelican State, but Taylor worked largely without legal sources because at the time they were inaccessible to scholars.

In exploring these cases and the opinions of the judges and justices,[4] the book outlines central tendencies in the law of slavery in Louisiana as it evolved from the territorial period to the Civil War. Slave law encompassed much more than the often-studied cases involving emancipation and slave crimes. Several other categories of slave law existed, including property, successions (estates), interstate commerce, insolvency, contracts, and torts. To understand these categories the historian must confront a complex variety of questions that also faced the judges and justices of the Supreme Court of Louisiana. Civil law changed through repeated exposure to common-law concepts after Louisiana joined the federal union and prospered under its rule. At the same time, the increasingly explosive issue of slavery rose to dominance on the stage of national politics. Did the workings of the civil law in Louisiana mean that the nature of slavery in the state differed substantially from elsewhere in the South? How did the law of slavery in Louisiana change through repeated exposure to common-law concepts? What were the implications of this development for slavery in the state and beyond? Finally, how did the presence of slavery operate to "Americanize" Louisiana law?

For several decades scholars have questioned whether slavery in Latin America was a milder form of bondage than in the American South. Some have contended that the Catholic church and Spanish law mitigated the harshness of slavery in Central and South America. Others have attacked that view, holding that the system of bondage, particularly on the sugar islands of the Caribbean, was especially brutal.[5] The debate, which is far from over, may be rooted in a tendency to judge the condition of slavery in any given locale simply by studying the law

4. The Constitution of 1812 designated those serving on the Supreme Court of Louisiana as "judges." In the Constitution of 1845 and subsequent Louisiana constitutions, they were called "justices." Benjamin Wall Dart, ed., *Constitution of the State of Louisiana,* Art. IV, Sec. 3, p. 503; Tit. IV, Art. 64, p. 514; Tit. IV, Art. 63, p. 528.

5. For a sampling of the debate over slavery in Latin America and the American South, see Frank Tannenbaum, *Slave and Citizen: The Negro in the Americas* (New York, 1946); Stanley M. Elkins, *Slavery: A Problem in American Institutional and Intellectual Life* (Chicago, 1959); David Brion Davis, *The Problem of Slavery in Western Culture* (Ithaca, N.Y., 1966); Herbert S. Klein, *Slavery in the Americas: A Comparative Study of Virginia and Cuba* (Chicago, 1967); Laura Foner and Eugene D. Genovese, eds., *Slavery in the New World: A Reader in Comparative History* (Englewood Cliffs, N.J., 1969); and Ann J. Lane, *The Debate over Slavery: Stanley Elkins and His Critics* (Urbana, Ill., 1971). For a more recent view, see Alan Watson, *Slave Law in the Americas* (Athens, Ga., 1989).

of slavery. Can the actual circumstances of slave life anywhere be discerned solely by a study of the law, divorced from the day-to-day operations of the society and without considering variations in treatment by individual owners? And how does one take into account the difference between what was written into law and the actual physical treatment of slaves?

The goal of this book is not to consider whether slavery was harsher or milder in Louisiana than in her sister states of the South, but to examine the operation of Louisiana law on slavery as seen in decisions of the Supreme Court of Louisiana and, conversely, to discover the effect of the institution of slavery on the development, and in some instances the "Americanization," of Louisiana law. It is my belief that in some aspects, such as in the law of slave crimes, slave law in Louisiana was harsher than its counterparts elsewhere; in other ways, such as in laws concerning emancipation, it was milder: in allowing slaves to purchase themselves and to sue directly in court for their freedom, Louisiana law placed more value on the humanity of slaves rather than on their status as property. Most often, however, Louisiana slave law was simply *different*.

When Louisiana became an American possession, Spanish civil law remained in force, and the Spanish legal heritage persisted in the early territorial period in slave law, as well as other areas of the legal culture. As a result, it was easier to emancipate a slave in Louisiana during the first four decades of the nineteenth century than in any other southern slave state. Yet while Louisiana slave law in this early period was in some ways unique among slave states, in other aspects its law closely resembled that of its neighbors. A continuous influx of American influence, intensified by the immigration to Louisiana of scores of attorneys trained in the common law, as well as the growing national controversy over the "peculiar institution," caused Louisiana slave law to be steadily "Americanized" to the extent that by the eve of the Civil War, slave law in Louisiana closely resembled the law of slavery in the other states that would soon leave the federal union. Americanization, however, was not a straight-line process. In several unique and fundamental areas of Louisiana law, change came slowly, if at all.

Studying change over time demands both a knowledge of what happened and an understanding of why and how change occurred. Because Louisiana did not have a tradition of English culture and laws, and because the state's legal heritage was distinctly foreign to the other states of the nation, it is important to understand the state's unique colonial heritage as well as the continuation of the civil law into the territorial period and beyond.

Finally, a word about the source materials. This study is based on the manuscript records of the Supreme Court of Louisiana, which are housed in Account No. 106 in the Earl K. Long Library of the University of New Orleans. Although scholars have had access to the printed reports of the decisions of the court, the original handwritten decisions only recently became available; this is the first book-length study of these incredibly rich and valuable records. The printed reports usually contain a brief and often sparse recitation of the facts of the case, the decision of the court, and the legal reasoning on which the court based its ruling. The handwritten case files ordinarily provide copies of the lower-court case, including attorneys' arguments, depositions, written interrogatories, and the clerk's summary of the testimony. Thus the typical handwritten case record runs between fifty and one hundred pages in length and offers a wealth of detail only suggested by the brief printed report of the case. When separated from the main corpus of case files of the Supreme Court of Louisiana, the materials used for this study occupied more than twenty-five linear feet of archival shelf space. To my knowledge, no one has ever done a study of slave law in any state in the American South using a body of original case records containing judicial decisions that span the entire antebellum period. Considering Louisiana's unique cultural and legal heritage, it is remarkable that no book-length study of the state's law of slavery exists.

Before these records became available to scholars, students of slave law in Louisiana had only legal indexes, such as the *Louisiana Digest,* and Helen T. Catterall's *Judicial Cases Concerning American Slavery and the Negro* to guide them to judicial decisions involving slavery.[6] The index in the *Louisiana Digest* is based on the published reports of cases and is far from complete; Catterall, too, was forced to rely on the reported cases, as she did not have access to the original manuscripts of the court.

6. *Louisiana Digest: 1809 to Date* (St. Paul, Minn., 1959); *Reports of Cases Argued and Determined in the Supreme Court of Louisiana and the Superior Court of the Territory of Orleans* (St. Paul, Minn., 1913); Helen T. Catterall, *Judicial Cases Concerning American Slavery and the Negro* (1926; rpr. New York, 1968).

Furthermore, there are a number of appeals involving slavery that were never reported and are therefore only available in manuscript form. These unreported cases are invisible in Catterall's work and in all law indexes. For this study, attempting to locate every existing case meant going through the entire body of manuscripts box by box. Moreover, neither Catterall's *Judicial Cases* nor the printed reports contain the docket numbers of the individual cases, and the manuscript records are only accessible by docket number. This necessitated searching the *Minute Books,* each of which was the clerk's handwritten account of the daily activities of the Supreme Court, for the docket number for each individual case. Finding the corresponding numbers was a tedious and time-consuming process. It is my hope that future researchers will find the list of cases in the Bibliography of this book a valuable aid.

ACKNOWLEDGMENTS

I HAVE BEEN FORTUNATE, BOTH PROFESSIONALLY AND personally, in having a number of colleagues, friends, and family members who have made this book a reality. I owe a tremendous debt to my mentor and friend, the late Hugh Franklin "Big Daddy" Rankin, who convinced me that I should become a historian. His good advice and steadfast faith in my ability continue to sustain and inspire me. I have also enjoyed my association with his wife, Betty Bursley Rankin, an expert on New Orleans jazz and my favorite disc jockey.

Bennett H. Wall has read the manuscript at least twice and has offered sage advice, wisdom, conviviality, and gentle but frequent threats to make use of a cattle prod to "persuade" me to finish. This book and my life have been enhanced by my friendship with him and his wife, Neva. I am thankful to them both.

The late Joe Gray Taylor, whose book *Negro Slavery in Louisiana* is still the classic work on the subject, was as generous with his offer to read and critique my work at an early stage as he was with his acerbic wit and his sarcastic sense of humor. I could barely read the pages he returned for the sea of red ink that overflowed the margins into the text. I am greatly indebted to him and his wife, Helen.

Paul Finkelman has read the manuscript at least three mind-numbing times, at least two more than professional responsibility or friendship required. He has encouraged me and rescued me from a number of egregious and embarrassing errors. I owe him a great debt of gratitude.

Richard H. Kilbourne, Jr., also read the entire manuscript and provided a great wealth of expertise on Louisiana law. I am thankful for his advice and observations.

The Murphy Institute of Political Economy at Tulane University has provided support for the last seven years, including the computer on which I completed the final draft and a generous subvention in support of publication. The Institute's director, Richard F. Teichgraeber III, has repeatedly taken time from his own study of slavery to give encouragement and advice. I am very much in his debt. His support of my professional activities since 1985 is very much appreciated and valued.

I am also grateful to the dean of the Tulane University School of Law, John R. Kramer, for his support, and to the faculty of the law school, especially Lloyd Bonfield, Harvey Couch, Raymond Diamond, Shael Herman, Cynthia Samuel, and George Strickler.

My good friend and colleague Edward F. Haas, Jr., suggested the topic, and Harold Hyman contributed the title. I am grateful to them both. I am also thankful to a number of historians who have read all or part of the manuscript in various stages: Warren Billings, John Boles, Catherine Clinton, Tony Freyer, Eugene Genovese, Perry Jamieson, Gary Mills, Lawrence Powell, Jonathan Prichett, Jim Viator, and William Wiecek. None of the persons mentioned are in any way responsible for my shortcomings and errors. Sometimes I was too stubborn to listen to them.

No researcher could have had a more extraordinary archivist than Marie E. Windell. She organized and indexed the antebellum records of the Supreme Court of Louisiana and is responsible for securing funding to have this priceless collection microfilmed. Her enthusiasm and meticulous attention to my research needs made the project seem less daunting. And she never let me know that when I believed that I had looked at most of the case records, hundreds remained.

David A. Combe, librarian of the Tulane Law School, generously loaned me a set of the *Louisiana Reports* and a copy of the Louisiana *Civil Code of 1825,* saving me dozens of trips across campus to check references. The staff of the law library, especially Kevin Hourihan, have also been extremely patient with my requests to locate little-used and mostly forgotten materials.

I also wish to thank Carol Billings of the law library of the Supreme Court of Louisiana, Jon Kukla of the Historic New Orleans Collection, and Marie Windell for their assistance in gathering illustrations.

I am grateful to two editors and one faculty adviser who gave permission to reprint portions of articles that appeared in their journals: to Glenn R. Conrad of the Center for Louisiana Studies at the University of Southwestern Louisiana and editor of *Louisiana History* for "'Open and Notorious Concubinage': The Emancipation of Slave Mistresses by Will and the Supreme Court in Antebellum Louisiana," *Louisiana History,* XXVIII (Spring, 1987), 165–82; to Diane Maleson of Temple University Law School and editor of the *American Journal of Legal History* for "'Guaranteed Against the Vices and Maladies Prescribed by Law': Consumer Protection, the Law of Slave Sales, and the Supreme Court in Antebellum Louisiana," *American Journal of Legal History,* XXXI (October, 1987), 305–21; and to Shael Herman of Tulane Law School, faculty adviser for the *Tulane Law Review,* for "The Long Arm of the Law: Slave Criminals and the Supreme Court in Antebellum Louisiana," *Tulane Law Review,* LX (June, 1986), 1247–68.

Mildred Covert expertly typed the original manuscript, and Carroll S. Zehner word processed a later version. Ruth A. Carter's expertise in computers and keen editorial eye not only have been invaluable, but have saved me from several embarrassing lapses.

And finally, I am grateful to Margaret Fisher Dalrymple of Louisiana State University Press for her encouragement and faith in my work, and to Gerry Anders, an expert and tactful copy editor.

Without the support of my family, this book would not be. Special thanks to my daughter, Ashley E. Schafer; my son, T. Gregory Schafer; and my son-in-law, John T. Suttles, Jr., who joined our family in 1989. Ashley, Greg, and John believed this book would be published, and for their faith I will always be appreciative. My mother, Beryl Kelleher De Gruy, and my brother, Cody A. Kelleher, have also provided much needed encouragement, as has the memory of my late father, Robert Cody Kelleher, M.D. My friendship with Fr. Terry Davis has been invaluable to me. My dear friend Margaret S. Kessels has been a mainstay throughout the last thirty years.

And finally, my deepest gratitude and most heartfelt thanks go to Timothy G. Schafer for all of the reasons he knows best. This book is for him.

Slavery, the Civil Law, and the Supreme Court of Louisiana

1

"SLAVES ARE REGARDED AS PERSONS AND PROPERTY"

Sources of Slave Law in American Louisiana

SLAVES FIRST ARRIVED IN FRENCH COLONIAL LOUISIANA in 1719, not far ahead of the first comprehensive code of laws to govern them. The 1724 Louisiana *Code Noir* had as its prototype a 1685 edict promulgated to establish an orderly system of slave labor and race relations for French possessions in the Caribbean. This first law of slavery in Louisiana established the Roman Catholic church in Louisiana, ordered the expulsion of Jews, and provided that slaves should be instructed in the Catholic faith and married under its laws. It also specified minimum food and clothing allowances and granted neglected slaves the right to complain to the public prosecutor should their maintenance be substandard. The code forbade the sale of young children separately from their mothers. Slaves were not to labor on Sunday, and those who were baptized had the privilege of burial in consecrated ground. Marriages between slaves were valid and binding under the law if the owners of both slaves consented. The French colonial slave's status was also shaped by what was forbidden: slaves could not own property through their labor or from inheritance; they could not hold office or be parties in a contract or litigants in court. In no case could slaves testify for or against whites, nor could they testify for or against any free person of color except in a case in which the charge against the free black was attempting to incite a slave insurrection. Restrictions existed for whites too: they could not marry or live in concubinage with mulattoes or blacks, whether slave or free, under penalty of a fine or loss of the slave involved. Under the 1724 Louisiana *Code Noir* only masters or mistresses over twenty-five years of age could emancipate a slave. The code required that such a slaveholder gain permission of the Conseil Supérieur (the governing body of the colony). Moreover, a slave's manumission demanded a legitimate reason, such as having saved the life of the owner; it was not to be done out of simple generosity.[1]

Several provisions of the Louisiana *Code Noir* of 1724 originated from the Roman law of slavery, particularly the legal disqualifications of slaves as witnesses, arbitrators, litigants, and parties in a contract. Under Roman law slaves had almost no civil rights. Roman law heavily influenced French law, but the French borrowings from the Roman law of slavery are unique in their selection of those aspects that were often detrimental to slaves. Unlike slaves under Roman law, those in French colonial Louisiana were unable to petition to be sold away from a cruel master or mistress, were unable to claim the right of self-purchase (practiced often in the Roman Empire), and could not be manumitted without permission of the government. Slaveholders were also unable to free their slaves by testamentary action.[2]

Louisiana became a Spanish possession in 1763, and gradually the law of Spain became established in the colony. Although Spanish slave law was also rooted in Roman law, the effect of the Roman heritage on Spanish law was much more beneficial to the slave. *Las Siete Partidas,* a digest of preexisting Spanish law, exhibited strong Roman influences. Both Roman law and Spanish law held that slavery was contrary to natural law and reason. The *Partidas* directed the judicial sale of slaves who proved cruel treatment by their owners. Under the *Partidas* slaveholders could manumit their slaves without government permission and without proof of meritorious acts. Most significantly, slaves under Spanish law had the right of self-purchase, or *coartación.* This important right enabled slaves to petition to have themselves appraised and to purchase

1. Taylor, *Negro Slavery in Louisiana,* 3, 17; Hans W. Baade, "The Law of Slavery in Spanish Luisiana, 1769–1803," in *Louisiana's Legal Heritage,* ed. Edward F. Haas, Jr. (Pensacola, Fla., 1983), 48–50; *Collection of Regulations, Edicts, Declarations, and Decrees Concerning the Commerce, Administration of Justice, and the Policy of the French Colonies of America* (Paris, 1765), hereinafter cited as *Code Noir;* "An Act to Amend the Act Entitled the 'Black Code' . . ." Act of March 19, 1816, *Louisiana Acts, 1816,* Secs. 1–2, p. 146.

2. W. W. Buckland, *The Roman Law of Slavery: The Condition of the Slave in Private Law from Augustus to Justinian* (Cambridge, Eng., 1908), 82–87. Alan Watson argues that ancient Rome was essentially not a racist society, which resulted in some of the less detrimental aspects of Roman slave law. He contends that the American South preferred to ignore the milder aspects of Roman slave law because slavery in the South was a racist system. Alan Watson, *Roman Slave Law* (Baltimore, 1987), xviii–xix; Baade, "Law of Slavery in Spanish Luisiana," in *Louisiana's Legal Heritage,* ed. Haas, 50.

themselves from even unwilling masters or mistresses at their judicially appraised market value. One effect of *coartación* was to give slaves working for their freedom an interest in the system, making them unlikely to participate in insurrectionary plots and motivating them to be industrious laborers. A small but steady stream of judicial decisions recognized and enforced the right of *coartación* throughout the Spanish colonial period. In contrast, the French *Code Noir* specifically prohibited self-purchase on the ground that it encouraged slaves to steal in order to gain their purchase price.[3]

Spain transferred Louisiana back to France in 1801 in a secret treaty, but France did not publicly take possession of the colony until November 30, 1803. By that time Napoleon had sold Louisiana to the United States, and on December 20, 1803, Pierre Clément de Laussat, colonial prefect of the French Republic, surrendered the colony to the Americans. During the twenty days when Louisiana was again a French colony, Laussat had reenacted the *Code Noir* and ordered its strict enforcement. The handbill announcing the reenactment stated that the police regulation of slaves and free blacks was dangerously lax or actually nonexistent.[4]

Laussat's reenactment of the *Code Noir* has gone largely unnoticed by scholars, perhaps because Louisianians ignored the proclamation at the time. The practice of *coartación* continued, and slaveowners continued to emancipate slaves between 1803 and 1806. Approximately two hundred slaves gained their freedom by either self-purchase or manumission during these three years. These emancipations suggest that Louisianians, including the notaries who processed the legal papers granting freedom, believed Spanish slave law to continue to be in effect in the new American possession until repealed and replaced by the new American territorial government or the federal government of the United States. Indeed, in *Paul* v. *Succession of Carrière* (1806), the newly created Superior Court of the Territory of Orleans declared Spanish law, rather than

3. Baade, "Law of Slavery in Spanish Luisiana," in *Louisiana's Legal Heritage,* ed. Haas, 50–53, 72; Stephen Webre, "The Problem of Indian Slavery in Spanish Louisiana, 1769–1803," *Louisiana History,* XXV (Spring, 1984), 134–35; Thomas N. Ingersoll, "Free Blacks in a Slave Society: New Orleans, 1718–1812," *William and Mary Quarterly,* XLVIII (April, 1991), 182.

4. Baade, "Law of Slavery in Spanish Luisiana,," in *Louisiana's Legal Heritage,* ed. Haas, 70–74; Pierre Clément de Laussat, *Memoirs of My Life,* ed. Robert D. Bush, trans. Agnes-Josephine Pastwa (Baton Rouge, 1978), 78–90.

French law, to be the law of the territory unless it conflicted with American law. As it happened, the first elected territorial legislature under American rule would restore the basic elements of French slave law.[5]

The early period of American rule was a time of uncertainty and confusion over which system of law was in effect in the territory. In 1806 the first elected territorial legislature, which was firmly in the control of the Louisiana creole inhabitants, passed a law to retain most elements of the Spanish civil-law system. Thomas Jefferson had appointed William C. C. Claiborne, a Virginia-trained attorney, as the first territorial governor of Louisiana. Claiborne immediately vetoed the bill because he planned to establish American common law in Louisiana. His veto created such tensions between the creoles and their new government that Jefferson briefly considered sending an army of thirty thousand to hold Louisiana for the United States. Why would the overwhelmingly French inhabitants of Louisiana want to retain the Spanish legal system? The underlying cause was the fear that the new government would prohibit slavery in Louisiana as it had in the Northwest Territory. Despite Article III of the treaty of Louisiana cession, which guaranteed the inhabitants of Louisiana "free enjoyment of their property," one of the first acts of the new American government had been to embargo slave importations into the territory. Louisianians saw this prohibition as a violation of the language and spirit of the treaty of cession and possibly the first step toward abolition of slavery itself. Accordingly, the act of 1806 was intended to prevent the establishment of English common law in civil matters in Louisiana and to protect slavery in the territory. The act reinforced Claiborne's opinion that Louisianians were an alien people accustomed to despotism and therefore unfit for freedom. In his view, they were not to be trusted with self-government until properly tutored by those experts in liberty, the superior Americans.[6]

The creoles had some reason to fear that slavery might be prohibited in Louisiana. In 1804 the great propagandist of the American and French revolutions, Thomas Paine, had attacked the slaveholding inhabitants of

5. Baade, "Law of Slavery in Spanish Luisiana," in *Louisiana's Legal Heritage,* ed. Haas, 72–73, 85*n 176;* Paul v. Succession of Carrière (1806) [unreported, unlocated].

6. George Dargo, *Jefferson's Louisiana: Politics and the Clash of Legal Traditions* (Cambridge, Mass., 1975), 30, 49. *Creole* is used here and elsewhere to mean native-born whites; native-born blacks or persons of color are called "creoles of color."

Louisiana. Paine said that the Louisiana creoles were an American minority who claimed their democratic rights to statehood and cultural autonomy in order to enslave another minority. Jefferson himself favored the closing of the foreign slave trade to Louisiana, although he did not oppose the institution of slavery in the territory. Louisianians, however, perceived the president's desire to close the foreign slave trade as evidence that the United States might prohibit slavery in Louisiana altogether. In the Act of 1806, they declared their desire for political self-determination, cultural autonomy, the right to select their own legal system in their own language, and the continuation of slavery. The crisis caused by Claiborne's veto did not subside until the creation of the *Digest of 1808,* which was based on Spanish law but reenacted many of the harshest provisions of French slave law, including measures so restrictive of self-purchase that *coartación* was effectively demolished and the right to sue for cruel treatment totally prohibited.[7]

In the earlier decades of the antebellum period, the lingering Roman, French, and Spanish influences upon Louisiana slave law set the state apart from her sister slave states: in some respects the law was kinder to slaves, in some considerably harsher, and in many simply different. Some of its more beneficial influences remained in the area of manumissions. For example, slaves in American Louisiana could enter into only one kind of contract—for their freedom. This right was quite limited, but it was unknown in other slave states. Slaves could not compel their owners to sell them if they managed to acquire their appraisal price, but if the master or mistress consented to the contract, the slave obtained the price the slaveholder set, and the contract was in the proper form for the transfer of real estate, it could be enforced. Some other differences from conventional southern slave law were decidedly not better for the

7. "An Act Prescribing the Rules and Conduct to Be Observed with Respect to Negroes and Other Slaves of This Territory," Act of June 7, 1806, *Orleans Territory Acts, 1806,* 150–90, hereinafter cited as *Black Code* to distinguish it from the 1724 French *Code Noir;* "An Act to Amend the Act Entitled 'An Act Prescribing the Rules and Conduct to Be Observed with Respect to Negroes . . . ,'" Act of April 14, 1807, *Orleans Territory Acts, 1807,* pp. 186–90. See also Mitchell Franklin, "The Eighteenth *Brumaire* in Louisiana: Talleyrand and the Spanish Medieval Legal System of 1806," *Tulane Law Review,* XVI (April, 1942), 516; Mitchell Franklin, "The Place of Thomas Jefferson in the Expulsion of Spanish Medieval Law from Louisiana," *Tulane Law Review,* XVI (April, 1942), 319, 321–26; Henry Plauché Dart, "The Influence of the Ancient Laws of Spain on the Jurisprudence of Louisiana," *Tulane Law Review,* VI (December, 1931), 84; Dargo, *Jefferson's Louisiana,* 29–30, 49–50.

slave. For example, slaves accused of crimes received harsher and less just treatment than in other slave states.[8]

American rule initiated an era of diminished rights for slaves as Louisiana planters suddenly found themselves in a position to make their own laws. In 1806 the territorial legislature passed a new *Black Code* that dealt mainly with the regulation and punishment of slaves. Legislators passed an act regarding the emancipation of slaves the following year. The *Black Code* and the 1807 act together destroyed two of the great freedoms of Spanish slave law and greatly weakened a third. First, the right of self-purchase ceased because slaves could no longer own property and slaveholders could no longer be compelled to free slaves who raised the money to purchase themselves. Second, the new law once again required judicial permission for manumission, predicated on the slave's having attained the age of thirty years and providing proof of good behavior for four years preceding the emancipation. An immediate and dramatic decline in the volume of manumissions resulted. Third, although slaves still had some recourse against a cruel master, it was now greatly limited. Whereas slaves in Spanish Louisiana could petition to be sold away from a vicious owner, in American Louisiana only the criminal conviction of cruel masters or mistresses could remove slaves from their power (even this limited protection was available only to Louisiana slaves and not to their counterparts in other slave states). Guilty verdicts of this nature were rare because often the only witnesses to the alleged brutality were slaves, who could not testify in court in such cases against free people, black or white. Also, white juries were often reluctant to convict slaveholders for doing as they pleased with their own property. By 1808, Louisiana slave law closely resembled French colonial slave law. Many of the relatively benign traces of Spanish law had disappeared.[9]

8. *Civil Code of the State of Louisiana* (New Orleans, 1825), Art. 174, p. 27, hereinafter cited as *Civil Code;* Daniel J. Flanigan, "Criminal Procedure in Slave Trials in the Antebellum South," *Journal of Southern History,* XL (November, 1974), 545–46.

9. Baade, "Law of Slavery in Spanish Luisiana," in *Louisiana's Legal Heritage,* ed. Haas, 74–75; *Black Code,* Sec. 16, p. 158. For the first time, free people of color were to have their status more restricted. The last article of the *Black Code* ordered free blacks not to imagine themselves equal to whites; on the contrary, they were to defer to whites on every occasion and treat them with respect; *Black Code,* Sec. 40, pp. 188–90. "An Act to Prescribe Certain Formalities Respecting Free Persons of Color," Act of March 31, 1808, *Orleans Territory Acts, 1808,* pp. 138–40, required free people of color to have the words "free man or woman of color" after their name in any legal proceeding. Notaries and clerks of court ordinarily abbreviated this requirement by inserting "f.m.c." or "f.w.c." after the names of free blacks.

VIEW OF THE PLACE DES ARMES, NEW ORLEANS, LOUISIANA.

The Place d'Armes (mislabeled "*des* Armes" by the artist) in New Orleans, *ca.* 1849. The Louisiana Supreme Court had its chambers in the Cabildo (immediately to the left of St. Louis Cathedral in the picture), which once housed the Spanish colonial government of Louisiana.

Courtesy of Marie E. Windell, University of New Orleans

Regulation and control of the area's burgeoning slave population was the main purpose of the *Black Code,* but the code did endow Louisiana slaves with a unique set of rights. The first few articles set forth rules for their protection and granted rights not given to slaves in the rest of the South, establishing minimum issuances of food and clothing, laborless Sundays, and the obligation of the owner to care for infirm and aged slaves. The new code protected slave children under ten from sale away from their mothers, and superannuated slaves were only to be sold together with a child of their choosing (these two provisions were not found in any other state's antebellum slave code). Slaves were specifically designated as real estate, which implied a tie with the land. Moreover, designating slaves as real estate, and therefore immovable property, meant that they were subject to the same laws in Louisiana as was real estate in such diverse matters as the transfer of property, mortgages, insolvency, seizure for debt, concubinage, and inheritance. For example, a sale of a slave had to be in writing, witnessed before a notary public, notarized, and recorded in the conveyance office; oral contracts for the sale of a slave were invalid. Although treating slaves as real estate offered no particular benefit to the slave, it ensured that the law operated on slave property and chattel, or movable property, in a different manner.[10]

Section 18 of the American *Black Code* clearly brought home the reality of slavery: "The condition of a slave being merely a passive one, his subordination to his master and to all who represent him, is not susceptible to any modification or restriction, . . . he owes to his master, and to all his family, a respect without bounds, and an absolute obedience."[11] The code remained in effect throughout the antebellum period

10. *Black Code,* Secs. 8–10, 18, pp. 154, 160; *A Digest of the Civil Laws Now in Force in the Territory of Orleans. . . .* (New Orleans, 1808) [hereinafter cited as *Digest of 1808*], Bk. I, Title VI, Chap. 3, Arts. 15–26, pp. 38–42. See also William Goodell, *The American Slave Code in Theory and Practice* (New York, 1853), 135–49, 177, 196. Kentucky also classified slaves as real estate: *Digest of the Statute Laws of Kentucky* (Frankfort, 1834), I, 566. Alabamians passed a law in 1852 that prohibited the sale of young slave children away from their mothers. According to James Benson Sellers, *Slavery in Alabama* (University, Ala., 1950), 167, the purpose of this act was to stem abolitionist criticism of a common practice.

Evidence of Louisiana's provision prohibiting the separation of elderly slaves from at least one of their children does not appear in the supreme court's records. As the children of superannuated slaves were likely to be adults, the chances of their having the same owner was less, which would have made the law more difficult to enforce.

11. *Black Code,* Sec. 18, p. 160. This section might as well have stipulated that slaves obey not only their master and the master's family, but any white. In a case involving assault and battery between two slaves, the First District Court of New Orleans held that when warned

in Louisiana, although it was altered and made more stringent by the state legislature from time to time. By the eve of the Civil War, as the state became more "Americanized," the Louisiana slave code had begun to resemble closely those of other slaveholding states in the American South.[12]

Why did the people of Louisiana turn away from some of their milder colonial traditions during the antebellum period? The years from the beginning of the territorial period to the Civil War were ones of continuous agricultural expansion for the area. Americans poured into the newly acquired lands; the climate and soil seemed ideally suited to the system of slave labor. Louisianians increasingly believed that slavery was an essential element not only for economic success but for social order, and that wholesale manumission would result in disaster. The state's law of slavery emphasized control of slave labor to ensure prosperity. This attitude is evident in *Marie, a Slave,* v. *Avart's Heirs,* an 1821 decision of the Supreme Court of Louisiana: "emancipated slaves, in a free country like ours, are not *exactly what we want to make our agriculture flourish*" (emphasis in original).[13] In *Henriette* v. *Heirs of Barnes* (1856) the court was even more specific: "its [emancipation's] tendency is to substitute a free colored population for the system of compulsory labor, which involves to such a vast extent the fortunes of our citizens and the production of our agricultural staples."[14] Indeed, the court considered slavery to be an integral part of Louisiana society, "an institution thoroughly interwoven with our interior lives."[15]

Slavery in the antebellum South was, of course, a system of coerced labor as well as racial control, and the high court of Louisiana recognized

---

by a white woman to stop fighting, the offending slave "should have immediately yielded to a white." Roebuck v. Curry, No. 458, 2 La. Ann. 998 (1847).

12. Historians disagree over the nature of slavery in Louisiana as compared with other slave states. Mary Veronica Miceli states that the position of slaves in French Louisiana was far superior to that of their counterparts in the British colonies. Miceli concludes that as more and more Anglo-Americans moved into Louisiana, the status of blacks declined steadily. Mary Veronica Miceli, "The Influence of the Roman Catholic Church on Slavery in Colonial Louisiana Under French Domination, 1718–1763" (Ph.D. dissertation, Tulane University, 1979), 178–81. *Cf.* David C. Rankin, "The Tannenbaum Thesis Reconsidered: Slavery and Race Relations in Antebellum Louisiana," *Southern Studies,* XVIII (Spring, 1979), 8, 17; Clement Eaton, *The Growth of Southern Civilization, 1790–1860* (New York, 1961), 132.

13. Taylor, *Negro Slavery in Louisiana,* xi; Marie, a Slave, v. Avart's Heirs, No. 488, 10 Mart. (o.s.) 25 (La. 1821).

14. Henriette, alias Mary, v. Heirs of Barnes, No. 3751, 11 La. Ann. 453 (1856).

15. Barclay, f.w.c., v. Sewell, No. 4622, 12 La. Ann. 262 (1857).

the importance of control. In *Poydras* v. *Mourain* (1836), an unsuccessful suit for freedom by twelve slaves, the court observed that there was "hardly any difference between the emancipated slave and the slave who cannot be compelled to labor," adding that "the obligation to work for a master is of the essence of slavery." Ultimately the purpose of antebellum slave law was to enforce that obligation as well as to provide social control. In 1829 the Supreme Court of Louisiana had made this position quite clear in *Dorothée* v. *Coquillon:* "the power of the master is absolute, and the slave cannot resist or be heard if he complains of that power." Hence a slave could not sue even for flagrant mistreatment—in *Poulard* v. *Délamare* (1838), the Louisiana Supreme Court dismissed a suit for cruelty by a slave petitioner. In American Louisiana a slave could not institute any legal action except to sue for freedom. The primary purposes of slave law were to keep slaves slaves and to protect the property rights of the owners. At the same time, slaveowners generally did not imagine themselves to be barbarous, and therefore paid some lip service to the humanity of the slaves.[16]

The Supreme Court of Louisiana presided over the legal system of the new American state. In 1805, the United States Congress had established the Superior Court of the Territory of Orleans as its highest appellate body. The Constitution of 1812 created the Supreme Court of Louisiana, and the Constitution of 1845 reorganized that court's personnel, expanded its jurisdiction, and streamlined its administrative procedures. This judicial body continued to operate without interruption until the court adjourned when New Orleans surrendered to Union forces in April, 1862.[17]

16. Poydras v. Mourain, No. 2871, 9 La. 492 (1836); Dorothée v. Coquillon, No. 1649, 7 Mart. (N.S.) 350 (La. 1829); Poulard v. Délamare, No. 3101, 12 La. 267 (1838); Mark V. Tushnet, *The American Law of Slavery, 1810–1860: Considerations of Humanity and Interest* (Princeton, 1981), 25, 62.

17. Henry Plauché Dart, "History of the Supreme Court of Louisiana," in *The Celebration of the Centenary of the Supreme Court of Louisiana* (New Orleans, 1913), 6–56; John Smith Kendall, *History of New Orleans* (Chicago, 1922), I, 272–73; Robert C. Reinders, "Slavery in New Orleans in the Decade Before the Civil War," *Mid-America,* XLIV (October, 1962), 221; Warren M. Billings, ed., *The Historic Rules of the Supreme Court of Louisiana, 1813–1879* (Lafayette, La., 1985); Mark Fernandez, "From Chaos to Continuity: Early Reforms of the Supreme Court of Louisiana, 1845–1852," *Louisiana History,* XXVIII (Winter, 1987), 19–36. For a general history of New Orleans just before the Civil War, see Robert C. Reinders, *End of an Era: New Orleans, 1850–1860* (New Orleans, 1964).

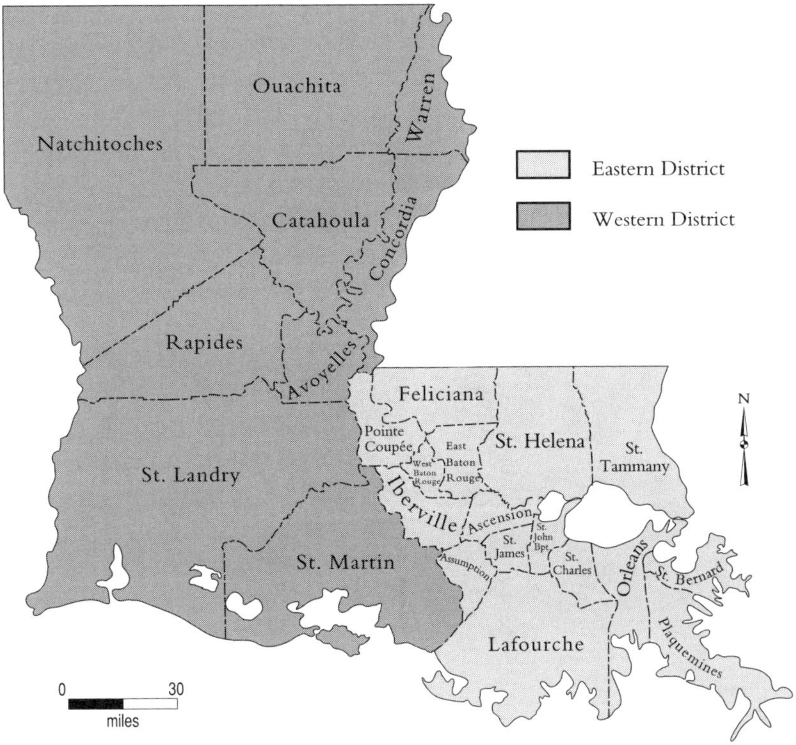

MAP 1. Constitution of 1812: Parish Boundaries and Judicial Districts.

Source: *Historical Records Survey, Works Progress Administration, "County-Parish Boundaries in Louisiana," October, 1939.*

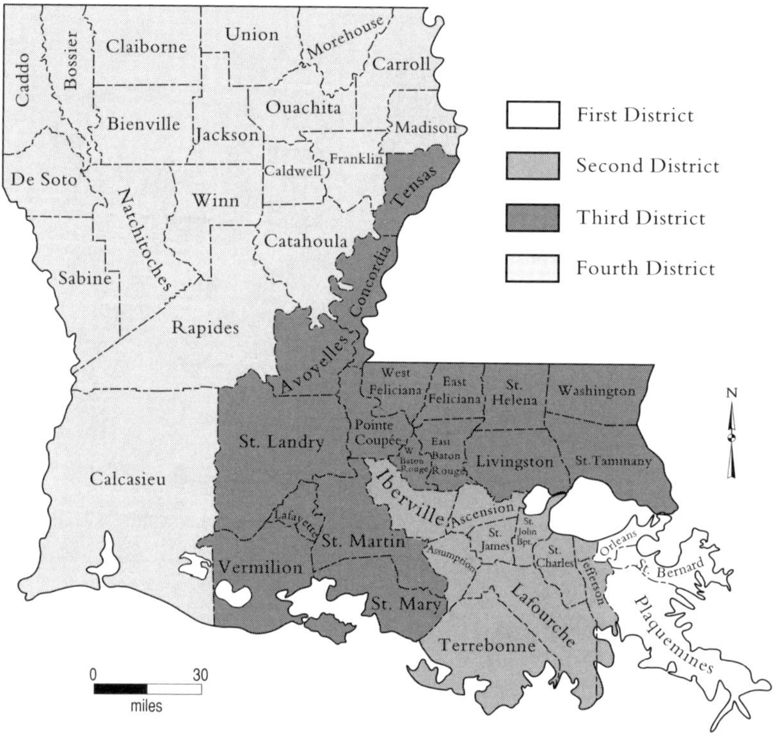

MAP 2. Constitutions of 1852 and 1864: Parish Boundaries and Judicial Districts.

Source: *Historical Records Survey, Works Progress Administration, "County-Parish Boundaries in Louisiana," October, 1939.*

From the creation of the Superior Court of the Territory of Orleans to the closing of the Supreme Court of Louisiana on the day of the surrender of New Orleans, it was overwhelmingly common-law-trained attorneys, most of whom were not native Louisianians, who staffed Louisiana's highest appellate court. The judges of the Superior Court of the Territory of Orleans were men who had first become attorneys in New York, Ohio, Georgia, North Carolina, and Kentucky. François-Xavier Martin, a judge of the Superior Court who later became chief judge of the Supreme Court of Louisiana, was a native of France but had been trained as a common-law attorney in North Carolina before coming to Louisiana. Pierre Dérbigny, who served on the court from 1813 to 1820, was also a native of France, and subsequently a resident of St. Domingue, but had studied law in Pittsburgh before coming to Louisiana. The court's first chief justice, George Eustis, was born in Massachusetts and held an LL.D. from Harvard Law School. Only one antebellum judge or justice of the Supreme Court of Louisiana, Cornelius Voorhies, was native-born and locally educated, and there is evidence of only one justice, Belgian-born Edward Simon, having had any formal training in civil law. This is not the place for a detailed study of the court's personnel, but it is enough to observe that the majority of the members of the court before the Civil War were American attorneys who were trained in common law and were not native Louisianians. Moreover, the entire structure of the Louisiana judicial system, with its system of parish (county), district, and appellate courts, was Anglo-American in nature.[18]

Common-law-trained judges and justices operating in a civil-law jurisdiction in the United States posed unusual problems in the development of Louisiana law, although the boundaries between civil and common law were not always clearly defined; it was not uncommon for Anglo-American jurists to borrow from civil-law jurisprudence, and the reverse was also not unusual. However, it is not surprising that the law of slavery in Louisiana became increasingly Americanized; indeed, it was one logical result of a judicial system administered by judges trained in the common law. How the court handled the approximately 1,200 appeals that involved slaves during the antebellum period, and how it interpreted civil-law institutions in a state where vestiges of French and

18. Willian Kernan Dart, "Justices of the Supreme Court," *Louisiana Reports,* CXXXIII (1913), 60–63; Billings, ed., *Historic Rules of the Supreme Court of Louisiana,* 44–50.

TABLE 1
Percentage of Louisiana Supreme Court Cases Involving Slaves, 1809–1871

Year	All Cases	Cases Involving Slaves	Percent
1809	24	3	12.5
1810	32	8	25
1811	55	7	12.7
1812	77	7	9
1813	27	1	3.7
1814	62	7	11.2
1815	41	3	7.3
1816	64	13	20.3
1817	67	9	13.4
1818	58	15	25.9
1819	96	16	16.7
1820	114	22	19.3
1821	128	16	12.5
1822	107	15	14
1823	160	14	8.8
1824	154	15	9.7
1825	162	10	6.2
1826	119	11	9.2
1827	171	13	7.6
1828	161	7	4.3
1829	165	18	10.9
1830	186	15	8.1
1831	193	17	8.8
1832	187	19	10.2
1833	118	14	11.9
1834	155	26	16.8
1835	168	10	5.6
1836	183	21	11.5
1837	206	11	5.3
1838	268	15	5.6
1839	267	17	6.5

TABLE 1 (*continued*)

Year	All Cases	Cases Involving Slaves	Percent
1840	381	25	6.6
1841	403	42	10.4
1842	353	25	7
1843	361	31	8.6
1844	228	29	12.7
1845	300	31	10.3
1846	434	19	4.6
1847	428	28	6.5
1848	429	29	6.8
1849	406	32	7.7
1850	414	31	7.4
1851	427	43	10.1
1852	476	25	5.3
1853	433	17	3.9
1854	444	21	4.7
1855	533	41	7.7
1856	515	43	8.3
1857	599	41	6.8
1858	521	36	6.9
1859	578	51	8.8
1860	423	64	15.1
1861	405	13	3.2
1862	62	6	9.7
	(court closed by Union occupation)		
1865	244	7	2.9
1866	326	7	2.1
1867	432	13	3
1868	551	10	1.8
1869	560	18	3.2
1870	567	14	2.5
1871	841	4	.4
Total	17,049	1,191	7.0

Spanish law coexisted with American law, is another part of the story of the development of the law of slavery in Louisiana.

Civil law was an integral part of Louisiana's French and Spanish colonial past. When Louisiana entered the federal union, many of the inhabitants feared the imposition of the American common-law system, which not only was in a language foreign to many of the inhabitants but was based on case decisions made by judges—British or American judges at that—rather than upon a written code of law. The people of Louisiana were accustomed to law based on civil-law principles.[19]

Accordingly, the Louisiana constitution of 1812 forbade the legislature from imposing any general and unspecific form of law, such as the common law, upon the state: "The Legislature shall never adopt any system or code of laws, by a general reference to the said system or code; but in all cases, shall specify the several provisions of the law it may enact." Both the framers and subsequent legislators intended to minimize judicial discretion by binding the high court to the *Civil Code* and legislative acts. The constitution limited the jurisdiction of the state's highest court to questions of law alone in civil cases and required it to justify each and every decision by citing the specific act of the legislature or article in the *Civil Code* upon which it was based, placing implied law and principles of equity outside of the Louisiana system. Equity, after all, was developed to enlarge and override a scheme of law considered too rigid in scope. Louisiana judges were forbidden to bend the law or to create it in this manner and were allowed only to interpret it—although in practice they continued to use traditional French and Spanish sources to support their decisions when it suited them. Later Louisiana constitutions contained the same restrictions. In the event the court might be tempted to overstep its authority, the articles limiting its power were immediately followed by one that outlined the process of impeachment for the court's justices.[20]

19. Dargo, *Jefferson's Louisiana*, 118. See also Edward F. Haas's Introduction to *Louisiana's Legal Heritage*, 1–6; and Elizabeth Gaspar Brown, "Legal Systems in Conflict: Orleans Territory, 1804–1812," *American Journal of Legal History*, I (January, 1957), 35–75. For an excellent discussion of the court-legislature struggle, see Richard Holcomb Kilbourne, Jr., *A History of the Louisiana Civil Code: The Formative Years, 1803–1839* (Baton Rouge, 1987). See also Thomas Jones Cross, "The Eclecticism of the Law of Louisiana," *American Law Review*, LV (May–June, 1921), 405–25.

20. Henry Plauché Dart, ed., *Constitutions of the State of Louisiana*, Art. IV, Sec. 11, p. 504; Art. V, Sec. 1, p. 504. Article 21 of the *Civil Code* allowed civil court judges to use equity

A significant element in the judicial history of antebellum Louisiana is the sometimes-elaborate attempts of the judges and justices of the supreme court to escape the legal straitjacket placed upon them by the state legislature and the consistent efforts of the legislature to keep the court under its control. Throughout the antebellum period the legislature repeatedly attempted to restrict the sources of Louisiana law; often these attempts were purposely misinterpreted or blatantly ignored by the state's highest court.

That the legislature wanted to limit the judicial discretion of the Supreme Court of Louisiana and to confine its function to interpreting the current statute law, rather than resorting to Roman, French, and Spanish writings and precedents, is quite clear. Most of the judges and justices, who had been trained in a common-law system in which precedent was all-important, now found themselves in a system in which precedent counted less as a source of law than the *Civil Code*. The first set of laws promulgated under American rule, the *Digest of 1808,* attempted to limit the court to the articles contained within the new compilation and to suppress the use of the old Roman, French, and Spanish sources. The stated purpose of the act of the Louisiana legislature that authorized the writing of the *Digest of 1808* was to collect laws "in a single work, which might serve as a guide for the decisions of the courts and jurors, without recurring to a multiplicity of books." The act also referred to "the confused state in which the civil laws of this territory were plunged by the effect of the changes which happened in its government."[21]

The old laws and traditions would fade slowly, not disappear abruptly as ordered by the *Digest of 1808*. In *Cottin* v. *Cottin* (1817), the Supreme

"where there is no express law . . . where positive law is silent," but the framers of the code and the Louisiana legislature attempted to provide detailed laws on all subjects. *Civil Code,* Art. 21, p. 6; Mitchell Franklin, "Equity in Louisiana: The Role of Article 21," *Tulane Law Review,* IX (June, 1935), 485–516.

21. "An Act Providing for the Promulgation of the Digest of the Civil Laws Now in Force in the Territory of Orleans," *Orleans Territory Acts, 1808,* pp. 120–28. Both the *Digest of 1808* and the 1825 *Civil Code* were originally written in French and translated into English. The Supreme Court of Louisiana expressed its contempt for English translation in an 1846 ruling: "The definition relied on from the English side of one of the articles of the Code proves nothing but the ignorance of the person who translated it from the French." Egerton v. Third Municipality, 1 La. Ann. 435, 437 (1846). See also Ferdinand Stone, "The Law with a Difference and How It Came About," in *The Past as Prelude: New Orleans, 1718–1968,* ed. Hodding Carter (New Orleans, 1968), 61.

Court of Louisiana held that the Spanish laws remained in force unless specifically in conflict with or repealed by the *Digest of 1808*.[22] This ruling allowed the high court to apply Spanish law to issues upon which the *Digest of 1808* was silent, and to use the old sources to augment the 1808 digest.

Members of the legislature wished to reform the digest to include "such of the laws as are still in force and not included therein," and accordingly, on March 14, 1822, they passed a resolution that appointed a committee to revise the *Digest of 1808*. The committee reported that in preparing a new code, they would draw upon the *Partidas,* the *Digest of 1808,* existing English laws, and the codes of France and of Rome.[23]

A civil-law digest is a compilation of preexisting law, rather than a coherent and complete code. The writers of the 1825 *Civil Code* intended to replace the old *Digest* with an instrument that was complete, coherent, and sufficient unto itself; courts should have no need to resort to their own jurisprudence or to Roman, French, or Spanish precedents outside of the new code. The very first article of the new code was a statement of legislative supremacy over the courts, "Law is a solemn expression of Legislative will," and one of the last articles was quite precise as to the intention that the code be the sole authority for Louisiana law: "From and after the promulgation of this Code, the Spanish, Roman, and French laws, which were in force in this state when Louisiana was ceded to the United States be and are hereby repealed in every case for which it has been especially provided in this Code, and that they shall not be invoked as laws, even under the pretense that their provisions are not contrary or repugnant to those of this Code."[24]

The Supreme Court of Louisiana was determined to have the final say on what was law in the state, and it refused to be confined in its choice of sources for that law. In order to gain judicial flexibility and escape the confines of the *Civil Code,* the justices freely used the old sources when it suited them. In *Fowler* v. *Griffith* (1827), the judges ignored the exclusivity of the *Civil Code* of 1825 and stated that those provisions of the Spanish law not repealed or in conflict with the *Civil Code,* as well as those articles of the 1808 code that were omitted from the new code,

22. Hayes v. Berwick, 2 Mart. (o.s.) 138 (La. 1812); Cottin v. Cottin, No. 223, 5 Mart. (o.s.) 93 (La. 1817).

23. Stone, "The Law with a Difference," in *Past as Prelude,* ed. Carter, 64–65.

24. *Civil Code,* Art. 1, 3521, 3522, pp. 533–35; Vernon V. Palmer, "The Death of a Code—The Birth of a Digest," *Tulane Law Review,* LXIII (December, 1988), 226.

continued in force. The legislature countered with an 1828 act that specifically abrogated all civil laws in force before the promulgation of the *Civil Code of 1825*.[25] After 1828, the judges began to resort to their own decisions for authority, citing those that were contrary to the new *Civil Code* in order to escape its restrictions. If the old sources were off limits, the judges' own decisions were not, and this ingenious resort to prior jurisprudence provided a way for the court to continue using the old sources of Louisiana law to gain judicial discretion when the parameters of the *Civil Code* grew too narrow. An old saying still common among Louisiana attorneys—"Precedent means nothing in Louisiana, and I'll quote you ten cases to prove it"—is indicative of the complexity of the unique admixture that was Louisiana law.

There are other instances of the judges of the Supreme Court of Louisiana asserting their authority in determining sources of Louisiana law. In *Reynolds* v. *Swain* (1839), the justices stated that in rejecting Roman, French, and Spanish law, "the legislature never intended to abrogate those *principles* of law which had been established or settled by the decisions of courts of justice."[26] Another instance of the high court's refusal to submit to the legislature's concept of what constituted Louisiana law was the court's Rule of 1840, which required that candidates for admission to the Louisiana bar be "well read" not only in the United States Constitution and the *Civil Code,* but also in *The Institutes of Justinian* (Roman law), the *Partidas,* and French legal treatises by Domat and Pothier.[27] If the court had been paying heed to the Act of 1828, which stated that the *Civil Code* of 1825 was the sole authority for Louisiana law, aspiring candidates for admission to the Louisiana bar would have had no need of the likes of Justinian, Domat, and Pothier. As late as 1855, in *Foley and Townsend* v. *Bourg,* the high court referred disdainfully to the *Civil Code* of 1825 as "this loose amended codification."[28]

Slavery was an exception to the presumption in natural law that all human beings are free. A system of slave law was necessary to maintain

25. Warren M. Billings, Review of Richard Holcomb Kilbourne, Jr.'s *A History of the Louisiana Civil Code: The Formative Years, 1803–1839,* in *Louisiana History,* XXX (Summer, 1989), 325; Fowler v. Griffith, No. 1419, 6 Mart. (N.S.) 89 (La. 1827); "An Act to Repeal Certain Articles of the Former Civil Code," Act of March 12, 1828, *Louisiana Acts, 1828,* p. 66.

26. Reynolds v. Swain, No. 3244, 13 La. 193 (1839); emphasis in original.

27. Billings, ed. *Historic Rules of the Supreme Court,* 9–10; Jean Domat, *Les Lois civiles dans leur ordre naturel* (Paris, 1689–97); Robert Joseph Pothier, *Oeuvres de Pothier* (Paris, 1760–78).

28. Foley and Townsend v. Bourg, No. 3841, 10 La. Ann. 129 (1855).

and underpin the institution of slavery because if slaves had fallen under the same laws as free people, they would have also been free. In Louisiana the state supreme court inextricably tied bondage to color and reflected the state's colonial traditions in its legal definition of slavery. In a series of decisions the judges defined who were and who were not slaves in Louisiana, as well as the legal presumptions associated with shades of skin color. In *Adéle* v. *Beauregard* (1810), the Superior Court of the Territory of Orleans declared that mulattoes and other persons of color were presumed free: "Persons of color are presumed free—Negroes otherwise." Judge François-Xavier Martin reasoned that persons of color might be descendants of Indians, whites, or free mulattoes. Martin, writing for the court, stated, "Slavery is an exception to the condition of the great masses of mankind . . . except as to Africans in the slaveholding States."[29]

In *Ulzere* v. *Poeyfarré* (1820), Judge Martin held that Indians could not be enslaved in Louisiana. The court also dealt with the status of mulattoes. In many slaveholding states the courts, just as they did with Negroes, presumed mulattoes to be slaves. In these states the burden of proof of freedom was on the person of mixed blood. Some southern states passed statutes specifying the amount of Negro blood necessary for one to be presumed a slave. In Virginia and Kentucky one-quarter Negro blood was enough to raise the presumption of slavery. Arkansas law decreed that even a trace of African blood implied slavery.[30]

Presumption of freedom did not mean that the Louisiana Supreme Court considered free people of color remotely equal to whites. In reality, antebellum Louisiana was a three-tiered society. In *State* v. *Harri-*

29. Tannenbaum, *Slave and Citizen,* 68; Tushnet, *American Law of Slavery,* 143–44; Adéle v. Beauregard, 1 Mart. (O.S.) 183 (La. 1810). However, proof of servile origin outweighed the presumption of freedom by color. English v. Latham, No. 289, 3 Mart. (N.S.) 88 (La. 1824). In an 1812 decision the Louisiana Supreme Court ruled that the testimony of a woman of color should be admitted in a case involving whites even though she claimed to have lost her free papers. The court presumed she was free because of her color. State v. Cecil, 2 Mart. (O.S.) 208 (La. 1812). In another case to determine whether a Negro was free or slave, the court ruled that because he was black, he should be presumed a slave. In this case the supreme court made an interesting observation concerning the effect of slavery: "Kept for a number of years, perhaps from his birth, in bondage, the spirit of the injured negro is said to have been borne down by the influence which long exerted mastery creates." Forsyth v. Nash, No. 150, 4 Mart. (O.S.) 385 (La. 1816).

30. Ulzere v. Poeyfarré, No. 468, 8 Mart. (O.S.) 155 (La. 1820), and No. 989, 2 Mart. (N.S.) 504 (La. 1824); Kenneth M. Stampp, *The Peculiar Institution: Slavery in the Antebellum South* (New York, 1956), 194–96.

son (1856), the court expressed the opinion that free people of color were totally different from slaves and that the difference was as great as the one between white men and slaves. Here was an area in which Americanization was incomplete. The dissenting opinion in this appeal was in harmony with other southern states, which tended to lump mulattoes together with Negroes. In his dissent, Justice Henry M. Spofford stated that slaves and free persons of color composed "a single, homogeneous class of beings, distinguished from all others by nature, custom and law and never confounded with citizens of the State. No white person can be a slave; no colored person can be a citizen." In equating blackness with slavery and persons of color with freedom the court was reflecting real conditions in southern Louisiana. In antebellum New Orleans, for example, perhaps 80 percent of the city's Negroes were slaves and 70 percent of its mulattoes were free.[31]

The central problem in slavery jurisprudence was the inherent contradiction of the status of the slave under the law. Slaves had personage before the law and at the same time were immovables in Louisiana.[32] A resolution of this conflict could have resulted if slaveowners had owned merely the *labor* of their slaves, rather than their persons—that is, if property rights had been restricted to slaves' labor. However, the court ignored this possibility, continuing to regard slaves as human property, which itself is a contradiction in terms. In *State* v. *Seaborne, alias Moore* (1843), the court stated that under Louisiana law, "slaves are regarded as both persons and property; the intention of the lawgivers must have undoubtedly been, to discharge the obligations which humanity and sound policy . . . imposed . . . of giving the most ample protection, both to the person of the slave, and to the property of the citizen." In *State* v. *Davis* (1859), a criminal prosecution of a white man for shooting a slave, the high court rejected the defense that there was no law against a free person shooting a slave. The court stated that "slaves are treated in our law as property, and also as persons," and ruled that the law against murder applied to slave and free alike. In fact, the Su-

31. State v. Harrison, a Slave, No. 4464, 11 La. Ann. 722 (1856); John W. Blassingame, *Black New Orleans, 1860–1880* (Chicago, 1973), 11. The high court did state that Louisiana free blacks were superior to those in other states. In a case involving the question of whether a free person of color could testify against a white, the court stated that in Louisiana free blacks were often educated, respected property owners. In other states, the court stated, free blacks were "degraded." State v. Levy and Dreyfous, Nos. 1414, 1416, 5 La. Ann. 64 (1850).

32. Stampp, *Peculiar Institution,* 193.

The sale of "estates, pictures, and slaves" in the same location attests to the status of slaves as property. By their dress, the slaves depicted as being sold here must have been imported from Africa.

Courtesy of the Historic New Orleans Collection, Museum/Research Center, Acc. No. 1953.149

preme Court of Louisiana treated slaves at times as persons and at times as property on a case-by-case basis depending on what the court considered appropriate to maintaining the property rights of the slaveowner and the regulatory needs of a slave society. In *Gomez* v. *Bonneval* (1819), the court invented the phrase "passive beings" rather than address the dilemma of whether slaves were exclusively people or property.[33] In a succession of cases, jurists created a web of euphemisms to soften the

33. Tushnet, *American Law of Slavery,* 6; State v. Seaborne, alias Moore, 8 Rob. 518 (La. 1843); State v. Davis, 14 La. Ann. 678 (1859); Mark Tushnet, "The American Law of Slavery, 1810–1860: A Study in the Persistence of Legal Autonomy," *Law and Society Review,* X (Fall, 1975), 122, 148; Gomez v. Bonneval, No. 364, 6 Martin (o.s.) 656 (La. 1819).

reality that slaves' status as property often precluded their legal consideration as persons.

The legal dichotomy between slaves as persons and slaves as property can also be seen in cases concerning slave homicide by another slave or a white person. Sometimes the dead slave's owner brought a civil suit for financial compensation for the loss of his property. At other times the alleged murderer was prosecuted on criminal charges. In Louisiana both methods were legally accepted, and the choice was up to the victim's owner. An owner who wished to see the killers brought to justice pressed criminal charges, and a criminal trial resulted; if financial compensation was paramount, the owner filed civil suit for the value of the murdered slave against the owner of the slave who committed the crime. The aggrieved slaveholder could also choose to pursue both avenues, seeking criminal justice *and* civil redress; although such double actions were unusual, they did occur. If the alleged murderer was white, the slaveowner's options were similar: bring criminal charges, sue for damages in a civil action, or both.

One of the best examples of the person-property dilemma appears in a ruling involving the blinding of the slave James by the slave Mangé. James's owner sued Mangé's owner for James's full value, claiming he was now worthless and a burden to support as a result of the blinding. In this case the court admitted the humanity of the slave in considering his feelings and well-being, and at the same time denied that they were relevant under the law. The judges reasoned that if they awarded James's owner his *full* value (as if he were not blind), then the owner of Mangé should own James. The court stated: "The principle of humanity, which would lead us to suppose that the mistress, [of James] whom he had long served, would treat her miserable, blind slave with more kindness than the defendant [Mangé's owner] to whom the judgment ought to transfer him, cannot be taken into consideration. . . . Cruelty and inhumanity ought not to be presumed against any person. A remedy for them can only be applied when they are legally proven." The court awarded James's owner $1,200 and transferred the title to James to the defendant. James's owner, of course, could have opted to take less than full value and retain possession of James.[34]

34. Tushnet, *American Law of Slavery,* 67; Jourdan v. Patton, No. 304, 5 Mart. (o.s.) 615 (La. 1818); Eugene D. Genovese, *Roll, Jordan, Roll: The World the Slaves Made* (New York,

The courts of the South admitted the humanity of slaves in various ways. Ironically, one way was in prosecuting them for criminal offenses. Property, whether chattel or real estate, cannot commit a crime. It follows that if slaves could be prosecuted for crimes, then they were persons and considered rational beings responsible for their actions.[35] The court also recognized the personage of slaves in suits for freedom. The very act of emancipation implied that the slave was a person. No southern court could seriously have believed that it could transform a thing into a person by one of its acts. In *Rachel, alias Betsy,* v. *St. Armand* (1820) the lower-court judge admitted that the matter before him was an "intricate and troubling case . . . when the freedom of a human creature is an issue."[36]

Attempts to treat slaves as things under the law sometimes met with dismissals from the Louisiana Supreme Court. "A slave is not a thing," the court stated in *Tom* v. *Slave Ernest* (1860). The dilemma of slave personage arose in *Folse* v. *New Orleans Coast and Lafourche Transportation Co.,* which hinged on the question of whether common carriers, such as steamboats and trains, had the obligation to carry slaves as passengers or as cargo; the court ruled that slaves were to be carried as "intelligent beings," as "passengers, and not packages." *Taylor* v. *Andrus* (1840) involved a slaveowner who attempted to recover the price of a hired slave who had been killed in performing duties for which his owner claimed he had not been hired. The court ruled: "An intelligent being like a slave cannot be assimilated to a horse or an inanimate object, the particular uses of which are limited. . . . A slave, although hired as

---

1976), 29, 30. The idea that James's owner could have chosen to demand less than his full value was suggested to me by Paul Finkelman. Mark Tushnet, in discussing *Jourdan* v. *Patton* in *American Law of Slavery,* 66–71, states that in this case the supreme court recognized the "sentiment that slavery could generate between master and slave" but denied that those ties were relevant because there was no reason to presume that the owner of the slave who blinded the plaintiff's slave would be cruel. This analysis does not take into account the possibility that if the "sentiment" between the mistress and the slave had been so strong, she could have demanded less than his full value, and title would not have been transferred.

35. Tushnet, *American Law of Slavery,* 74. For examples, see Howes v. *Red Chief,* No. 5944, 6487, 15 La. Ann. 321 (1860); State v. Peter, a Slave, No. 6175, 14 La. Ann. 521 (1859); State v. Kitty, No. 5154, 12 La. Ann. 805 (1857); Maille v. Blas, No. 5975, 15 La. Ann. 100 (1860); and State v. Dick, No. 1224, 4 La. Ann. 182 (1849).

36. Tushnet, *American Law of Slavery,* 6; Rachel, alias Betsy, v. St. Armand, No. 478, 8 Mart. (o.s.) 363 (La. 1820).

possessing a particular talent, is expected to render numberless other services." The deceased slave's owner not only lost the case but had to pay court costs.[37]

It is clear that even among the judges and justices of the Supreme Court of Louisiana, there was great confusion regarding legal definitions of slaves as property and as persons. Even when they could agree that slaves were a form of property, they could not always agree on what type of property they were. This confusion is inherent in the civil-law classification of slaves as immovables as well as real estate, which was just one form of immovable. The civil law concept of "immeubles" was defined in the *Digest of 1808* and the *Civil Code.* The redactors of the codes defined immovables as land and buildings immovable by their nature, but acknowledged that certain kinds of property could be deemed immovable by destination, such as livestock, farm implements, seeds, animal feed, sawmills, sugar refineries, and "all such movables as the owner has attached permanently to the . . . building." Chapter 2, article 19 of the *Digest of 1808* stated: "Slaves in this territory are considered as immovable by the operation of the law, on account of their value and utility for the cultivation of the lands." Article 461 of the *Civil Code* agreed: "Slaves, though movables by their nature, are considered as immovables, by the operation of the law."[38]

The 1806 Louisiana *Black Code* defined slaves as real estate: "Slaves shall always be reputed and considered real estates [*sic*]." In *Stephens* v. *Graves* (1854), a case involving the status of slaves brought to Louisiana from Kentucky, the court stated, "The moment those slaves touched our soil, they ceased to be personal property. . . . Slaves are regarded as real estate."[39] Five years later, in *Boatner* v. *Wade* (1859), the Supreme Court of Louisiana expanded its confusing and ambiguous attempt to define the nature of slave property, holding that slaves were "a kind of property which may be removed from place to place, with the utmost facility," implying logically that slaves were movable because they were trans-

37. Tom v. Slave Ernest, No. 6009, 15 La. Ann. 44 (1860); Folse v. New Orleans Coast and Lafourche Transportation Co., No. 301, 19 La. Ann. 199 (1867); Taylor v. Andrus, 16 La. 15 (1840).

38. *Digest of 1808,* Chap. 2, Arts. 13–21, pp. 96–98; *Civil Code,* Arts. 453–461, pp. 67–68.

39. *Black Code,* Sec. 10, p. 154; Tannenbaum, *Slave and Citizen,* 79; Stephens v. Graves, No. 3449, 9 La. Ann. 239 (1854).

portable. In *Girard* v. *City of New Orleans* (1847), the executor of an estate wanted to remove slaves from the deceased's land, although expressly forbidden to do so by the testator in his will. The supreme court ruled that the slaves were not tied to the land and the executor could enjoy the fruits of their labor elsewhere. "Slaves are in no sense real estate; they are considered immovables . . . but neither in common parlance, nor in law, are they designated by the term real estate." In another decision the court stated what slaves were not. In *Smoot* v. *Baldwin* (1823), a title squabble over a slave, the court ruled that the "slave [was] not personal property—clearly not so by our law."[40]

The Louisiana Supreme Court never made sense of the confusion implied in the term "human property." Untroubled by this conflict in most of the 1,200 decisions involving slaves, the court ignored the contradiction and considered only the specific issues at hand. Throughout the antebellum period, hundreds of slaves appeared before the court for a variety of reasons; in most instances they were the object at issue in the legal action.

The court's ambiguity in dealing with slaves sometimes as property, sometimes as persons, and sometimes as both is quite significant. Treating slaves solely as property was difficult, even though the *Black Code* clearly stated that they were real estate. The wording of the *Civil Code* of 1825—that slaves, "though movables by their nature," were "immovables by the operation of law"—more accurately reflected their status. The ambiguous stance of the court in dealing with slaves was no accident; it reflected the property interests of the slaveholding class, who were the leaders of antebellum Louisiana, a society convinced that slavery was the only way to achieve economic prosperity and social order. And Louisianians, despite their unique legal and cultural heritage and their singular civil-law system, were no less susceptible to the lure of economic gain than were southerners of English background and common-law traditions.[41]

An analysis of Louisiana Supreme Court cases about slavery provides a revealing study of bondage in the state. Slaves came before the high court for reasons as various as was the experience of slavery itself. There

40. Boatner v. Wade, 14 La. Ann. 695 (1859); Girard v. City of New Orleans, No. 18, 2 La. Ann. 897 (1847); Smoot v. Baldwin, Nos. 247, 273, 1 Mart. (N.S.) 528 (La. 1823).

41. *Civil Code,* Art. 461, p. 72; *Black Code,* Sec. 10, p. 154.

are cases involving slaves as criminals and as victims, as defective merchandise, as stolen goods, as self-stealers (if slaves ran away, they "stole" themselves), as concubines, as property to be seized for debts, and as objects of disputes over ownership. Slaves sued their owners for their freedom and were objects of lawsuits in which their masters or mistresses attempted to emancipate them. For a people whose very legal status was ambiguous, there was never a scarcity of slaves involved in litigation in antebellum Louisiana. Their lowly position under Louisiana law did not prevent them from occupying a significant portion of the court's time.

2

"DETAILS ARE OF A MOST REVOLTING CHARACTER"

Cruelty to Slaves and Legal Intervention

ONE OF THE PRIMARY PURPOSES OF THE *BLACK CODE* was to create a legal apparatus for the control and discipline of slaves. Slavery, by its very nature, required such regulation. Discipline was an essential element of the slave system if slaves were to earn a profit for their masters. Control of slave behavior also maintained the image of white superiority and the prescribed and delicate etiquette of relations between the races. In addition, whites believed that making slaves "stand in fear" was a necessary precaution to prevent slave insurrections.

Breaches of discipline necessitated punishment, which was most often physical in nature. All such punishments were inherently cruel, and if the chastiser was a martinet, extreme—even barbarous—cruelty was always possible. The *Black Code* prohibited treatment harsher than what was acceptable in American Louisiana, but recalcitrant slaves and hot-tempered masters were a combination that could convert control into brutality. According to the *Black Code,* slaves were "passive" creatures whose subordination to their master and "to all who represent him" was "not susceptible of any modification." Hence, even minor insubordination might occasion excessive punishment. The *Digest of 1808,* a compilation of the civil law in territorial Louisiana, reinforced the *Black Code:* "The slave is entirely subject to the will of his master who may correct him and chastise him, though not with unusual rigor, nor so as to maim or mutilate him, or expose him to the danger of loss of life, or to cause him death." The *Digest* also provided, if the presiding judge so ordered, for the court-ordered sale of slaves whose owners had been convicted of cruel treatment. No other American state had such a provision.[1]

1. *Black Code,* "Crimes and Offenses," Sec. 16, pp. 206–207; *Digest of 1808,* Tit. VI, Chap. 3, Arts. 16, 27, pp. 40, 42; Stampp, *Peculiar Institution,* 141.

The *Black Code* also prohibited the maiming or killing of slaves by their owners or others. Persons who treated slaves with cruelty risked a fine of between $200 and $500. The *Code* excepted certain types of physical chastisement from its definition of cruel punishment: "flogging, or striking with a whip, leather thong, switch or small stick." Other exceptions included placing a slave in fetters or in confinement. It is indicative of legislative sentiment concerning cruelty to slaves that Louisiana lawmakers passed an act in 1821 mandating a fine of $200 or imprisonment for six months for a person convicted of "wantonly or maliciously kill[ing] any horse, mare, gelding, mule, or jack-ass." Those convicted of this crime were also liable to the owner of the animal for its value. To "cruelly beat, maim, or disable" an animal subjected the offender to a $100 fine and liability for damages to the animal.[2]

Evidence that excessive violence and cruel treatment of slaves were not uncommon in Louisiana abounds in plantation diaries and other manuscript sources. The most famous case involved the notorious Madame Lalaurie. A New Orleans court found this sadistic woman guilty of abusing her slaves and ordered their sale away from her. Lalaurie's relatives purchased the slaves and returned them to her. She chained them to the walls of her Royal Street home, where she reportedly alternated between striking them and harsher forms of torture. On April 10, 1834, an elderly slave, fettered in a garret, somehow managed to set fire to Lalaurie's house. The New Orleans *Bee* described the events that followed:

> The conflagration at the house occupied by the woman Lalaurie . . . has been the means of discovering one of those atrocities, the details of which seem to be too incredible for human belief. We would shrink from the task of detailing the painful circumstances connected therewith, were it not that a sense of duty . . . renders it indispensible to do so.
>
> The flames having spread with alarming rapidity, . . . the horrible suspicion [was] entertained among the spectators, that some of the inmates of the premises . . . were incarcerated therein. Upon entering one of the apartments, the most appalling spectacle met their eyes. Seven slaves more or less horribly mutilated, were seen suspended by the neck, with their limbs apparently

2. *Black Code,* "Crimes and Offenses," Sec. 17, p. 208, Sec. 16, pp. 206–207.

> stretched and torn from one extremity to the other. The slaves were the property of the demon, in the shape of a woman. They had been confined by her for several months . . . and had been merely kept in existence to prolong their sufferings and make them taste all that the most refined cruelty could inflict.

Those who came to fight the fire turned into an angry mob when they observed the pitiful condition of the slaves. Madame Lalaurie barely escaped the city, just ahead of a furious band of pursuers who had seen the horror. The crowd destroyed her furniture by dropping it from the balcony to the courtyard below, then proceeded to demolish most of the house.[3]

Section 16 of the *Black Code* authorized criminal prosecution for the mutilation, severe ill-treatment, or killing of a slave. Section 17 held that if a slave were "mutilated, beaten or ill-treated" when no witnesses were present, the owner or person responsible for managing the slave would be prosecuted for cruelty unless he or she could produce evidence to the contrary. Since slaves could not testify in court against whites, this provision was intended to protect slaves in situations in which they were the only witnesses to the cruel treatment. However, the creators of the *Code* left a loophole: an owner prosecuted under such circumstances could clear himself "by his own oath." Although this provision drastically weakened the law, and although few slaveowners were ever prosecuted for cruelty, neither Louisiana law nor the state's courts ever ruled out the possibility as did North Carolina judge Thomas Ruffin in *State v. Mann* (1829). In this often-quoted decision, Ruffin held that slaveowners could not be held criminally responsible for an assault and battery on one of their own slaves because such a ruling contradicted the absolute power of the slaveholder, which was necessary "to render the submission of the slave perfect."[4]

3. New Orleans *Bee,* April 11, 12, 1834; Stampp, *Peculiar Institution,* 182, 188; Taylor, *Negro Slavery in Louisiana,* 225–27. Fred Darkis contends that Mme Lalaurie was the victim of a "bad press"; Fred R. Darkis, "Madame Lalaurie of New Orleans," *Louisiana History,* XXIII (Fall, 1982), 383.

4. Black Code, "Crimes and Offenses," Secs. 16, 17, pp. 206–208; State v. Mann, 2 Dev. 263 (N.C. 1829). South Carolina was the only other state with the provision that slaveholders could clear themselves from a charge of cruelty to their slaves by a personal oath; Goodell, *American Slave Code,* 280; State v. Raines, 3 McC. 538 (S.C. 1826). For an overview of prosecutions for cruelty to slaves in common-law states, see Andrew Fede, "Legitimized Violent Slave Abuse in the American South, 1619–1865: A Case Study of Law and Social Change in Six Southern States," *American Journal of Legal History,* XXIX (April, 1985), 93–150.

Plenty of evidence of ill treatment exists in the records of appeals of civil cases to the court. Some cases reveal unprovoked or senseless violence on the part of owners, overseers, or strangers. In many other instances, cruelty to a slave resulted from a white's overreaction to a minor infraction.

Three factors prevented the Supreme Court of Louisiana from hearing many appeals from criminal trials for cruelty to a slave during the antebellum period. The most obvious is that there were few prosecutions of this nature at the lower level. Since slaves were often the only witnesses to such incidents, and since Louisiana law prohibited them from testifying against whites, finding legally competent witnesses was difficult. Often white witnesses, many of whom felt that slave discipline was a private matter between slaveholders and their property, were reluctant to testify. A second factor is that such prosecutions as occurred in the lower courts probably often ended in acquittal. As we will see, white juries could simply refuse to convict despite overwhelming evidence of brutality. Of course, prosecutions that ended in acquittal were not appealed, and therefore do not appear in the records of the supreme court. The third reason for the scarcity of criminal appeals is technical. The first constitution of the state of Louisiana (1812) limited the jurisdiction of the state supreme court to civil appeals. Until the Constitution of 1845 gave the high court criminal jurisdiction, the court heard no criminal appeals. Appeals of criminal prosecutions for cruelty to slaves were therefore limited to the sixteen-year period from 1846 to 1862, although the court heard appeals of civil suits that involved death or injury to slaves throughout the antebellum period.[5] The court was quite willing to sustain the property rights of slaveowners in civil suits when their slaves were injured or killed by others, but the justices had little opportunity to affirm convictions of whites in criminal prosecutions. There were only six criminal appeals of cruelty convictions to the court from 1846 to 1862. Each involved a slave who had died from the abuse he received.

The first such appeal occurred in *State* v. *Morris* (1849). The defendant allegedly had beaten his slave to death "in a cruel and barbarous manner . . . causing sundry dangerous and severe bruises and wounds upon the thigh, loins, and other parts of the body." A hole in the ab-

5. Benjamin Wall Dart, ed., *Constitutions of the State of Louisiana,* Art. IV, Sec. 2, p. 503; Tit. IV, Art. 63, p. 514.

domen, the size of a dollar and appearing to have been "gouged out," was the immediate cause of death. No one witnessed the alleged cruel treatment of the slave, and Morris presented his oath in an affidavit denying his responsibility for it. The district judge instructed the jury that the oath was not conclusive evidence of the defendant's innocence. The jury found Morris guilty. He appealed, claiming that section 17 of the *Black Code* held that the owner's oath could not only repeal the presumption of guilt created by the same section, but was intended to be conclusive proof of the defendant's innocence. Justice George King, writing for the court, denied such an interpretation of section 17:

> Such does not appear to us to be a just interpretation of the act. The law creates a presumption of the master's guilt, which, in the absence of this express legislation, would not arise. It is founded upon the relation of master and slave, and the power of the former to maltreat the latter secretly and without the possibility, in many instances, of otherwise establishing his guilt.
>
> He is consequently held answerable for the cruel treatment received by his slave while under his charge, and when no person is present, and is presumed to be guilty of the offence, "unless" in the words of the act, "he can prove the contrary."
>
> It has been correctly urged by the Attorney General, that the interpretation contended for by the defendant would enable the master to escape punishment by interposing his oath, when his guilt could be satisfactorily established by other testimony, which could not have been contemplated by the legislature. . . . In such cases the legislature could not have intended that the owner should escape punishment by interposing his own oath; or that the jury should acquit, notwithstanding their convictions, from the testimony, of the guilt of the accused.

State v. *Morris* is one of only a handful of cases in the appellate court records of the American South in which a state supreme court upheld the conviction of a slaveholder for cruelty to his slave. Overseers, poor whites, and free persons of color were more likely to be successfully prosecuted for abuse of slaves than slaveowners.[6]

6. State v. Morris, No. 1293, 4 La. Ann. 177 (1849); Fede, "Legitimized Violent Slave Abuse," 96, 133. For cases in other states involving convictions of owners, see *State* v. *Hoover,* 4 Dev. and Batt. 365 (N.C., 1839), and *Souther* v. *Commonwealth,* 7 Grant 672 (Va., 1851).

Seven years elapsed before the court heard the next appeal of a conviction for cruelty, *State* v. *Bass and McNabb* (1856). William Bass and his stepfather, Harry McNabb, both described as yeomen, were convicted of killing a slave named Joe, allegedly a runaway. Bass shot Joe out of a tree with a shotgun loaded with "divers leaden bullets." The slave had climbed the tree in order to escape pursuing hounds. Bass's primary defense was that "he was but a boy" and also an orphan. The prosecutor charged McNabb with aiding and abetting Bass in the shooting. The jury acquitted McNabb but found Bass guilty with a recommendation of clemency, as Bass was an "orphan boy of tender age." The Morehouse District Court judge sentenced Bass to only thirty days in jail and a fine of $300. The state appealed to the supreme court on the basis that the district court judge had given Bass such a light sentence because the judge had allowed Bass's counsel inappropriately to introduce damaging testimony about the character of the victim in an attempt to justify the shooting. However, Justice Henry Spofford, writing for the court, upheld the decision of the trial court.[7]

Two of the other four criminal prosecutions for killing a slave involved free blacks. In *State* v. *Taylor, f.m.c.* (1856), the First District Court of New Orleans found the free man of color (f.m.c.) Joseph Jerry Taylor guilty of manslaughter in the death of Henry Cruize, a slave. Taylor had killed Cruize by throwing a brick at his head. The judge sentenced him to the penitentiary for seven years at hard labor, and his attorneys appealed. The primary witness at the trial had been a mulatto named Charles Robinson, who said that he had been a slave but that his mistress had freed him upon her death. Attorneys for Taylor objected to his testimony, saying that Robinson had offered no proof that he was free, and if he were a slave, he could not testify. Justice Spofford rejected this argument, stating that the objection to Robinson's testimony came only after the testimony, too late to sustain such an objection. The court affirmed the judgment of the lower court.[8]

The other criminal appeal involving a free black, *State* v. *Populus, f.m.c.*, occurred the following year. The Rapides Parish District Court convicted Joseph Populus of killing the slave David by stabbing him with a "dirk knife." The convicting jury recommended him to the

7. State v. Bass and McNabb, No. 4603, 11 La. Ann. 478 (1856).
8. State v. Taylor, f.m.c., No. 4132, 11 La. Ann. 430 (1856).

mercy of the court, and the judge sentenced him to twelve months at hard labor. His attorneys appealed on the grounds that the judge had not sequestered the jury after he had charged them. The jurors had gone home for the night and had returned the next morning to render their verdict. The supreme court found this irregularity sufficient grounds to grant a petition for a new trial. No record of the subsequent proceeding exists.[9]

During the next term, in *State* v. *Ward and White* (1858), the court heard an appeal from two defendants in the second criminal conviction for cruelty to a slave by those who owned him. The St. Martin parish jury found George White and Clarence Ward guilty of "inflicting inhuman and cruel treatment" on a slave under sections 16 and 17 of the *Black Code,* and the judge fined each $400. The slave had died from his wounds. White appealed the conviction on a legal technicality, asserting that an 1855 legislative act relative to crimes had repealed sections 16 and 17 of the *Black Code.* White also asserted that if not repealed, sections 16 and 17 did not require a criminal prosecution for cruelty. He claimed that he was entitled to a civil trial for damages rather than a criminal prosecution. Chief Justice Edwin Merrick rejected these arguments. He found that the act of 1855 did not repeal sections 16 and 17, and he wrote a strong opinion in favor of a criminal prosecution: "We know no law which requires the prosecution under these sections of the Act of 1806 to be conducted as a civil suit. On the contrary, we think that the terms, conviction and offence, used in them, imply a prosecution by information or indictment. Moreover, the first offence specified in section 16, viz, the offence of killing the slave of another, could be prosecuted in no other manner."[10]

The last criminal prosecution for killing a slave, *State* v. *Davis,* occurred in 1859. The record of the lower-court case no longer exists. The opinion of the Louisiana Supreme Court indicates that a grand jury indicted W. H. Davis for felonious assault on a slave "by willfully shooting at him with a shotgun loaded with gunpowder and divers leaden shot." Davis' attorneys filed a motion to quash the indictment, asserting that no law existed that forbade a free person from purposefully shooting at a slave with intent to kill. The Morehouse Parish District Court

9. State v. Populus, f.m.c., No. 250, 12 La. Ann. 710 (1857).
10. State v. Ward and White, 13 La. Ann. 573 (1858).

ordered Davis' indictment quashed, but the supreme court reversed this order, reinstated the indictment, and remanded the case to the lower court for prosecution. Associate Justice James Cole wrote for the court: "Slaves are treated in our law as property, and, also as persons; this section [of the act of 1855 pertaining to crimes] then applies to an assault upon a slave or upon a free person."[11]

Owners of slaves abused by others often chose to bring a civil action for the value of the slave in question if he were dead, or for the amount the injury had diminished his value. It is in these cases that evidence of cruel treatment most often appears, and it is clear that the property value of the slave took precedence over obtaining a just punishment for the perpetrator of the barbarous treatment. Even a purely civil matter would have brought the incident to the attention of the public prosecutor, who could have chosen to begin a criminal prosecution. The scarcity of criminal prosecutions was the result of solidarity among whites and especially among slaveowners, which often prevented whites who had witnessed the atrocities or who had seen the physical evidence of them from pressing charges or even reporting the abuse to the authorities.[12]

Appeals to the Supreme Court of Louisiana in cases involving cruel treatment or senseless, unprovoked violence against slaves can be divided into three categories: abuse by strangers, by overseers, and by masters. The last classification was the least frequent, no doubt because slaves, who could not testify in court, were often the only witnesses to such incidents, and masters were unlikely to report the abuse themselves. On the other hand, masters were much more likely to report acts of violence by others that injured or killed their valuable slave property.

Slaves who stole animals or produce risked gunshot wounds and even death, although their infractions might have been minor. In *Allain, f.m.c.,* v. *Young* (1821), the Louisiana Supreme Court heard an appeal

11. State v. Davis, 14 La. Ann. 678 (1859); "An Act Relative to Crimes and Offenses," Act of March 14, 1855, *Louisiana Acts, 1855,* Sec. 9, p. 131. The judge in *State* v. *Hale,* a North Carolina case, ruled that an assault on a slave by a person or persons other than the owner was an indictable offense. State v. Hale, 2 Hawks 582 (N.C. 1823).

12. *Black Code,* "Crimes and Offenses," Sec. 16, pp. 206–208. Fede, "Legitimized Violent Slave Abuse," 113, suggests that slaveowners chose civil remedies if the offender had the financial means to compensate for the damages to or loss of the slave, but chose criminal prosecution to serve as a deterrent to poor whites who would have been unable to come up with a sufficient amount to justify a civil suit for the value of the slave.

from a free black slaveowner named François Allain, whose slave Régese had such a bad character, so witnesses testified, that no one would accept him as a gift. Régese regularly stole cattle and hogs from neighboring farms, slaughtered them, and sold the meat. From the record it is not clear whether Régese acted without his master's knowledge or Allain, too, profited from the sale of the stolen meat. When a man named Young caught Régese with stolen animals, Régese attempted to seize Young's gun, and Young shot and killed him. Allain sued Young for Régese's value, which he estimated at $2,000. The judge of the lower court held for the defendant, reasoning that Régese died while committing a felony. Allain appealed, but Chief Judge George Mathews affirmed the decision: "If a slave of bad character . . . pursued on suspicion of felony attempts to seize a gun . . . [and] is killed in the pursuit, the supreme court will not disturb a verdict for the defendant, who killed him."[13]

Régese had been involved in an extensive scheme to steal from others. In most other cases involving animal stealing, thieves were committing petty larceny, usually pilfering chickens for their own use. The court did not condone excessive violence in these instances. *Déslonde, f.m.c.,* v. *LeBéret* (1833) involved a free man of color who sued Pierre LeBéret for shooting and killing his slave Isaac for attempting to steal one of LeBéret's chickens. LeBéret caught the slave in the act, bound him with a rope, and shot him execution-style. LeBéret claimed the act was justified, saying that Isaac was "in the habit of stealing and carrying away the defendant's property in the night." The supreme court remanded the case to the lower court to ascertain the value of Isaac, presumably to award damages to Déslonde. There is no record of subsequent action by the lower court.[14]

In the 1850s, the Supreme Court of Louisiana heard several appeals in which owners sued others for shooting their slaves for stealing animals or produce. Stealing sugarcane resulted in the death of a slave, which instigated a lawsuit, *Carmouche* v. *Bouis* (1851). Narcisse Carmouche brought a civil action against his neighbors, Francis P. Bouis and his son

13. Allain, f.m.c., v. Young, No. 537, 9 Mart. (O.S.) 221 (La. 1821). For a similar case see Hébert v. Esnard, No. 1818, 8 Mart. (N.S.) 498 (La. 1830). It was against the law for slaves to sell or barter produce without permission from their masters; *Black Code,* Sec. 14, pp. 156–58.

14. Déslonde, f.m.c., v. LeBéret, No. 2300, 5 La. 96 (1833). For a similar case, see Richardson v. Dukes, 4 McCord 156 (S.C. 1827).

Louis, for the value of a slave named John. Testimony indicated that a gang of slaves had been making nightly raids on Bouis' sugar plantation to steal cane. Determined to put an end to the depredations, Bouis ordered his son and his overseer to arm themselves and keep watch over his fields. Both were instructed not to shoot at trespassing slaves, but merely to fire warning shots to frighten them. When Bouis' son saw John climbing the sugarcane field's fence, he fired without taking aim and by chance mortally wounded the slave. The Pointe Coupée Parish court awarded Carmouche $800, and Bouis appealed. Bouis contended that he had the right to defend his property. However, the justices of the supreme court ruled that he was liable for the death and resulting property loss to Carmouche. The difference between this case and *Allain, f.m.c.* v. *Young* lay in the nature of the slaves' acts: Régese's attempt to seize a firearm was a felony; John's offense was petty theft. Justice Isaac Preston, writing for the court, held that homicide was not necessary to prevent a misdemeanor, and that the killing of John was unnecessary for the defense of Bouis' person, family, or property.[15]

Eight years later the court heard an appeal from the District Court of Plaquemines Parish, *McCutcheon* v. *Angelo* (1859), which involved the shooting and blinding of a slave named John Hall, the property of S. D. McCutcheon. The plaintiff brought a civil action for $3,000—$2,000 for the alleged value of the slave and $1,000 for his future maintenance, as McCutcheon claimed John was worthless as a result of his injuries. Angelo claimed that he shot the slave because he had observed him lurking about his chicken house. When the slave realized that Angelo had seen him, he fled, ignoring Angelo's order to stop, whereupon Angelo shot him. The attending physician testified that Hall had been wounded eight times, including one shot in one eye and two in the other. The lower-court judge awarded McCutcheon $1,500, stating that Angelo had used "excessive force for petty larceny." In his appeal Angelo asserted that his actions were justified, as the slave was in the act of committing a felony and had refused to obey Angelo's order to halt. The supreme court ordered Angelo to pay the damages assessed by the lower court. Chief Justice Merrick wrote the opinion dismissing the defendant's assertion that chicken stealing was a felony and rejecting An-

15. Carmouche v. Bouis, No. 2032, 6 La. Ann. 95 (1851). For an almost identical case involving a slave shot in the act of stealing a hog, see Bibb v. Hebert, No. 753, 3 La. Ann. 132 (1848). See also Jennings v. Fundeburg, 4 McCord 161 (S.C. 1827).

gelo's contention that the shooting was justified by the slave's refusal to stop when commanded: "it is true that it is provided by law that 'if any slave shall be found absent from his usual place of working or residence, without some white person accompanying him, and shall refuse to submit himself to examination, any freeholder shall be permitted to seize and correct him; and if he should resist or attempt to escape, the freeholder is authorized to make use of arms, but to avoid killing the slave; but should the slave assault and strike him, he is authorized to kill him.'" Merrick made no mention of *Jourdan* v. *Patton* (1818), in which the court ordered an owner who was fully compensated for the blinding of her slave to transfer title to the owner of the slave who caused the injury. In that case the supreme court considered the well-being of the slave, who had been owned by the same mistress for many years, but denied that the slave's future situation had any relevance under the law. The difference between *Jourdan* and *McCutcheon* was that in *Jourdan* the slave was injured by another slave, but in *McCutcheon* the slave was injured by the very party to whom title would have been transferred. Although in *Jourdan* the court stated that "cruelty and inhumanity ought not to be presumed against any person," in *McCutcheon* Angelo's excessive punishment of chicken stealing went far beyond mere presumption that further abuse of the slave might occur.[16]

During the same term that the court decided *McCutcheon,* it also heard the appeal of *Gardiner* v. *Thibodeau* (1859), a civil suit in which Edward C. Gardiner sought to recover the value of his slave Charles. The slave had been in the act of stealing chickens when Jean Thibodeau shot and killed him. A witness stated that after the shooting, "there were chicken feathers from the [chicken] yard to the place where the negro was lying." Thibodeau admitted that he had shot Charles because he ordered the slave to halt but the man continued to flee. The District Court of St. Landry Parish found for the defendant, and Gardiner appealed. Citing an 1857 act that held that "it shall be lawful to fire upon runaway negroes, who may be armed, when pursued, if they refuse to surrender," Thibodeau contended that he was justified in shooting Charles because he was running away and was armed. Chief Justice Merrick rejected this argument:

16. McCutcheon v. Angelo, No. 5425, 14 La. Ann. 34 (1859); Jourdan v. Patton, No. 304, 5 Mart. (o.s.) 615 (La. 1818). See also chap. 1, note 34.

> It is proved that a knife was found in the pocket of his coat after the body of the negro was removed to the residence of the plaintiff. The coat was lying at the feet of the boy, and the knife was a butcher knife, six or seven inches long. This does not bring the case within the statute. The defendant did not pretend (as we have seen), that he killed the slave because he was a runaway and armed, but because he was stealing his chickens, and run [*sic*], and did not stop when commanded.
>
> If it be assumed, that the negro had his coat on when he was stealing the chickens, and the knife was in the pocket, the defence still fails, because it is not shown that the slave was a runaway. So far from being a runaway, the proof makes it sufficiently certain that he was out for no other purpose than that of stealing chickens; two of which were found by his house. The proof shows, that he was addicted to theft; but there is none tending to show that he was a runaway. Our law does not justify the killing of any one for a theft, and the defendant is left without sufficient justification.

The supreme court reversed the decision and awarded Gardiner $1,150. Citing *McCutcheon* v. *Angelo* in his ruling, Merrick ordered Thibodeau to reimburse Gardiner for Charles's value.[17]

In *Dupérrier* v. *Dautrive* (1856), the owner of another slave who disobeyed an order to halt was unable to recover from those who shot the luckless man. Dupérrier claimed that the defendants had "wantonly shot and mortally wounded" his slave while they were riding patrol for the city of New Iberia. When the patrol spotted the slave, they ordered him to halt, but he galloped away on a horse, whereupon members of the patrol fired upon him. Testimony established that his master had sent him into town on horseback to run an errand. When the patrol ordered him to stop, his horse, which was newly broken, bolted; members of the patrol fired at him three times with shotguns. The slave returned home and died of his wounds the next day. The District Court of St. Martin Parish held for the defendants, who, the court reasoned, believed the slave was a fugitive and were only doing their duty. Unrest among the slaves in and around New Iberia and rumors of slave insurrection had caused the patrols to take their responsibilities more seriously than

17. Gardiner v. Thibodeau, 14 La. Ann. 732 (1859); "An Act Relative to Slaves," Act of March 19, 1857, *Louisiana Acts, 1857,* Sec. 41, p. 233.

usual. The supreme court affirmed the judgment, stating that the recent disorders called for strict enforcement of the laws for policing slaves. The justices cited section 65 of the Act of 1855, "An Act Relative to Slaves and Colored Persons," which provided that any white who found a slave away from his usual residence who resisted arrest might "make use of arms" to seize and subdue him. The use of weapons, the justices reasoned, implied the risk of killing, and therefore applied to this case.[18]

The supreme court heard several appeals involving slaveholders who sued their overseers for brutality and injury to their slaves. Slaves' hatred toward overseers in the American South is legendary. Historians have charged that overseers had a marked preference for using physical force in managing their charges. Since slaves generally did not accord overseers the same respect they gave owners, physical coercion was often necessary to induce obedience. Details from the lower-court cases reveal that many overseers deserved their reputation for harsh and often excessive measures to maintain discipline and maximize productivity. The *Black Code* dealt with situations in which persons beat slaves belonging to others without sufficient provocation: section 33 provided not only for financial compensation if a slave were injured or killed, but also for criminal prosecution of the offender. Yet not one case of abuse by an overseer that was appealed to the supreme court involved criminal prosecution; all were civil suits to regain the value of the lost labor of slaves temporarily incapacitated by mistreatment, or the full value of slaves permanently disabled or killed. Often the slaveholder asked merely that the court reduce the overseer's salary as compensation for the loss. The lack of criminal prosecutions despite overpowering evidence of barbarous treatment demonstrates both the failure of slave law to protect the basic right to be treated humanely and the resultant inadequacy of the courts in dealing with cruelty to slaves.[19]

18. Dupérrier v. Dautrive, 12 La. Ann. 664 (1856); "An Act Relative to Slaves and Free Colored Persons," Act of March 15, 1855, *Louisiana Acts, 1855,* Sec. 65, p. 386. See also Witsell v. Earnest, 1 N. and McCord 182 (S.C. 1818). St. Martin Parish and neighboring parishes were shaken by rumors of slave revolts in the fall of 1856. The patrol shot the slave in *Dupérrier* in August, 1855. Harvey Wish, "The Slave Insurrection Panic of 1856," *Journal of Southern History,* V (May, 1939), 217–18.

19. Stampp, *Peculiar Institution,* 183; Alton V. Moody, "Slavery on Louisiana Sugar Plantations," *Louisiana Historical Quarterly,* VII (April, 1924), 210; William Kaufman Scarborough, *The Overseer: Plantation Management in the Old South* (Athens, 1984), 78–29; *Black Code,* Sec. 33, p. 176.

It is also worth noting that in these cases the supreme court ruled overwhelmingly in favor of the slaveowners, regardless of the decision of the lower court. There is no evidence of a shift in jurisprudence during the antebellum period: despite changing times and personnel, the court almost always supported the property interests of the masters against their overseers. Only unusual circumstances produced any other result.

Coincidentally, the earliest case involving an overseer killing a slave was one of the exceptions to this pattern. In *Martineau* v. *Hooper* (1818, 1820), the plaintiff sued his overseer for killing one of his slaves. The jury in the first case found the overseer blameless and ruled against Martineau. On appeal the supreme court refused to rule because the clerk of the district court had failed to provide a transcript of one witness' testimony. The district court retried the case in 1820, the jury again found for the defendant, and Martineau appealed. Witnesses testified that Harry, the slave, was so insubordinate that his master was afraid to return to his plantation and had ordered the overseer, Hooper, to subdue him. Evidence indicated that the slave was so out of control that he had laid hands on his master. Believing that the recalcitrant slave would resist him, Hooper took the precaution of loading his gun, although he left it in the house before going outside to whip him. Harry did resist, and a scuffle ensued during which the overseer threatened to kill him. Harry took flight, and Hooper ran to the house, got his gun, and fatally wounded the slave. Chief Judge Mathews, writing for the court, held Hooper blameless, as the slave was "in an actual state of rebellion." It was imperative, he ruled, that a slave who set such an example not go unpunished. Mathews reasoned that Hooper had acted as though the slave were his own and that two juries had excused him for refusing to allow "this rebel slave" to escape with impunity.[20]

Martineau v. *Hooper* was an exceptional decision based on the interest of the slaveholding community in maintaining slave discipline by not allowing an ungovernable slave to go unpunished. The court was willing to allow a slaveholder to suffer a loss of his property for the general safety of the community. Otherwise, however, the justices ordinarily ruled in favor of slaveowners. In 1827 the court heard an appeal involv-

20. Martineau v. Hooper, No. 49, 5 Mart. (o.s.) 668 (La. 1818); No. 49, 8 Mart. (o.s.) 699 (La. 1820).

ing an overseer, *Perrie* v. *Williams and Adams*. Lucy Perrie, an absentee owner, sued her overseer, James Williams, and her neighbor, Arthur Adams, both of whom allegedly had shot her slave Milo, killing him. In her petition, Perrie claimed that Williams was an incompetent overseer who "cruelly treated and unnecessarily abused her slaves, . . . drove them off the plantation, and made a poor crop." She alleged that Williams had severely whipped and shot at two other slaves on her plantation. Adams, for his part, admitted the shooting, but said it was justified because Perrie's slaves often stole his cattle for food; their rations, he added, were meager. The lower court jury found Williams and Adams liable, and the judge awarded Perrie $900, $450 each from Williams and Adams. Only Williams appealed. Chief Judge Mathews affirmed the judgment of the lower court on the grounds that Perrie had a reasonable claim for damages because of the "unjustifiable violence and injury done directly to the property of the plaintiff."[21]

Womack v. *Nicholson* (1842) was a civil action brought by Abraham Womack, the owner of a slave named Nancy, against Peter Nicholson for the value of Nancy and for other damages. Womack had hired Nancy to Nicholson, whose overseer beat the pregnant slave woman so severely that she delivered her baby prematurely; she and the infant subsequently died. Nicholson denied the allegations, stating that Womack had represented Nancy as being "humble, tractable, and healthy," when in fact she was not only sickly but "insolent, disobedient, and in the habit of running away." The defendant claimed that Womack owed him $500 for days of lost labor, as well as maintenance and medical care for the slave. The Caddo Parish jury found in favor of the plaintiff for the sum of $558, and the defendant appealed. The testimony of witnesses established that Nancy was an intractable slave and had run away several times from the defendant. One witness stated that Nancy "required more whipping than ordinary negroes" and that another planter who had hired her returned her to Womack because of "her vicious and unmanageable character." When Nicholson found Nancy so insubordinate that she was useless, he ordered Mr. Churchman, his overseer, to return her to her owner. A neighbor subsequently found her lying by the side of the road, her head gashed, bruised, and swollen, with both old and fresh marks of the lash on her body. The neighbor summoned a physi-

21. Perrie v. Williams and Adams, No. 1444, 5 Mart. (N.S.) 694 (La. 1827).

cian, who found symptoms of dropsy (congestive heart failure), as well as evidence of a severe beating. Womack brought Nancy to his plantation, where she continued to exhibit symptoms of dropsy. He never summoned a physician, and Nancy died two months later. The Caddo Parish jury believed that the beating Nicholson's overseer administered to Nancy caused her death, but the supreme court reversed the decision, stating that although the beating most likely caused the death of Nancy's baby, Nancy herself had died of a preexisting disease, dropsy. The court held that Womack's neglect in failing to call a physician cost him full recovery of Nancy's value. The court lowered the award to $158.50, the cost of medical care for Nancy at the neighbor's house as a result of the overseer's beating. In overturning the lower court, Associate Judge Alonzo Morphy, writing for the court, held that the decision of the jury was a "manifest error" contrary to the evidence as to the cause of Nancy's death. Although the Supreme Court of Louisiana could review both law and fact, it could not overturn the verdict of a lower court on the basis of fact unless the judgment was clearly wrong—a "manifest error."[22]

Occasionally a master who believed that his overseer had abused a slave retaliated by withholding the overseer's salary. In *Hendricks* v. *Phillips* (1848), the overseer Hendricks sued Phillips, his employer, for back wages. Phillips admitted that Hendricks had been his overseer but stated that Hendricks had treated his slaves with such cruelty that he had made a reconventional demand (a civil-law term for countersuit) for the amount of the overseer's wages. Witnesses testified that Hendricks was a capable overseer who made a good crop, but they admitted that he had treated one slave woman with great brutality. Condemning the conduct of the overseer, Justice Thomas Slidell observed that "the details are of a most revolting character, and exhibited conduct on the part of the overseer utterly undefensible." Since the lower-court record no longer exists, we do not know what the "revolting" details were, except that witnesses' testimony was "extremely unfavorable to him [the overseer] with regard to the cruel treatment of the negro." Citing article 173 of the *Civil Code,* which prohibited masters and, by implication, those to whom masters delegated power, from inflicting excessively rigorous

22. Womack v. Nicholson, No. 949, 3 Rob. 248 (La. 1842); Benjamin Wall Dart, ed., *Constitutions of the State of Louisiana,* Tit. IV, Art. 63, p. 514, Tit. IV, Art. 62, p. 528.

Thomas Slidell, chief justice of the Louisiana Supreme Court from 1853 to 1855.
Photo by Warren Gravois. Courtesy of the Librarian, Law Library of Louisiana

punishment, as well as the *Black Code,* section 33, which made anyone cruelly chastising the slave of another liable for the value of the slave, Justice Slidell reversed the decision of the Catahoula Parish District Court, which had lowered the overseer's salary by the amount of the value of labor lost during the slave woman's convalescence; the supreme court ruled that testimony in the case established that the overseer had permanently disabled the slave, and that Phillips was entitled to her value as well as medical expenses. The court awarded Phillips the entire amount of the overseer's wages plus $100.[23]

The following year the court heard another appeal involving an overseer, *Blanchard* v. *Dixon* (1849). In this civil suit Blanchard alleged that Dixon, who was the overseer of the plaintiff's neighbor, had shot one of Blanchard's slaves without provocation. The overseer had seen the slave on the road in front of Blanchard's residence. He demanded a pass from the slave, who answered in French, which the overseer did not understand. However, Dixon believed from the tone of the reply that the slave was insolent, whereupon he demanded that the slave halt. In response to this order the slave took flight, and the overseer ran to his house for his gun, mounted a horse, and pursued the slave until he was sufficiently close to shoot him, fracturing his knee. Witnesses testified that the slave had been well-behaved and submissive before the incident. The overseer cited the *Black Code,* Sections 30 and 32, to justify the use of force in arresting a slave absent from his master's premises without a pass. The district court found for the overseer, but the supreme court reversed the judgment. Associate Justice George Rogers King compared the case with *Allain* v. *Young,* in which a white man had shot a slave who was out without a pass. The difference between the two cases, he reasoned, was that in *Allain* the slave had attempted to seize a firearm and was in the act of committing a felony, whereas in *Blanchard* the slave was guilty of no crime but failing to halt and be examined. As a physician had declared the injury to be permanent, King awarded Blanchard $700 in damages, two-thirds of the slave's value, plus $50 in medical expenses.[24]

The supreme court cited both *Allain* and *Blanchard* in the next appeal

23. Hendricks v. Phillips, No. 98, 3 La. Ann. 618 (1848). The court heard an appeal in an almost identical case in which an overseer shot the slave Alfred: Taylor v. Patterson, No. 3473, 9 La. Ann. 251 (1854).

24. Blanchard v. Dixon, No. 1135, 4 La. Ann. 57 (1849).

it considered of a case in which an overseer had shot a slave without provocation. *Arnandez* v. *Lawes* (1850) involved two slaves belonging to Jean Baptiste Arnandez. They were catching driftwood at their master's order when the overseer of a plantation across the river called them ashore and demanded their passes. Although both slaves produced written permits from Arnandez to be on the river, the overseer, Thomas B. Lawes, ordered two armed men standing nearby to restrain both slaves. One of the slaves, William, became frightened and fled. He had gone only a few feet when he apparently realized that running might make the situation worse; he turned to submit to Lawes just as the overseer fired several times, mortally wounding him. The lower court ruled in favor of the owner and awarded him $1,000 in damages; Lawes appealed on the grounds that under section 32 of the *Black Code* it was not a crime to shoot a slave who refused to halt. Associate Justice Pierre Adolphe Rost rejected this argument, calling Lawes's actions "useless, barbarous, unjustified violence." In a rare action, Rost amended the judgment and raised the award to Arnandez to $1,200.[25]

The following year the court heard another appeal from an overseer who shot a slave for a minor offense. In *Benjamin* v. *Davis* (1851), Herman P. Benjamin sued his overseer for the value of his slave Ned. The slave had misbehaved and had subsequently fled because Davis planned to whip him. The following day, the overseer armed himself and a companion; the two mounted horses and tracked Ned down with "negro dogs." After bragging to witnesses that they were off to hunt runaways, they returned with a mortally wounded Ned across Davis' saddle. Davis claimed the slave was a fugitive and as such could be shot with impunity according to the *Black Code*. The West Feliciana District Court jury found for the defendant, and Benjamin appealed. Justice Rost, writing for the court, reversed the decision of the lower court, calling the shooting "totally unjustified." Citing *Carmouche* v. *Bouis,* he questioned what excuse two able-bodied armed and mounted men with dogs might have had in firing upon an old, unarmed slave. Calling the verdict of the lower court "clearly erroneous," Rost awarded Benjamin $350.[26]

Six months later Rost wrote another decision involving an overseer's cruel treatment of the slaves in his charge, *Dwyer* v. *Cane* (1851). The

25. Arnandez v. Lawes, No. 1572, 5 La. Ann. 127 (1850).

26. *Black Code,* Sec. 35, p. 180; Benjamin v. Davis, No. 2141, 6 La. Ann. 472 (1851).

overseer, Samuel E. Dwyer, sued his former employer, who had fired him and refused to pay his back wages. Despite the fact that Dwyer had made a good crop, "he inflicted cruel and unusual punishments upon the male slaves, and . . . his conduct with the women of the plantation was grossly and openly immoral." Dwyer lost in the district court and appealed to the supreme court. Justice Rost, writing for the court, acknowledged that Dwyer was not guilty of such mismanagement that he should have been dismissed, because he "made a good crop of cotton." However, Rost rejected the overseer's demand for reinstatement and back wages: "Cruelty to slaves is a sufficient cause of dismissal, and *honeste vivere* [a Roman law term meaning 'to live virtuously'] forms part of the duties of an overseer."[27]

In 1855 the supreme court heard two appeals in which owners claimed that overseers had caused the loss of one of their slaves through excessive punishment. In *Kennedy* v. *Mason,* the plaintiff claimed $600 from the estate of the owner of the plantation as the final amount due for his wages. The agent of the owner filed a reconventional demand for $1000, the value of a slave named Jim Crack, who allegedly had died at the hands of the overseer as a punishment for having run away. Witnesses stated that despite extremely cold weather, Kennedy stripped the slave, tied him "with his belly down to the cold ground," and beat him steadily for an hour and a half with a handsaw and a whip. Following the beating, Kennedy rubbed him with a mixture called No. 6 and administered a dose of castor oil; fellow slaves put Jim Crack in his bed, where he died within a few hours. The lower court found in favor of the unpaid overseer, but the supreme court reversed the decision. The physician who conducted the postmortem examination concluded that the whipping alone did not cause Crack's death, but that the combination of the whipping and exposure to the frigid weather was fatal: "I saw that he had been whipped and considerably bruised on his buttock, and each side of his shoulders. The buttock and sides of the shoulders did not appear much cut, but considerably bruised, from which the blood oozed and stuck to the shirt in a few places. That amount of whipping under ordinary circumstances, would not produce death. I thought it imprudent to whip the boy at that time and under the circumstances. From

27. Dwyer v. Cane, No. 222, 6 La. Ann. 707 (1851); emphasis in original. Cruelty to slaves was not an uncommon cause of dismissal; see Scarborough, *Overseer,* 96.

internal and external indications, I think it more likely that death was caused by a congestive chill, than by the whipping; but more likely death in this case was caused by a combination of all the circumstances." In overturning the decision of the Ouachita Parish District Court, Justice Cornelius Voorhies wrote: "Under this state of facts we do not think it is unreasonable to infer that the slave's death was caused by the severity of the punishment inflicted upon him, combined with his exposure to the weather. Had the plaintiff taken proper care of him after he retired to his cabin, he might have averted the unfortunate consequence: but he did not. This was gross negligence on his part." The high court allowed the reconventional demand of the owner's agent for the full value of Jim Crack. The overseer requested a rehearing on the grounds that Jim Crack had been a frequent runaway and was therefore virtually worthless. A witness testified that she had known the slave since he was a child, and "with his character and habits he was entirely worthless." Notwithstanding, Justice Voorhies refused to grant a rehearing.[28]

During the same month, the court heard *Kemp* v. *Hutchinson*. The overseer had whipped a slave named Big Nancy twice in one day for stealing, and was threatening a third flogging if she did not produce the allegedly stolen articles. She denied the theft but said she would try to find the articles. Instead, she threw herself into a river and drowned. The difference between *Kemp* and *Kennedy* v. *Mason,* Associate Justice Alexander Buchanan reasoned, was that there was no proof that the overseer caused Big Nancy's death, which Justice Buchanan termed a "voluntary act." Buchanan ruled that the overseer was not responsible for the woman's death: "The power of correction of a slave, vested in his master by our law, was held, in the case of *Kennedy* v. *Mason,* to be delegated to an overseer, from the nature of his employment. In the exercise of that power, the owner of the slave or his delegate, is only held to be responsible for the immediate and necessary consequences of his acts." Buchanan ordered Hutchinson to pay the overseer the wages he had withheld.[29]

28. Kennedy v. Mason, No. 362, 10 La. Ann. 519 (1855). "No. 6" may refer to one of the six basic medicines of the "system," namely brandy or wine, thought "to strengthen the internal system and the weakened patient." Todd L. Savitt, *Medicine and Slavery: The Diseases and Health Care of Blacks in Antebellum Virginia* (Urbana, Ill., 1978), 170*n37*. Another court record indicates that a slave was rubbed with a mixture of brandy and cayenne pepper. Cayenne was No. 2 of the "system." Buddy v. *Vanleer,* No. 1901, 6 La. Ann. 34 (1851).

29. Kemp v. Hutchinson, No. 452, 10 La. Ann. 494 (1855).

The following year the court heard the appeal that most clearly demonstrates the inability of the legal system to deal with excessive cruelty to slaves. The unreported case of *Humphreys* v. *Utz* (1856) is remarkable for several reasons, among them for providing compelling evidence that the Supreme Court of Louisiana had an unspoken policy of underreporting or omitting entirely from its official reports certain kinds of cases involving cruelty to slaves. Cases of flagrant sexual abuse were one category that made the justices reticent. For example, in *Hendricks* v. *Phillips* (1848), the court stated that the overseer's behavior with a slave woman was "of a most revolting character, and exhibited conduct on the part of the overseer utterly indefensible," but we are not given the "revolting" details, and the record of the trial court has vanished. In *Dwyer* v. *Cane,* the court again relied on generalizations—"He inflicted cruel and unusual punishment upon the male slaves . . . and his conduct with the women of the plantation was grossly and openly immoral"—and again the trial-court record, where we might learn specifics, has disappeared. In citing "cruel and unusual punishment," though, the justices touched on a second phenomenon they disliked to report: extreme (and almost certainly sadistic) physical brutality. Several appeals involving beatings of slaves, even to death, were dutifully reported, but when the issue was torture, not merely harsh discipline, things were different. *Humphreys* v. *Utz* was a torture case that speaks volumes about the court's tacit policy on reporting. For here at last the grisly details have somehow survived: we have the complete trial-court record, the briefs to the supreme court, the court's handwritten decision, even a sheet of scratch paper on which the trial jury figured the amount of damages—and the case went unreported.

Humphreys was a suit for civil damages of $5,000 brought by J. C. and G. W. Humphreys, absentee owners of Burkland Plantation in Madison Parish, against Henry Utz, their overseer, for damages he allegedly caused by inflicting "cruel treatment of an unusual inhuman and outrageous nature . . . upon two of the negroes placed under his care." The Humphreys brothers charged that one of the slaves, "Ginger Pop," died from Utz's cruelty. Specifically, they claimed that Utz had killed Ginger Pop by "nailing the privates of said negro to the bedstead and then inflicting blows upon him until said negro pulled loose from the post to which he had been pinned by driving an iron tack or nail through his penis." The Humphreyses further alleged that Utz had "inflicted a similar outrage upon a certain negro boy named Dave," who also belonged to them.[30]

Utz denied the allegations of cruelty. He claimed that the brothers had hired him to manage the plantation for the year 1853 for a salary of $800. He said he had served as overseer until he was "wrongfully discharged" on August 19, 1853, and he made a reconventional demand for his salary. He stated that he "was at all times attentive to his business, kind to the sick and humain [*sic*] to all," and that the plaintiffs were bent on ruining his reputation as "a careful manager of negroes, and a good cultivator of the soil." He alleged that the slaves of Burkland Plantation "had the reputation of being difficult to manage, and several of them were habitual runaways." Utz asked for $6,000 in damages from the Humphreyses for the harm done to his reputation.

A witness to the incident testified that Ginger Pop was a habitual runaway, and apparently Utz had tried to discipline him in other ways, once attempting to nail his ear to the gallery of the plantation house and once taking "the butt end of his cowhide and [whipping him] on the head as long as he could stand over him." Gabriel Utz, brother to the defendant and himself an overseer on a neighboring plantation, testified that Ginger Pop was always running away; besides, Gabriel added, Henry Utz had told him that he only tacked Ginger Pop's penis to the bedpost to scare him, and "that it had done more good than all the whippings, that it had calmed him." Gabriel Utz also testified that Ginger Pop would have been worth from $800 to $1,000 if he were not a habitual runaway, but with his character, he was "worth little or nothing."

On the night Ginger Pop died, Utz told a witness "that he was *damd* [*sic*] glad of it and wished he could get clear of Shed and Maria [other slaves on the plantation] the same way, deft [*sic*] told witness next morning that he had slept the happiest nights [*sic*] sleep he had since he had been on the place." Ginger Pop died on June 10; the Humphreyses called a physician to conduct a postmortem examination on August 20, but the decomposition of the body prevented him from coming to any conclu-

30. Humphreys v. Utz, Unreported Louisiana Supreme Court Case No. 3910 (1856). It is unclear whether Utz nailed the slave's penis itself, or only the foreskin, to the bedpost. One witness said that Utz "had drove a tack through the skin of his [Ginger Pop's] penis to the Bed Rail and hit him two or three licks until he pulled loose." Either way, Utz's action was barbarous even by the standards of the times.

sion regarding the cause of death. Utz claimed Ginger Pop had died of a "congestive chill," although he admitted that "he had worn him out." The Humphreys brothers fired Utz the same day.

The trial-court jury found for Utz in the amount of 388.86. They arrived at this figure by calculating Utz's wages from January 1 to August 20—$508.83—and then deducting damages to Ginger Pop of $120. Why did the Madison Parish jury find for Utz despite overwhelming evidence to the contrary? Why was Utz never convicted of cruelty in a criminal trial? The answer to both questions lies in the brief to the supreme court by the Humphreyses' attorney, Andrew R. Hynes:

> It will be remembered that the Mssrs. Humphreys reside in the State of Mississippi and seldom visit the Burkland plantation, and were not present at the trial of this suit in the District Court. The Grand Jury acting in and for the Parish of Madison, indicted the defendant for cruel treatment of the slaves of the plaintiff, and the Jury impanelled to try the case brought in a verdict of "Not Guilty," although the proof was direct and overwhelming. It will be remembered that in a sparsely populated country, where the owners of property are non-residents, the Jurors of the country are almost entirely made up of Overseers, and that perhaps no class is so clannish or so disposed to protect each other in their difficulties. Whenever a planter shall in a contest with an overseer resort to a jury, there can be no doubt as to what the verdict will be, and the only hope left to the country is that the purity of the Bench will correct the evil.[31]

Justice Buchanan wrote the decision of the court. He acknowledged that Ginger Pop was "an incorrigible runaway . . . a vicious and worthless subject," and he stated that there was no proof that the actual death of the slave had been caused by Utz's cruel treatment. However, Buchanan did not allow Utz to avoid the consequences of his actions: "Yet

31. Hynes's assessment of the cause of Utz's acquittal from criminal charges may well be accurate. Although the record of the criminal trial has vanished, the census indicates that at least six of the eleven jurors in the civil trial were overseers. The 1850 census for Madison Parish lists only 389 persons qualified to vote, meaning white males twenty-one or older. The census also indicates that there were 66 overseers in the parish. Although we cannot know how many overseers were in the jury pool at any given time, the possibility of having several on a jury was obviously high. The total population of Madison Parish in 1850 was 8,773, of whom 1,416 were white, 7,353 were slaves, and 4 were free persons of color.

acts of revolting brutality have been proved, which entirely exceed the limits of that repressive and correctional discipline which is necessary to the management of the agricultural laborers of the South . . . [which] should be strict . . . but . . . tempered with mercy. The evil passions of men become infuriated to reckless ferocity by unbridled indulgence: and the very helplessness of the slave . . . is sometimes found to encourage . . . cold blooded refinements of torture. He who cannot protect himself has a double claim to protection." Buchanan reversed the decision of the trial court and ruled that the Humphreyses' discharge of Utz was justified. Ordering Utz to pay his wages to the date of his discharge to the plaintiffs—$508.83—Buchanan also ruled that Utz pay costs in both courts.[32]

Humphreys v. *Utz* provides rare documentary evidence, considered too horrible to be published, of the barbarous treatment that some slaves endured. It also reveals a jury unwilling to award the owner of such a slave more than token damages for such abuse. From the appellate brief, we learn that Utz was the defendant in a criminal trial as well as in the civil suit for damages. The result of this trial is a clear illustration of a criminal justice system that utterly failed to protect slaves from even the most savage treatment: Utz was acquitted; despite overwhelming evidence against him, the jury simply refused to convict.

The following year, in *Miller* v. *Stewart* (1857), another overseer sued his employer for his wages of $800 for two years' service, and the owner filed a reconventional demand for $1,250, claiming the overseer was liable for the death of one of his slaves. In the appeal, the overseer claimed that the slave, Tom, had attacked him, was incorrigible, and had resisted when he attempted to whip him. During the scuffle Tom bit off the tip of Miller's finger and scratched his face. Finally Miller subdued the slave, loaded him with chains, staked him to the ground, and gave him a severe lashing. An eyewitness claimed that Miller whipped Tom from his neck to his heels and that the stripes were so close together that a person could not put a finger between them. This witness testified that he had never seen a slave whipped with such brutality. The two physicians who conducted the postmortem agreed that either the flogging itself or exhaustion and overexertion from the scourging caused Tom's death. The

32. Humphreys v. Utz, Unreported Louisiana Supreme Court case No. 3910 (1856).

Carroll Parish jury awarded Miller $344.15, the amount of the wages he had earned from the time of his employment to the time of his discharge, and Stewart appealed. Citing *Kennedy* v. *Mason* and describing the overseer's actions as "gross negligence," Justice Voorhies awarded Stewart $1,200—the assessed value of the slave—deducting $344, wages Stewart owed the overseer. In his decision, Voorhies quoted section 16 of the "Crimes and Offenses" section of the *Black Code* and questioned the overseer's allegations that Tom was a troublemaker: "The overseer may correct and chastise the slaves of the planter who employs him, but he cannot do so 'with unusual rigor, nor so to maim or mutilate them, or to expose them to the danger of loss of life, or to cause their death.' . . . There is not a scintilla of evidence showing that the slave *Tom* was vicious or that his character was bad; nor was there any attempt to show the nature of the offence which brought upon him such severe punishment."[33]

The supreme court heard the last case involving improper conduct by an overseer toward a slave in *Kessee* v. *Mayfield and Cage* (1859). Kessee sued the defendants for his wages of $800 for one year as overseer of their plantation. The owners had employed him on April 10, 1856, and discharged him, Kessee alleged, for no reason on June 22, 1856. Kessee's attorneys cited *Civil Code* article 2720, which required an employer who fired an employee without cause to honor the terms of the contract of hiring, paying him wages for the entire time provided for in the agreement. The defendants asserted that they had fired Kessee for good cause: incompetence, disregarding defendant's instructions, and cruelty to the slaves. Mayfield and Cage were willing to pay Kessee for the two months he had worked for them, but Kessee claimed wages for the whole year. Although the owners introduced no evidence to prove their allegations that the overseer was cruel or incompetent, evidence supported their claim that he disregarded their instructions. The defendants had strictly ordered him not to discipline the slaves with his own hand. Drivers were to flog the slaves if they should need chastisement. Witnesses stated that Kessee ignored these instructions and lashed the slaves himself. The District Court of Terrebonne Parish found that the owners

33. Miller v. Stewart, No. 4946, 12 La. Ann. 170 (1857); *Black Code,* "Crimes and Offenses," Sec. 16, pp. 206–208.

had discharged Kessee for good cause and denied him any wages whatever. The supreme court reversed this ruling and granted Kessee wages for the period he had actually worked. In its ruling the court stated that although article 2720 applied only to persons fired with no cause, it seemed unfair not to grant Kessee wages to the time of his discharge.[34]

Cases in which masters were accused of abusing their own slaves reached litigation infrequently during the antebellum period. The supreme court heard only three appeals of such civil suits during the whole time. In the first, *Markham* v. *Close* (1831), the plaintiff presented a petition to the District Court of Opelousas in which he alleged that his neighbor, Close, had cruelly beaten his own slave, Augustin. Markham requested that the court take the slave away from Close and sell him. Close did not deny the beating but claimed that the slave had been a fugitive for some time and deserved the punishment. Witnesses testified that the flogging was so severe that Augustin was incapable of sitting or lying on his back, and that Close had lashed him on three separate occasions. His back was "very much cut and skinned . . . the weather being warm, the wounds smelled badly." The district court judge placed the case on its docket as a civil action, and although Close protested that the proceedings were unknown to the law and that Markham had no right to institute such a suit, the lower court ordered Close to sell the slave. He appealed to the supreme court. Associate Judge Alexander Porter, writing for the court, found that Markham's petition was "an anomalous action, instituted in civil form to punish a criminal offense." Porter stated that Markham had no interest in the slave but had presented himself to the court as a public prosecutor. He acknowledged that evidence supported Markham's claim that Close had been excessively cruel to the slave, and added: "It is greatly to be deplored, that owners of slaves should abuse their authority." However, Porter denied that Markham had any right to institute such a suit. Excessive cruelty, Porter reasoned, was a public offense that had to be prosecuted criminally, according to section 16 of the *Black Code*. Judge Porter also cited article 192 of the *Civil Code,* which stated that a master could not be compelled to sell his slave unless he was actually convicted of cruel treatment. In

34. Kessee v. Mayfield and Cage No. 6022, 14 La. Ann. 90 (1859); *Civil Code,* Art. 2720, p. 418. Disobeying orders not to whip slaves was another common cause of dismissal for overseers; Scarborough, *Overseer,* 93–94.

such cases the judge could order the sale of a slave at public auction "in order to place him out of the reach of the power which his master has abused." Without a criminal conviction, no court could order sale of the slave. Markham could not take the law into his own hands in this manner, Porter ruled. Reversing the lower court's decision, Porter found that although Markham's motives might have been admirable, in another instance a person bringing a similar suit might be motivated by "envy, malice, and all uncharitableness." There is no record of any subsequent criminal prosecution against Close.[35]

In 1857 the court heard *Barrow* v. *McDonald,* a lawsuit for damages for the "malicious killing" of a slave by one of his owners. The plaintiff, Robert Ruffin Barrow, owned a three-fourths interest in the slave; the defendant, who managed one of Barrow's four sugar plantations, owned one-fourth. Barrow estimated his losses at $1,500. Barrow and McDonald were business partners and owned the sugar plantation upon which the killing occurred in the same proportions that they owned the slave. The judge in the Terrebonne District Court ruled that the damages should properly be a part of the action (which was in progress) to dissolve the partnership between the two men, and not a separate action. The supreme court agreed with this assessment and affirmed the judgment.[36]

The high court heard the last appeal involving cruelty to a slave by a master in *Ney* v. *Richard* (1860), a civil action that arose because of the improper handling of a criminal case. The sheriff of St. Landry Parish arrested Adele Roy Ney for cruel treatment of her slave Frozine. The parish court judge released Ney after she posted bail. At the same time, he ordered Frozine to be incarcerated in parish prison pending the outcome of the trial. His purpose was to furnish the slave protection from Ney. Ney's husband filed an action against the parish judge and the sheriff. The district court judge ruled that sequestering the slave to remove her from Ney's power was the proper action under the circumstances, and Ney appealed. The supreme court ruled that the district court erred

35. Markham v. Close, 2 La. 581 (1831); *Black Code,* "Crimes and Offenses," Sec. 16, pp. 206–208; *Civil Code,* Art. 192, pp. 29–30.

36. Barrow v. McDonald, No. 4854, 12 La. Ann. 110 (1857). Barrow was a wealthy Terrebonne Parish slaveowner who owned four sugar plantations: Residence, Myrtle Grove, Caillou Grove, and Point Farm; Scarborough, *Overseer,* 187.

in its ruling because no law existed to remove a slave from the power of his or her master without a criminal conviction for cruelty. The court ordered the release of the slave to the Neys. No record exists of an appeal of the criminal prosecution.[37]

Louisiana law provided slaves few protections against cruel treatment, although the legal machinery was in place had witnesses, prosecutors, and judges chosen to use it. Evidence in appeals to the Supreme Court of Louisiana shows that strangers, neighbors, overseers, and owners abused slaves at times, ignoring such protective laws as existed. Most of these cases involved irate owners bringing civil actions to recover damages for slaves injured or killed by others. The court heard no criminal appeals until after 1846 because it lacked jurisdiction, and even after 1846 heard few criminal appeals of this nature. Masters were apparently more interested in financial compensation than justice. Since lower-court records of criminal prosecutions are not accessible or have not survived, these appeals are the only solid evidence of prosecutions for cruelty to slaves in Louisiana. Of course, we have no way of knowing how many persons accused of brutal cruelty and incontrovertibly guilty of it were acquitted because, as with Henry Utz, a jury simply refused to convict. Certainly, though, *Humphreys* v. *Utz* demonstrates the failure of the law to provide even the most basic protection for slaves.

Slaveowners created the legal system that prohibited cruel treatment, and the judiciary as a whole seems to have been very reluctant to interfere with what many judges and juries perceived as a matter between owners and their property. The courts were quite willing to support the slaveowners' financial interest in injured or dead slaves, which was a simple issue of awarding property damages, but only the most atrocious crimes occasionally resulted in criminal prosecutions; in all criminal prosecutions of a slaveowner, the cruel treatment had caused the death of the slave.

Ironically, even though the legal status of slaves in Louisiana was insignificant compared with that of their powerful owners, the law abundantly protected the slaveholders *from* their slaves. The paradox of the slave's being at once person and property often disappeared when he or she committed a crime. In that instance the slave was almost invariably

37. Ney v. Richard, 15 La. Ann. 603 (1860).

a person in the eyes of the law. By contrast, when a slave was victimized by an owner's cruelty, Louisiana was far more cognizant of the slave as property. Thus, again, the legal system was rendered inadequate to protect slaves' most basic rights; for when the limited right of slaves to life conflicted with the property interests of slaveholders, the outcome was seldom in doubt.

3

"NO PROCEEDINGS . . . SHALL BE ANNULLED OR IMPEDED BY ANY ERROR OF FORM"

The Treatment of Slaves Accused of Crimes

SLAVES COULD COUNT ON BEING CONSIDERED PERSONS rather than property under Louisiana law when they committed a crime. Paradoxically, this affirmation of their humanity placed them in jeopardy; as persons, they could be tried, convicted, and punished for their actions. The *Black Code* and other legislative measures made criminal certain acts by blacks that were not considered crimes for whites. Furthermore, the punishments for blacks were usually more severe than for whites who committed similar offenses. Disgruntled owners of convicted slaves could and did appeal to the Supreme Court of Louisiana for redress, usually without success. In Louisiana, unlike its southern counterparts, the state supreme court was influenced by a unique legal heritage, a singular system of laws, and stringent state constitutional restrictions. These exceptional features prevented antebellum Louisiana's criminal jurisprudence from falling into the pattern of southern appellate-court justice for slaves.

One way to look at "justice" for slaves accused of crimes is to understand that the overriding purpose of criminal law for slaves was to protect slaveowners' property and to maintain discipline and order in slave communities. In this light, criminal procedure for slaves was primarily a mechanism for determining whether property should be condemned, much as in real-property law when private property is taken for public use without the owner's consent—a forced sale with compensation to the property owner. Slave trials, then, were similar to a procedure for eminent domain, a taking of property by the state in the public interest, which explains why procedural rules were so often ignored in antebellum slave trials. So although slaves accused of crimes were vulnerable to criminal prosecution as persons, the legal procedure to determine their fate was strikingly like compensated property condemnations.

The *Black Code* of 1806 mandated execution or corporal punishment for criminal offenses committed by slaves. An 1855 revision of the law of slave crimes gave the court the option of execution *or* imprisonment in the state penitentiary for a capital offense. For example, a slave who struck his master "so as to cause a contusion of blood" received a death sentence under the 1806 *Black Code;* under the 1855 revision, the judge could sentence him to execution or to imprisonment at hard labor for not less than ten years. Laws to compensate owners of convicted slaves also changed during the antebellum period. Under the 1806 *Black Code,* the court appraised condemned slaves and compensated their owners for the assessed value, up to $500 (owners of slaves executed for participation in a rebellion, however, could not be compensated). An act of 1855 changed the limit to two-thirds of the slave's value, up to $750, and ordered appraisals of slaves sentenced to be executed or imprisoned for life. This act required the owner of such a slave to surrender title to the state before being compensated for the loss of property—more evidence of a similarity to a procedure of eminent domain, in which the state must compensate the property owner for the property seized.[1]

Some historians believe that in southern states where slaves were tried in the same courts and under the same laws as whites, appellate courts often upheld the procedural rights of slaves in major criminal cases, and that these courts often used procedural errors to mitigate harsh local justice. These scholars' studies have found that common-law protections often benefited the slave defendants. A study of the Tennessee Supreme Court, for example, found treatment of slave defendants to be essentially fair, and the reversal rate of slave convictions higher than that of whites.[2]

1. Stampp, *Peculiar Institution,* 210; *Black Code,* "Crimes and Offenses," Secs. 9, 12, pp. 200, 202–204; "An Act to Repeal All Laws or Provisions of Laws Prescribing Remunerating the Owners of Slaves Sentenced to Death or Killed While Run Away," Act of January 8, 1813, *Louisiana Acts, 1813,* Secs. 1, 2, p. 16; "An Act Relative to Slaves and Free Colored Persons," Act of March 15, 1855, *Louisiana Acts, 1855,* Secs. 3, 52, 53, pp. 378, 384–85.

2. A. E. Keir Nash, "The Texas Supreme Court and Trial Rights of Blacks, 1845–1860," *Journal of American History,* LVIII (December, 1971), 622; A. E. Keir Nash, "Fairness and Formalism in the Trials of Blacks in the State Supreme Courts of the Old South," *Virginia Law Review,* LVI (February, 1970), 65–66. See also A. E. Keir Nash, "A More Equitable Past? Southern Supreme Courts and the Protection of the Antebellum Negro," *North Carolina Law Review,* XLVII (February, 1970), 197–242, and Flanigan, "Criminal Procedure in Slave Trials," 538. Recent scholarship analyzing black justice at the local level concludes that slave justice in the lower courts was rarely just, that in fact black justice was a contradiction in terms. Michael Stephen Hindus, "Black Justice Under White Law: Criminal Prosecutions of Blacks in Ante-

Colonial Louisianians were unfamiliar with such English-common-law rights as presumption of innocence, trial by jury, an independent judiciary, and the right of appeal in criminal cases. These protections did not exist in the French or Spanish systems of law. During the Spanish colonial period in Louisiana, criminal law was brutal. Torture was legal, and sentences were meted out solely at the judge's discretion. In capital cases Spanish judges could choose decapitation by sword, burning at the stake, or death by wild beasts. Although there is no evidence of a sentence of decapitation or death by wild beasts, one slave in Spanish Louisiana was burned at the stake in the judge's presence. Judges in eighteenth-century France were instruments of the crown and considered a part of the prosecution team. Under French law the burden of proof rested on the accused to prove innocence, not on the state to prove guilt. Despite extensive reforms in Gallic law after the French Revolution, civil law assumed that the accused in a criminal trial was guilty until proved otherwise.[3]

Louisiana's colonial criminal law was so contrary to the United States Constitution, the Bill of Rights, and general American concepts of criminal justice that Governor Claiborne insisted that the Territorial Legislature pass the Crimes Act in 1805. This measure introduced common-law principles in criminal prosecutions in Louisiana for white defendants and for free persons of color. Common-law concepts of criminal procedure and trial by jury were so unfamiliar to Louisianians that in 1806 Governor Claiborne commissioned Lewis Kerr to write a detailed exposition of the Crimes Act.[4]

---

bellum South Carolina," *Journal of American History,* LXIII (December, 1976), 599; Michael Stephen Hindus, *Prison and Plantation: Crime, Justice, and Authority in Massachusetts and South Carolina, 1767–1878* (Chapel Hill, 1980), 161. *Cf.* Arthur Fletcher Howington, "The Treatment of Slaves and Free Blacks in the State and Local Courts of Tennessee" (Ph.D. dissertation, Vanderbilt University, 1982), 212, 214, 201, 288–89; Howington found slave justice in the lower courts comparable to that for whites.

3. John Henry Wigmore, "Louisiana: The Story of Its Legal System," *Southern Law Quarterly,* I (January, 1916), 8; Henry Plauché Dart, *The Colonial Legal Systems of Arkansas, Louisiana, and Texas* (New Orleans, 1926), 8; A. Esmein, *A History of Continental Criminal Procedure* (New York, 1968), 8, 10, 12, 58, 397–99; John Henry Wigmore, *A Treatise on the System of Evidence in Trials at Common Law* (Boston, 1904), 530.

4. "An Act for the Punishment of Crimes and Misdemeanors," Act of May 4, 1805, *Orleans Territorial Acts, 1805,* Sec. 33, p. 440; Lewis Kerr, *An Exposition of the Criminal Laws of the Territory of Orleans. . . .* (New Orleans, 1806), iv–vi.

In *State* v. *Peggy* (1820), a slave was sentenced to wear this thirteen-and-a-half-pound ball on her ankle as part of her punishment for manslaughter. The case did not come before the state supreme court, which was limited to civil appeals before 1846.

Courtesy of the Historic New Orleans Collection, Museum/Research Center, Acc. No. 90-58-L

The right of appellate review was absent from the Crimes Act, and the Louisiana Constitution of 1812 limited the state supreme court's jurisdiction to *civil* cases exceeding $300. Thus, the Louisiana Supreme Court heard no appeals from slaves or free people convicted of capital crimes until 1846. In its first term, in *Laverty* v. *Duplessis* (1813), the court refused to enlarge its authority by considering a criminal appeal, ruling that the case was not within its appellate jurisdiction. The revised Constitution of 1845, which became effective in March, 1846, extended the court's appellate jurisdiction to criminal cases in which the punishment was incarceration at hard labor or execution. The right to an appellate review of a conviction for a capital crime was assumed under the common-law system and guaranteed by the structure of the federal court system created by the United States Constitution; state constitutions also created state supreme courts for review of criminal as well as civil appeals. However, no such appeal was possible in Louisiana until the Constitution of 1845 went into effect. The only recourse available to the convicted person was to petition for a new trial by entering a writ of error in the same court that had convicted him or her in the first place.[5] Because all criminal appeals the Louisiana Supreme Court heard occurred between 1846 and 1861, there is little evidence of change in jurisprudential thought.

The powers of the court were further limited to "questions of law alone," so the only legal basis for reversal was manifest judicial error (of course, it was necessary to review the facts to determine whether the law was applicable to the case). Even if the court (beginning in 1846) felt proof of guilt was insufficient, it could not overturn a lower court's decision on those grounds, because it could not use common-law reasoning to fill in the gaps in state law. Similarly, along with other antebellum courts—and courts today, for that matter—the Supreme Court of Louisiana could not affirm a conviction for an act, no matter how blatantly wrong, unless a specific statute prohibited it. In *State* v. *King* (1857), *State* v. *Kitty* (1857), and *State* v. *Henderson* (1858), the court overturned convictions of slaves accused of capital offenses because the state legislature had repealed the law creating the crimes that King, Kitty, and Henderson allegedly committed, but had accidentally failed to pass a saving clause for pending prosecutions. *King* and *Henderson* were prosecutions for assault with intent to kill, and *Kitty* was a case of a slavewoman convicted of poisoning a white man. The purpose of the flawed legislation, "An Act Relative to Slaves and Free Colored Persons," had

5. Benjamin Wall Dart, ed., *Constitutions of the State of Louisiana,* Art. IV, Sec. 2, p. 503; Tit. IV, Art. 63, p. 514; "An Act to Establish a Court of Errors and Appeals in Criminal Matters . . . ," Act of April 6, 1843, *Louisiana Acts, 1843,* pp. 59–61; Laverty v. Duplessis, 3 Mart. (o.s.) 42 (La. 1813). The court reiterated *Laverty* in Hyde v. Jenkins, 6 La. 427 (1834), and State v. Judge of the Commercial Court (Stiles), 15 La. 192 (1840). The statement that the Louisiana Supreme Court did not hear any criminal appeals (slave or free) until 1846 appears to be incorrect if one notices that note 23 of this chapter shows five cases reported before that time. However, two were heard by the Superior Court of the Territory of Orleans; the three remaining were cases of the Court of Errors and Appeals, an appellate court created by the Louisiana legislature on April 6, 1843. This tribunal sat for the last time in February, 1846; its jurisdiction was transferred to the Louisiana Supreme Court by the new state constitution of 1845 which went into effect in March, 1846. Cases of the Court of Errors and Appeals are included here merely for interest.

been to provide a more comprehensive criminal code for slaves than the *Black Code*. Using the omission of the saving clause for pending prosecutions was an act of resistance by the justices to the legislature's attempt to define law in Louisiana.[6]

Did Louisiana's French and Spanish heritage create a more enlightened treatment of slaves accused of crimes than in the essentially Anglo-Saxon South? An examination of the Louisiana system for criminal trials and appeals of slaves reveals that the English common-law tradition furnished the greater protection. Louisiana blacks in bondage were more vulnerable than whites and free persons of color to prosecution for crime because they were treated separately and specially. The Crimes Act of 1805 applied only to whites and free blacks accused of crimes. Slaves were subject to the *Black Code,* which established special tribunals to try slaves accused of capital crimes. The *Black Code* stipulated the composition of these tribunals, and section 20 of the "Crimes and Offenses" part of the *Code* specifically exempted their proceedings from being annulled "by any error of form." Slaves were to be tried by the parish (county) judge or by two justices of the peace and three to five freeholders.[7] The law required members of the special courts to be slaveowners, and as the antebellum period progressed, their number was increased. Special tribunals composed of two justices of the peace and ten slaveholders of the appropriate parish heard most slave prosecutions appealed

6. Albert Voorhies, *A Treatise on the Criminal Jurisprudence of Louisiana* (New Orleans, 1860), 39; Tushnet, *American Law of Slavery,* 126–27 [for a critique of Tushnet, see Andrew Fede, "Toward a Solution of the Slave Law Dilemma: A Critique of Tushnet's *The American Law of Slavery,*" *Law and History Review,* II (Fall, 1984), 301]; State v. King, No. 597, 12 La. Ann. 593 (1857); State v. Kitty, No. 5154, 12 La. Ann. 805 (1857); State v. Henderson, No. 5621, 13 La. Ann. 489 (1858). In *Norris* v. *Crocker,* the United States Supreme Court made a similar ruling regarding a saving clause: Norris v. Crocker, 54 U.S. (13 How.) 429 (1852).

7. Elkins, *Slavery: A Problem in American Institutional and Intellectual Life,* 54–55*n45*. For the opposite view, see Flanigan, "Criminal Procedure in Slave Trials," 545*n25,* and Rankin, "The Tannenbaum Thesis Reconsidered," 31. Mary Frances Berry and John W. Blassingame, in *Long Memory: The Black Experience in America* (New York, 1982), 231, state that the purpose of slave trials was to determine the amount of compensation due the owner rather than meting out black justice. This was not true of Louisiana, where compensation was fixed by law throughout the antebellum period; see Klady v. McGuire, 1 Rob. 25 (1841); McDowell v. Couch, No. 2093, 6 La. Ann. 365 (1851). The rationale behind the low maximum figure of $750 was that slaves who committed capital crimes had almost no value; Flanigan, "Criminal Procedure in Slave Trials," 559. Tushnet, *American Law of Slavery,* 124, states that in 1846 Louisiana established special courts to try slaves convicted of capital offenses. Actually, the *Black Code* (1806) established these tribunals; *Black Code,* "Crimes and Offenses," Secs. 1–4, pp. 190–96.

to the supreme court. The slaveholding requirement worked simultaneously for and against the accused bondsman. Slaveowners knew well the monetary value of slaves and the importance of their labor to an owner, and they were reluctant to jeopardize the economic interest of other masters by imprisonment or execution of an expensive slave. However, slaveholders were also by definition staunch supporters of the system of bondage, a system in which control of slave conduct was absolutely essential.

Different rules applied to slave trials than to trials of whites or free blacks. Throughout the antebellum period, slaves tried by the special tribunals did not have the basic common-law right to challenge jurors, either peremptorily or for cause, although whites and free persons of color could issue both types of challenges. In 1855 the Louisiana legislature passed a law to allow jury challenges for cause by slaves, but this statute only partially corrected the problem, since the two presiding justices were judges as well as jurors, and as such were not subject to challenge. Also, this system allowed the justices to sit again in the trial of a case that had previously ended in a mistrial. The supreme court generally used a different set of rules for its reasoning in slave trials. Although the court freely cited common-law principles and decisions as a basis for its judgments in the appeals of whites and free persons of color convicted of crimes, it rarely did so in reviewing decisions by the special tribunals. Although there were exceptions, in most decisions the court, if it mentioned any precedents, confined itself to citing its own decisions in other slave appeals. By this practice, the court denied slaves the protection of common-law precedents of states that tried slaves under the same rules and in the same courts as whites—protection that the free people of Louisiana, black and white, received.[8]

All of these factors reinforce the view that slave trials were more in the nature of property condemnations than what is normally thought of as American criminal justice. Although purporting to mete out justice for slaves, the special tribunals in Louisiana were essentially part of a system dedicated to protecting white property, rather than to adminis-

8. Moody, "Slavery on Louisiana Sugar Plantations," 218–19; Kerr, *Exposition of the Criminal Laws*, 206–12; "An Act Relative to Slaves and Free Colored Persons," Act of March 15, 1855, *Louisiana Acts, 1855*, pp. 377–91. For example, in *Borie, f.m.c.,* v. *Bush* (mistakenly reported as "Bore"), the Supreme Court of Louisiana upheld the right of free persons of color accused of criminal acts to a trial by jury. Of course, as people of color could not serve on juries, it was not a jury of Borie's peers. Borie, f.m.c., v. Bush, No. 3039, 6 Mart. (N.S.) 1 (La. 1827).

tering justice to bondservants. In fact, the tribunals were actually designed to dispense with procedural niceties and render verdicts based on the opinion of the white community in which they functioned. Slaves tried in the same courts and under the same rules as whites would have been more likely to benefit from the procedural system that applied to whites. By the beginning of the Civil War, all southern states except South Carolina, Virginia, and Louisiana had abolished special slave tribunals and tried slaves in the same courts as whites. In *State* v. *Kentuck* (1853), a slave appealed a conviction for assault on a white man with a knife. The Supreme Court of Louisiana admitted that its responsibility in slave appeals was less than in that of whites: "The law . . . does not demand on the trial of slaves, in the tribunals established for that purpose, an observance of the technical rules which regulate criminal proceedings in the higher courts." The court based its decision on an 1846 act of the legislature stating that "no [slave] proceedings . . . shall be annulled or impeded by any error of form." This act echoed the provision in the 1806 *Black Code:* "No proceedings had by competent judges in consequence of this act, shall be annulled, avoided, or in any way impeded by any error of form in the drawing of the same."[9]

Not surprisingly, the court rarely reversed the judgments of the special slave courts because of procedural irregularities, and it often affirmed them despite such irregularities. In fact, the high court rarely questioned the decisions by the slave tribunals for *any* reason—further cause to view these proceedings as property condemnations. If local slave justice was harsh, the Louisiana Supreme Court made little attempt to mitigate its effects. Although it is possible that many slaves brought before the special courts were guilty as charged, the supreme court did not insist on procedural fairness to ensure a just trial. It is more accurate, then, to say that slaves were merely amenable to criminal prosecutions, rather than that they had "rights." They were equal to whites under the law only in their vulnerability to being jailed and sentenced.

One way to judge the relative fairness of slave trials in Louisiana is to examine appeals questioning the admission of allegedly involuntary confessions that had led to convictions by the special courts. An exami-

9. Flanigan, "Criminal Procedure in Slave Trials," 553, 559; Stampp, *Peculiar Institution,* 225; State v. Kentuck, No. 3039, 8 La. Ann. 308 (1853); Tushnet, *American Law of Slavery,* 124; "An Act Relative to Trials of Slaves," Act of June 1, 1846, *Louisiana Acts, 1846,* Sec. 28, p. 115; *Black Code,* "Crimes and Offenses," Sec. 20, p. 210.

nation of such cases indicates that common-law rules of evidence were often ignored in slave trials in Louisiana—another indication that the special tribunals were quasi-judicial proceedings in which evidentiary burdens were relaxed. More often than not, the Supreme Court of Louisiana upheld convictions of slaves based on confessions that appear from the record to have been coerced. A brief sampling of similar cases in other slave states suggests that slave confessions obtained under duress were less likely to be allowed into evidence in those states than in Louisiana. And the overwhelming majority of appeals that overturned convictions based on coerced confessions occurred in states where slaves were tried in the same courts and under the same procedural rules as whites.[10]

The first appeal in Louisiana of a slave's conviction based on a coerced confession was *State* v. *Gilbert* (1847). Gilbert's alleged crime was an attempt to rape a white woman. The first special tribunal could not agree on a verdict; a second tribunal found him guilty on the basis of the slave's confession. At the hearing, a witness testified that Gilbert had confessed "while undergoing corporal punishment." Associate Justice George King, who wrote the decision of the court, overturned the conviction and remanded the case for a new proceeding, with instructions not to admit the confession, as it had been obtained "under the influence of threats or violence."[11]

The following year, the court heard *State* v. *Nelson, Edwin, and Henry* (1848), a murder case in which there was no *corpus delicti*. A special tribunal had tried three slaves, Nelson, Edwin, and Henry, for choking, beating, and drowning two white men. Nelson confessed to the overseer

10. State v. Clarissa, a Slave, 11 Ala. 57 (1847); Wyatt, a Slave, v. State, 25 Ala. 9 (1854); Bob, a Slave, v. State, 32 Ala. 560 (1858); Dinah, a Slave, v. State, 39 Ala. 359 (1864); William, a Slave, v. State, 39 Ala. 532 (1865); Simon, a Slave, v. State, 5 Fla. 285 (1853); Isham, a Slave, v. State, 6 How. Miss. 35 (1841); Peter, a Slave, v. State, 4 S. and M. 31 (Miss. 1844); Van Buren, a Slave, v. State, 24 Miss. 512 (1852); Jordan, a Slave, v. State, 32 Miss. 382 (1856); Simon, a Slave, v. State, 37 Miss. 288 (1858); State v. George, a Slave, 5 Jones N.C. 233 (1858); Ann v. State, 11 Humphreys 159 (Tenn. 1850). However, two Georgia decisions concerning coerced confessions affirm judgments based on such confessions: Berry v. State, 10 Ga. 511 (1851); Jim, a Slave, v. State, 15 Ga. 535 (1854). In *Jim* the Georgia Supreme Court held that if a slaveowner "exceed[ed] the bounds of reason . . . in his chastisement, the slave must submit, as the child submits. . . . He cannot, himself, undertake to redress his wrong . . . because, to allow it, would be to make him the judge . . . to encourage servile insurrection and bloodshed."

11. State v. Gilbert, No. 343, 2 La. Ann. 244 (1847).

(who was also the son of Nelson's master), but only after being placed in the stocks and warned that "it would be better for him to tell what he had done." Edwin confessed in prison, an act that his attorney claimed was prompted by being "under duress." Associate Justice King remanded Nelson's case for a new trial because he believed the confession was coerced and therefore should not have been admitted into evidence:

> The well settled rule of law is, that only such confessions of the accused as have been voluntarily made, uninfluenced by either hope or fear, can be given in evidence against him, and they must be shown to have been thus made, before they can be received. The circumstances of this case do not authorize the conclusion that, threats or violence were used to extort confessions. The accused, *Nelson,* was in the stocks, it is true, but only for safekeeping. As regards him, the only enquiry is, whether the inducement held out to him to confess was such as should have excluded the confession from evidence. Saying to a prisoner that "it would be better for him to confess," or words to that effect, has been repeatedly held to be such an inducement offered to the prisoner as will exclude his confession; and, although opposite opinions have been entertained as to the question, whether a confession made to a person who has no authority over the prisoner, upon an inducement offered by that person, is receivable, yet it seems to be settled that, if the inducement be offered by a master to a servant, or by any other person having authority over the prisoner, the confession will not be deemed voluntary, and will be rejected.

Justice King affirmed Edwin's conviction because the court believed that he had confessed "freely and repeatedly": "As regards the slave *Edwin,* his confessions were repeated and voluntary. No inducements were held out to him to confess, and he was under no other constraint than that necessary for his safe custody." The tribunal had acquitted Henry because, even though there was no less proof to implicate him than the others, he had not confessed; the tribunal had convicted Edwin and Nelson only on the basis of their confessions.[12]

The supreme court remanded *State* v. *Slave Isaac* (1848) for a new trial because of the coerced confession of the slave Isaac, whom the spe-

12. State v. Nelson, Edwin, and Henry, Slaves, No. 741, 3 La. Ann. 497 (1848).

cial tribunal had found guilty of stabbing the slave Jim to death. After his master tied his hands, Isaac confessed and began to justify the slaying to his master, who interrupted him and told Isaac that he intended to turn him over for punishment. Justice King, writing for the court, reversed the conviction because Isaac's master had not allowed him to complete his statement:

> The confessions of the slave made to his master were objected to, on the ground that they were made under the influence of fear, and that he was not permitted to complete his statement. The witness testified: "That the accused came to him the morning after the affray, and told him that he had killed the slave *Jim,* and commenced justifying the act, when the witness stopped him, and told him that he intended to deliver him over to be punished." The confession appears to have been voluntary, but should have been excluded on the ground that it was interrupted and never completed. When confessions of guilt are given in evidence, the whole must be taken together. If the parts relied on to establish the guilt of the prisoner be received, the explanations with which they were accompanied cannot be rejected. Although all the parts of the confession are not entitled to equal weight, the whole must be submitted to the jury, who are to determine, under all the circumstances, how much of the entire statement is worthy of belief. . . . In the present instance the prisoner was not permitted to make a full statement. It is evident that he intended to state circumstances in justification, which the witness refused to hear. A full explanation might have established a complete justification, and the narrative might have been so consistent and probable as to command the belief of the jury. Having been deprived of the benefit of the explanations with which he intended to accompany his admission, and which, if they had been made, would have been admissible in evidence, justice requires that his incomplete disclosure, consisting only of the fact unfavorable to himself, should not go to the jury.

Justice King remanded the case for a new trial, with orders to the special tribunal to exclude the confession.[13]

13. State v. Slave Isaac, No. 828, 3 La. Ann. 359 (1848).

In *State* v. *Hannah* (1855) the Louisiana Supreme Court allowed use of an accused slave's confession. A special tribunal had convicted Hannah, a female slave of the Episcopal bishop and later Confederate general Leonidas Polk, of murdering a slave named Wilson, who resided on a nearby plantation. Apparently Hannah had assaulted Wilson with an "iron or steel dirk," mortally wounding him. The special tribunal found her guilty and sentenced her to life imprisonment at hard labor. She appealed, saying that the tribunal should not have admitted her confession, which was made to her master's son. Associate Justice Abner N. Ogden ruled the confession voluntary and affirmed the decision. The difference between Hannah's confession and Nelson's was that Hannah was offered no inducements to encourage her to confess:

> It is contended, that a confession to one having the power of a master, is not of that voluntary character which the law requires to render such confession evidence against the accused. As it is shown affirmatively that no inducements or promises were held out to induce the confession, and that neither threats nor violence were used to extort it, it must be considered as entirely voluntary. The proposition seems to us inadmissible, that the relation of the master to his slave is such, as to render objectionable, evidence of that character. On the contrary, as it is alike the interest and the duty of the master to protect and defend his slaves, confessions made to the master and voluntarily deposed to by him, ought to have the highest moral weight as evidence. . . . There may be, no doubt, cases where the confession having been made in reference to the defence to be made for the slave, it ought to be received and weighed with great caution, but to exclude entirely confessions made to the master on the ground of his relation to the accused, is not required by any motive of justice or humanity to the slave, and is opposed to sound reason and public policy.[14]

In *State* v. *Adeline, a Slave* (1856), a special tribunal convicted a slave named Adeline of manslaughter of a white man and sentenced her to twenty-five years in prison. When she had seen the arresting officers coming for her, she had become very agitated and said she knew they were there to take her to the "calaboose." She stated that she knew what

14. State v. Hannah, No. 3829, 10 La. Ann. 131 (1855).

she had done and would do it again. Adeline told the officers she had killed the deceased with a sword cane and had subsequently thrown the murder weapon down a well. Chief Justice Edwin Merrick ruled that this confession was freely given and affirmed the conviction: "Her confessions do not appear to have been given under fear, or to have been drawn out by promises, and we see no error in the ruling of the Judge *a quo* in regard to them. We may add that it appears, by the bill of exceptions, that her confessions were corroborated by the discovery of a sword corresponding with the one described by her on searching the well." Adeline's attorney objected to the length of the prison sentence, claiming that twenty-five years exceeded the period fixed by law for manslaughter. Chief Justice Merrick rejected this argument because Adeline was not a free person:

> The longest period affixed by law for the punishment of the crime of manslaughter, coupled with a discretionary fine of $2000, in the case of free persons, is twenty years. But in the case of slaves, a less restricted discretion is conferred upon the tribunal organized for the trial of slaves. By the 7th section of the Act of 6th of April, 1843, it is provided that "In all cases where capital punishment or imprisonment at hard labor for life is inflicted for any crime committed by a slave, the jury trying the same shall in its discretion pronounce sentence of death, imprisonment at hard labor for life, or for a shorter term, in prison or in irons in the service of his master, or order that corporeal punishment be inflicted."

Adeline's master also objected to being deprived of her services without compensation for such a lengthy period. Louisiana law compensated masters for slaves executed or imprisoned for life, but not for a specified term of years. Merrick expressed sympathy for this position, but directed Adeline's owner to appeal to the legislature for redress:

> And it may be added, if imprisonment for a long period of years is resorted to as a punishment, the owner is deprived of his slave for the most valuable period of its life without any indemnity.
>
> As the punishment of imprisonment is more merciful, perhaps, than any corporeal punishment which the jury could inflict commensurate with the offence committed, the argument appears to be more in the interest of the master than the accused, and one

Detail from a drawing by Saint-Aulaire *ca.* 1820 shows a slave woman wearing an iron collar. Fetters were often used as punishment for slave crimes, sometimes augmenting prison sentences at hard labor.

Courtesy of the Historic New Orleans Collection, Museum/Research Center, Acc. No. 1937.2.3

> which could be addressed to the Legislature with more hopes of success than to this tribunal.[15]

State v. *Jonas and Sam, Slaves* (1851) is the worst example from the antebellum period of a special tribunal's allowing a questionable confession that was upheld on appeal to the supreme court. The case involved two slaves whom the tribunal had convicted of killing a white man. Jonas voluntarily told his captors the details of the homicide. He and Sam had been fugitives from Arkansas. A white man named William Bozeman came upon them while they were preparing a meal. Bozeman went to use his gun to capture them, but both runaways were also armed, and Sam shot Bozeman. After the shooting, the fugitives threw Bozeman's gun into a river, hid their own, and fled, but a man named Cook captured them two days later, brought them to Shreveport, and detained them in jail, where Jonas made his confession.

When confronted with Jonas' account, Sam became sullen and refused to speak, at which time one of the men interrogating him took out a pocketknife, caught hold of Sam, and said, "I can make him talk." Others present told him to put away the knife, which he did. Sam continued to remain silent. At this point one of those present "spoke of using a handsaw and sending for a rope." The next day, while visiting the site of the homicide—Jonas had led the authorities to the hidden weapons—Sam confessed to the man who had held the knife on him. Associate Justice Isaac Preston, writing for the court, found that Sam had confessed voluntarily, and not under duress, although he admitted that such issues were less important in slave trials. He also regretted what he felt was the court's past leniency toward whites who claimed that authorities coerced them to confess:

> The true ground upon which confessions, extorted by violence or induced by promises, are excluded as evidence, is, that the vio-

15. State v. Adeline, a Slave, No. 4503, 11 La. Ann. 736 (1856). A twenty-five-year prison sentence was probably in effect a death sentence. Prison conditions during the antebellum period in Louisiana were extremely unhealthy for whites and blacks alike. Prisons seem to have been uniformly unheated, damp, filthy, vermin-infested, unsanitary, and cramped. Some jailers kept prisoners in stocks. See Cox v. Myers, No. 1234, 4 La. Ann. 144 (1849); Hitchcock v. North, No. 5659, 5 Rob. 328 (La. 1843); Lewis v. City of New Orleans, No. 4679, 12 La. Ann. 190 (1857); Johnson v. Municipality #1, No. 1444, 5 La. Ann. 100 (1850). In these four cases slaves died as a result of unwholesome prison conditions.

lence and hope destroy all confidence in the confessions. *In favorem vitae,* too much strictness has been observed on this subject as to free persons. Upon true principles, the objections should go rather to the credit of the confessions than to their admission as evidence. We are not prepared to say the same strictness should be observed, so as to exclude the confessions of slaves as evidence; humanity and charity ought to be extended to them; but if their confessions are obtained without a violation of either, and under such circumstances as to force the belief that the confessions are true, they should be received as evidence. The bill of exceptions does not satisfy us, that these principles were not observed on the trial of the prisoners, and for these reasons and those given by the tribunal, we cannot say that the confessions should not have been received in evidence.

Preston affirmed the conviction with the recommendation that Jonas' owner should lay his case before the governor because "it might be deemed advisable to commute his [Jonas'] punishment." Preston made no recommendation to lessen Sam's sentence.[16]

The Louisiana Supreme Court remanded *State* v. *George* (1860), an arson and burglary case, for a new trial because of what it considered to be an involuntary confession. A special tribunal convicted the slave George of burning a sawmill and breaking into the millowner's house and stealing $128 in gold, silver, and bank notes. The tribunal sentenced him to death. Justice Albert Voorhies (the son of former justice Cornelius Voorhies) granted him a new trial, stating that his confession had been obtained by "influences of promises and threats." However, since the stolen items were recovered using information the slave's confession provided, the outcome of the new trial may have been identical.[17]

During the antebellum period, there were only two appeals of cases involving allegedly forced confessions by whites accused of capital crimes against whites, *State* v. *Simon* (1860) and *State* v. *Mulholland* (1861). In both, the accused confessed voluntarily to a police officer. The

16. State v. Jonas and Sam, Slaves, No. 279, 6 La. Ann. 695 (1851). See also State v. Jackson, a Slave, No. 2124, 6 La. Ann. 593 (1851) at note 27, and State v. Slaves Bob, Joe, and Catherine, No. 4411, 11 La. Ann. 192 (1856) at note 35.

17. State v. George, No. 6501, 15 La. Ann. 145 (1860).

appeals asserted that the mere presence of such a figure of authority was threatening to the accused. The Louisiana Supreme Court denied both appeals. In *Simon,* Justice Albert Voorhies reasoned that it was "the common law rule" that voluntary confessions were admissible as evidence, even if the confession were made to one in authority. The court used similar reasoning in *Mulholland.*[18] Although it is difficult to ascertain whether force was indeed used in these instances, the court was no more likely to reverse convictions of whites than of slaves on grounds of coercion, suggesting that judges were generally less concerned with procedural niceties than is the case today. However, whites and free persons of color accused of crimes had the benefit of common-law protections, peremptory challenges, trial by jury, an attorney of their own choosing, and probably, a better understanding of their rights. Moreover, it is perhaps revealing that the argument advanced in *Simon* and *Mulholland*—that the mere presence of a person in authority could be coercive—was never offered in an appeal in behalf of a convicted slave.

The antebellum Supreme Court of Louisiana heard appeals involving slaves accused of everything from chicken stealing to arson, rape, and murder. An analysis of the court's decisions, crime by crime, reveals an overriding concern with social control and with property damage resulting from slave crime. Even when procedural errors were flagrant and punishments harsh, the court rarely reversed the verdicts of the special tribunals established ostensibly to ensure justice for slaves. The court's reluctance to intervene is especially evident in cases of assault and murder in which both defendant and victim were black. Rape, by legal definition, was confined to white victims (the crime of rape against women of color—free or slave—did not exist under Louisiana law), and since slaves under the law could own nothing, they could have nothing stolen from them by a fellow slave. Free blacks, however, could lose property by theft, since they were legally capable of owning it.

The Louisiana Supreme Court heard only one criminal case involving assault by a slave on a free person of color. In *State* v. *Harris* (1852), the high court affirmed a life sentence for the slave defendant despite the fact that the victim's injuries were minor. Two other slave assault cases, *Jourdan* v. *Patton* (1818) and *Roebuck* v. *Curry* (1847), came before the court

18. State v. Simon, 15 La. Ann. 568 (1860); State v. Mulholland, 16 La. Ann. 376 (1861).

as civil suits in which the owner of the victim sued the master of the alleged criminal for loss of the victim's services while injured and for diminution of his value.[19]

The supreme court heard twenty-one cases involving slaves killing other slaves during the antebellum period. Of these, ten were civil actions for the value of the deceased slaves by their owners and eleven were criminal prosecutions (two of the twenty-one involved the same slave—the owner sued in a civil action for the value of the dead slave and pressed charges that led to criminal prosecution against the alleged murderer). This nearly even split between civil and criminal cases underscores the person-property contradiction inherent in slave law. Murder and manslaughter cases in which the accused and the victim were slaves belonging to different owners were the most common criminal prosecutions involving black defendants that reached the Louisiana Supreme Court during the antebellum period. The civil suits arose because the *Civil Code* held slaveowners to strict liability for their slaves' acts: "The master shall be answerable for all the damages occasioned by an offense or quasi-offence committed by his slave, independent of the punishment inflicted on the slave." In the ten civil cases where slaves met their deaths at the hands of other slaves, the following causes were among those cited: accident, marital infidelity, larceny (unspecified), street brawling, and quarreling at a slave "frolic." In two separate cases slaves—on direct orders from their masters—shot fellow slaves from a neighboring plantation for stealing hogs. One slave killed another who had been ordered to hold him down to be whipped. In two appeals no motives were stated.[20]

It is in appeals where both the accused and the victim were slaves that one might expect to see the best examples of justice for slaves, especially at the appellate level. Violence among slaves did not personally

19. State v. Harris, Unreported Louisiana Supreme Court Case No. 2400 (1852); Jourdan v. Patton, No. 304, 5 Mart. (o.s.) 615 (La. 1818); Roebuck v. Curry, No. 458, 2 La. Ann. 998 (1847).

20. *Civil Code,* Art, 180, p. 28; Audige v. Gaillard, f.w.c., No. 2865, 8 La. Ann. 71 (1853); Griffing v. Routh, No. 3921, 11 La. Ann. 135 (1856); Arnoult v. Deschapelles, No. 1057, 4 La. Ann. 41 (1849); Maille v. Blas, No. 5975, 15 La. Ann. 100 (1860); Steel v. Cazeau, No. 402, 8 Mart. (o.s.) 318 (La. 1820); Bibb v. Hebert, No. 753, 3 La. Ann. 132 (1848); Bernard v. Pyburn, No. 4028, 15 La. 126 (1840); McDowell v. Couch, No. 2039, 6 La. Ann. 365 (1851) [see also State v. Jerry, No. 1302, 4 La. Ann. 190 (1849)]; Ford v. Simmons, No. 636, 13 La. Ann. 397 (1858); Jones and Daugharty v. Goza, No. 90, 16 La. Ann. 428 (1862).

threaten whites, except in the sense that order and peace were disturbed and labor and valuable property lost or damaged. Justice for blacks or whites demanded that in trials for capital crimes procedural rules be strictly followed. Louisiana law, however, exempted the special tribunals from such rules, and the high court was clearly reluctant to overturn their verdicts on the basis of technical error. Of the eleven appeals in cases of slave-on-slave killing, nine were filed by defendants on grounds of procedural irregularities. Six of the nine involved capital punishment; in the other three, the sentences were either twenty years' or life imprisonment—which, given prison conditions and slave life expectancy, amounted to the same thing. Procedural complaints in these cases included illegal arrest, improper arraignment, improperly constituted tribunal, confession obtained under duress, biased jury, being tried under a repealed or unconstitutional law, improper sentence, and error in setting date of execution. Although such irregularities obviously could have had a direct bearing on justice, the high court upheld the special tribunals' decisions in all but one of the nine cases.[21] On the other hand, the justices did not often use procedural errors to acquit whites accused of homicide or manslaughter against whites, either. In twenty-six cases heard by the court during the antebellum period involving whites, only two convictions were reversed and seven remanded for new trials.[22]

21. State v. Isaac, No. 828, 3 La. Ann. 359 (1848); State v. Oscar, a Slave, No. 5407, 13 La. Ann. 297 (1858); State v. Jerry, No. 129, 3 La. Ann. 576 (1848); State v. Dick, No. 1224, 4 La. Ann. 182 (1849); State v. Henry, No. 6239, 15 La. Ann. 297 (1860); State v. Jerry, No. 1302, 4 La. Ann. 190 (1849) [an entirely different case from State v. Jerry (1848)]; State v. Lewis, No. 584, 3 La. Ann. 398 (1848); State v. Harrison, No. 4464, 11 La. Ann. 722 (1856); State v. Hannah, a Slave, No. 3829, 10 La. Ann. 131 (1855). The supreme court affirmed the special tribunals' verdicts in all of these cases except *Isaac,* which the justices remanded for a new trial after considering three claims of procedural irregularity: a biased tribunal that was also improperly constituted, and a coerced confession; the outcome of the new trial is unknown. A tenth appeal went unreported, and the decision by the high court has been lost: State v. Slave Leonidas, Unreported Louisiana Supreme Court Case No. 429 (*ca.* 1862). Since this case was filed only one month before the court adjourned because of the Civil War, it may never have been tried. The other appeal to come before the supreme court in a case of a slave killing a slave was the exceptional *State* v. *Slave Jack* (1859), discussed in the next paragraph.

22. Territory v. Mather, 2 Mart. (o.s.) 48 (1811); Territory v. McFarlane, 1 Mart. (o.s.) 221 (1811); State v. Hornsby, No. 19, 8 Rob. 554 (La. 1844); State v. Kennedy, No. 18, 8 Rob. 590 (La. 1844); State v. McCoy, 8 Rob. 545 (La. 1844); State v. Patza, No. 983, 3 La. Ann. 512 (1848); State v. Cummings, No. 794, 5 La. Ann. 330 (1850); State v. Chandler, No. 1536, 5 La. Ann. 489 (1850); State v. Bradley, No. 1509, 6 La. Ann. 554 (1851); State v. Price, No. 159, 6 La. Ann. 691 (1851); State v. Green, No. 2748, 7 La. Ann. 518 (1852); State v. Parker, No. 2392, 7 La. Ann. 83 (1852); State v. DeAngelo, No. 3135, 9 La. Ann. 46 (1854); State v. Brien, No. 4061, 10 La. Ann. 454 (1855); State v. Chopin, No. 4113, 10 La. Ann. 458 (1855);

State v. *Slave Jack* (1859), in which both the accused and the victim were slaves, is particularly illustrative of the reasoning of the justices in applying the law. Jack was found guilty of manslaughter, a capital offense for slaves, and sentenced to five years' hard labor and ten lashes every sixty days while incarcerated. The question here was not the verdict, but the sentence: according to the *Black Code,* a conviction of manslaughter required execution, and on this basis the state appealed. However, Justice Albert Voorhies ruled that an act of March 19, 1857, relative to criminal procedure for slaves, allowed juries to commute the sentence for a crime punishable by execution or life in prison to a lesser penalty. Voorhies ordered the district-court judge to pass sentence in accordance with the verdict of the jury:

> The statute leaves it to the sound discretion of the jury to *substitute* the lesser for the greater penalty: that is the meaning of the commutation of punishment there provided for. And as regards the limits imposed by law in the exercise of the discretionary power of punishment, vested in the special tribunal for the trial of slaves, the 29th section of the Act of 1857, p. 232, is explicit:—"Whenever the punishment is left by law to the discretion of the court, it shall in no case extend to the privation of life or limb."[23]

The Supreme Court of Louisiana did reverse two particularly outrageous verdicts in which slaves, although acquitted, were nevertheless sentenced to be punished. In *State* v. *Solomon* (1860), a special tribunal in Morehouse Parish tried the slave Solomon for murder. Although the court found him innocent, members of the tribunal nevertheless sentenced him to be whipped. Punishment of an innocent slave caused the Supreme Court of Louisiana to affirm the acquittal and reverse the sentence of corporal punishment. In their ruling, the justices commented that "the course pursued by the special tribunal . . . is unwarranted in

---

State v. Heas, No. 3830, 10 La. Ann. 195 (1855); State v. Maxent and Guesnon, No. 4110, 10 La. Ann. 743 (1855); State v. Jackson, 12 La. Ann. 679 (1856); State v. Shields, No. 4171, 11 La. Ann. 395 (1856); State v. Munce, No. 499, 12 La. Ann. 625 (1856); State v. Scott, No. 4964, 12 La. Ann. 274 (1857); State v. Brunetto, No. 5376, 13 La. Ann. 45 (1858); State v. Bennett, 14 La. Ann. 651 (1859); State v. Mullen, No. 6146, 14 La. Ann. 570 (1859); State v. Swift, No. 6318, 14 La. Ann. 827 (1859); State v. Brown, No. 317, 16 La. Ann. 384 (1861).

23. State v. Slave Jack, No. 5926, 14 La. Ann. 385 (1859), emphasis in original; *Black Code,* "Crimes and Offenses," Sec. 11, p. 202; "An Act Relative to Slaves," Act of March 19, 1857, *Louisiana Acts, 1857,* Sec. 35, p. 233.

law. A slave cannot be subject to punishment when he is acquitted of the charges preferred against him."[24] In *State* v. *Charles* (1859) a special tribunal acquitted the slave Charles of assaulting his overseer "so as to cause a shedding of blood" but still sentenced him to 154 lashes, albeit "not so as to break the skin of said slave." The tribunal apparently felt that Charles had laid hands on a white man, and no matter how great the provocation, this could not go unpunished. The tribunal based its sentence on section 28 of the act of March 19, 1857: "Be it further enacted . . . [if] such court [a slave tribunal] shall not convict or acquit the accused on an offence punishable with death, it shall have the power to decree the infliction of corporeal punishment as it may consider deserved by the prisoner." Justice Cole denied the tribunal's authority to impose such a sentence after acquitting the defendant. Cole explained his decision:

> The idea of the legislator seems to have been, that when the evidence was such that the jury were of opinion that the accused was not absolutely guilty of the offence charged, but, still, that he had committed an offence which ought to be punished in a lighter form, than by death or hard labor, that then they should have the right to inflict corporal punisment [*sic*]. . . .
>
> As, then, the jury acquitted the prisoner of an offence punishable with death it had not the right to inflict corporal punishment.[25]

The court heard only two appeals for convictions of arson by slaves. In both cases the justices showed little concern about procedural fairness. Particularly egregious was *State* v. *Jackson* (1851), in which a special tribunal had convicted a slave of setting fire to a home and sentenced him to life imprisonment at hard labor. Jackson's attorney appealed, charging several errors in the trial. Eliza, Jackson's wife, had been severely threatened and whipped until she disclosed her husband's crime. (Article 2260 of the *Civil Code* prohibited husbands and wives from tes-

24. State v. Slave Solomon, 15 La. Ann. 463 (1860). The Supreme Court of Louisiana remanded one more slave case for a new trial because of procedural irregularities. This case, heard in Monroe, was among those subject to dislocation following the Civil War. The slaves Lethe, Biner, Hal, and Chloe were convicted of an unspecified capital crime. The defense charged there was error in the procedure, and the high court ordered a new trial. State v. Lethe, Biner, Hal, and Chloe, Slaves, No. 3083, 9 La. Ann. 182 (1854).

25. State v. Charles, 14 La. Ann. 649 (1859); "An Act Relative to Slaves," Act of March 19, 1857, *Louisiana Acts, 1857,* Sec. 28, p. 232.

tifying for or against each other, but article 182 held that slave marriages had no civil effect; therefore, the trial court could ignore the husband-wife relationship in accepting Eliza's testimony.) Jackson himself had not confessed until he was threatened with hanging. Moreover, the trial was conducted in the office of the mayor of Baton Rouge to ensure maximum publicity.

Even though circumstantial evidence indicated that Jackson may have committed the crime, this whole proceeding was a mockery; testimony obtained by whipping and a confession prompted by threats of hanging were more than sufficient to render the trial unjust. Jackson's attorney also appealed on the basis that he had discovered new evidence concerning Eliza's character. He told the court that a special tribunal had recently convicted Eliza of committing an assault "upon the person of a white woman," and that she had lied in that proceeding. He characterized her as so "bad, vicious and wanton, as to have compelled her mistress to have her tried and confined for days at a time." Jackson's attorney concluded that this new evidence and the fact that the slave woman had been whipped into testifying against Jackson should induce the court to ignore her testimony. Writing for the court, Justice Preston brushed aside this argument, citing the act of 1846: "No [slave] proceedings . . . shall be annulled or impeded by any error in form." The justices apparently simply ignored the issue of Jackson's own coerced confession. As for the trial's being held in the mayor's office, Preston commented that "publicity in trials is the greatest protection of innocence, and security to the community that crimes should not go unwhipt [*sic*] of justice." In a unanimous ruling, the court upheld the conviction.[26] Jackson may have been guilty. Nevertheless, his conviction was so unjustly achieved that it is difficult to understand this ruling by the high court as anything other than a tacit admission that procedural due process did not necessarily apply to slaves.

Larceny was the most common slave crime against property and the most usual slave offense to come before the supreme court during the antebellum period. According to articles 179 and 180 of the *Civil Code,* owners were personally responsible for damages inflicted as a direct result of the "offenses and quasi-offenses" of their slaves. Therefore, all

26. State v. Jackson, a Slave, No. 2124, 6 La. Ann. 593 (1851); *Civil Code,* Art. 2260, p. 353, Art. 182, p. 28. For the other appeal involving arson by a slave, see State v. George, No. 6501, 15 La. Ann. 145 (1860).

sixteen cases heard by the court involving slave larceny were civil actions to recover stolen goods or damages incurred by the thefts. In three appeals, witnesses described slaves as being "the head of a gang of thieves," "addicted to robbery," and "*un peu voleur*" (light-fingered). Four cases involved animal stealing, and two were trials to recover sums of money stolen by slaves: in *Déslondes* v. *Wilson* (1833), the slave Philippe was drowned trying to escape on a steamboat with $3,000 in stolen money, and in *Bertin* v. *Phillips* (1846), the slave Fleming and two other slaves broke into the safe in the office of the quartermaster of the United States and stole several thousand dollars.[27]

Five cases concerning slave larceny involved slaves who allegedly had broken into stores. In *Hewet* v. *Wilson* (1834), a slave named Big Sam reportedly stole $5,000 worth of dry goods, including lengths of fabric and combs. His owner alleged that the overseer—who was also charged in the larceny—ran Big Sam over the state line to avoid prosecution. In *Moffat* v. *Vion* (1833), a group of slave women stole $419.59 worth of fabric from the New Orleans store of the plaintiff. The proprietor had put a special mark on his inventory, and when several pieces appeared at the store of one of his competitors, Moffat sued the slave women's owner to recover the stolen goods. In *Hart* v. *St. Romes and Dubuys* (1835), five slaves belonging to different owners broke into a New Orleans store and stole $2,556.79 worth of pistols, buttons, suspenders, jewelry, knives, thimbles, and other assorted items. In all of these cases the court held the owners of the thieves liable for civil damages. That owners were responsible for damages and losses caused by their slaves was true from the original *Code Noir* until the end of the antebellum period and was a feature of slave law unique to Louisiana. It was part of

27. *Civil Code,* Art. 178, p. 28; Hindus, "Black Justice Under White Law," 583; Stampp, *Peculiar Institution,* 127. Other cases involving evidence of larceny by slaves are Ogden v. Michel, No. 5127, 4 Rob. 154 (La. 1843); Blondeau v. Galez, No. 484, 8 Mart. (O.S.) 313 (La. 1820); Back v. Meek, No. 1941, 1 La. 309 (1830); Smith v. Taylor, No. 5755, 10 Rob. 133 (La. 1844); Déslonde, f.m.c., v. LeBéret, No. 2300, 5 La. 96 (1833); Allain v. Young, No. 527, 9 Mart. (O.S.) 221 (La. 1821); Perrie v. Williams and Adams, No. 1444, 5 Mart. (N.S.) 694 (La. 1827); Musson v. Clayton, No. 5888, 1 La. Ann. 122 (1846); Déslondes v. Wilson, No. 2496, 5 La. 397 (1833); Bertin v. Phillips, No. 5728 1 La. Ann. 173 (1846). In this last case, Fleming was sentenced to two hours in the pillory, eight days in jail, and six months of wearing an iron collar with prongs. This was not his first conviction for theft. He had previously been sentenced to twenty-five lashes and wearing an iron collar for one year for the same offense. Prior to these convictions he had spent ten years in jail for participating in a mutiny. One witness stated that "the boy is to a thief invaluable, but to an honest man worthless."

a whole system of order created by the *Civil Code,* which also included provisions regarding harm caused by minors, interdicted persons (persons unable to manage their own affairs), and animals. When owners were answerable for the damages occasioned by their slaves, there were fewer reasons to make the slaves amenable to criminal prosecution for their actions—and slaves in general were too valuable as property to let them rot in jail or to lose them permanently to the executioner.[28]

The supreme court heard appeals of convictions for assaults on whites by slaves ten times during the antebellum period. Four of the cases were civil matters in which the victim sued the slave's owner for damages. In *Hynson* v. *Meuillon, f.m.c.* (1847), a white woman sued for damages for an assault by a slave named John, who she alleged had proceeded to "beat, wound and ill treat her, so that her life was greatly despaired of—that with shears, knives, clubs and other weapons said slave inflicted . . . divers large incisions, gashes, contusions." She also alleged that he had attempted to rape her. A special tribunal found the slave guilty in an unappealed criminal prosecution, and the judge sentenced him to wear a ball and chain and to labor in the penitentiary for fifteen years. The victim sued the slave's owner for damages and obtained a judgment against Meuillon of $500. According to *Civil Code* article 181, a slaveholder could abandon his slave to the plaintiff in such circumstances and be absolved of further financial responsibility. When Meuillon abandoned the slave, the plaintiff claimed that article 181 implied physical delivery of the slave—an impossibility, since the slave was serving his sentence in the penitentiary. Associate Justice Rost ruled that although the confinement of the slave operated a "hardship" in this case, the abandonment of the slave was compensation for the damages in-

28. Hewet v. Wilson, No. 65, 7 La. 71 (1834); Moffat v. Vion, No. 2357, 5 La. 346 (1833); Hart v. St. Romes and Dubuys, No. 2663, 7 La. 586 (1835); *Civil Code,* Arts. 180, 181, 2300, pp. 28, 359–60; *Code Noir,* Art. 31, pp. 174–76; Shael Herman, David Combe, and Thomas E. Carbonneau, *The Louisiana Civil Code: A Humanistic Appraisal* (New Orleans, 1981), 8–9. Two slaves named Dick and Sam robbed a Royal Street store of weapons worth $1,284, including ten shotguns, six rifles, sixteen pistols, and ammunition; Patterson v. Behan and Freeland, No. 3141, 12 La. 227 (1838). One slave took a promissory note for $720 from the pocket of a sleeping white man, for which he received thirty-nine lashes; Lewis v. Peytavin, No. 1152, 4 Mart. (N.S.) 3 (La. 1825). In one instance a white man was sued for the value of goods stolen by him in the company of several slaves; Devine v. Kelly, No. 2363, 4 La. 206 (1831). For common-law ruling on the fellow servant issue, see Paul Finkelman, "Slaves as Fellow Servants: Ideology, Law, and Industrialization," *American Journal of Legal History,* XXXI (October, 1987), 269–305.

curred by the plaintiff. "It is the inconvenience of all fixed rules of damages, that they, at times, fall short of the actual damages sustained."[29]

During the same term the court heard a civil appeal, *Collingsworth* v. *Covington* (1847), in which an overseer sued his employer for $5,000 for injuries received in a knife attack by one of the slaves under his management. The owner, Covington, contended that his overseer had been in charge of the slave and therefore was responsible for his actions. The Tensas Parish court found for the owner, and the overseer appealed. Justice King, writing for the supreme court, held Covington to strict liability for the actions of his slave and reversed the judgment, noting that

> the plaintiff was a good manager, attentive to the health, discipline, and good government, of the slaves under his charge, and exercised no unnecessary severity; that *Covington* had rendered his slaves unmanageable by over indulgence; and that the loose discipline which he maintained on his plantation, was a source of complaint and dissatisfaction among his neighbors. This evidence is uncontradicted, and the veracity of the witnesses, by whom it is given, unimpeached. The judge below has assigned no reason for rejecting the plaintiff's demand, but probably considered, as has been contended by the counsel for the defendant, that masters are not responsible for the damage caused by their slaves, in cases like the present.
>
> In our opinion, the judge erred. Masters are expressly made answerable for the damage occasioned by the offences or quasi-offences committed by their slaves, but with the right reserved to them of liberating themselves from that responsibility, by abandoning the slave. No exception to this rule is established which precludes an overseer or other person, having a slave under his

29. Hynson v. Meuillon, f.m.c., No. 98, 2 La. Ann. 798 (1847). In one case an intoxicated slave assaulted his overseer with a knife: Behan v. Freeland and Faures, No. 3187, 12 La. 211 (1838). In another, a slave named John assaulted a white man, Henry J. Andrews, by beating him on the head with a "green dog wood stick." Apparently John was a runaway at the time and Andrews was attempting to arrest him. A lower-court jury awarded Andrews $200 damages in addition to his medical expenses, all to be paid by John's owner. The supreme court decision on this Monroe case appears to have been lost, or perhaps the case was never decided as a result of the Civil War. Andrews v. Kemp, Unreported Louisiana Supreme Court Case No. 812 (filed July, 1860).

> charge, from obtaining reparation in damages for injuries caused by the latter.[30]

In three instances of assaults by slaves on whites, the Supreme Court of Louisiana remanded the cases for new trials. *State* v. *Peyton* (1862) involved a slave who was accused of shooting at a white man with a double-barreled shotgun. At the arraignment a mob burst into the courtroom to seize Peyton and hang him "in spite of the law, the court, the sheriff or anything else." When the sheriff attempted to remove Peyton from the courtroom for his own safety, the would-be lynchers seized the slave. The presiding judge was able to quiet them by agreeing to try the accused quickly. A hastily convened special tribunal found him guilty, and the judge sentenced him to death; the trial was so speedy that the court failed to notify Peyton's master, and the slave did not have the benefit of counsel. The supreme court remanded the case for a new trial, stating that Peyton's conviction was under duress by a mob. The circumstances were less dramatic in the other two cases. In *State* v. *Slave Bill* (1860), the defendant was accused of stabbing and biting a white man. The first attempt to try the case ended in a mistrial; the second resulted in Bill's conviction, but three jurors admitted that they had decided his guilt before the trial began. The supreme court ordered a new trial. Similarly, in *State* v. *George* (1844), a slave convicted by a special tribunal and sentenced to death for striking his overseer had not been allowed to challenge a member of that court who had already decided his guilt. The high court sent the case back to the parish to be tried again.[31]

Two cases in which slaves assaulted whites have already been noted as exceptional in that their outcomes turned on a legal fluke. In *State* v. *King* (1857) and *State* v. *Henderson* (1858), the defendants both stood convicted of assault with intent to kill: Henderson had stabbed his master with a pocketknife; King had stabbed a man named Elias Smith with a butcher knife. The supreme court reversed both convictions on the ground that they rested on a statute that had been repealed. On March

30. Collingsworth v. Covington, No. 469, 2 La. Ann. 406 (1847). In one civil suit heard by the Louisiana Supreme Court over a disputed sale, the object of the legal action was the slave Nelson, who had assaulted his master with an axe but was found innocent by a special tribunal by reason of insanity. Berret v. Adams, No. 3806, 10 La. Ann. 77 (1855).

31. State v. Peyton, a Slave, Unreported Louisiana Supreme Court Case No. 388 (1862); State v. Slave Bill, No. 6560, 15 La. Ann. 114 (1860); State v. George, 8 Rob. 535 (La. 1844).

19, 1857, in passing an act revising laws concerning crimes by slaves, the Louisiana legislature had repealed a section of the old law listing such crimes and the penalties for them. Section 43 of the new act stated that "all laws or parts of laws conflicting with the provisions of this Act, and all laws on the same subject-matter . . . be repealed." The legislators failed to make an exception for the act just passed, which was a new list of criminal offenses to replace the repealed one. Thus, the new list was also repealed and the actions of King and Henderson were left uncovered by the law. Obviously, the lawmakers never intended to allow a slave to stab a white person with impunity, and the court's ruling served to alert them to the omission.[32]

Two other slaves who assaulted whites were not so fortunate as to escape through a legal loophole. In *State* v. *Kentuck* (1853), the court denied an appeal by the slave Kentuck for having stabbed the white overseer of the brickyard where Kentuck worked. The appeal alleged irregularity in appointing an attorney for the slave, but the court quoted the familiar act of 1846 provision that errors of form were not grounds for overturning a slave conviction. Although a witness testified that the wound, which was to the victim's hand, was "of a slight character," Justice James Campbell affirmed the conviction, and the state subsequently executed Kentuck. In *State* v. *Sam* (1855), the slave Sam, out in the middle of the night, attempted to assault his overseer when ordered to return to his cabin. The lower court would not allow Sam's owner to testify because of his possible prejudicial financial interest. The owner appealed on the basis that all evidence that might exonerate the slave should have been admitted. The high court denied the appeal.[33]

Three cases of slaves attempting to poison whites came before the Louisiana Supreme Court during the antebellum period. One, *Barnett* v. *Macoin* (1840), was a civil suit that listed attempted poisoning as a reason for rescinding the sale of the suspected slave. Another was the criminal case *State* v. *Kitty* (1857), of which more later. Also a criminal proceed-

32. State v. King, No. 597, 12 La. Ann. 593 (1857); State v. Henderson, No. 5621, 13 La. Ann. 489 (1858); "An Act Relative to Slaves," Act of March 19, 1857, *Louisiana Acts, 1857,* pp. 229–34.

33. State v. Kentuck, a Slave, No. 3039, 8 La. Ann. 308 (1853); State v. Sam, Unreported Louisiana Supreme Court Case No. 4041 (1855). In *Elijah, a Slave,* v. *The State,* a Tennessee case, the court remanded the case of a slave whose master was not allowed to testify against him; 20 Tenn. 102 (1839). In *State* v. *Charity,* 2 Dev. 543 (N.C. 1830), the court prohibited a master from testifying for or against his slave.

ing was *State* v. *Slaves Bob, Joe, and Catherine* (1856), in which three slaves stood trial for administering "Jamestown Weed" (jimsonweed, highly poisonous) to their overseer in his coffee. The overseer testified that he felt "a swimming in his head," realized that he had been poisoned, and sent the slave Bob for a physician. A witness testified that Bob purposely rode slowly; the physician finally came, however, and the overseer recovered. The overseer whipped Bob, Joe, and Catherine for the incident, and Bob confessed after a hundred lashes. A witness stated that the lashing had not intimidated Bob, that in fact the slave laughed at the overseer, who then put him in the stocks. The special tribunal found Bob guilty and sentenced him to death by hanging. It could not agree on the guilt or innocence of Joe and Catherine, but nevertheless sentenced Joe to the stocks every Sunday for three months and Catherine to thirty-nine lashes. Despite the forced confession of Bob and the sentencing of Joe and Catherine without their guilt having been ascertained, Associate Justice Henry Spofford dismissed the appeal, stating: "Our appellate jurisdiction in criminal cases is limited to questions of law . . . presented by bills of exception or assignment of errors." Since the slaves' attorney failed to present either to the court, apparently through his own incompetence, Spofford refused to consider the appeal or remand the case for a new trial.[34]

No Louisiana law made rape of a black woman, slave or free, a crime. Rape was specifically limited to white women under the state's law. Eight rape or attempted rape cases in which the accused was a slave and the alleged victim was white came before the court during the antebellum period. Seven of the eight were criminal prosecutions (the eighth was the civil suit by the victim for damages, *Hynson* v. *Meuillon, f.m.c.*, discussed earlier). In *State* v. *Bill* (1844), the slave Bill was sentenced to death by the special tribunal for attempting to commit a rape on a six-year-old white girl. His attorney appealed on the grounds that a child must have attained the age of ten to be capable of being raped. He cited a dictionary definition of *woman* as being a female of ten years or older. The Court of Errors and Appeals, whose jurisdiction was incorporated into the supreme court in 1845, rejected this reasoning, citing two Louisiana statutes that did not confine rape to a specified age. The court went on to cite English law and French law (which, the court observed,

34. Barnett v. Macoin, No. 3591, 14 La. 428 (1840); State v. Kitty, No. 5154, 12 La. Ann. 805 (1857); State v. Slaves Bob, Joe, and Catherine, No. 4411, 11 La. Ann. 192 (1856).

"is equally the law with the English"), and concluded, "Ubi lex non distinguit, non debemis distinguere" (Where the law does not distinguish [as to the age of a rape victim], we ought not to distinguish). Furthermore, the court stated that "whatever doubt might be entertained with regard to a white man, it appears to this Court that there can be none where a slave is the party accused" because in the *Black Code* victims of rape were described as "any white woman or girl." The justices then proceeded to cite several lexicographers, including Webster, as to the definition of the word *girl*. The court affirmed the judgment and ordered the accused to be executed.[35]

In a similar but unreported case, *State* v. *David* (1862), a special tribunal convicted the slave David of assault with intent to commit rape of a white girl under ten years of age and sentenced him to receive two hundred lashes (twenty-five per week) and ten years in prison at hard labor. At the trial the slave's attorney implied that although the child had initially resisted the attack, she ultimately consented to the act, and that resistance was an essential element in finding the slave guilty. The presiding judge instructed the members of the special tribunal that under Louisiana law a child under the age of ten could not consent to such an act, and the tribunal found David guilty. The attorney appealed, charging error in the instructions. The Louisiana Supreme Court affirmed the judgment. The court also affirmed four other judgments involving special tribunals' convictions of slaves for rape or attempted rape, *State* v. *Dick* (1855), *State* v. *Ned* (1856), *State* v. *Oscar* (1858), and *State* v. *Joshua* (1860). In all four, procedural errors were the basis of appeals. The tribunals ordered three of these slave defendants to be executed and one to life at hard labor in the penitentiary.[36]

Two of the seven convictions for rape or attempted rape by slaves were remanded for new trials because of errors in the procedure by the special tribunals. The first of these two cases, *State* v. *Gilbert* (1847),

35. State v. Bill, 8 Rob. 527 (La. 1844); *Black Code,* "Crimes and Offenses," Sec. 7, pp. 198–200. An 1855 and an 1857 statute stated that rape victims were "only white females": "An Act Relative to Slaves and Free Persons of Color," Act of March 15, 1855, *Louisiana Acts, 1855,* Sec. 6, p. 378; "An Act Relative to Slaves," Act of March 19, 1857, *Louisiana Acts, 1857,* Sec. 6, p. 230.

36. State v. David, Slave of Drake, Unreported Louisiana Supreme Court Case No. 312 (1862); State v. Dick, No. 3647, 10 La. Ann. 461 (1855). State v. Ned, Unreported Louisiana Supreme Court Case No. 4629 (1856); State v. Oscar, No. 5407, 13 La. Ann. 297 (1858); State v. Joshua, No. 6530, 15 La. Ann. 118 (1860).

involved a slave convicted of rape and sentenced to hang. The Louisiana Supreme Court found that Gilbert's confession had been obtained by threats and violence. The court sent the case to the special tribunal to be tried again, with instructions that the confession not be admitted as evidence.[37] In *State* v. *Peter, a Slave* (1859), the accused slave's master was not allowed to testify because of his financial interest in the slave. A special tribunal found Peter guilty of attempting to rape a thirteen-year-old white girl. The girl's father had handcuffed the slave and threatened him until he confessed. The Louisiana Supreme Court ruled that Peter could not be deprived of the eyewitness testimony of his owner, who claimed she had seen him at the plow at the time of the alleged incident. The high court remanded the case with instructions to the special tribunal to allow the owner's testimony. In an unusual recognition of the slave's humanity, Justice James Cole stated:

> Slaves are prosecuted as persons, and they ought not to be deprived of the testimony of their owners, because the verdict may injure them [the owners] in a pecuniary view. The point at issue is not their [the slaves'] value, but their guilt or innocence.
>
> The rights of a slave to have all the testimony that may establish his innocence are superior to the principle which would exclude his owners on the ground of interest, and their testimony ought to be received, subject to the credibility the jury may attach to it.[38]

Four instances of slaves murdering whites came before the court during the antebellum period. Three of the four cases were criminal prosecutions. The other, *Hardy* v. *Voorhies* (1859), was a civil suit from the District Court of Lafayette Parish in which the district attorney brought a *mandamus* action to have the sheriff execute a slave woman previously convicted of murder. Two slaves, Modeste and Joseph, had been convicted of murdering their mistress. Both were sentenced to hang, but Modeste's execution was to be delayed until fifteen days after the child she was carrying was born. Modeste either miscarried or had feigned pregnancy, because no child was born. The sheriff refused to execute her, saying that the condition for execution (of giving birth to a child)

37. State v. Gilbert, No. 343, 2 La. Ann. 244 (1847).

38. State v. Peter, a Slave, No. 6175, 14 La. Ann. 521 (1859). Allowing the owner's testimony was a departure from the old common-law rule that interested parties were prohibited from testifying. See Elijah, a Slave, v. the State, 20 Tenn. 102 (1839).

had never been fulfilled. The Supreme Court of Louisiana ruled that the governor of Louisiana or the justices of the peace who had presided at the special tribunal that had convicted Modeste could set a date for her sentence to be carried out, but that the district court had no jurisdiction over slave tribunals. The court therefore ordered the *mandamus* to be dismissed. No record exists of Modeste's ultimate fate.[39]

In all three of the criminal prosecutions for slaves murdering whites, procedural errors were the basis for appeals of convictions to the state supreme court. The court's record is, at best, ambiguous. Two of the cases, *State* v. *Jonas and Sam* (1851) and *State* v. *Adeline* (1856), have already been discussed. Both were appealed on the basis of forced confessions, and in both, the judgment of the special tribunal was affirmed.[40]

In only one case, *State* v. *Kitty* (1857), did the court reverse the conviction of a slave for killing a white. The slave Kitty was convicted and sentenced to life imprisonment at hard labor for poisoning a white man. Until she confessed, it had been thought that the man died of natural causes. The supreme court ruled that her confession had not been forced (as claimed in the appeal) but nevertheless reversed Kitty's conviction because the statute on which it was based had been repealed—this was the same legislative error that led to reversals in *State* v. *King* and *State* v. *Henderson.* Kitty's acquittal reflected the constitutional limits imposed on the court: simply because of a mistake of the legislature, the justices must acquit a slave accused of killing a white. Yet despite the court's ongoing rivalry with the legislature, there was no other choice. As the court noted in *King,* it was "dangerous to the liberties of the people" for the judicial branch to consider the motives of the legislature: "We regret to be obliged to set the prisoner at liberty, but it is far wiser and safer for society . . . to allow him to be liberated, than to violate a great principle in the interpretation of Statutes." The great principle was simply that the court was constitutionally restricted to questions of law in criminal cases. Crimes had to be defined by the legislature, and proper indictments had to cite a particular law or statute. If no law existed to convict, acquittal was the only judgment the court could render.[41]

39. Hardy v. Voorhies, 14 La. Ann. 776 (1859).

40. State v. Jonas and Sam, Slaves, No. 379, 6 La. Ann. 695 (1851); State v. Adeline, a Slave, No. 4503, 11 La. Ann. 736 (1856).

41. State v. Kitty, No. 5154, 12 La. Ann. 805 (1857); State v. Slave King, No. 597, 12 La. Ann. 593 (1857).

Ample evidence of Louisiana slaves' precarious status exists in cases involving slaves accused and convicted of crimes. The number of civil suits for damages caused by the criminal acts of slaves underscores their status as at once persons and property at law. Although special courts were created ostensibly to protect slaves and ensure justice, their real purpose was more to condemn slave property, as is evidenced by the court's disregard for procedural due process in many appeals of slave convictions. The slave appellant before the supreme court was handicapped by a law that did not demand a careful observance of procedural rules in slave trials. Reversals of convictions of the special slave tribunals were infrequent. Free defendants, white or black, despite being tried in regular courts and having the advantage of common-law protections, fared little better than slaves in the few antebellum cases available. Slaves, however, had no opportunity to be tried by a jury of their peers, and Louisiana law specifically exempted the enforcement of slaves' procedural rights.[42] Under Louisiana law, more of their possible actions merited criminal penalties, and they could not enlist the aid of favorable slave testimony (even their own) if it contradicted the testimony of whites. These disabilities reinforced the lowly status of Louisiana slaves and made the law operate more harshly on them than on whites.

42. *Black Code,* "Crimes and Offenses," Sec. 20, p. 210; "An Act Relative to the Trials of Slaves," Act of June 1, 1846, *Louisiana Acts, 1846,* Sec. 28, p. 115.

4

"THE SLAVE WHO ABSCONDS . . . STEALS HIMSELF"

Slave Stealers and Fugitive Slaves

IT IS SYMBOLIC OF THE UNIQUE LEGAL STATUS OF SLAVES in antebellum society that if they could be considered criminals for stealing, they could at times also be stolen goods themselves. Slaves were, after all, valuable property, and keeping slaves one did not own and appropriating their labor brought daily gain to those who held them, and loss to the rightful owner. Slaves were often stolen outright, either for the purpose of using their services or to realize a quick profit by selling them. In 1839 the New Orleans *Daily Picayune* commented on the frequency of thefts of slaves: "We believe there are worthless scamps prowling about in this community who make a business of stealing Negroes and who exist on the fruits of their infamous labor."[1]

Because the Supreme Court of Louisiana lacked criminal jurisdiction until after the Constitution of 1845 went into effect, many appeals that the court heard involving slave stealing took the form of civil lawsuits for damages for the loss of labor and property—the fact that slaves *were* property meant that their owners could sue to recover their losses in this manner. In these appeals, the court upheld the property rights of masters and mistresses if the facts supported their claims for damages, and ordered return of the slave when possible. This type of lawsuit reflects another legal contortion of slave law—in Louisiana, civil litigation over stolen goods was relatively rare, indicating that actions involving slave stealing were concerned less with bringing the thieves to justice than with recovering the value of the slaves, if they were permanently lost to their owners, or damages caused by the loss of their labor.

Slave stealing was a serious offense. Masters feared it. The mere suspicion that John Gardiner might steal slaves was enough to have him

1. New Orleans *Daily Picayune*, May 31, 1839.

severely beaten twice. Gardiner had a contract to saw lumber on the Lafourche Parish plantation of Benjamin Cross. The lumberman enjoyed the company of Cross's slaves, attending a "negro ball" and often visiting their cabins. Cross claimed Gardiner excited the slaves to "insubordination, disobedience and disorder." When the planter ordered him to stop frequenting the slave quarters, Gardiner said he "would be damned if he would not go as often as he pleased." Cross forced him to submit to being tied up and whipped him once on the plantation with the "lashe [*sic*] of a negro whip," claiming he feared the lumberman would "run off" (steal) some of his slaves. He also accused Gardiner of writing passes for slaves to leave the plantation without permission, and even alleged that Gardiner had attempted to incite the slaves to insurrection. Two days after the first whipping, Cross found Gardiner in a Thibodaux billiard room. The lumberman called the planter "a damned old son of a bitch," and Cross hit him ten or twelve times with a three-and-a-half-foot stick called a "black-jack vine." In *Gardiner* v. *Cross* (1844), Gardiner brought a civil action for assault and battery and slander for $5,000 damages against Cross. The lower-court jury awarded him $800. The supreme court affirmed the decision. Presiding Judge François-Xavier Martin, writing for the court, observed: "Whatever may be the character of a white man, it cannot follow, that anyone has the right of inflicting on him such a chastisement."[2]

In all, the court heard twenty cases of slave stealing during the antebellum period. Eight were civil actions and eleven were criminal prosecutions (one of the criminal cases came before the court twice). In three of the civil actions the court found the claims of the plaintiff unfounded.[3] In the other five, the court decided in favor of awarding damages to the

2. Gardiner v. Cross, No. 5435, 6 Rob. 454 (La. 1844). Being whipped was considered particularly degrading tơ a white man. Clement Stachlin trespassed on the property of a plantation owner. When he was observed, he used abusive language to the planter and attempted to steal his skiff. The slaveowner ordered his driver (a slave) to whip Stachlin with his driving lash, which drew blood. Stachlin sued for damages of $1,000 for the indignity of having been whipped by a slave and as if he were a slave. A lower-court jury awarded him $1,000, and the planter appealed. The supreme court affirmed the judgment, stating that being whipped by a slave as if he were a Negro caused Stachlin "to lower [his] . . . own estimation of himself . . . to the condition of a slave of the worst character, by causing a slave, the driver of slaves, to inflict the lash upon him." The court added that "if masters are to be permitted to cause even the worst of white men to be thus treated by their slaves, the sooner we get rid of slavery the better." Stachlin v. Destrehan, No. 539, 2 La. Ann. 1019 (1847).

3. Kemper's Heirs v. Hulick, 16 La. 44 (1840) and 19 La. 349 (1841); McGowan v. Laughlan, No. 4938, 12 La. Ann. 242 (1857); Hull v. McLauren, No. 6812, 17 La. Ann. 35 (1865).

slaveholders. For example, in *Frierson* v. *Irvin* (1847), Samuel T. Frierson of Alabama was able to prove ownership of the slave Sam, whom Patrick Delane stole from Frierson's Alabama plantation and whom Frierson found in New Orleans in possession of one Patrick Irvin. Delane made "artful promises of freedom" to Sam, a "bright mulatto" cook and house servant, and then sold him at a New Orleans auction to Irvin. The lower court confirmed Frierson's ownership of Sam and awarded him the slave's wages of fifteen dollars a month from the date of the theft. At issue was the admission into evidence of three depositions that had been taken in Alabama. The commission to take the depositions had been issued to E. R. Clyde; the depositions were taken by R. J. Clyde. Because of this discrepancy, the lower court had refused to admit the depositions. The supreme court ruled that the irregularity in names was not a basis for refusing to admit the depositions. Remanding the case for a new trial, Chief Justice George Eustis ordered the lower court to admit the depositions. The final outcome of the trial cannot be determined.[4]

In its criminal aspect, slave stealing involved severe penalties. In 1819 the Louisiana legislature passed a law prescribing imprisonment at hard labor for not less than two years or more than twenty years for any person convicted of stealing a slave or helping a slave to run away. This law remained in force throughout the antebellum period. Because of the lack of criminal jurisdiction, the first appeal of a criminal conviction did not occur until 1844, before the Court of Errors and Appeals. After the supreme court received appellate jurisdiction in criminal cases, it heard eleven of these appeals between 1846 and 1862.[5] As in other decisions in

4. Frierson v. Irvin, No. 1050, 4 La. Ann. 277 (1849) and No. 1696, 5 La. Ann. 525 (1850). For other cases of slave stealing as seen in civil suits, see McGrew v. Browder, No. 863, 2 Mart. (N.S.) 17 (La. 1823); Harper v. Destrehan, No. 965, 2 Mart. (N.S.) 389 (La. 1824); and McAlpin v. Jones, No. 398, 10 La. Ann. 552 (1855). An irate woman sued the man she married for the theft of her slaves' labor when she discovered he was a bigamist. She also sued him for the use of her furniture. The Louisiana Supreme Court declared her marriage contract void and awarded her damages: Fox v. Dawson's Curator, No. 470, 8 Mart. (O.S.) 94 (La. 1820). See also Brownson v. Fenwick, 19 La. 431 (1841).

5. "An Act to Amend the Several Acts Enacted for the Punishment of the Crimes and Misdemeanors, Committed by Free Persons, and for Other Purposes," Act of March 6, 1819, *Louisiana Acts, 1819,* Sec. 5, p. 64; State v. Lennon, 8 Rob. 543 (La. 1844); State v. Dubord, No. 563, 2 La. Ann. 732 (1847); State v. Ritchie, No. 971, 3 La. Ann. 511, 715 (1848); State v. Barton, alias Bennet, alias Angel, No. 928, 4 La. Ann. 31 (1849); State v. Capers, No. 2146, 6 La. Ann. 267, 269 (1851); State v. Benjamin, No. 2512, 7 La. Ann. 47 (1852); State v. Thomp-

criminal appeals involving white defendants, the high court made liberal use of common-law rules and precedents from other states, as well as various treatises. In many cases involving slave stealing, Louisiana law afforded whites more protection than slaves accused of crimes, including a jury of their peers and the use of specific common-law precedents.

Of the eleven appeals of criminal prosecutions for slave stealing that came before the Supreme Court of Louisiana during the antebellum period, all but two were appealed by defendants on the basis of procedural irregularities in the trials. The alleged errors included improper jury selection, irregular form of indictment, being tried under the wrong statute or a repealed statute, being convicted of two crimes impossible to commit at the same time, and receiving an improper verdict. The court remanded only three cases for new trials because of judicial errors.

In *State* v. *Ritchie* (1848), the accused "did inveigle, steal and carry away" a slave named John from John's owner, Philip Millaudon. The jury found Ritchie guilty of taking the slave and disposing of him. On appeal to the supreme court, however, Associate Justice George Rogers King ruled that the jury had erred in neglecting to add that Ritchie had deprived Millaudon of the use of the slave. King observed that without the "depriving" phrase, Ritchie could have taken the slave with Millaudon's consent. Since the verdict was "so uncertain and imperfect," King remanded the case for a new trial—at which Ritchie's attorney attempted to prevent the state from presenting any case, on the basis that Ritchie had already been tried for the offense. King rejected this argument, stating that his previous ruling was not an acquittal and did not preclude a new trial for the same offense. In his ruling King cited several cases from other states, as well as *Chitty's Criminal Law*. On rehearing, the court cited two Louisiana cases as well as another common-law text, *Wharton's Criminal Law*.[6]

In *State* v. *Adams* (1859), James Adams was convicted for "feloniously and willfully attempting to carry a slave out of the state by land." The court remanded this case because Chief Justice Eustis ruled that the district court judge had erred in refusing to allow a witness for the prose-

son, alias Robinson and Baer, No. 5799, 13 La. Ann. 515 (1858); State v. Adams, No. 321, 14 La. Ann. 620 (1859); State v. Marion Fuller, 14 La. Ann. 667 (1859); State v. Robert Fuller, 14 La. Ann. 720, 726 (1859); State v. Gore, No. 6507, 15 La. Ann. 79 (1860).

6. State v. Ritchie, No. 971, 3 La. Ann. 511 (1848).

cution to answer a question to determine whether he wanted to see the defendant convicted. Eustis ruled that the question was a proper attempt to ascertain prejudice on the part of the witness.[7]

In *State* v. *Capers* (1851), the East Baton Rouge District Court convicted Joseph J. Capers of "inveigling, stealing, and carrying away" John Buhler's slave Betsey, estimated to be worth $400. The defendant appealed on the grounds that the indictment did not clearly identify the location of the crime. Associate Justice Isaac Preston ruled that the district court judge had erred in allowing the indictment, and remanded the case for a new trial.[8]

Except for *Ritchie, Adams,* and *Capers,* the supreme court upheld the lower courts in appeals of cases involving criminal charges of slave stealing. For example, in *State* v. *Thompson, alias Robinson, and Baer* (1858), a jury convicted William Thompson and S. J. Baer of stealing a slave and aiding the same slave to run away. The judge sentenced both men to five years at hard labor in the state penitentiary for stealing John, the property of the New Orleans Gaslight Company, valued at $1,000. Baer alone appealed to the Louisiana Supreme Court, on the grounds that the two crimes were impossible to commit at once. Associate Justice James Cole observed that stealing a slave and aiding a slave to escape were not incompatible crimes. Quoting the decision of the district court judge, "The object of the law is to secure to the owner the enjoyment of slave property," Cole affirmed the conviction.[9]

In *State* v. *Benjamin* (1852), the Pointe Coupée District Court convicted a planter named Harman B. Benjamin of abducting the slave Maria in July, 1849, and helping her to run away "so that the owner was deprived of her services. These terms imply, that the acts were criminal." Maria's owner found her in Benjamin's slave quarters in February, 1850. The lower court held that being in possession of recently stolen goods created the strong presumption that the holder of the purloined item was the thief. The jury convicted Benjamin and sentenced him to two years imprisonment at hard labor. He appealed on the basis that Maria had been a runaway at the time she was found on his plantation, and that there was no proof he knew she was in his quarters. Citing its earlier decision in *Ritchie* (1848), as well as *Greenleaf on Evidence* (a com-

7. State v. Adams, No. 321, 14 La. Ann. 620 (1859).
8. State v. Capers, No. 2146, 6 La. Ann. 267, 269 (1851).
9. State v. Thompson, alias Robinson, and Baer, No. 5799, 13 La. Ann. 515 (1858).

mon-law treatise), the supreme court affirmed the judgment. Essentially repeating the lower court's reasoning, the justices stated that the "possession of property recently stolen, raises a presumption, that the possessor is the thief, until the possession is otherwise explained."[10]

In *State* v. *Gore* (1860), W. Perry Gore appealed the decision of the District Court of East Feliciana Parish, which had found him guilty of stealing the "copper-colored" slave Jerry from slave dealers Heckle and Wilson and had sentenced him to five years in the penitentiary. Witnesses testified that Gore took the slave, valued at $1,000, from East Feliciana Parish to New Orleans and rented him a room in a boardinghouse. The owner of the slave found him in New Orleans and had Gore arrested. Gore appealed his conviction, claiming that he had been convicted under a law that had been repealed. He was referring to "An Act Relative to Crimes and Offenses" (1855), which he claimed repealed the law of 1819 concerning slave stealing. The 1855 statute was a general revision of the criminal law of Louisiana for whites; Gore claimed that slave stealing fell under the act's section 26, which dealt with larceny of the personal goods of another. Chief Justice Edwin Merrick rejected this argument, stating that "slaves are not classed under our law as goods or personal chattels" and therefore did not fall under the 1855 statute. Citing several of the high court's own cases, including *State* v. *Adams* (1859), Merrick affirmed Gore's conviction.[11]

The civil suits for slave stealing that came before the Louisiana Supreme Court, petitioning as they did for damages resulting from the loss of the slave and/or the slave's labor, underline again and again the fact that slaves were legally property, and much like any other valuable asset were subject to being illegally possessed or stolen outright. However, this human property had one exceptional feature: it could steal itself.

Fugitive slaves stole their labor from their masters simply by their absence. By running away, slaves were at the same time the thief and the stolen goods. Fugitive slaves were the objects of a number of appeals of civil cases heard by the Supreme Court of Louisiana during the antebellum period. This litigation fell into three categories of suits: those

10. State v. Benjamin, No. 2512, 7 La. Ann. 47 (1852); Simon Greenleaf, *Treatise on the Law of Evidence* (Boston, 1842), 3449. *Greenleaf on Evidence* is the way the court cited the latter.

11. State v. Gore, No. 6507, 15 La. Ann. 79 (1860); "An Act Relative to Crimes and Offenses," Act of March 14, 1855, *Louisiana Acts, 1855,* Sec. 26, p. 133.

concerning fugitives who made their escape on steamboats, those concerning slaves who were considered defective merchandise after a sale because they ran away (see chapter 5), and those in a large miscellaneous group that involved everything from harboring a slave to a sheriff's selling an unclaimed fugitive. The volume of these cases is evidence that some slaves were frequent runaways and that attempts to keep them under the rigid supervision required by law often failed.

On October 8, 1842, the following classified advertisements appeared in the New Orleans *Daily Picayune:*

> $50 REWARD
>
> Ran from the subscriber on the 5th instant., the griffe boy JIM, about 5 feet five inches high, and about 26 years old; an intelligent and shrewd fellow; has a downcast look when spoken to; and is supposed to endeavor to make his way to some free State. . . . Masters of vessels and steamboats will please pay attention that such a boy may not be carried off on board their vessels. . . .
>
> $20 REWARD
>
> Will be paid for the recovery of the negro GEORGE, who ran away from the steamer "Brilliant" 10 days ago. George is 25 years old; black, with flat nose; and is about 5 feet 7 inches high; both his legs are sore. He was a fireman on the "Brilliant," and may try to get employment as such on other boats. Masters of steamboats are requested to look out for him.
>
> $50 REWARD
>
> Absconded from Pass Christian, on or about the 28th of June, a mulattress named MINERVA—the property of Mrs. Sarah Hanna. . . . She is about 20 years old; hair long and curly; shows her teeth much when speaking; two front upper teeth much separated; cheek bones high, and rather good looking. She is known to be in possession of free papers, and to have made application to several steamboats for a passage to Chester, Illinois, once by a white man, dressed in gentleman's clothes. Captains of steamboats are particularly cautioned. Twenty-five dollars reward will be given for her apprehension and delivery to the subscriber, if apprehended in the State, or one hundred dollars if apprehended out of it.

> $50 REWARD
>
> Will be paid for the apprehension and delivery, in jail, of the mulatto man named ALPHEUS; . . . aged about 25 years, 5 feet, 6 inches high, stout built, forehead and cheek bones broad, chin rather pointed; wears his hair long and no whiskers at present; he has a large scar on his left arm; walks quick, and had good clothing. . . . It is believed that he can read and write. Captains of steamboats and vessels are particularly cautioned against receiving him. He will probably attempt to go up the river.[12]

Advertisements such as these appeared regularly in Louisiana newspapers throughout the antebellum period. The frequency with which they arose indicates that attempts to escape bondage by steamboat were not uncommon, and the number of long-running advertisements implies that some fugitives made good their escapes or at least managed to elude capture for a considerable length of time. The slave Minerva (above) absconded on June 28, 1842; the item advertising for her return appeared each day in the New Orleans *Daily Picayune* from July 14 until December 17. Of course, the disappearance of a long-running ad does not tell us whether Minerva's owner regained possession of her or simply gave up hope for her return.[13]

A fugitive slave in antebellum Louisiana who attempted to flee to a free state—or who simply decamped to see friends and relatives or ran to escape punishment or hard work—faced almost insurmountable obstacles. Any white could stop persons of color, free or slave, and demand proof of freedom or a pass (written permission from their owners to be wherever they were). The fugitive slave also had the patrols to avoid. Even if he or she could escape detection, sheer geographical distance to a free jurisdiction for a runaway on foot could be an insuperable barrier to attaining liberty. A combination of factors made the steamboats plying the myriad waterways of Louisiana an attractive alternative to being on foot: speedy transportation (by antebellum standards) away from an area where the slave's status was known; routes that often included a journey to or near a free state or territory; the willingness of

12. New Orleans *Daily Picayune,* October 8, 1842. The discrepancy between the reward offered in the heading of the ad for Minerva and those promised in the ad's text is in the original.

13. New Orleans *Daily Picayune,* July 14, 1842–December 17, 1842.

steamer captains, who sorely needed labor, to risk heavy fines and civil liability to allow bondsmen to join their crews without demanding the written permission of their owners or proof of their free status as prescribed by law; and crew members who were sometimes sympathetic to fleeing fugitives.

Advertisements for fugitives believed to have relied upon steamboats to run from slavery indicate three methods of escape. The first and most usual involved slaves who represented themselves as free and hired on as crew members on boats traveling between Louisiana and a free state or territory. When the vessel sailed into free waters, the fugitive would disembark and attempt to disappear. Another, more daring, way to escape was to pretend to be free and book passage to a free port or to a city such as Louisville, which was across the river from a free state; occasionally light-skinned slaves even represented themselves as white passengers when purchasing a ticket and while on board. The third escape mode was simply to hide aboard a vessel, with or without knowledge of the crew. If the stowaway managed to escape detection until the ship docked in a free territory, he or she would leave the hiding place and attempt to flee into the surrounding area.

Louisiana and other slave states imposed regulations on ship captains and vessel owners to prevent fugitives from using steamboats to escape bondage. In all of these states, including Louisiana, the intent of the law was the same—to make captains and shipowners liable for slaves' lost labor or, if a slave made good an escape, for the total value of the fugitive. The procedure for filing suit against violators differed somewhat in Louisiana because of its civil-law heritage; in Missouri, for example, aggrieved slaveowners often brought such lawsuits as actions of trespass (a common-law term meaning an act causing damage to the person or property of another), whereas in Louisiana the form of action was by petition. Whatever the technical details, the results were similar. This is one area in which the presence of slavery worked as a force to "Americanize" Louisiana jurisprudence, and with time the state's law as it concerned fugitive slaves aboard steam vessels came to closely resemble that of other slave states.[14]

14. *Code of Practice in Civil Cases for the State of Louisiana* (New Orleans, 1824), Art. 171, pp. 141–42. In Virginia the use of the act of trespass was established by statute: "An Act Authorizing Representatives to Sustain or Revive Actions in Certain Acts of Trespass," Act of

An 1816 statute allowed both criminal penalties and civil damages for ship captains who hired blacks on board their ships without permission of their masters if they were slaves or proof of freedom if they were free persons of color. The penalty for violating this law was a sentence of between three and seven years in jail, as well as paying damages to the owner of the slave. The same jury that pronounced the verdict on the criminal prosecution was to determine the amount of civil damages. The act further required the captain to provide to the mayor of New Orleans or the parish (county) judge of the place where the ship was located a written description the slave or free person of color, along with either proof of freedom for the free person of color or written permission from

March 9, 1827, *Virginia Acts, 1827,* p. 27. For cases about steamboats and slaves in other states, see Eaton v. Vaughan, 9 Mo. 743 (1846); Calvert v. Rider, 20 Mo. 146 (1854); Edwards v. Vail, 3 J. J. Marsh 595 (Ken. 1836); Bracken v. Steamboat *Gulnare,* 16 B. Mon. 444 (Ken. 1855); Meekin v. Thomas, 17 B. Mon. 710 (Ken. 1857); Ellis v. Walsh, 4 Richardson 486 (S.C. 1851); Duncan v. State, 7 Humphreys 148 (Tenn. 1846); Scruggs v. Davis, 5 Sneed 261 (Tenn. 1857); Case v. Woolley, 6 Dana 17 (Va. 1837); Steam Navigation Co. v. Hungerford, 6 Gill and John. 291 (Md. 1834); State v. Baltimore and Susquehanna Steam Co., 13 Md. 181 (1859); Page v. Vandegrift, 5 Harrington 176 (Del. 1849); Gibbons v. Morse, 2 Halsted 253 (N.J. 1821); Cutter v. Moore, 3 Halsted 219 (N.J. 1825); Gibbs v. Mennard, 6 Paige 258 (N.Y. 1837); Mangham v. Cox and Waring, 29 Ala. 81 (1856); and Massey v. Cole, 29 Ala. 364 (1856). Other slaves states' laws concerning slaves and steamboats include: "An Act to Prevent the Stealing of Slaves and Carrying Them Off by Water," Act of February 11, 1828, *Florida Acts, 1828,* pp. 92–94. This act called for "death as a felon" for a ship captain who allowed a slave on board without written consent of the owner; it also prescribed a $500 fine if a slave was found concealed aboard a ship. See also "An Act to Amend the Act Entitled 'An Act to Prevent the Masters of Vessels and Others from Removing Persons of Color from This State,'" Act of February 12, 1828, *Kentucky Acts, 1828,* pp. 178–79; "An Act to Amend the Act Entitled 'An Act More Effectually to Prevent the Owners of Steam Boats and Stages from Carrying Off Slaves Without the Knowledge or Consent of Their Masters,'" Act of November 12, 1833, *Tennessee Acts, 1833,* p. 75; and "An Act to Prevent the Transportation of Slaves Upon Railroads, Steam Boats or Stage Coaches Without Written Permission from Their Owners," Act of January 12, 1841, *North Carolina Acts, 1841,* pp. 99–100. The latter act also provided for a $500 fine for violators and the value of the slave if he or she escaped permanently. "An Act to Amend an Act Entitled 'An Act Reducing into One the Several Acts Concerning Slaves, Free Negroes, and Mulattoes,'" Act of February 24, 1827, *Virginia Acts, 1827,* pp. 23–25; "An Act to Amend the Several Acts Concerning Free Negroes and Mulattoes," Act of March 11, 1834, *Virginia Acts, 1834,* pp. 77–81, created a presumption that if a runaway was found concealed aboard a ship, the captain was presumed to have knowingly accepted the slave aboard. "An Act to Prevent the Citizens of New York from Carrying Slaves Out of This Commonwealth . . . ," Act of March 13, 1841, *Virginia Acts, 1841,* pp. 79–82, instituted a $500 fine for captains who accepted slaves on board their ships without written permission of their owners.

the owner of the slave to remove him or her from the state. (The section requiring free persons of color to file evidence of their status had no counterpart in the law of other states and was no doubt a reflection of Louisiana's large population in that category.) Failure to comply with this law resulted in a $500 fine for each slave removed from the state, in addition to damages. Before the legislature passed the 1816 statute, slaveowners could sue ship captains for accepting slaves on board without consent of their masters under several general provisions of the *Black Code,* such as hiring a slave's services without the owner's permission.[15]

In 1835 the legislature expanded the liability to include shipowners as well as captains from whose vessels slaves managed to escape. This act allowed owners of escaped slaves to "recover the full value of the slave or slaves so carried away" and gave the aggrieved slaveowner a "tacit lien" on the vessel involved. In 1839 Louisiana lawmakers passed additional legislation aimed at steamboat captains and owners, requiring them to post a bond of $1,000 if they regularly operated vessels that hired slaves as crew members on voyages that left Louisiana waters. Captains and owners who failed to provide this security could be fined $1,000 and jailed for six months at hard labor. Shipowners and captains were also liable for the value of slaves taken out of the state if they escaped.[16]

An 1840 revision of the 1816, 1835, and 1839 laws still required captains of ships to demand that slaves produce the written consent of their owners before hiring them but eliminated criminal penalties for neglecting to do so. If a slaveowner found one of his or her slaves on a ship whose destination was either beyond or within Louisiana, the new statute created the presumption that the captain and owner of the vessel had allowed the slave on board and concealed the fugitive with the purpose of depriving his master of his services or had allowed the slave to remain

15. "An Act to Take the Most Effective Measures in Order to Prevent the Transportation or Carrying Away of Slaves Out of This State . . . ," Act of February 13, 1816, *Louisiana Acts, 1816,* pp. 8–14; *Black Code,* Sec. 12, p. 156.

16. "An Act to Amend the Act Entitled 'An Act to Take the Most Effective Measures in Order to Prevent the Transportation, or Carrying Away of Slaves Out of the State' . . . Approved 13 February 1816," Act of March 26, 1835, *Louisiana Acts, 1835,* pp. 152–53; "An Act to Prevent the Carrying Away of Slaves, and for Other Purposes," Act of March 19, 1839, *Louisiana Acts, 1839,* pp. 118–20. To avoid confusion between slave masters and ship masters, I have not used the maritime-law term *masters* in referring to vessel captains.

on board after discovery with the purpose of depriving the slaveowner of the slave's services. This presumption, according to the act, could not be refuted without "corroborating circumstances" or the testimony of two witnesses who were not employees of the vessel involved. Failure to comply with this law made captains and owners liable for a fine of $500, to be paid to the owner of the slave, in addition to the wages of the slaves during their absence. Accepting a fugitive slave also made the captain and shipowner liable for the value of the slave if the runaway was injured or killed while in the ship's employ, as well as for any damages occasioned by the slave's actions while on board. Furthermore, the slaveowner was entitled to damages and to a privilege on the vessel involved (a privilege is a civil-law concept that entitles a creditor to be preferred over other creditors by the very nature of the debt). Thirty-one appeals of violations of these statutes appeared before the Supreme Court of Louisiana during the antebellum period, an indication that slave labor on steamboats was in such demand that at least some captains were willing to risk the penalties prescribed by law. The court found for the allegedly aggrieved slaveowner fourteen times and held the steamboat captains and shipowners not to be liable an equal number of times, the remaining three appeals being either remanded for further action or nonsuited. In most of the appeals won by ship captains, the captains were able to prove conclusively either that they had no way of knowing fugitives were aboard their ships or that they had done everything possible after discovery of a runaway slave to keep him secured until the slave's owner could retrieve the fugitive. The crucial issue was the loss of labor of the slave while runaway, or the loss of the slave entirely if killed or escaped permanently.[17]

17. "An Act . . . Passed for the Purpose of Preventing Slaves from Being Transported or Conducted Out of the State," Act of March 25, 1840, *Louisiana Acts, 1840,* pp. 89–91. The Louisiana legislature was also concerned about steamboats bringing free persons of color into the state. In 1842 the lawmakers passed an act prohibiting ship captains from entering Louisiana waters with free blacks as passengers or crew on board their vessels. If captains disregarded this prohibition, the act required the harbormaster to notify the justice of the peace in the area, who was to issue a warrant for the arrest of the persons of color, who would then be confined in the parish jail until the vessel was ready to depart the state: "An Act More Effectually to Prevent Free Persons of Color from Entering into This State . . . ," Act of March 16, 1842, *Louisiana Acts, 1842,* pp. 308–18. Louisiana law held slaveowners to strict liability for the actions of their slaves whether authorized or not, a provision unknown in the laws of other slave states; *Digest of 1808,* Tit. I, Chap. III, Arts. 20–22; *Civil Code,* Arts. 179–81, p. 28.

Shipowners and captains faced a difficult task in ensuring that no runaway slaves boarded their vessels. According to an article in the New Orleans *Daily Picayune,* some steamboat crews encouraged slaves to run away from their plantations, come to New Orleans, and board their ships. These crew members, the article alleged, concealed the slaves on board until the ship arrived in a free state, where they allowed the slaves to run away.[18]

Compounding the problems of the owners and captains was the danger of working on a steamboat, considered such a hazardous occupation that life insurance for slave sailors was more expensive than for any other slave employment. The supreme court heard seven cases involving slaves severely injured or killed while legally hired to steamboats. Aboard the steamboat *Two Friends* a slave was seriously wounded by the ship's engine or flywheel. In another case the slave Jack Little, or "Brickyard Jack," was "cordelling" (towing) the schooner *Maryland* to track it around a bend in the Mississippi River at night when the ship sheered, pulling Jack from the levee into the river, where he drowned. Jack's owner claimed that the victim had been a first-rate hand at sugar making; he testified that he allowed his slaves to work at night (for fifty cents and all the beef, bread, and grog they wanted) because it was the only time they had in which to make something for themselves, so that "it was hard to be too strict with them." Jasmin, described by his owner as an "extraordinarily fine Negro," a creole (native-born) slave worth $1,200, was hired out as a steward, cook, and foreman on the *American Eagle.* He was scalded and died of his injuries when the vessel's boiler burst following a collision with another steamboat. A boiler explosion also took the life of another slave; witnesses in *Poree* v. *Cannon* (1859) stated that "his nostrils were filled with hot ashes." In *England* v. *Gripon* (1860), a slave fell overboard and drowned because the steamboat had no lifeboat to save him. In *Howes* v. Red Chief (1860), a slave transferring corn from one steamboat to another in bad weather slipped on a wet plank, fell into the Mississippi, and drowned. In *Huntington* v. *Ricard* (1851), a slave died when a vessel was lost at sea, apparently because it was unsuited for oceangoing service and was improperly loaded. One slave hired to a steamboat inadvertently caused his own demise: Preston

18. New Orleans *Daily Picayune,* July 27, 1854.

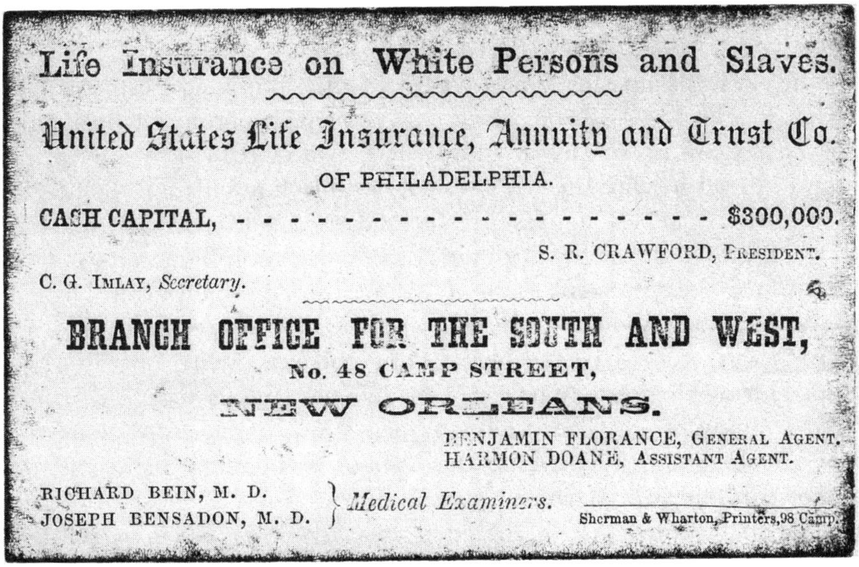

Life Insurance on White Persons and Slaves.

United States Life Insurance, Annuity and Trust Co.

OF PHILADELPHIA.

CASH CAPITAL, - $300,000.

S. R. CRAWFORD, President.

C. G. Imlay, *Secretary*.

BRANCH OFFICE FOR THE SOUTH AND WEST,

No. 48 CAMP STREET,

NEW ORLEANS.

BENJAMIN FLORANCE, General Agent.
HARMON DOANE, Assistant Agent.

RICHARD BEIN, M. D.
JOSEPH BENSADON, M. D. } *Medical Examiners.*

Sherman & Wharton, Printers, 98 Camp.

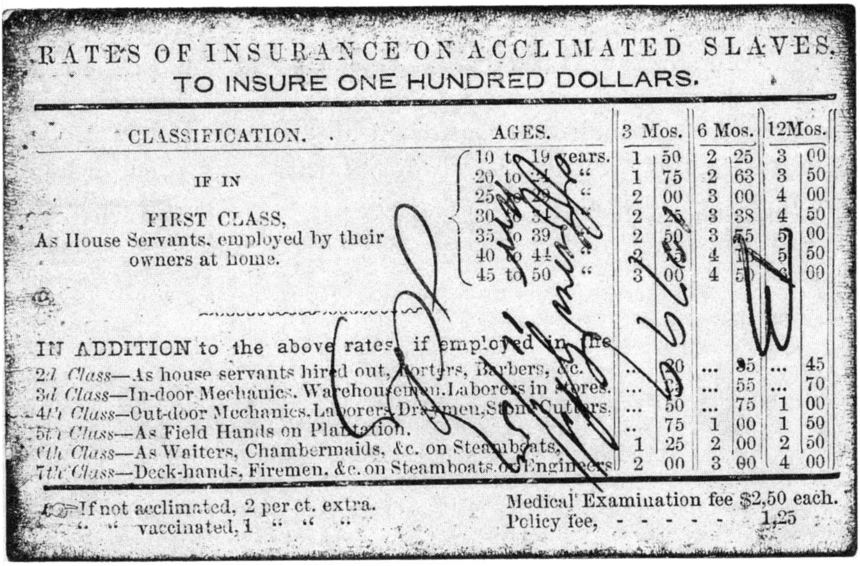

RATES OF INSURANCE ON ACCLIMATED SLAVES,
TO INSURE ONE HUNDRED DOLLARS.

CLASSIFICATION.	AGES.	3 Mos.		6 Mos.		12Mos.	
IF IN FIRST CLASS, As House Servants, employed by their owners at home.	10 to 19 years.	1	50	2	25	3	00
	20 to 24 "	1	75	2	63	3	50
	25 to 29 "	2	00	3	00	4	00
	30 to 34 "	2	25	3	38	4	50
	35 to 39 "	2	50	3	[illegible]	5	00
	40 to 44 "	2	[illegible]	4	[illegible]	5	50
	45 to 50 "	3	00	4	50	6	00
IN ADDITION to the above rates, if employed in the							
2d *Class*—As house servants hired out, Porters, Barbers, &c.		...	30	...	35	...	45
3d *Class*—In-door Mechanics, Warehousemen, Laborers in stores.		...	[illegible]	...	55	...	70
4th *Class*—Out-door Mechanics, Laborers, Draymen, Stone Cutters.		...	50	...	75	1	00
5th *Class*—As Field Hands on Plantation.		..	75	1	00	1	50
6th *Class*—As Waiters, Chambermaids, &c. on Steamboats.		1	25	2	00	2	50
7th *Class*—Deck-hands, Firemen, &c. on Steamboats or Engineers		2	00	3	00	4	00

☞ If not acclimated, 2 per ct. extra.
" " vaccinated, 1 " " "

Medical Examination fee $2,50 each.
Policy fee, - - - - - 1,25

Front and back of a Philadelphia insurance company's rate card found in *Summers* v. *U.S. Life Insurance, Annuity & Trust Co.* (1858). Note that the premiums for slaves working aboard steamboats were double and triple those for field hands, the next most hazardous category.

Courtesy of the Supreme Court of Louisiana Collection of Legal Archives

was sitting on a barrel of pork drinking liquor; he fell asleep and when called was startled, fell overboard, and drowned.[19]

The earliest Louisiana appeal concerning fugitives and steam vessels, *Bayon* v. *Prévost* (1815), involved a slave named Joseph, a tailor, who ran away from his master in Lafourche Parish in 1814. Probably planning to blend in with the city's skilled free-black population, he fled to New Orleans, where he was arrested and confined in the city jail. His owner's family physician, Dr. François Prévost, took it upon himself to remove the slave and return him to his master, Antoine Bayon. During the steamboat voyage to Lafourche Parish, Joseph appeared to be very ill with dysentery—so enfeebled that he collapsed while boarding the ship. During the journey he either made a miraculous recovery or had been feigning illness, because he escaped at one of the stops along the way. Bayon sued Prévost after this "act of friendship" for negligence in not confining the slave and putting him in irons. Prévost's attorney alleged that Prévost had been acting as a *negotiorum gestor,* a civil-law term meaning a voluntary agent for another, who without authority took charge of a situation for another in his or her interest. Presiding Judge George Mathews ruled that as a *negotiorum gestor,* Prévost was not liable for the loss of the slave. Citing the *Digest of 1808,* Mathews ruled that Prévost had handled the situation with "all the care of a prudent father of a family," for the slave had appeared too ill to put in irons.

19. Rice v. Cade, 10 La. 228 (1836) [which coincidentally affirmed the right of slaves to be paid for Sunday work]; Morgan's Syndics v. Fiveash, No. 1700, 7 Mart. (N.S.) 410 (La. 1829); Lacoste v. Sellick, No. 6101, 1 La. Ann. 336 (1846); Poree v. Cannon, No. 6006, 14 La. Ann. 501 (1859); England v. Gripon, No. 6316, 15 La. Ann. 304 (1860); Howes v. *Red Chief,* Nos. 5944, 6487, 15 La. Ann. 321 (1860); Huntington v. Ricard, No. 2288, 6 La. Ann. 806 (1851); Barry v. Kimball, No. 3500, 10 La. Ann. 787 (1855), and No. 4684, 12 La. Ann. 372 (1857). For other maritime accidents involving slaves, see Livaudais v. Scott and *America,* No. 1754, 8 Mart. (N.S.) 166 (La. 1829); Myers v. Slack, No. 2401, 5 La. 53 (1833); Lobdell v. Bullitt and *James Monroe,* No. 3316, 13 La. 348 (1839); Ricard, f.m.c., v. Kimball (*John Linton*), No. 4717, Rob. 142 (La. 1843); Hudson v. Grout, 5 Rob. 499 (1843); Dowty v. Templeton, No. 3131, 9 La. Ann. 549 (1854); Pousargues v. *Natchez,* No. 6250, 15 La. Ann. 80 (1860); and Pelham v. *Messenger,* No. 6629, 16 La. Ann. 99 (1861). For similar cases involving slaves and railroads, see Lesseps v. Pontchartrain Railroad Company, No. 3698, 17 La. 361 (1841); Fleytas v. Pontchartrain Railroad Company, No. 3772, 18 La. 339 (1841). For cases where it was not known whether slaves drowned or ran away from a steamboat, see Nicholls v. Roland, No. 649, 11 Mart. (O.S.) 190 (La. 1822), and Downey v. Stacy, No. 5969, 1 La. Ann. 426 (1846). For slave life insurance rates, see Summers v. United States Insurance, Annuity and Trust Co., No. 5423, 13 La. Ann. 504 (1858). The information on life insurance for slaves engaged in various forms of labor is not contained in the printed report of this case, but in a pocket insurance card enclosed in the original lower-court case record (see illustration, p. 103).

Mathews affirmed the judgment of the lower court, which had held Prévost blameless.[20]

McMaster v. *Beckwith* (1831) was a typical case of an owner's suing a ship captain for the loss of his slave. In 1830 Samuel McMaster sued Captain Beckwith of the steamboat *Louisiana* for hiring his slave John Scott, a twenty-five-year-old carpenter, without McMaster's consent or knowledge. When the *Louisiana* stopped at Louisville, Scott left the ship and disappeared, probably to freedom just across the Ohio River in Indiana. McMaster sued Beckwith for $1,500—$400 for the price he had paid for the slave and $1,100 for damages. The lower court awarded him $800 despite proof that McMaster had purchased the slave as a runaway who had been confined to jail for safekeeping. In the act of sale transferring Scott to McMaster, Scott's former owner specifically stated that the slave was a frequent fugitive, and therefore the warranty required by Louisiana law for slave sales did not apply. Although Judge Martin ruled that Beckwith was negligent in hiring the slave without McMaster's permission, he also ruled that the district court judge should not have awarded damages above the actual purchase price of $400 because McMaster had purchased Scott knowing he was "addicted to running away." Martin reduced the award to $400.[21]

Two years later, in *Hurst* v. *Wallace* (1833), the court exonerated a captain of responsibility for the loss of slaves brought aboard his ship. In this case a person who pretended to be the master of two slaves traveled with them on the steamboat *Hercules* from New Orleans to Louisville. The three disembarked at their destination and disappeared. The owner of the slaves sued the captain of the steamboat, claiming he had not filed a description of the slaves as well as written permission from their master, as required by the act of 1816. Chief Judge Mathews affirmed a judgment for the defendant, stating that he had no way of knowing that the man who boarded the ship with the slaves was not their master. Mathews reasoned that the 1816 statute should not be construed to prohibit masters from traveling by boat with their slaves without following the formalities prescribed by the 1816 statute. Further-

20. Bayon v. Prévost, No. 115, 4 Mart. (o.s.) 58 (La. 1815); *Digest of 1808,* Tit. IV, Sec. 1, Art. 8, p. 318. *Bayon* v. *Prévost* is one of only a handful of cases on *negotiorum gestor* in Louisiana law.

21. McMaster v. Beckwith, No. 2017, 2 La. 329 (1831). For a complete discussion of the Louisiana warranty in slave sales, see chapter 5.

more, he ruled that the damages to the slaves' owner was not the fault of the captain, but of the person who pretended to be their owner.[22]

Seven years later, in *Burke, f.w.c.,* v. *Clarke* (1837), the court heard an appeal in which Captain Clarke of the *Freedom* helped a slave hired to his ship to escape. The captain had agreed to hire the slave Eliza, owned by a free woman of color named Burke, as a chambermaid aboard the *Freedom* for a voyage from New Orleans to Louisville and back. Clarke agreed to turn the slave over to an agent of Burke's upon return to New Orleans. Instead, he took her on another voyage, during which she disappeared on the way to Cincinnati. A witness testified that Clarke had refused to hand Eliza over to the plaintiff's agent at the end of the first voyage, saying "he would keep her all the summer, and take her to Cincinnati, where she would be safe." Clarke assured the agent that there was no danger that Eliza would escape, as he planned to moor the steamboat in the middle of the river and never allow the slave on shore unless he accompanied her personally. However, witnesses testified that he moored the boat close to the riverbank, allowing her to escape. The first mate stated that Clarke had allowed Eliza to disembark whenever she pleased, and had not ordered anyone to watch her when she went ashore. One member of the crew, a free man of color, testified that he heard Burke and Clarke agree that Eliza's wages would be twelve dollars per month.

The lower court found in favor of the plaintiff, and Clarke and the owner of the steamboat appealed on the grounds that there was no evidence that Clarke helped Eliza to escape. The co-owner of the *Freedom* also appealed, on the grounds that he was not responsible for the actions of Captain Clarke. The high court rejected these arguments, stating that Clarke and the co-owner had entered into a commercial partnership and as such were both bound for the acts of each other. However, Judge Martin, writing for the court, reasoned that the lower court's award of $1,000 (the value of the slave) plus $82.50 wages and $100 damages was excessive: "The master of a vessel who does not deliver goods which he has received on freight, cannot be made to pay higher damages than the value of the goods at the place of delivery. The rule must be the same in the case of a master who undertakes to carry a slave as a passenger; he must pay the value of the slave and no more." Martin reduced the

22. Hurst v. Wallace, No. 2402, 5 La. 98 (1833).

plaintiff's award to the slave's value of $1,000, plus $12, one month's wages.[23]

Holmes v. Chieftain (1845) involved a fugitive slave named George, alias Granville, who entertained those aboard the *Chieftain* by "dancing and patting for the amusement of the passengers," who rewarded him with "drams." His owner, Pleasant H. Harbour, recovered him in Golconda, Illinois, in 1842, and through his agent, Holmes, sued the steamboat's captain and owner under the act of 1840 for $500 for taking George on board without Harbour's knowledge or consent, and also for $600 in damages, which included expenses of advertising, recovery, and lost services. The lower court awarded the plaintiff the $500 fine and $300 in expenses. The state supreme court affirmed the judgment of $800. The defendant had appealed on the grounds that the names George and Granville had neither of them appeared on the original suit, causing confusion in identifying the slave in question, and that the veracity of one of the plaintiff's witnesses was questionable. Associate Judge King rejected both arguments, stating that there was no problem identifying the slave and dismissing the question of the witness' credibility, since the jury had found him convincing.[24]

In *Emmerling* v. *Beebe* (1840), Louis Emmerling, owner of the slave Peter, sued Junius Beebe for hiring Peter to work aboard the *Tiger* without Emmerling's knowledge or consent. Peter disappeared after working on the *Tiger* for ten months. The ship's captain said that the slave had exhibited free papers and claimed his name was James Rivers. Another witness stated that when the boat was in port Peter frequented the "grog shops" all day and did not seem to fear being on shore. He testified that the slave often shipped with a Negro woman, who passed as his wife, although he also lived with another woman, a slave on a nearby plantation. Emmerling sued for $2,600 ($2,000 value and $600 wages), but the District Court of New Orleans awarded him only $150, and he appealed. Beebe's attorney argued that the loss was the "fault of the plaintiff who permitted him [Peter] to palm himself off on the community as a free man." Associate Justice Henry Bullard affirmed the judgment, stating that since the slave had been allowed to hire his own time

23. Burke, f.w.c., v. Clarke, No. 3112, 11 La. 206 (1837).

24. Holmes v. *Chieftain,* No. 5837, 1 La. Ann. 136 (1845). *Patting* more than likely refers to "hamboning," a dance in which the chest is patted rhythmically.

on the levee and had exhibited free papers, it was difficult to know he was not free.[25]

Captains who failed to demand proof of freedom could not escape liability. *Buel* v. New York (1841) involved a house servant, cook, and dray driver named Prince, who hired himself on the steamboat *New York* without his master's knowledge or consent. Calling himself Ned, he went aboard with a trunk and bundle and told the vessel's engineer that he was free and that he had just arrived in New Orleans on a steamer from Cincinnati. The captain of the *New York* had given explicit instructions that no one was to hire a person of color without demanding free papers. The engineer, accepting Prince's statement that he was free, failed to demand papers. The captain did not discover that Prince had no proof of freedom until the *New York* was in Kentucky. He put the slave in irons, transferred him to the *Black Hawk,* and paid his passage to New Orleans. Somehow Prince escaped, and his owner never recovered him. Prince's owner sued the *New York*'s captain and owners for $1,700 ($1,500 value and $200 spent attempting to recover the slave). Buel recovered that amount from the judgment of the lower court. Associate Judge Edward Simon affirmed the judgment, stating that the captain was responsible for the actions of those in his employ according to *Civil Code* article 2299. Simon reasoned that the captain had seen the slave on board for several days but had failed to demand proof of freedom.[26]

The Supreme Court of Louisiana did not always hold ship captains liable if fugitives secreted themselves on board steamboats without the captain's knowledge, especially if the captain took prompt action to secure the runaways and have them returned to their owners. In *Winston* v. *Foster* (1843), the owner of the slave Thomas Taylor sued Captain Foster of the *St. Mary* for receiving Taylor on his ship to "carry said boy Tom from the State of Louisiana to some one of the Northern Atlantic States of the Union to wit to New York." Taylor's owner, Thomas B. Winston, sued for $400 damages and expenses of recovering the slave and $800, the bondsman's value, claiming that the "boy [is] now worth but very little . . . in consequence of his having discovered that the way

25. Emmerling v. Beebe, No. 3642, 15 La. 251 (1840).

26. Buel v. *New York,* No. 3689, 17 La. 541 (1841); *Civil Code,* Art. 2299, p. 359. See also Slatter v. Holton, No. 3894, 19 La. 39 (1841); Feltus v. Anders (*Swallow*), No. 4576, 5 Rob. 7 (La. 1843).

to escape from the State is so easy." Winston also demanded that Foster pay the $500 fine under the act of 1840 for accepting the slave aboard without demanding proof of freedom. In advertising for Tom, Winston had described the bondsman as "a confirmed and incorrigible runaway" who had lately "been badly ruptured" and "may be wearing a Warner's Patent Truss." The ad stated that Tom had just been purchased from Natchez and his wife remained in that city. Testimony proved that the ship's cook had accepted Tom aboard the ship; about twenty miles from the mouth of the Mississippi River, the captain discovered that Tom had no free papers, and he sent him back to New Orleans on a towboat to be lodged in prison. The lower court found the captain responsible for the cook's actions and fined him the $500 but denied Winston damages and the value of Tom, since he had recovered the slave. The supreme court reversed this decision and held that the captain had not incurred the $500 fine, because his actions following the discovery of the slave nullified the presumption that he had intended to deprive the master of the slave's services. Judge Alonzo Morphy found that the difference between this case and *Buel* v. New York was that in *Buel* the plaintiff never recovered his slave. In this case, the plaintiff recovered her slave, and the court ruled that the captain's actions did not merit the fine.[27]

The idea that running away and experiencing freedom lessened the value of a slave surfaced again in *Spalding* v. *Taylor* (St. Missouri) (1846). A ship's steward saw no need to demand proof of freedom from a man named Felix. He hired Felix without asking to examine his papers. The captain testified, "*God, the boy is so white that you can't tell if he is a white man or a slave*" (emphasis in original). Another witness stated that Felix appeared to have Indian or Spanish blood, that no one would suspect he was of African origin, and that a great many creoles were darker than Felix. Another witness said that Felix dressed like a gentleman and that nothing in his manner or appearance suggested he was a slave. The captain stated that because of Felix's blue eyes and straight hair, he would have allowed him to sit at the table with even the female passengers had he booked passage. Testimony proved Felix had hired his own time for several years on ships that traveled to free states. Justice Pierre A. Rost denied Felix's master recovery, noting that any slave who

27. Winston v. Foster, No. 4617, 5 Rob. 113 (La. 1843). For another case where a captain's swift action in jailing a runaway rendered him blameless, see Botts v. Cockrane, No. 1013, 4 La. Ann. 35 (1849).

lived as free and went to other states where slavery was prohibited was totally worthless: "We . . . are satisfied that, on account of his color and of his vices, the slave was of very little value at any time. After he had been suffered by the plaintiff to live and act like a freeman, and to go and remain as long as he pleased in States where slavery is prohibited, he must have been utterly worthless, and the jury erred in coming to a different conclusion."[28]

In *Buddy* v. Vanleer (1851), a trilingual slave named Ned, who was an excellent judge of hides and deerskins and a "good cook," died of cholera while working on the *A. W. Vanleer* without his owner's knowledge or consent. When the captain discovered Ned's illness, he gave him a great deal of care, including rubbing him down with a mixture of brandy and cayenne pepper and administering "Dr. Cannon's anti-cholera preparation." However, the slave died, and his master sued the steamboat's captain and owners for $1,300 ($1,000 for Ned's value and $300 damages). The lower court awarded him $1,000, but the supreme court remanded the case for a new trial to determine the value of the slave's lost labor to the owner as well as damage to the character of the slave because of his absence from his owner. "His character as a slave may have been injured by their negligence." Associate Justice Preston observed that there was an epidemic of cholera in New Orleans at the time Ned left and that there was no connection between Ned's death and his employment on the steamboat. Preston cited *Winston* v. *Foster* and held that the captain's actions proved he was not attempting to remove the slave from the state or to deprive his owner of his services. Preston remanded the case and instructed the lower court to award Ned's owner only his wages while absent, as well as damages, but not his value.[29]

Williamson v. *Norton* (1852) involved another light-skinned slave fugitive, named Robert. He booked cabin passage aboard the steamboat *Western World* and throughout the voyage called himself Henry Smith. He ate at the first table all the way from New Orleans to Memphis, usually seating himself near the ladies. Witnesses described him as being creole in appearance, "a shade lighter than a new saddle" and looking like a white raised in a southern climate or perhaps a person of Spanish

28. Spalding v. Taylor (*St. Missouri*), No. 5628, 1 La. Ann. 195 (1846).

29. Buddy v. *Vanleer,* No. 1901, 6 La. Ann. 34 (1851). See also Roundtree v. *Brilliant,* No. 2804, 8 La. Ann. 289 (1853); and Goldenbow v. Wright (*Lady Washington*), No. 3108, 13 La. 371 (1839).

or Mexican origin. He was "genteelly dressed and of a very genteel deportment." Near Memphis the steward expressed his fears to the captain that the man was a slave. At this report the captain put Robert ashore and had him jailed as a probable runaway. Many passengers protested, stating that Robert could not be a Negro, that he had "no appearance of African blood," and that he had "more the appearance of a gentleman than a plebeian." Finding that the captain should have noticed Robert's "colored blood," the lower court awarded his owner $275 in damages. In his decision on the appeal, Justice Rost noted that he believed the defendant had been deceived by the appearance of the slave and should not be fined under the law of 1840 because he lacked criminal intent. However, Rost ruled, Robert's owner deserved the $275 damages because of the inconvenience and loss of the slave's labor. Rost noted that this decision split the court 2–2, thereby affirming the judgment of the lower court, as required in the Constitution of 1845. One of the dissenters, Justice Preston, reversed the decision on the rehearing of the case. Preston noted that none of the passengers of the crowded steamer had noticed that Robert was not white, even after traveling several hundred miles with him. Preston awarded the owner no damages, reasoning that the captain had acted with ordinary prudence and that "all discoveries are easy after they are made": "The master and officers of a steamboat, crowded with freight and passengers, have too much to do to scrutinize minutely the hair, skin, and complexion of every one on board; and, if they act with ordinary care, are excusable, even if they overlook that which requires, out of their peculiar line, minute inspection to ascertain."[30]

Daret v. *Gray* (1857) involved four members of a slave family—a mulatto man, his wife, and their two children—who in March of 1854 booked passage to Aspinwall (now Colón, Panama) on the oceangoing steamboat *Eldorado*. Captain Gray checked their free papers, which later proved to be excellent forgeries of the signatures of two prominent New Orleans notaries. Their owner, Dr. H. Daret, discovered the slaves' plan of escape and telegraphed officials at the mouth of the Mississippi River to arrest them. As soon as the message reached the captain, he returned to New Orleans and restored the slaves to their owner. Claiming that the near-escape lowered the value of the slaves—whom he had since sold

30. Williamson v. Norton (*Western World*), No. 2427, 7 La. Ann. 393 (1852); Benjamin Wall Dart, ed., *Constitutions of the State of Louisiana*, Tit. IV, Art. 68, p. 514.

at a substantial loss—Daret sued for $445.25, which included diminution of the value of the slaves, jail fees, and the cost of the telegram. Chief Justice Merrick held that the slaves were already "corrupt," having exhibited "viciousness of character" when they procured forged papers and left their master's house:

> The proof, it is true, shows that the plaintiff sold the slaves and that he suffered large deductions from their apparent value, on account of their having runaway [*sic*]. The habit of running away is a vice inherent in the slave. That vice had developed itself before the slaves went on board the defendant's ship. It was when they procured their forged papers and clandestinely left their master's house to go on board of the ship, that they became runaways. They were corrupt when they imposed their purchased forgeries upon the officers of the ship, and the captain of the ship cannot be held responsible for the deterioration in the value of the slaves, which he had no agency in producing, and who was only made, by a neglect of a form of law, the instrument of giving greater publicity to such defects.

Merrick awarded Daret $34, the actual expense involved in recovering the four slaves. Even this small award seems unfair to the captain, who had no way of knowing that the papers were forged.[31]

During the same term the court heard *Owen* v. *Brown* (1857). Three slaves, Tom, Brun, and John, had run away from the Carroll Parish plantation of Shapley Owen. They drifted down the Mississippi River in a stolen skiff until they arrived at Island 95, where Gershen Brown captured them, hid them for a time, then put them to work cutting wood. Brown made no attempt to inform Owen of their whereabouts. Two months later Brown allowed Tom to leave the island in a small boat. He made his way to New Orleans and embarked on the steamboat *Niagara* to Cairo, Illinois. Several weeks later Brown released the other two slaves when he saw a group of men, including Owen, Owen's two sons, and two slaves coming toward the island. The two fugitives fled to Vicksburg, where they were captured two days later. Owen retrieved

31. Daret v. Gray (*El Dorado*), No. 4681, 12 La. Ann. 394 (1857). The slave husband, a bilingual personal servant and carriage driver (and a former racehorse jockey), was about to be sold by Daret, who planned to retain the wife and children. The threatened separation may have precipitated the attempt to escape.

them. The planter sued Brown for $1,500—the value of Tom—and the wages of all three for the time Brown had them in his possession ($30 per month). The lower court allowed him $1,300 for Tom and $160 for the fugitives' wages. Owen also successfully sued the owners of the *Niagara* for carrying Tom away without Owen's knowledge or consent, and recovered $600 for the price of Tom. Brown asked for a new trial, but the lower court denied it. Chief Justice Merrick overruled the lower court, reasoning that as the steamboat owner had already paid the plaintiff for the slave, the payment in effect transferred title to the slave to the owners of the steamboat. Ruling it unfair for the planter to recover twice, Merrick remanded the case against Brown to the lower court to reassess the amount of the judgment against him.[32]

Mariacq v. Wright (1858) involved a fugitive slave who made himself so indispensable on board the steamboat *H. M. Wright* that the captain offered to purchase him for $1,000 after discovering him to be a runaway. Jacko, a bilingual slave described as "handsome," "quite intelligent," with a "jet black countenance," ran away from Jean Louis Mariacq of English Turn in Plaquemines Parish. Mariacq advertised for Jacko, warning that the runaway would attempt to find work as a steward on a steamboat, as he had done twice before. Jacko presented a forged pass to the master of the *H. M. Wright,* who hired him. The captain testified that Jacko was a good servant and that he "would have trusted him with anything on the boat," even his keys. Mariacq sued the captain, and the lower court awarded him $500 (under the act of 1840) and $140 in wages—$20 per month for the seven months Jacko was absent. The supreme court affirmed the judgment but on a rehearing awarded Mariacq only wages, stating that it was not the captain's intent to deprive Mariacq of the slave, and that because the captain and owners lacked "guilty intent," the court had erred in ordering them to pay the fine:

> But upon a survey of all the provisions of this obscurely framed law it would seem that the Legislature did not intend that the bare fact should constitute the offence or give rise to the severe penalty, but that the fact must be coupled with an intent, of which intent the fact was to be presumptive evidence, to be rebutted only on

32. Owen v. Brown, No. 4927, 12 La. Ann. 172 (1857).

> the testimony of two witnesses not employed on the boat, corroborated by circumstances.
>
> The fact gives rise to a presumption that the captain or owners received the slave on board "*with the intention of depriving his master of him and of transporting him out of the State, or from one part of the State to the other.*" Section 1. The ingredient of a guilty intent is, therefore, a necessary element in ascertaining whether the penalty was incurred.[33]

In *Beverley* v. Empire (1860), Robert Beverley sued the captain of the *Empire* for $1,200, the price of the slave Charles, who was lost allegedly as a result of the captain's negligence. When steamboats sailed from New Orleans to Cincinnati, it was the usual policy to leave slave members of the crew in Kentucky, rather than risk taking them to a free state, where it was almost impossible to prevent their escape. The captain ignored the precaution of removing the slaves before entering Ohio, and Charles escaped. The lower court awarded Beverley $1,200. Chief Justice Merrick cited common law and civil law in upholding the decision of the lower court. He noted that under common law, "the defendants were bound to take the same care to preserve the thing which a good and prudent father of a family would take of his own." Merrick went on, "By our law the lessee is liable for the injuries and losses sustained through his own fault."[34]

In *Folse* v. *New Orleans Coast and Lafourche Transportation Co.* (1867), the captain of the steamboat *Music* accepted the slave Henry as a runaway from another steamboat and agreed to return him to his owner's plantation on Bayou Lafourche. The captain handcuffed Henry to the hog-chain of the boat and put him under guard of the ship's free black porter, who had the key to the handcuffs. Henry asked permission to use the bathroom, and the porter removed the handcuffs but held on to Henry's

33. Mariacq v. *Wright,* No. 4645, 13 La. Ann. 27 (1858); emphasis in original of the court's opinion.

34. Beverley v. *Empire,* No. 6323, 15 La. Ann. 432 (1860). See Paul Finkelman, *An Imperfect Union: Slavery, Federalism, and Comity* (Chapel Hill, 1981), 162–64. For other cases involving fugitive slaves and steamboats, see Palfrey v. Kerr, No. 1783, 8 Mart. (N.S.) 503 (La. 1830); Duncan v. Hawks (*Molaeska*), No. 3912, 18 La. 548 (1841); Milo v. Lynch, 9 Rob. 98 (La. 1844); Lusk v. Swon, No. 2852, 9 La. Ann. 367 (1854); Farwell v. Harris and Morgan, No. 4490, 12 La. Ann. 50 (1857); Lusk v. Church, No. 5332, 13 La. Ann. 360 (1858); Chaffe v. *St. Charles,* No. 646, 13 La. Ann. 415 (1858); and Mouras v. *A. C. Brewer,* No. 6856, 17 La. Ann. 82 (1865).

coattails. The steamboat was in port at the time and Henry bolted, leaving the porter with nothing but a handful of his ripped jacket. The lower court found the ship's owners not to be negligent, and Henry's owner could not recover. While the appeal of this case was in progress, the court adjourned when New Orleans fell to Union troops in April, 1862. The reconstituted supreme court affirmed the decision in 1867.[35]

In *Fisk* v. *Bergerot* (1869), F. M. Fisk sued A. Bergerot, the owner of an oceangoing steamer, for carrying away his female slave without his knowledge or consent in 1858. In 1854 Fisk had decided to sell the slave and accordingly placed her in a New Orleans slave yard. She escaped in April and concealed herself in the city until December, when she sailed aboard Bergerot's ship, bound for Le Havre. She facilitated her escape by disguising herself in male attire and was never captured. Citing *Civil Code* article 3502 on prescription, the lower court ruled that suit was instituted more than one year after the incident; the case had prescribed. After the Civil War the supreme court affirmed the decision.[36]

Several fugitive-slave cases that came before the Louisiana Supreme Court during the antebellum period do not fall neatly into categories. For example, in 1833 Charles Caffin's slave Isaac, alias Chambers, ran away. Caffin heard nothing of the slave until 1846, when he read an advertisement by a sheriff in Canton, Mississippi, who was holding Isaac as a runaway. Caffin reclaimed his slave and returned to his home in New Orleans. He was subsequently sued by Jacob Oates in *Oates* v. *Caffin* (1848). Oates claimed to have had possession of the slave, whom he called Chambers, from 1836 to 1845, at which time the slave had run away from him. Oates had bought "Chambers" in 1836 in St. Augustine, Florida, along with several other slaves. The lower court awarded possession of this well-traveled slave to his original owner, Caffin. The decision was affirmed by the Louisiana Supreme Court. Justice Rost reasoned that Louisiana's law of slavery was derived from Roman law, in which "the slave who absconds from his master steals himself . . .

35. Folse v. New Orleans Coast and Lafourche Transportation Co., No. 301, 19 La. Ann. 199 (1867).

36. Fisk v. Bergerot, No. 6814, 21 La. Ann. 111 (1869). Although prescription had a special meaning in civil law, in this case it simply meant that the plaintiff had exceeded the allowable time limit for filing suit. See also Strawbridge v. Turner, No. 2803, 8 La. 537 (1835), and Temple v. Smith, No. 343, 7 La. Ann. 562 (1852).

and neither possession nor title can be acquired to him." Rost added: "Should the law be otherwise, no one can possess a fugitive slave as owner."

This case was a possessory action, a civil-law process in which a person instituted litigation to be reinstated in the possession of an immovable. But Oates's possession of the slave had occurred in Mississippi, and Louisiana law had no extraterritorial effect. The issue thus was not just whether a possessory action could be brought to recover a fugitive slave, but whether Oates had the right to institute such an action. Addressing the problem of jurisdiction, Rost cited *Prigg* v. *Pennsylvania,* 16 Peters 608 (1842), which he interpreted to mean that Isaac "was held to labor under our laws, and the authorities of the state of Mississippi were at all times bound to deliver him to the party to whom the labor is due." Rost also cited Story's *Commentaries on the Constitution of the United States* and article IV, section 2 of the United States Constitution, the fugitive-slave clause, as well as two of the Louisiana Supreme Court's own decisions and the *Siete Partidas,* because issues of common law, civil law, and constitutional law were intertwined. A note at the end of this decision states that Chief Justice Eustis concurred in the judgment.[37]

In *Reynolds* v. *Brenford* and *Reynolds* v. *Batson* (1856), an anonymous letter informed Major Walker Reynolds of Alabama that his slaves Ned and Dick, missing for eleven years, were in New Orleans in possession of William Batson. Ned and Dick were brothers; they had disappeared from Reynolds' plantation in 1845, when they were eleven and seventeen years old, respectively, and Reynolds believed that they had run away. Batson claimed he had bought the slaves at auction in New Orleans one month later. He testified that he employed the brothers as stevedores on steamboats at $150 to $180 per year. During this ten-year period, Dick ran away from Batson two or three times, and Batson "could hardly give a bad enough character of Ned." He described Dick as being "self-willing & saucy" and said he had seen the bondsman "get hold of a white man & whip him." The anonymous letter to Reynolds—written, it turned out, by a slave carpenter in Ned and Dick's behalf—stated that the brothers asked their old master's forgiveness

37. Oates v. Caffin, No. 627, 3 La. Ann. 339 (1848). For similar cases, see Brack v. Wood, 11 La. Ann. 512 (1856); Templet v. Baker, 12 La. Ann. 658 (1856); Bradford's Heirs v. Clark, No. 41, 7 La. 147 (1834); and Hudnall v. Watts, DeSaulles, and Jones, No. 2776, 8 La. Ann. 5 (1853).

and promised never to run away again. They expressed a desire to return "home" to Reynolds' plantation because they longed to see their mother, Venus, and their brothers, all owned by Reynolds. Reynolds sued Batson for possession of the slaves. However, the lower court ruled that Batson had purchased the slaves in good faith and that his peaceful ownership of them for ten years gave him a valid title by prescription, a civil-law concept in which property can be acquired by continuous possession for a specified number of years. The new chief justice, Merrick, affirmed the judgment. This decision was not contradictory to *Oates* v. *Caffin,* which was a possessory action. The issue in *Batson* was prescription. According to *Civil Code* article 3444, the property of slaves by prescription was acquired in five years between parties who both resided within the state, and ten years if one of them lived outside of the state. Neither Oates nor Reynolds resided in Louisiana, but in *Oates* v. *Caffin,* Oates had held Isaac for only nine years. In all such cases, the claimant must have held title to the slave at issue and have purchased the slave in good faith, believing the purchase to be valid. The crucial distinction between *Batson* and *Oates* was that Chief Justice Merrick found no evidence that Ned and Dick had been fugitives. On the contrary, Merrick ruled, their first appearance in Louisiana had been as slaves being sold at auction. Since the slaves were not fugitives, Batson could acquire title to them by prescription of ten years if in "good faith." He could have gained title in thirty years even if in "bad faith," a "bad faith" possession being the civil-law equivalent of the common-law concept of "adverse possession."[38]

In *Hill* v. *White* (1856), Sarah Hill of Nashville sent her slave Edmund downriver to be sold by New Orleans slave dealer James White. Edmund told White he had left his clothes on the steamboat, and White allowed him to retrieve them while in the custody of a fellow slave. It was common practice among slave dealers to have a slave who was "kind of head over the rest of the negroes, to send on errands, and to send with slaves . . . for their baggage and clothes." Edmund escaped while on the levee, probably on a boat, and his owner never recovered

38. Reynolds v. Brenford, Reynolds v. Batson, No. 4291, 11 La. Ann. 729 (1856); *Civil Code,* Art. 3444, p. 522. For a similar case, see Cavelier v. Davenport and Moss, No. 6099, 2 La. Ann. 584 (1847). In common law, adverse possession is a method of acquiring and holding real property "in opposition to all the world." An example would be squatter's rights. In Louisiana, adverse possession was called "acquisitive prescription."

Edwin Thomas Merrick, chief justice of the Louisiana Supreme Court from 1855 to 1865.

Photo by Warren Gravois. Courtesy of the librarian, Law Library of Louisiana

him. The plaintiff's agent, who had brought Edmund to New Orleans, said "that the boy was too white to keep" (he had blue eyes and straight hair) and the reason his owner sent him to New Orleans to be sold was because she feared losing him. No one told Edmund the purpose of the journey until he arrived at White's slave market: "This trick was at once calculated to excite an apprehension of some impending evil, to be evaded by flight." The lower court awarded Hill $1,100, ruling that White was negligent in allowing the slave to be placed in the care of another bondsman. Justice Spofford, writing for the high court, reversed the decision, reasoning that White could not have known the slave might run, as Hill had represented the slave as being "humble and obedient, as having been raised on a plantation, being a good ploughman." Also, Spofford observed, he was "so nearly white it was easy for him to make his escape."[39]

In *Griffing* v. *Routh* (1856), fellow slaves stabbed a hapless runaway while he hid in a pile of hay in a barn on a neighboring plantation. The overseer had sent two slaves, the driver and another, to search for the man, who was a habitual runaway. The driver thrust a broadsword used for pruning hedges into the straw to see whether the fugitive was concealed there, and in doing so plunged the weapon into the man's abdomen, wounding him so severely that he died a few hours later. The owner of the dead slave sued the driver's owner for $1,200, the value of the slave. The lower court found for the plaintiff, and the defendant appealed. The supreme court affirmed the judgment of the Tensas Parish District Court, reasoning that the defendant's slave had committed a "grossly negligent and wanton act" and that his master was liable for this "inexcusable negligence and barbarity." In his ruling Justice Spofford cited *Civil Code* articles 180 and 181, which stated that masters were liable for damages resulting from "offenses and quasi-offenses" committed by their slaves. Spofford ordered Routh to either pay for the value of the deceased slave or abandon his guilty slaves to Griffing. The latter alternative was possible under article 181, which permitted a master to discharge his liability for his slave's action by abandoning the guilty slave to the injured party. This provision was unique to Louisiana.[40]

39. Hill v. White, No. 4489, 11 La. Ann. 170 (1856).
40. Griffing v. Routh, No. 3921, 11 La. Ann. 135 (1856); *Civil Code,* Art. 180, p. 28.

Concealing or "harboring" a fugitive slave was an offense that merited criminal penalties. An 1807 act of the territorial legislature provided that any person concealing a slave was to compensate the slave's master at the rate of $2 per day of concealment and was responsible for any damages caused by the slave during that time. In 1809 the legislature amended this act and made harboring a slave punishable by a fine of not less than $100 and not more than $300.[41] Persons unable to pay the fine were subject to between fifteen days and three months in prison. *Roquet* v. *Richardson* (1832) was a civil suit in which the runaway slave's owner sued for damages and expenses associated with recovering the slave. Richardson allegedly concealed and employed the twelve-year-old slave girl Rachael for nearly a year. Rachael had run away from her mistress, Roquet, in New Orleans in January, 1830. Roquet discovered her in the employ of Richardson on his plantation at Terre-aux-Boeufs, in St. Bernard Parish, the following December. Rachael had cajoled a cartman into allowing her to ride with him to St. Bernard and had told Richardson that she was the daughter of a free woman in Kentucky who had drowned. She cooked for the other slaves on Richardson's plantation; a witness testified she worked as hard as an adult slave. Roquet proved that she had spent $100 to recover Rachael by advertising in the newspapers. The lower court ruled Richardson blameless, as there were no newspapers in his area, but the supreme court reversed the judgment and awarded Roquet $100 damages and possession of Rachael. In his reasoning, Chief Judge Mathews observed that the amount claimed by Roquet ($100) was within the limits of the 1807 and 1809 acts. However, Mathews also noted that the statutes of 1807 and 1809 were criminal in nature, whereas *Roquet* v. *Richardson* was a civil suit. The judge ruled that Richardson's actions did not constitute criminal concealment but were nevertheless negligent; therefore, Roquet should recover civil damages actually suffered by her.[42]

Leigh, f.w.c., v. *Meurice* 1851) began after a fifteen-year-old slave named Ellen, property of a free woman of color, Sarah A. Leigh, ran away. Ellen's mother, Phoebe, property of Dr. Joseph Meurice, man-

41. "An Act to Amend the Act Entitled 'An Act Prescribing the Rules and Conduct to be Observed with Respect to Negroes . . . ,'" Act of April 14, 1807, *Louisiana Acts, 1807,* pp. 186–88; "An Act to Provide for the Delivery of Fugitive Slaves to Their Owners . . . ," Act of February 21, 1809, *Louisiana Acts, 1809,* pp. 190–94.

42. Roquet v. Richardson, No. 2252, 3 La. 452 (1832).

aged to hide Ellen in her room for about a month. When someone discovered the girl, a special tribunal tried and convicted Phoebe of harboring her daughter. Since Phoebe was a slave, she could not be fined for the offense. Her owner, however, was judged to be responsible for damages caused by Phoebe, according to *Civil Code* article 180. Leigh sued Meurice for one month's wages and for the cost of advertising for Ellen as a runaway. The lower court awarded Ellen's mistress $63. The supreme court reduced the judgment and awarded Leigh only $17. Justice Rost based the lowered amount on damages done to Ellen's value because of her experience as a fugitive: "The fact that the mother harbored and concealed the slave of the plaintiff, even for a month, no doubt injured her character and qualities as a servant; and the depreciation is sufficiently proved by witnesses to require us to allow something on that account. And, although we may differ with the district court as to the means of arriving at the same result, yet we think that his judgment has done justice to the parties." Justice Rost noted an important distinction in his ruling: that according to *Civil Code* article 2300, slaveowners were not answerable for criminal penalties that might have been imposed upon their slaves, but were liable for civil damages occasioned by their slaves' negligence.[43]

In the same session, the supreme court heard *Vinot* v. *Bertrand, f.w.c.* Adelaide Vinot sued Célèste Bertrand, a free woman of color, for $493 for harboring Vinot's slave Mathilda. The slaveowner claimed that Mathilda ran away in October, 1847, and that Bertrand received and harbored her from then until May, 1848. Vinot sued for wages of two dollars a day ($408) plus the $50 reward for return of the slave and $35 for advertisements. The ad had stated that Mathilda had "very large breasts which hang down . . . is an elegant washer and ironer . . . she has an Italian for a husband in this city who it is supposed is harboring her." Bertrand testified that she did not think the slave was a fugitive—despite the fact that she wore an iron collar for having run away in a previous incident—because Mathilda showed her a pass. The pass later proved to be a forgery. The lower court ruled that Bertrand did not criminally conceal the slave under the acts of 1807 and 1809 and denied Vinot recovery. The supreme court reversed the decision. The high

43. Leigh, f.w.c., v. Meurice, No. 2191, 6 La. Ann. 476 (1851); *Civil Code,* Art. 2300, 180, pp. 359–60, 28.

court estimated Mathilda's value at $500 and allowed Vinot to recover interest of $17 on the sum for the time the slave was absent. Citing *Roquet* v. *Richardson,* the court held that although Bertrand's actions were not criminal in nature, she was nevertheless responsible for damages caused by Mathilda's absence from her mistress because Bertrand had not ascertained that the pass was genuine.[44]

Sections 28 and 29 of the *Black Code* required sheriffs to advertise fugitive slaves in French and English in at least two newspapers during three successive months, and then once a month for the remainder of the year. A sheriff could sell an unclaimed slave two years after the date of the first advertisement. In *Labranche* v. *Watkins* (1816), Sheriff William Watkins failed to advertise a slave as required and sold him before the two years had elapsed. Lem, alias Tom, the "American born" slave of Alexander Labranche, ran away early in 1813. He was caught and jailed in Ascension Parish in July, 1813. Sheriff Watkins, who apparently wanted the slave himself, only advertised Lem once. Less than two years after he imprisoned the slave, the sheriff sold him for one-third of his value ($250) to Henry Wiatt, who the same day sold him back to Watkins. Labranche successfully sued, recovering possession of the slave and $185.25 damages. The court denied Watkins even Lem's maintenance, as testimony proved the sheriff kept him at work and therefore benefited from his services. Ruling that Watkins's appeal was frivolous, Judge Martin affirmed the judgment and added 10 percent interest to the damages from the date of suit.[45]

One runaway slave died in prison as a result of a sheriff's failure to advertise. In August, 1847, the sheriff of Orleans Parish placed Ned, slave of George W. Johnson, in the police jail of Municipality No. 1 (the area of the French Quarter). The sheriff failed to advertise the slave, and when Johnson sent his overseer to inquire if the slave was detained there, the sheriff turned him away. The slave died in November of a disease that Johnson, in *Johnson* v. *Municipality # 1* (1850), claimed Ned had contracted as a result of prison conditions. Testimony indicated that the plaintiff's agent found the slave in a very cold room with only one blanket; he was "so emaciated and feeble as then to be unable to get up on

44. Vinot v. Bertrand, f.w.c., No. 2171, 6 La. Ann. 474 (1851). See also Meunier v. Dupérron, No. 38, 3 Mart. (o.s.) 285 (La. 1814).

45. *Black Code,* Secs. 28–29, pp. 170–72; Labranche v. Watkins, No. 159, 4 Mart. (o.s.) 391 (La. 1816).

his knees without the assistance of another man." The district-court judge awarded Johnson $600 and stated that the prison conditions were "neither fit not decent for a human being of any color." The district-court judge's reasoning in setting this price involved the diminution of the slave's value as a result of his becoming a fugitive: "The plaintiff estimates his slave at nine hundred dollars; his witnesses adopt a higher figure. There is no doubt that his value was seriously diminished by his having absconded, and the estimate, both of the plaintiff and his witnesses, appear to have been made without reference to that fact. The plaintiff has probably claimed all that his slave was worth, under any circumstances. On the other hand, the defendant's witness states, that he has seen runaway negroes sold for three hundred dollars." Chief Justice Eustis affirmed the judgment without comment.[46]

An unclaimed fugitive slave who was sold at a sheriff's sale became the object of an 1858 lawsuit, *Landry* v. *Klopman*. Daniel, a cooper, ran away from Tasimere Landry, a sugar planter, in Ascension Parish in April or May of 1854. Authorities caught and imprisoned him in Vicksburg, Mississippi, in July. The sheriff advertised him for thirty consecutive days and once a month for six months thereafter (as required by Mississippi law), after which A. Mizel, a New Orleans slave dealer, purchased him for $809. Mizel sold Daniel to L. Klopman of New Orleans in March, 1855, for $1,100. That same month Landry spotted Daniel working in Klopman's French Quarter store and sued for possession of the slave, claiming to be his rightful owner. Landry's attorney cited the fugitive-slave clause of the Constitution in support of his claim. He won in the lower court, but the supreme court reversed the judgment. Chief Justice Merrick rejected the plaintiff's use of the fugitive-slave clause to support his claim:

> The history of the Constitution of the United States shows that this clause was introduced into "the Constitution solely for the benefit of the slave holding States to enable them to reclaim their fugitive slaves who should escape into other States where slavery is not tolerated." Story Const., sec. 952.
>
> And the language of the clause clearly shows that this was the intention. It declares that no person held to labor shall, in conse-

46. Johnson v. Municipality #1, No. 1444, 5 La. Ann. 100 (1850). See also Fleming v. Loccard, No. 123, 10 Mart. (o.s.) 308 (La. 1821).

> quence of any law or regulation, *be discharged from such service or labor.* The regulation here spoken of is one therefore between the slave and his master; the slave is not to be discharged from labor, but is to be given up. Now this cannot in our opinion be applied to controversies arising between two persons claiming the ownership of a slave depending upon the laws of different States although the slave was a fugitive from labor; for the slave is not discharged from labor or service, but the right to his service or labor is the subject-matter of a controversy between others, in which, in a legal point of view, he has no interest.
>
> If we hold the contrary, these consequences follow: a slave, the moment he becomes a fugitive, acquires a sacred character under the Constitution and is above the laws and *extra commercium.* He cannot be sold as property nor punished for crime. . . .
>
> It is thus evident that the Article of the Constitution is not to be taken literally but to be interpreted according to its true meaning and intent.

Merrick ruled that since the sale was made in compliance with Mississippi law, Klopman's title was valid. He was to keep the slave and Landry was allowed the proceeds of the sheriff's sale ($809). Merrick referred to *Oates* v. *Caffin,* in which the court had ruled that no one could acquire title to a fugitive slave. Merrick observed that as "under our system, a single decision is not considered conclusive on any question of law." Thus a review of the issue was necessary. The chief justice held that the law of Mississippi regarding the sale of an unclaimed fugitive was a valid law, a law not purposefully designed to deprive an owner of his property. "It appears to us that the comity which exists between different States requires us to enforce rights . . . adverse to a citizen of Louisiana."[47]

One slave ran *to* jail to escape harsh treatment by her mistress. In *McCarthy* v. *Sheriff (Lewis)* (1850), the bondswoman Jane "failed in her duty to her mistress," Eugenie McCarthy, who responded by sending her to the police jail to be whipped. The sheriff gave her twenty-five lashes, "but lightly as is usual when owner not present." Apparently the chastisement did not satisfy her mistress, who "gave her blows with her own hand." Jane had run away at least once before, just after being sold

47. Landry v. Klopman, No. 5272, 13 La. Ann. 345 (1858); emphasis in original of Merrick's opinion.

to McCarthy in May, 1847, and after this latest treatment she ran again, on September 7, 1848—this time to the police jail of Orleans Parish. She begged to be admitted to the prison, complaining of cruel treatment by her mistress, whose name she steadfastly refused to tell the jailer. At first he was reluctant to accept her without her mistress' consent, but he feared that "there were Some Abolitionistes [*sic*] in the Neighborhood wishing to decoy her away," and he confined her to a cell. Jane became ill in prison, and within a short time her illness became serious. The sheriff discovered the identity of her owner and sent the slave woman home thirteen days later. She died of gangrene of the intestines, aggravated by the filthiness of the prison (she came home "covered with her own excrements . . . which had been permitted to harden"). McCarthy sued the jailer for Jane's value ($700), claiming the slave was a good washer and ironer and American cook worth "six bitts [*sic*] per day." The lower court ruled that the sheriff was not guilty of wrongly admitting her or of neglecting her, as he did not know the identity of her owner and the disease she contracted was not contagious. The supreme court affirmed this decision. In the dictum, Justice Thomas Slidell noted that McCarthy was entitled to the equivalent of the slave's wages while incarcerated: "As to the question of wages it may be that the defendant became answerable for them; but we deem it unnecessary to express an opinion on this point. For if we thought they ought to have been allowed in the court below, the amount would be so small, say not more at the utmost than seven or eight dollars, that according to our uniform practice we would decline reversing the judgment on that ground."[48]

Sheriff's duties in disciplining slaves and incarcerating fugitives for safekeeping occasionally became a subject for lawsuits. In *Perrine, f.w.c.,* v. *Planchard* (1860), a jailer accidentally whipped Constance Perrine, a free woman of color, as a runaway slave in the police jail of New Orleans. The sheriff had arrrested and jailed the pregnant free black woman for being drunk and disturbing the peace. Anaise, the runaway slave of a Mr. Rousseau, shared her cell. Rousseau instructed the jailer, Edward Planchard, to give Anaise ten lashes before bringing her out to him.

48. McCarthy v. Sheriff (Lewis), No. 1355, 1377, 5 La. Ann. 115 (1850). For other miscellaneous cases involving fugitive slaves, see Dossat v. Guillotte, No. 81, 4 Mart. (o.s.) 203 (La. 1816); Griffin v. Waters, No. 634, 1 Rob. 149 (La. 1841); Womack v. Nicholson, No. 934, 3 Rob. 248 (La. 1842) [see chapter 2, note 22]; Cartwright v. McMillan and Nichols, No. 906, 3 La. Ann. 685 (1848); Bacon v. Leeds, No. 2295, 6 La. Ann. 804 (1851); and Callaway v. Bobo, Sheriff, 15 La. Ann. 467 (1860).

Planchard mistakenly began to whip Perrine, who repeatedly claimed to be free. Planchard went out to Rousseau and told him of her claims, to which he replied, "Yes, she has the habit of saying so, but she is not yet free." Planchard completed the whipping and "stretched her upon a platform where only slaves are whipped." Perrine sued. The lower court held that although Planchard's actions were not malicious in intent, Perrine had been injured and should recover $500 in lost wages, medical expenses, and damages. The supreme court affirmed the judgment but lowered the award to $150 ($100 of actual medical expenses and $50 for twenty-five days' lost wages). In his ruling Justice Albert Duffel cited *Civil Code* article 2294: "Every act whatever of man, that causes damages to another, obliges him, by whose fault it happened, to repair it."[49]

The most effective method for slaves to resist the South's peculiar institution was to steal themselves, and deprive the owner of their most valuable asset—their labor. The court's awards for the value of slaves' services while they were fugitive is evidence that running away was an effective and costly form of resistance. The volume of appeals to the Supreme Court of Louisiana that involved fugitive slaves, which reflects a much larger number of lower-court actions, clearly demonstrates that many slaves effectively became runaways. Some escaped permanently, despite their color's branding them as slaves, despite the distance to the free states, and despite the fact that in the Deep South every white was a potential informer or captor.

The judicial concept of slaves stealing themselves is an example of one of many instances in which slave law contorted itself into a conceptual peculiarity to accommodate a social institution that the law itself was powerless and unwilling to change. Since the courts in the slave states never really came to grips with the concept of property in human beings, legal fictions arose to attempt to rationalize what in effect was a system contrary to the idea that all persons have a right to their own bodies and the fruits of their own labor. The concept that slaves could "steal themselves" was a contrivance to make sense of what was essentially not theoretically sound.

49. Perrine, f.w.c., v. Planchard, No. 6031, 15 La. Ann. 133 (1860); *Civil Code,* Art. 2294, p. 359.

5

"GUARANTEED AGAINST THE VICES AND MALADIES PRESCRIBED BY LAW"

Warranties in Slave Sales

AN EXAMINATION OF ALL LOUISIANA SUPREME COURT cases concerning slaves reveals that the transfer of slaves from one owner to another was big business in Louisiana. Hundreds of appeals centered on slaves as property that was regularly mortgaged, hired, stolen, bartered, wagered, seized for debt, and fought over in succession (estate) and divorce contests. Of all the appeals of cases involving slavery, warranties in the sale of slaves were by far the most common issue before the court.

The Louisiana *Digest of 1808* and the *Civil Code* contained specialized regulations involving slave sales. Unlike other southern slave states, Louisiana had a Romanist background for its law of sales and had, both through legislative acts and the *Civil Code,* a comprehensive system that not only defined the relationships between slaves and their masters but carefully regulated the transfer of slave property as well.[1] In the complexity and extent of its regulation of slave sales, Louisiana law was unique; moreover, in this area the state's law did not become more like that of the common-law states but retained its special characteristics throughout the antebellum period. Among the most remarkable of these characteristics was the protection of purchasers of slaves by implied warranties.

The redactors of the *Digest of 1808* drew heavily on both Roman and

1. *Digest of 1808,* Tit. VI, Chap. III, Sec. III, Arts. 65–81, pp. 355–60; *Civil Code,* Arts. 174, 175, 176, p. 27; Art. 461, p. 68; Arts. 537, 539, pp. 80–81; Art. 588, p. 89; Art. 631, p. 95; Art. 945, p. 142; Art. 1462, p. 222; Art. 1775, p. 269; Arts. 1783, 1785, p. 292; Art. 2335, p. 365; Art. 2346, p. 366; Art. 2415, p. 377; Arts. 2500, 2502, 2505, p. 398; Arts. 3435, 3436, 3439, 3444, 3445, pp. 521–22; Art. 3465, p. 525; Arts. 3510, 3511, p. 532.

French law in constructing the articles on which these implied warranties rested. Roman law was specific on the regulation of slave sales:

> Let those who sell slaves inform the purchasers what are the diseases and defects of each, who is a runaway or given to wandering off. . . .
>
> And when the slaves are sold, let them declare all these matters openly and correctly. But if a slave is sold contrary to these provisions or contrary to what was said or promised when he was sold, in respect of which a legal duty is alleged, we will grant to the buyer and to all whom the matter concerns an action for the redhibition of the slave.

French law also carefully regulated sales. Article 1641 of the *Code Napoléon* stated:

> The vendor should procure for the buyer a useful possession. He responds therefore for hidden defects which render the thing unsuitable for any service or which considerably diminish such use. This is what is called the warranty against vices.

The next article of the *Code Napoléon* explained the conditions under which the vendor was to be responsible for the defects of the object sold—that they were concealed from and unknown to the buyer, that they were harmful to the usefulness of the object, and that they "preexisted the sale." Article 1643 held that this warranty was implicit in every sale and that it was applicable to all goods sold. Under French civil law, the buyer of a defective product could either sue to have the sale rescinded and the purchase price returned, or demand a reduction of price. Subsequent articles delineated specific rules regarding the "vices of animals" (meaning disease or disability) giving rise to either rescission of a sale or reduction of the purchase price.[2]

The redactors of the *Digest of 1808* borrowed both the Roman and the French concepts and applied them to Louisiana slave sales because they found in them better protection for purchasers of slaves than existed in common law.

Slaves at Roman law fell into a peculiar dual category. They were considered primarily as objects, lacking rights or legal capacities. How-

2. Watson, *Roman Slave Law,* 49; Marcel Planiol, *Treatise on the Civil Law* (Baton Rouge, 1939), II, iii, 819–23.

ever, Roman law also held that slaves were capable of reason, will, and a capacity to act. They were indisputably an important article of commerce and, as such, were the subject of a body of specialized legislation. In the law of slave sales, a person could achieve ownership of a slave only by a solemn juristic act. Conversely, the buyer was well protected in the purchase of a slave. Two of the most important actions Roman law granted to the purchaser were the *actio redhibitoria* and its companion, the *actio quanti*. These special regulations for the sale of slaves placed the vendor under the obligation to declare a long list of physical, moral, and mental defects with which a slave might be afflicted; the law also required the vendor to declare that no defects existed unless specifically stated. If the seller did not meet these requirements, or if an undeclared flaw became apparent, the buyer could cancel the sale (*actio redhibitoria*) and return the slave or demand compensation for the diminution of the imperfect slave's value (*actio quanti*). In some cases, both cancellation and compensation were allowed. The concept of a warranty of quality in the sale of slaves was originally intended to protect the purchaser from the shoddy practices of the Roman slave trader. One of the most interesting aspects of implied warranty under Roman law was that it was initially used solely in slave sales, and only later in sales of animals. Eventually, it came to be applied to all sales, including sales of land.[3]

The *Digest of 1808* incorporated what was already the law of implied warranty in sales at the time of the cession of Louisiana to the United States. The implied warranty was as much a liability as an asset in transferring slave property. But many slave sales involved two transactions: the sale by the slaveowner to the slave trader, and a subsequent sale by the trader to a new owner. These two transfers were likely to occur in different states. One would expect that the law of slave sales would favor the seller in those states that were the largest exporters of slaves in the domestic slave trade, and to favor the purchaser in those states that were mainly importing states. However, in other importing states, such as Mississippi and Texas, caveat emptor ruled the law of slave sales. Only in Louisiana did the right of redhibition exist.[4]

3. Buckland, *Roman Law of Slavery,* 52–67. See also Leonard Oppenheim, "The Law of Slaves: A Comparative Study of the Roman and Louisiana Systems," *Tulane Law Review,* XIV (April, 1940), 384–406.

4. Andrew Fede, "Legal Protection for Slave Buyers in the U.S. South: A Caveat Concerning *Caveat Emptor,*" *American Journal of Legal History,* XXXI (October, 1987), 342.

Louisiana's slave imports always greatly exceeded her exports.[5] Despite the uniqueness of their legal heritage and way of operating, the Louisiana *Civil Code* and the state's statute law protected the slave buyer in much the same spirit as the laws of other slave-importing states.[6] In other words, Louisianians retained their Roman-law heritage in the area of slave sales because it suited the interests of the slaveholding class to do so. Other features of Roman slave law, such as those that granted slaves the capacity to own inherited property, make loans, accept payment, and pay debts, were not consistent with the interests of antebellum Louisiana slaveholders and therefore were never integrated into Louisiana slave law.[7]

The *Digest of 1808* and the *Civil Code* divided defects of slaves into "vices of body" and "vices of character." The first article in the section entitled "Of the Vices of the Thing Sold" stated: "Redhibition is called the avoidance of a sale on account of some vice or defect in the thing sold, which renders it either absolutely useless, or its use so inconvenient and imperfect, that it must be supposed that the buyer would not have purchased it, had he known of the vice." Subsequent articles excepted apparent defects (those obvious upon simple inspection) and vices or maladies declared by the vendor. The *Code* divided the defects of slaves and animals into "vices of body" and "vices of character," absolute and relative. Absolute vices of slaves—leprosy, madness, and epilepsy—were those defects that gave rise to the redhibitory action simply by their existence. Relative vices were those that forced the seller to accept a reduced price, depending on the degree of defectiveness. Articles 2502 through 2505 of the Louisiana *Civil Code* expanded the specific terms that applied to slaves:

> The absolute vices of slaves are leprosy, madness, and epilepsy.
> The absolute vices of horses and mules are short wind, glanders,

5. Stampp, *Peculiar Institution,* 238.

6. This similarity should not be seen as including Louisiana in a distinctively southern legal heritage, whether we perceive that tradition to be based on evidence other than legal issues involving slavery, as do James Ely and David Bodenhamer, or on Paul Finkelman's theory that slavery and race are central to the understanding of the South's unique legal past. David J. Bodenhamer and James W. Ely, Jr., *Ambivalent Legacy: A Legal History of the South* (Jackson, Miss., 1984); Paul Finkelman, "Exploring Southern Legal History," *North Carolina Law Review,* LXIV (November, 1985), 77–116. In many areas of slave law and other law, Louisiana fails to fit the southern pattern.

7. Buckland, *Roman Law of Slavery,* 190–91; Oppenheim, "Law of Slaves," 390; *Digest of 1808,* Tit. VI, Chap. III, Sec. III, Art. 78, p. 358.

> and founder. The vices of character which give rise to the redhibition of slaves, are confined to the cases in which it is proved: That the slave has committed a capital crime; Or, that he is addicted to theft; Or, that he is in the habit of running away. The slave shall be considered as being in the habit of running away, when he shall have absented himself from his master's house twice for several days, or once for more than a month.[8]

Louisiana law, then, considered slaves defective merchandise in a sale if they exhibited specified imperfections. It is symbolic that the first case in *Martin's Reports for the Supreme Court of the Territory of Orleans, Deweese* v. *Morgan* (1809), was a redhibition action for disease.[9] Such cases were more numerous than all other slavery-related cases that the Supreme Court of Louisiana heard during the antebellum period. Although slaves were probably ignorant of the intricacies of redhibition law, the volume of redhibition-illness cases (in the 1850s several appeals came before the supreme court each month) suggests that some bondsmen knew that diseased slaves could be returned to their sellers. We can never know how many slaves, unhappy at being sold, exaggerated or feigned illness in order to be returned to their former owners. This qualification must be borne in mind when evaluating the claims of the allegedly aggrieved party; similarly, the primitive state of medical practice at the time must be taken into consideration when evaluating the testimony of physicians in these cases.

The motives of vendors who sold diseased slaves must also be called into question. Although honest mistakes were made, the large number of redhibition-illness cases indicates that owners, slave dealers, and auctioneers knowingly sold unwell slaves in at least some instances to avoid the financial loss they would have incurred by keeping a slave with a serious or terminal illness or selling the slave at a more realistic price. The law required the purchaser of a defective slave to attempt to return the slave to the seller. If the vendor refused to accept the slave and return the sale price, the buyer's only alternatives were to accept the situation or file a civil suit. The burden of proof was on the purchaser, and the courts rigidly applied the specifications of the law in determining

8. *Civil Code,* Arts. 2496–2505, pp. 388–89.

9. Deweese v. Morgan, No. 2351, 1 Mart. (o.s.) 1 (1809). For health problems relating to slaves, see Todd L. Savitt, *Medicine and Slavery: The Diseases and Health Care of Blacks in Antebellum Virginia* (Urbana, Ill., 1978).

whether to grant a rescission. In the case of a diseased slave, the purchaser also had to prove that he had provided the ailing slave with proper medical attention. The primitive state of antebellum medicine may well have limited a plaintiff's chance of establishing that the disease existed before the sale.

To gain a rescission of a fugitive slave and a refund of purchase price, the purchaser had to capture the runaway, return him or her to the vendor, and prove that the slave was in the habit of running away before the sale. Because of these difficulties, many buyers who purchased their slaves on credit simply defaulted on payment, forcing the seller either to accept the returned slave or file suit directly against the purchaser.

Of the 166 appeals to the supreme court of suits brought to cancel sales of slaves alleged to be defective merchandise because of disease, 47 involved some form of tuberculosis. Among these 47 cases, 31 of the slaves in question died shortly after being sold. Two typical instances of redhibition for consumption came before the court in the 1850s. In *Bloodgood* v. *Wilson* (1855), John Bloodgood of Mobile purchased fourteen-year-old Ellen Jackson in June, 1851, for $650. She died of consumption the following October, and Bloodgood sued the vendor for her purchase price and $100 for medical and burial expenses. Although the physician who examined her nine days after the sale for insurance purposes had warned Bloodgood that she exhibited symptoms of consumption, Bloodgood made no attempt to return her. Instead, he put her to work in the reeling room of a cotton factory. She received neither special treatment nor medical care until August. The lower court denied Bloodgood recovery because he never attempted to return the slave and failed to provide medical care until she was dying. Justice Abner Ogden affirmed this decision, stating that "it would not be consistent with the principles established by frequent decrees of this court, to render the defendant liable under such circumstances."[10]

Alfred A. Williams purchased a slave named Jack for $1,183 in January, 1853. Upon discovering that Jack had tuberculosis six months later, Williams attempted to return him to the original owner, who refused to accept him. The slave died in June, 1854, and in *Williams* v. *Talbot*

10. Bloodgood v. Wilson, No. 3272, 10 La. Ann. 302 (1855). For a complete listing of cases concerning slaves and redhibition, see Judith Kelleher Schafer, "The Long Arm of the Law: Slavery and the Supreme Court in Antebellum Louisiana, 1809–1862" (Ph.D. dissertation, Tulane University, 1985), 427–30.

(1857), Williams sued for a rescission of the sale. Testimony proved that a previous purchaser had returned Jack because he was "unsound" and spitting blood. However, witnesses also stated that Williams kept Jack hard at work for months after he became ill, chopping wood, driving a cart, and tending a kettle in the sugarhouse. Williams called no physician until the slave was acutely ill. Williams' neglect cost him a rescission in the Second District Court of New Orleans, and on appeal, Justice James Cole, writing for the court, affirmed the judgment: "Humanity and a just regard to the rights of vendors requires that parties should not recover, who have permitted many months to elapse, after the first development of disease, before invoking medical aid."[11]

Occasionally, outright fraud is evident in redhibition cases. In *Gause* v. *Bullard* (1861), Daugherty Gause sued to have the $1,600 sale of the slave Hyman canceled because he had four front teeth missing as a result of scurvy. Gause claimed that the seller had concealed this flaw by placing wooden false teeth in the bondsman's mouth just before the sale. His main complaint, however, was that the slave became ill two days after the sale and died of pneumonia seven days later. According to *Civil Code* article 2508, since the disease manifested itself within three days after the sale, it created "the legal presumption that the germ of the malady was in the system before the transfer." The supreme court ruled that the defendant had failed to provide evidence that refuted this presumption, although Bullard persuaded a physician, who never saw the slave, to testify that the disease could have occurred suddenly as a result of "the probable effect of the atmosphere." Justice Duffel brushed this testimony aside, observing that the defendant had presented nothing "more than a speculative and possible case," and affirmed the judgment.[12]

Various conditions and diseases involving the central nervous system were bases for redhibitory actions. This is a difficult topic because of the level of medical knowledge, attitudes about mental illness, whites' assumptions concerning the intellectual inferiority of slaves, and the possibility of either an incorrect diagnosis by a medical doctor or purposeful deception by a slave. Two examples illustrate the problem of second-guessing a physician's diagnosis a century and a half after the fact.

In *Buhler* v. *McHatton* (1854), John Buhler sued J. A. McHatton,

11. Williams v. Talbot, No. 4628, 12 La. Ann. 407 (1857).
12. Gause v. Bullard, No. 6533, 16 La. Ann. 107 (1861).

claiming that the slave Jane, whom he had purchased from McHatton, was mad. Testimony proved that the bondswoman behaved "oddly and strangely" and that she refused "from religious scruples, to eat or take medicines on Fridays, and later on Saturday, saying that God had appeared to her and forbidden it." On one occasion she burned her clothes. Witnesses testified that Jane was "sound in mind and body and considered a very valuable servant" before she was taken from Kentucky to Louisiana and sold. A physician stated that the "girl labored under an aberation [*sic*] of mind, which they ascribed to religious enthusiasm and grief at being separated from her children." (Although Louisiana law prohibited separating mothers and children by sale until the children reached the age of ten, nothing prevented a slave trader from purchasing a mother without her young children outside of Louisiana and subsequently selling the slave mother in the state.) Buhler was unable to prove that the slave was insane. Associate Justice James Campbell affirmed the lower court's refusal to rescind the sale because there was no proof that the alleged insanity existed before the sale.[13]

William C. Adams purchased the slave Nelson from Joseph Berret for $500, much below the usual price for the 1850s. The result was a lawsuit, *Berret* v. *Adams* (1855). Shortly after the sale, Adams claimed Nelson was "incurably insane" and attempted to return him to Berret, who refused to accept him, saying that if he ever caught Nelson on his property he would kill him. The slave subsequently returned to his new master, who drove him away. Eventually Adams placed him in the Plaquemines Parish jail, where he died of dropsy. Testimony proved that Berret had warned the prospective purchaser that Nelson was subject to "fits of insanity," and furthermore, that Adams knew the slave was allegedly insane because only six months before the sale he had sat on a jury that tried Nelson for assaulting his former master with an axe and biting the man's thumb and chest. Nelson's defense of insanity in this trial had won him an acquittal. Witnesses testified to his bizarre behavior, which included returning his ration of pork, claiming he was accustomed to eating "shrimps," and throwing himself in the fire under the chimney of the sugarhouse because the overseer threatened to whip him. When spoken to, "he would break out in a big laugh and he would open his mouth and poke his fingers down his mouth and would not speak." He also could not be made to work. Witnesses testified that Nelson

13. Buhler v. McHatton, No. 3448, 9 La. Ann. 192 (1854).

would be worth $1,200 "if sound." Berret sued Adams for refusing to pay him the $500. The Iberville Parish judge charged the jury that if they felt Adams purchased the slave knowing that he was mentally unsound, they must rule in favor of Berret, which they did. Justice Alexander Buchanan, writing for the supreme court, affirmed the judgment, citing *Civil Code* article 2498, which held that if a purchaser was aware of a defect at the time of sale, the usual warranty did not apply: "[only] a special warranty can . . . enable the buyer to rescind the sale, or reduce the price, on account of such defect."[14]

Epilepsy was the basis for several redhibitory actions. A typical case, *Metoyer* v. *Caretta* (1859), involved the slave Ellen Dorn, age nineteen. Her new owner claimed she had epilepsy and "other fits," and the attending physician testified that he had witnessed a seizure during which she foamed at the mouth, her eyes rolled back in her head, and her muscles contracted. He was convinced she had epilepsy and was not feigning the disorder: he had applied a hot coal to her leg during the seizure and she had not winced. The physician for the vendor testified that her "fits" were not epilepsy. He stated that there were many types of "fits" with many causes, including "excess of love," "use of ardent drink," and "hysterical attacks," none of which were incurable. The lower court believed the first physician, and the buyer recovered his purchase price. The Louisiana Supreme Court did not disturb the verdict.[15]

In *Brabo* v. *Martin* (1833), a physician testified that the slave Nelly, age thirty, had epilepsy, was "subject to fits of derangement," and was "entirely out of her mind." He claimed she also had "trembling imbecility," ate mud, and had "nervous spasms." A lay witness alleged Nelly was neither ill nor mad but was playing a "trick." A police officer testified that two years before the sale at issue, he found her screaming and rolling on the ground saying that she wanted to be sold, that her owner was "too severe for her." The officer further testified that the slave woman often feigned illness to avoid work and encourage her master to sell her, and that the threat of chastisement cured her quickly. The lower-court jury denied recovery to her new owner because he was unable to prove she had epilepsy, an "absolute vice of body," and the Louisiana Supreme Court did not disturb this judgment.[16]

Epidemic diseases were the basis of several redhibitory actions that

14. Berret v. Adams, No. 3806, 10 La. Ann. 77 (1855).
15. Metoyer v. Caretta, Unreported Louisiana Supreme Court Case No. 5665 (1859).
16. Brabo v. Martin, No. 2458, La. 275 (1833).

reached the state supreme court. In *Dohan* v. *Wilson* (1859), a Tensas Parish planter, Daniel Dohan, purchased three young slave women from a New Orleans slave dealer. Dohan brought them to his plantation, and within fifteen days two of them, worth $1,150 each, died of cholera. One of Dohan's slave men, valued at $1,350, also caught the disease and died. As soon as the third slave became ill, Dohan took the precaution of making his unaffected slaves leave their cabins and camp out in different parts of the nearby woods, but some of them still contracted the disease. Testimony proved that there had been no cholera in Tensas Parish for seven years before the arrival of the two slave women. Dohan won a rescission of the sale of the two slaves by the lower court and an award for the value of the other dead slave. The supreme court affirmed the judgment. In the dictum, Chief Justice Edwin Merrick stated that "a disease making its appearance within fifteen days after the sale, is presumed to have existed on the day of sale."[17]

"Vices of character" also gave rise to numerous redhibition suits. Under Louisiana law, slaves were defective merchandise if they were habitual fugitives. According to the *Civil Code,* being "in the habit of running away" was an absolute vice of character that allowed the purchaser of such a slave to bring a legal action to rescind the sale and to have the purchase price returned or reduced. To establish that the slave was a habitual runaway required proof that the habit existed before the sale, specifically that the slave in question "shall have absented himself from his master's house twice for several days, or once for more than a month."[18]

The Louisiana Supreme Court heard fifty actions of redhibition, each involving one or more slaves alleged to be habitual runaways; these cases became more numerous during the late antebellum period as the population of slaves grew. A typical assertion was that the slave was "addicted to every sort of vice and defect and in the habit of running away."[19] Slightly more than half of these redhibitory actions were successful. Among those that were not, many failed because the slave did not fit the exact legal definition of a habitual runaway given in the *Civil Code.* Sometimes the sale itself precipitated the flight of slaves who had never

17. Dohan v. Wilson, No. 5368, 14 La. Ann. 353 (1859).

18. *Civil Code,* Art. 2505, p. 389.

19. Andry v. Foy, No. 342, 6 Mart. (o.s.) 689 (La. 1819) and 7 Mart. (o.s.) 33 (La. 1819). The fifty redhibition appeals to the supreme court involved a total of fifty-five runaway slaves, among whom men outnumbered women by forty-five to ten.

absented themselves before the transaction. In other cases, although the slaves whose sale was at issue had run away before the purchase, they had not been gone often enough or long enough to quality as habitual runaways. For example, before Carmelite Bocod purchased him, the teenaged slave Bob ran away once for a few days. Soon after the transfer he became a fugitive again. In *Bocod* v. *Jacobs* (1831), the lower court found that Bob's actions demonstrated a preexisting habit of running away and granted Bocod rescission of the sale. Jacobs appealed. Judge François-Xavier Martin reversed the verdict, commenting that "the mere fact of running away immediately after the sale, added to a single instance before, may not be received as evidence of an anterior habit. It may be the consequence of the displeasure of being sold—of his dislike of the new owner."[20]

In *Hiligsberg* v. *New Orleans Canal and Banking Company* (1834), Lucian G. Hiligsberg sued for rescission of the sale of the slave Turner. Although testimony proved the slave had run twice before the sale, it failed to establish the length of his absences. After the sale, the slave ran three or four times, usually to his former home. The last time he left his new master, he vanished. The lower court ruled that Hiligsberg had not proved Turner to be a habitual runaway, and the sale was not rescinded. Chief Judge Mathews affirmed the judgment: "We are of the opinion that the plaintiff has not made out his case by evidences [*sic*] as required by law." The very specific evidentiary burdens on the party who sought to rescind the sale suggest that in some cases the court construed the warranty in such a manner as to greatly limit its application.[21]

The Louisiana Supreme Court during the antebellum period heard twelve cases that involved buyers claiming that the slaves they had purchased were habitual runaways even though they could only prove the slaves became fugitives *after* the sale. In *Fazende* v. *Hagan* (1844), a Charleston slave trader, John Hagan, brought a ten-year-old orphan named Ben to New Orleans and sold him to Theodule Fazende for $390. Ben first ran away twenty days after the sale; the boy returned to Hagan's slave yard. Fazende reclaimed him, and ten or fifteen days later Ben again became a fugitive and "threw himself into the river and got drownded [*sic*]" as he attempted to flee his purchaser. Fazende won his

20. Bocod v. Jacobs, No. 2101, 2 La. 408 (1831).
21. Hiligsberg v. New Orleans Canal and Banking Co., No. 2555, 6 La. 228 (1834).

action for rescission by default in the New Orleans District Court because Hagan failed to appear, but the supreme court remanded the case, stating that there was "not a tittle of evidence" that Ben had ever run away before the sale. The court observed that "the habit of running away in a boy of ten years of age is supposed to be extremely rare . . . absenting himself from his new master, and going to his former [master]; is perhaps not conclusive evidence of an intention to run away"—another example of the court's limiting the scope of the warranty. Chief Judge Martin remanded the case for a new trial because Fazende failed to prove his case.[22]

The slave Agnes absented herself permanently when, according to witnesses, she intentionally drowned herself and her child, Virginia, in a "deep water hole" near her former owner's plantation eleven days after she was sold, but before her new owner took possession of her. Efforts to prove that she "was afflicted with the absolute vice of madness" failed. On the contrary, witnesses in *Walker* v. *Hays* (1860), stated that she possessed "unusual good sense." Chief Justice Merrick refused to cancel her sale, saying that "the only evidence of insanity or madness . . . was the unnatural act of drowning herself and her child." Citing *Civil Code* article 2442, Merrick ruled the contract of sale was therefore complete, and the property was at the risk of the buyer.[23]

Thomas W. Collins, a New Orleans slave trader, brought the Georgia slave Hillery to the city and sold him to John J. Blair of DeSoto Parish in December, 1857. The slave ran repeatedly after the sale and died in November, 1858, of what a physician called "chronic peritonitis, brought on by exposure," contracted while hiding in the woods. The previous spring, Blair had written Collins "that he was compelled to throw the negro back on his hands." He asked Collins to cancel the sale and send him another slave. Collins agreed to cancel the sale and send Blair another slave, but asked that the planter keep Hillery until the cholera epidemic raging in New Orleans had subsided. After the slave died, Blair won his suit, *Blair* v. *Collins* (1860), to have the sale rescinded

22. Fazende v. Hagan, No. 4824, 9 Rob. 306 (La. 1844). Another slave was killed while attempting to escape his new master. Testimony proved the bondsman was a "good slave" and not a habitual runaway. The court observed that the new owner had no grounds for redhibition, but was simply trying to recover his loss. Dugas v. Estiletts, 5 La. Ann. 559 (1850).

23. Walker v. Hays, No. 6606, 15 La. Ann. 640 (1860); *Civil Code,* Art. 2442, p. 381.

because the trader had agreed before the slave died to accept him; the supreme court ordered Collins to give Blair a refund or another slave.[24]

In all successful cases that came before the supreme court involving suits to rescind sales of slaves alleged to be habitual runaways, the petitioner was able to prove the slave in question was a fugitive both before and after the sale. For example, in *Andry* v. *Foy* (1819), Prosper Foy sold Manuel Andry nine slaves for $10,500. Six of the nine absconded shortly after the sale, and Andry sued for a rescission. Foy admitted that four of the six qualified as habitual runaways under the law. One of the other two, Foy claimed, was not a habitual fugitive, as he had only run away twice during the four years prior to sale. The other, a fourteen-year-old named Horace, had run on only one occasion. Foy's attorney argued, "If a gentleman should happen to get *in liquor once or twice* in four years, would any person pretend to say that he is in the habit of getting drunk?" (emphasis in original). Testimony proved that Horace indeed had run only once, but for more than the required month—he was actually absent for seven months, during which time he traveled to New York, Liverpool, and finally Charleston, where he was captured. The lower court ruled that this absence "excited as much apprehension and alarm as evidence of three ordinary acts of running away." The lower court granted a rescission of the sale of all six slaves named in the lawsuit and awarded $6,500 to Andry. In affirming this decision, Judge Martin gave the opinion of the high court: "It is clear that the disposition of six of these slaves to run away was known to the vendor, and that he did not communicate it to the vendees."[25]

At issue in *Thomas* v. *Selser* (1842) were five slaves that Nimrod R. Selser bought from Hiram J. Thomas. One of the five, Caleb, ran away shortly after the sale and never returned. Selser defaulted on the note he had signed to Thomas in payment for Caleb, and Thomas sued. Selser in turn claimed Caleb was "addicted to running away" and sued for rescission of the sale. Selser's son-in-law testified that he had heard a conversation in which Thomas admitted that the slave had absented himself four or five times before the sale but alleged that "it was generally from the fear of being whipped, and that he did not stay away for

24. Blair v. Collins, No. 6449, 15 La. Ann. 683 (1860).
25. Andry v. Foy, No. 342, 7 Mart. (o.s.) 33 (La. 1819).

five or six days at a time." In this conversation, Thomas stated that he did not consider the slave a runaway. Testimony proved that Caleb's owner before Thomas, a Dr. Campbell of Mississippi, had trusted him with transporting his produce to market and securing the family's stores at home. Under Campbell, Caleb had absented himself only once, for a night, because he had quarreled with his wife. The lower court refused to cancel the sale, and ordered Selser to pay the note. Judge Alonzo Morphy affirmed the judgment, ruling that the only basis of Selser's case was the hearsay testimony of his own son-in-law, which a disinterested witness (Campbell) had contradicted.[26]

In February, 1853, Hosea George purchased a mulatto blacksmith, Jacob, from the slave dealers Moses Greenwood and Company for $1,500. The traders sold Jacob fully guaranteed "against the vices and maladies prescribed by law." A little more than a month after the sale, Jacob ran away "without provocation," and George never recovered him. He sued to have the sale canceled in *George* v. *Greenwood* (1856), on the basis that Jacob was a habitual runaway. At the trial a witness stated that the slave had spoken of himself as a runaway and had admitted he had once been captured in the "Cherokee Nation." Jacob's reported admissions were stricken from the record because he was a slave and the *Civil Code* prohibited slaves from being witnesses in civil actions. However, other testimony proved that Jacob had indeed fled to the Indian territory before the sale and had to be put in irons to be returned to New Orleans. The chains were removed just before the sale. His original owner admitted to a witness that the slave was "ungovernable and that he could not control him and had to iron him to get him out of the nation." The lower court not only voided the sale and returned the purchase price to George, but also recommended that the slave dealers bring legal action against their vendor. To the charge that the plaintiff should have attempted to return the slave to the traders, Justice Alexander Buchanan replied that he could not order George to attempt to return the slave because it was impossible to do so: "The slave appears to be in the Indian territory, and beyond the reach of any civil process."[27]

One slave dealer, Bernard Kendig, regularly purchased slaves with known defects at a low price, then resold them fully guaranteed to un-

26. Thomas v. Selser, No. 4774, 1 Rob. 425 (La. 1842).
27. George v. Greenwood, No. 3687, 11 La. Ann. 299 (1856); *Civil Code,* Art. 177, p. 28.

suspecting buyers at handsome profits. Legally defective slaves sold as fully guaranteed netted Kendig an average profit of 37 percent; he realized only 23 percent on the sale of slaves with no vices of body or character. For example, Kendig sold the slave Dick to James H. Riggin for $1,000 with a full guarantee even though he had purchased Dick from a fellow slave dealer with no guarantee "and full knowledge of the existing vice." Seven months after the sale, Dick ran away for three months. When Riggin found him, he was "in a dying condition," and he "died in about three days of inflammation of the bowels [caused by] exposure, cold, eating indigestible food, and various other causes." Testimony in *Riggin* v. *Kendig* (1857) proved the slave had run away repeatedly before the sale and was sold as a runaway to Kendig by another slave trader. On the day of trial, the judge of the Fourth District Court of New Orleans demanded that Kendig produce his bill of sale of Dick from his fellow slave dealer. Kendig produced a bill of sale that fully guaranteed the slave, but the bill turned out to be for another slave. At this point Kendig, after searching through his papers, declared the bill of sale for Dick "lost or mislaid." The lower court refused to grant Riggin a rescission, but Justice Cole reversed the judgment, stating that Kendig knew Dick was a "notorious runaway" and concealed the fact from the purchaser. The court also knew that Kendig was a "negro trader" and had purchased Dick from a slave trader who knew him to be a runaway: "We think that Kendig was cognizant of this vice of Dick when he sold him, fully guaranteed, to plaintiff. They were both negro traders of the city, and that class of society is not easily imposed upon." Justice Spofford dissented in this case, citing *Civil Code* articles 2510 and 2511. Article 2510 stated that if a thing "affected with these vices has perished through the badness of its quality, the seller must sustain the loss." However, article 2511 held that if the thing purchased "perished by a fortuitous event, *before the purchaser has instituted his redhibitory action,* the loss must be borne by him" (emphasis in original of Spofford's dissent).[28]

28. Richard Tansey, "Bernard Kendig and the New Orleans Slave Trade," *Louisiana History,* XXIII (Spring, 1982), 163*n,* 170*n,* 171–74; Riggin v. Kendig, No. 4718, 12 La. Ann. 451 (1857); *Civil Code,* Arts. 2510, 2511, p. 390. The distinction between a preexisting condition and a disease that developed after a sale was made clear in *Kiper* v. *Nutall and Peniston* (1841). The defendant claimed that the slave was unhealthy at the time of the sale, but the court held that she died of a new disease, a "fortuitous event" within the meaning of article 2511 of the

Kendig also sold the slave Jim to Thomas Gatlin of Arkansas, who sued in *Gatlin* v. *Kendig* (1866) to cancel the sale on the grounds that the slave was a habitual fugitive. Gatlin testified that two months after he purchased Jim, the bondsman ran away "without chastisement." Six months later Gatlin found him in a Texas jail suffering from a severe gunshot wound inflicted when he was attempting to avoid capture. The Arkansas planter sued to rescind the sale and recover his purchase price of $1,200, medical expenses, and jail fees. Testimony showed that Kendig had sold Jim once before to a Texas judge, who had returned him to Kendig only a few days before the sale to Gatlin because he was a frequent fugitive. The lower court canceled the sale because Kendig obviously knew of the vice and concealed it from Gatlin. The supreme court affirmed the judgment.[29]

In several cases that reached the high court, the seller warned the purchaser that the slave had a history of running away. In *Bayon* v. *Towles* (1826), the vendor described the slave listed in the act of sale as "a runaway and drunkard." The vendor assured the buyer that the slave never wandered far ("petit marronnage") and that he always returned of his own accord. Testimony later indicated that he had run as far as the "Choctaw Nation" while owned by the vendor, and had to be captured and returned. The lower court canceled the sale, but Judge Martin reversed the judgment because the purchaser "had acknowledged, under his hand, before a notary and two witnesses, that the vendor informed him of an absolute and unqualified running away."[30]

In 1824 a St. Tammany Parish planter purchased the slave January for $300. January ran away soon after the sale; his new master captured him and put him in the police jail. While incarcerated he contracted smallpox. The sheriff transferred him to a hospital, where he died. The planter sued for cancellation of the sale in *Bonnet* v. *Ramsay* (1827), claiming January was a habitual runaway. The auctioneer who had sold the slave stated that January was a good "drayman, horsler and field

---

Civil Code. Furthermore, the defendant did not summon a physician until the slave was moribund, which alone could have cost him a rescission. Kiper v. Nutall and Peniston, No. 850, 1 Rob. 46 (La. 1841).

29. Gatlin v. Kendig, No. 6894, 18 La. Ann. 118 (1866). This lawsuit was filed in November, 1860, but because of the Civil War was not decided until 1866.

30. Bayon v. Towles, 5 Mart. (N.S.) 1 (La. 1826).

hand" but was guaranteed against illness only, not against running away. He claimed that he sold the slave as a runaway, as evidenced by a much-reduced purchase price. Bonnet alleged that the vendor told him that the slave had absented himself only once, to visit his mother, and that he had returned voluntarily a short time later. However, testimony established that January had often absented himself for a month at a time before the sale. The defendant also argued that the case had prescribed because the plaintiff had failed to file the lawsuit within the one-year period required by Louisiana law. Ramsay had sold Bonnet the slave on July 3, 1824. The sheriff did not serve Ramsay with the lawsuit until July 6, 1825. Chief Judge Mathews ruled that "prescription had elapsed without interruption, and must be held to protect the defendant in this suit."[31]

In three cases involving actions for redhibition on the basis that the slave was a habitual runaway, two bondsmen and one bondswoman were actually sold directly from jails where they had been imprisoned as fugitives. In these instances the vendor concealed the fact that the slaves were fugitives from the purchaser, and the high court affirmed lower-court judgments canceling the sales. In *Macarty* v. *Bagnieres* (1810), heard before the Superior Court for the Territory of Orleans, the fact that the vendor had kept the slave at issue in jail for five months preceding the sale led the judges to conclude that he knew the slave was a runaway: "We must believe that the defendant was conscious that the negro had such a habit or disposition to run away, as rendered it dangerous to allow him that degree of freedom without which a negro is of little service." Bagnieres' unwillingness to "trust him [the slave] out of jail" indicated that he was aware the slave "was addicted to running away." Citing Roman law, the judges affirmed the decision for the plaintiff.[32]

In *Pilié* v. *Férrière* (1829), the purchaser claimed that the attributes of the slave purchased were misrepresented and that the slave was a habitual runaway. The thirteen-year-old Celestine was sold to Joseph Pilié

31. Bonnet v. Ramsay, No. 1468, 6 Mart (N.S.) 129 (La. 1827).

32. Macarty v. Bagnieres, No. 2320, 1 Mart. (O.S.) 149 (La. 1810). The two similar cases were Sikes v. Allen, No. 1016, 2 Mart. (N.S.) 622 (La. 1824), and Farmer v. Fisk, No. 5248, 9 Rob. 351 (La. 1844). In Fisk v. Proctor, No. 927, 4 La. Ann. 562 (1849), Fisk sued his vendor but was denied recovery because he sued for damages and not redhibition.

by Joseph Lalande Férrière as a laundress and cook. Pilié claimed that "she possessed these qualities very defectively, if at all." Celestine ran away immediately after the sale, was captured, and absented herself again for more than one month. Pilié sued for a rescission of the sale on the basis that the slave's abilities had been misrepresented and that she habitually ran away. Férrìere claimed that the slave girl ran to escape cruel treatment by her new owner. A witness testified that Pilié sent her to jail to be chastised after she was caught. Another witness claimed she saw Celestine "freshly whipped," with blood on her clothes. A free woman of color testified that the slave girl had been given lashes for washing poorly (Louisiana was the only southern state to allow free persons of color to testify in actions involving whites). The lower court awarded Pilié $170, the value by which it felt Celestine's worth was diminished by her vices. The defendant appealed, claiming the court had erred by admitting the testimony of the free woman of color, whom the defendant alleged was a slave. Justice Alexander Porter admitted that "the evidence is contradictory, and does not authorize us to disturb the verdict." As to the defendant's allegations that one of the witnesses was a slave, the court noted that the bill of exceptions failed to state whether the woman was a mulatto or a Negro. The court referred to the legal presumption that mulattoes were free, a presumption in Louisiana since *Adéle* v. *Beauregard* (1810). Since the bill of exceptions failed to state the color of the witness, the judges ruled that "the actual enjoyment of freedom by the witness . . . [is] *prima facie* evidence of her competency."[33]

Redhibition actions were possible under Louisiana law if a slave was "addicted to theft." In several cases purchasers of bondsmen and bondswomen sued for cancellation of sales because the slave was both a thief and a runaway. In at least one case such an action was taken by a plaintiff seeking adjustment of a dowry settlement. A Pointe Coupée Parish man, James Mitchel, sued his father-in-law for $3,500, the price of three slaves given to Mitchel's wife as part of her dowry. A dowry in Louisiana was "the effects which the wife brought to the husband to support the expenses of marriage." The bride's father gave the dowry to the husband for his enjoyment as long as the marriage lasted. Furthermore, according to *Civil Code* article 2325, "Those who settle a dowry are bound to the warranty of the things thus settled." Article 2325, there-

33. Pilié v. Férrière, No. 1724, 7 Mart. (N.S.) 648 (La. 1829).

fore, made Jewel, the father-in-law, responsible for the defects in the slaves. In *Mitchel* v. *Jewel* (1820, 1822), Mitchel claimed the slave Tom was "addicted to every vice" and alleged that Jewel had purchased Tom in Charleston "at a place called the sugar house, where runaway and bad negroes are confined." Jewel had placed the slave Jack in irons for having run away. Mitchel alleged that Jack's chains were only removed when the appraisers for the marriage contract arrived, and were immediately replaced after their departure. Since the transfer, both Tom and Jack and the third slave, Jenny, allegedly had absented themselves often. In the trial court, a jury denied Mitchel any restitution; the Louisiana Supreme Court required Jewel to make restitution to Mitchel for the value of Tom had he been of good character, but sustained the gift of Jack and Jenny. Judge Porter noted that Jewel had purchased Tom "as one of the worst character, and that Jewel acknowledged the negro was addicted to robbery." However, the judges believed the testimony of Jewel's overseer, who stated that Jack had only run away once because he had "sore eyes, and [was] being too hard pushed." This was not sufficient evidence to establish a habit of running away, in Porter's opinion. He found no redhibitory vice in Jenny.[34]

In *Chrétien* v. *Théard* (1822), Gerald Chrétien sued to obtain rescission of the sale of a slave man named LaFortune, represented as a carpenter and joiner but, claimed the purchaser, in reality "a drunkard, runaway and thief." The lower court ruled that Chrétien had not proved his allegations, and the Louisiana Supreme Court affirmed the judgment. In the dictum, Judge Porter commented: "It is well known that most slaves will steal small articles from their owners as well as others when they find an opportunity . . . if sales were set aside for that, there would be no security in slave sales."[35] This statement demonstrates that the court recognized that slave discipline was much more stringent in law than in actuality.

Andrew Skillman purchased the slave Henry, alias Charles, who promptly ran away. Skillman was never able to recover him and refused to honor the promissory note for $600 that he had given for the slave. The vendor, Annias Dunbar, sued for payment in *Dunbar* v. *Skillman* (1828). Skillman alleged that the slave was a thief and a runaway, and he

34. *Civil Code,* Art. 2505, p. 389; Mitchel v. Jewel, No. 406, 9 Mart. (o.s.) 185 (La. 1820), and No. 499, 10 Mart. (o.s.) 645 (La. 1822); *Civil Code,* Arts. 2317, 2325, pp. 362–63.

35. Chrétien v. Théard, No. 612, 11 Mart. (o.s.) 11 (La. 1822).

asked the court for a rescission of the sale and a judgment for $1,500 because Henry had "enticed off" Phillis, age twenty, Andrew, age sixteen, and Maria, age eighteen, when he ran away; none was ever recovered. A former owner testified that Henry was a good body servant and pastry cook, but if used as a field hand, he would run away. Skillman had put him in the field. Henry's former mistress testified that the bondsman was so clever that she once had "a mind to educate him and put him to work in a store" (another witness stated that Henry was enough of a rascal without an education). Dunbar claimed that she had warned Skillman of the slave's faults before the sale, that everyone in the neighborhood knew of the bondsman's bad character, and that Skillman was aware of the slave's vices, as Henry was in chains when Skillman purchased him. The lower court ruled that the sale was without fraud and ordered Skillman to pay the note. On appeal, Chief Judge Mathews affirmed the judgment plus 10 percent damages for frivolous appeal. "A complete disclosure was made by the plaintiff, of the vices inherent in the slave at the time of the bargain between him and the defendant," Mathews observed.[36]

The slave Jim was the object of another lawsuit to cancel a sale. His new master, James B. Smith, alleged he was "addicted" to theft, drunkenness, and running away. In *Smith* v. *Taylor* (1845), testimony established that Jim had a habit of riding the master's horses at night and visiting other plantations without permission. The slave absconded twice from his new owner and also stole a hog. A witness stated that Jim's former master had tied him up before the sale for stealing. Taylor, a New Orleans slave trader, had sold Jim just before the sale to Smith; the previous purchaser had returned Jim because he was a "bad negro." The East Feliciana court canceled the sale. Associate Justice Bullard, writing for the court, affirmed the judgment because Taylor concealed Jim's faults from the purchaser.[37]

The volume and variety of Louisiana redhibition cases involving vices of body and vices of character demonstrate just how troublesome buying and selling human property could be and how carefully the Supreme

36. Dunbar v. Skillman, No. 1575, 6 Mart. (N.S.) 539 (La. 1828). Teaching a slave to read and write was not illegal in Louisiana until 1830. "An Act To Punish Certain Crimes . . . and for Other Purposes," Act of March 16, 1830, *Louisiana Acts, 1830,* Sec. 3, p. 96.

37. Smith v. Taylor, No. 5755, 10 Rob. 133 (La. 1845).

Court of Louisiana applied the law of redhibition in slave sales. During the antebellum period the court heard more than 1,200 appeals that concerned slaves: cases involving slaves as criminals, as victims, as stolen goods, as fugitives, as contraband, as concubines, as goods seized for debts, and as plaintiffs suing for emancipation. However, redhibition cases involving slave sales came before the court more often than any other kind of slave-related appeal. The number of slave-redhibition cases is clear evidence that slaves were significant financial investments and that many slave dealers, auctioneers, and individuals were willing to sell a diseased, disabled, or refractory slave rather than retain such a slave or accept a lowered sale price by admitting his or her legal defects.

An examination of redhibition cases indicates that slave sales were regulated in Louisiana in much the same way as the sale of any other property. The *Civil Code* listed the conditions for slave-redhibition actions, and the supreme court interpreted the law in a cut-and-dried manner. The court was highly circumspect in applying redhibition law, adhering to a strict construction of the redhibition articles found in the *Code,* with little or no jurisprudential innovation.

In the regulation of slave sales, Louisiana law retained its civil-law principles, grounded firmly on Roman slave law. Unlike other areas of slave law, redhibition law in slave sales showed little change over time, nor did the law of slave sales in Louisiana begin to resemble that of her sister states. In this area, Louisiana's legal heritage was strong enough to resist "Americanization" and useful enough to the state's slaveholders to ensure its retention.

Although redhibition was a double-edged sword that could hurt slaveowners trying to divest themselves of a diseased or recalcitrant slave, there is no evidence the unique system of implied warranty had any effect on the burgeoning New Orleans slave market. Although quantification is impossible, many slave sales that gave rise to redhibition involved slaves brought into Louisiana from other states and sold to Louisiana buyers. In these instances the implied warranty would have protected the residents of the state from purchasing slaves with hidden defects. The high number of appeals of redhibition cases indicates the importance of New Orleans as the premier slave market of the Deep South. More important for legal development, the presence of a large interstate slave trade meant that codal institutions, such as redhibition, might have lain dormant but for the volume of that trade. This is an instance in which the existence of slavery acted as a force to strengthen Louisiana's civil-law traditions rather than contributing to the Americanization of the state's jurisprudence. In turn, the very presence of redhibition in Louisiana contracts may have enhanced the development of the New Orleans slave market, as its guarantees would have been attractive to those wishing to purchase slaves.

6

"MARKED IN A MANNER UNUSUAL AMONGST CIVILISED PEOPLE"

The Foreign and Domestic Slave Trade in Louisiana

IF UNDER LOUISIANA LAW SLAVES COULD BE BOTH PERsons and property, victims and criminals, stolen goods and self-stealers, as well as defective merchandise because of vices of character or body, they were also objects to be bartered and wagered, bought, sold, mortgaged, seized for debt, and disposed of as liquid assets.[1] The very fact that the possibility of being sold existed and was sanctioned by law emphasized the property aspect of slavery.

New Orleans was the center for slave sales in Louisiana and the Deep South. Hundreds of slaves changed hands in Louisiana each year in the decades before the Civil War. Court records show that some slaves were sold repeatedly. For example, Dr. Gideon C. Forsyth of English Turn in Plaquemines Parish purchased the seventeen-year-old mulatto Fanny in 1840. In 1841 he sold her at auction at the Arcade in New Orleans for $835. Her purchaser, Nathaniel N. Wilkinson, returned her after a few days, saying she did not "suit" him. Fanny was auctioned off again a few days later, this time for $600. Forsyth successfully sued Wilkinson for the difference and for an additional $128.25 for the advertisements and auctioneer's commission that the second sale necessitated. Judge Alonzo Morphy affirmed the decision. It is not possible to ascertain whether Fanny was sold on any other occasion before or after these three sales.[2] This and many other cases heard by the Supreme Court of

1. One slave was bartered for a quantity of sugar, another for $104 and a gold watch. Brinigar v. Griffin, No. 302, 2 La. Ann. 154 (1847); Mayes v. Calvit, No. 58, 5 Mart. (o.s.) 699 (La. 1818). Eighteen-year-old Calem's bill of sale was held as the stakes in an 1813 horse race: Vernot (also Vernaught) v. Yocum, No. 14, 3 Mart. (o.s.) 406 (La. 1814).

2. Vernon A. Wegener, "Negro Slavery in New Orleans" (M.A. thesis, Tulane University, 1935), 28; Judith Kelleher Schafer, "New Orleans Slavery in 1850 as Seen in Advertisements," *Journal of Southern History,* XLVII (February, 1981), 35–36; Forsyth v. Wilkinson, No.

Louisiana during the antebellum period illustrate varied aspects of the foreign, interstate, and intrastate trade in slaves, the business practices of several prominent slave dealers, and the effect of sales on slave families and slave communities.

One of the first acts of the United States government after the acquisition of Louisiana in 1803 was to prohibit the foreign slave trade in the new territory. This action caused great discontent among a population already suspicious of the intentions of the Americans. The inhabitants believed the prohibition would mean economic ruin. Their protests went unheeded, however, and in 1807 the United States Congress broadened the ban, voting to prohibit the importation of foreign slaves nationwide as of January 1, 1808.[3]

The prohibition act stipulated that illegally imported slaves were to be sold for the benefit of the state and the informer (if any). Congress had hotly debated this provision. Many northern legislators abhorred the idea that the states should be in the business of selling slaves and profiting from it. Some suggested compromises that would have provided for illegally imported slaves to be freed or sent to areas where slavery was being gradually abolished. Furthermore, the idea that the helpless victims of those who violated federal law would be sold into a life of slavery offended some northern legislators. A more fundamental irritant to northern sensibilities was that forfeiture of the unlawfully imported slaves implied that they were property. However, southern lawmakers were adamant that blacks brought into the country unlawfully would remain slaves, and ultimately Congress left the disposition of confiscated slaves to the legislature of the states.[4] All that the law abolishing the trade meant to slaves who were brought illegally into the United States was that they would have different vendors and other purchasers than they would have had if the persons attempting to smuggle

---

5291, 5 Rob. 263 (La. 1843). Reinders, "Slavery in New Orleans," 211, states that by 1850 New Orleans was the greatest slave-trading center in the entire South.

3. Taylor, *Negro Slavery in Louisiana,* 35; Joe Gray Taylor, "The Foreign Slave Trade in Louisiana After 1808," *Louisiana History,* I (Winter, 1960), 36–43; Paul Finkelman, "Slavery and the Constitutional Convention: Making a Covenant with Death," in *Beyond Confederation: Origins of the Constitution and American National Identity,* ed. Richard Beeman, Stephen Botein, and Edward C. Carter II (Chapel Hill, 1987), 218.

4. Stampp, *Peculiar Institution,* 271; David Brion Davis, *The Problem of Slavery in the Age of Revolution, 1770–1823* (Ithaca, N.Y., 1975), 136–37; John Hope Franklin, *From Slavery to Freedom: A History of Negro Americans* (New York, 1980), 104.

A slave dealer's "pen" typical of the domestic slave trade period.

Courtesy of the Historic New Orleans Collection, Museum/Research Center, Acc. No. 1958.43.24

them into the country had not been caught. They were still destined for a life of slavery.

The arrival of the St. Domingue refugees and their slaves in New Orleans in 1809 precipitated an immediate reconsideration of the federal act of 1807 prohibiting the importation of foreign slaves. Fleeing French St. Domingue (Haiti) during the slave revolt that occurred during the 1790s, the refugees first sought asylum in Cuba but were expelled from that country in 1809 because of tensions between France and Spain. In that year, 9,059 of them arrived in New Orleans, of whom 2,731 were white, 3,102 were free people of color, and 3,226 were slaves—doubling the population of free persons of color and substantially increasing the population of whites and slaves in New Orleans overnight. Although some of the refugees settled elsewhere, the city's total population rose from 17,001 to 24,552 as a result of this mass immigration.

The creole population realized that the white refugees would reinforce their numbers and serve as a bulwark against the Americans pouring into the territory. They pressured Governor William Claiborne to petition Congress not to apply the law of 1807 to the slaves brought in by the refugees. Instead, Claiborne reported to President Jefferson that "many good Americans are dissatisfied with so great an influx of foreigners." For those who had hoped that immigration from the United States would "Americanize" Louisiana, the flood of French refugees seemed a major setback. However, Claiborne desperately needed to gain the support of the creole population, who resented American rule, and in the end he sponsored a bill to exempt the St. Domingue slaves from the law prohibiting foreign slave importation. Congress passed the exemption with no opposition, and the refugees kept their slaves.[5]

It was not until 1818 that Congress approved funds and empowered the president to dispatch armed patrols to intercept slave ships bound to the United States from foreign countries. Two years later Congress passed a statute that made participation in the African slave trade an act of piracy punishable by death. Meanwhile, the Louisiana territorial legislature did not enact the necessary enabling legislation for the federal act of 1807 until March, 1810, when it decreed that illegally imported slaves were to be sold and the proceeds of the sale placed in the territorial treasury. In 1814 the Louisiana state legislature amended this act to provide for half of the proceeds from such sales to be paid to the informer and the other half to the state. In 1818 the legislature amended the act again: now half the money derived from the sale of illegally imported Africans was to be paid to the capturing ship captain and the other half to Charity Hospital of New Orleans.[6] In effect, this law would encourage ship captains to aid in enforcing the act.

5. Paul F. Lachance, "The 1809 Immigration of Saint-Domingue Refugees to New Orleans: Reception, Integration, and Impact," *Louisiana History,* XXIX (Spring, 1988), 110–26; "House Debate on Emigrants from Cuba," *Annals of Congress,* June 28, 1809, p. 463; "An Act for the Remission of Certain Penalties and Forfeitures, and for Other Purposes," Act of June 28, 1809, *Annals of Congress,* 2508.

6. Davis, *Problem of Slavery in the Age of Revolution,* 137; Stampp, *Peculiar Institution,* 271; "An Act Respecting Slaves Imported into This Territory in Violation of the Act of Congress . . . ," Act of March 16, 1810, *Orleans Territory Acts, 1810,* pp. 18–22; "An Act to Amend the First Section of the Act Entitled 'An Act Respecting Slaves Imported into this Territory in Violation of the Act of Congress . . . ,'" Act of March 7, 1814, *Louisiana Acts, 1814,* p. 78; "An Act Respecting Slaves, Imported into This State in Violation of the Act of the Congress of the United States . . . ," Act of March 13, 1818, *Louisiana Acts, 1818,* pp. 66–68; Voorhies, *Treatise on the Criminal Jurisprudence of Louisiana,* 303–304. See also Warren S. Howard, *American Slavers and the Federal Law, 1837–1862* (Berkeley, 1963), 26–27. W. E. B. Du Bois estimated that 270,000 blacks were smuggled into the United States between 1808 and 1860; W. E. B. Du Bois, *The Suppression of the African Slave Trade to the United States of America, 1638–1870* (New York, 1896), 112–30.

Louisianians were particularly aggrieved by the ban on slave importations imposed on them by their new federal government, as the prohibition coincidentally occurred just after the agricultural basis of Louisiana's economy had shifted to the highly labor-intensive cash crops of cotton and sugar from the less profitable tobacco and indigo. The French had encouraged the planting of perique tobacco, and the Spanish, hoping to make tobacco Louisiana's cash crop, subsidized it and required its sale in a protected market. Sugar and cotton were grown in Louisiana only in small quantities during the eighteenth century. The development of the cotton gin and a viable process for granulating sugar, both of which occurred in the 1790s, ensured a massive shift to sugarcane in south Louisiana and cotton north of Baton Rouge. Louisiana's new crops created a need for expanded slave imports that was felt to be "acute" by 1800; without more slaves, agricultural prosperity would vanish. In that same year the Spanish governor of Louisiana wrote that "the province of Louisiana cannot be self-supporting without the admission of Negroes." A traveler to the territory in 1803 observed that the price of slaves in Louisiana at the time of the Louisiana Purchase was two to three times higher than in the American South. Not surprisingly, Louisianians ignored the ban on foreign slaves whenever possible and purchased large numbers of smuggled slaves.[7]

Five cases heard by the Supreme Court of Louisiana between 1809 and 1820 involved alleged violations of the act of 1807. In 1809 the ship *Clara,* owned by Fort and Giraud of New York, was seized and sold for illegally importing slaves into Louisiana. The record of this case has been lost, and no additional details are available.[8] Further evidence of illegal importation of slaves can be found in *Sierra* v. *Llort* (1817). Fernando Antoine De Sierra, a Havana merchant, alleged that he was the owner of the frigate *Rosalia,* which had sailed from the coast of Africa in 1813 carrying 800 quintals (hundredweights) of ivory and 599 Negroes, 564 of whom survived the voyage. When the ship neared Louisiana, pirates captured it and towed it to Barataria. The famous outlaw and adventurer Jean Lafitte was operating a ring of smugglers and pirates in Barataria Bay at the time. He used his blacksmith shop in New Or-

7. Charles Edwards O'Neill *et al., Louisiana: A History,* ed. Bennett H. Wall (Arlington Heights, Ill., 1990), 73–74, 147; Paul F. Lachance, "The Politics of Fear: French Louisianians and the Slave Trade, 1786–1800," *Plantation Society,* I (June, 1979), 173, 185; Joe Gray Taylor, *Louisiana: A History* (New York, 1976), 47.

8. Brown v. Fort and Giraud, No. 2288, 1 Mart. (o.s.) 34 (La. 1809).

leans as a depot for selling smuggled slaves. This trade must have had considerable volume, as New Orleans merchants complained that the pirate's refusal to accept anything other than specie created a critical shortage of hard money in New Orleans. Details are sketchy in the *Rosalia* case, but Antonio Llort claimed two of the slaves. Perhaps he had purchased them from the pirates, or possibly he was a smuggler himself. Sierra sued Llort for possession of the slaves and petitioned the court to postpone the trial until depositions he had requested in support of his case arrived from Havana. The lower court made an error in setting the trial date after the continuance. Judge François-Xavier Martin remanded the case to await the evidence from Havana. The importance of this case lies in the evidence of slave smuggling and piracy, rather than in the legal outcome.[9]

In 1818 the attorney general of Louisiana seized the slave Edward and petitioned the state supreme court for permission to have him forfeited and sold for the benefit of the state because he had been illegally imported from "the coast of Africa" in 1815. His owner, Peter Lamouison, alleged that in 1815 he was captain of a "Carthagenian privateer" that was captured by a gunboat of the United States and that he was taken to New Orleans along with Edward, his slave, and "unjustly detained." Lamouison was subsequently released. He told the court that he had not intended to violate Louisiana law regarding foreign slave importations and had planned to send Edward away at the first opportunity. Witnesses testified in *State* v. *Edward* (1818) that the captain had been in and out of New Orleans on business several times, and Edward had always accompanied him. Chief Judge George Mathews ruled that the captain had not intended to violate the antiimportation law, dismissed the attorney general's suit, and restored the slave to Lamouison. Neither Lamouison nor Edward appeared in the 1820 Louisiana census.[10]

Six months later, in *State, Snipes,* et al. v. *Five African Negroes* (1818), the court dealt with a flagrant violation of the act closing the foreign slave trade. Dempsey Snipes and three other men sued to have five allegedly smuggled slaves sold to enable them to collect their half of the proceeds as informers. When the suit began, the court could not determine who the Africans' owner was, and as they were without any

9. Sierra v. Llort, No. 336, 4 Mart. (o.s.) 587 (La. 1817); *Dictionary of American Biography* (1933), X, 540–41; Taylor, "Foreign Slave Trade in Louisiana," 38.

10. State v. Edward, No. 276, 5 Mart. (o.s.) 474 (La. 1818).

George Mathews, chief judge of the Louisiana Supreme Court from 1813 to 1836.

Photo by Warren Gravois. Courtesy of the Librarian, Law Library of Louisiana

means, it appointed an attorney to defend them. Joseph Parrott, the court-appointed defender of the young slaves—three boys and two girls, ranging in age from ten to sixteen—claimed that since they were illegally imported, they were free, reasoning that the only difference to them if the law were enforced was that they would have a different vendor and purchaser. To complicate matters, a Spaniard named Juan Constante, a Havana shipowner, claimed the slaves were his property, "piratically" stolen from him by a "Mexican Corsair" and taken to Texas. Testimony established that Constante dispatched the schooner *La Patronilla* to the coast of Guinea in 1816, where it took aboard 200 slaves to be brought to Cuba. The surviving 186 slaves were next seen in "Galvis Town" in April, 1817, on the same ship, commanded by one Captain Champlain. A witness testified that he had seen seventeen of the slaves near Opelousas, Louisiana. The five in question were found hidden in the sugarhouse of Captain John Theall of Opelousas by Snipes and the other plaintiffs in the suit, who took the youths away in a boat and delivered them to the sheriff.[11]

It is clear that the young slaves were freshly imported from Africa. Theall testified that the five were unable to understand English and "still had the scars or marks of his [their] country" on them. He also alleged that they were "destitute of shame more so than negroes commonly are that have lived among whites," probably a reference to their nakedness. A witness stated that Theall planned to take them to Mississippi and sell them for $500 each. Other witnesses testified that the Africans were "marked in a manner unusual amongst civilised people," probably a reference to ritual scars. Another witness alleged that the cargo of slaves had been sold in Galveston "to certain Italians" who brought them to Opelousas, where the sheriff seized them. The First District Court of New Orleans held that it had no jurisdiction in the case because it was a matter of admiralty and involved diversity of citizenship, therefore falling under federal jurisdiction.

Snipes and the other informers filed their appeal to the Louisiana Supreme Court in September, 1817. At that date the law stipulating that half of the proceeds of the sale of illegally imported slaves were to go to the informer and half to the state was still in force. While the appeal was

11. State, Snipes, et al. v. Five African Negroes, Unreported Louisiana Supreme Court Case No. 61 (1818). Slave mortality aboard ship was usually higher than that reported for the *Patronilla;* see Howard, *American Slavers,* App. D., 238.

under consideration, the law of March, 1818, was passed, changing the beneficiaries of the sales to Charity Hospital and the capturing ship captain, but Snipes and two of the other informers persisted in their appeal. Parrott subsequently filed a claim for the Africans' freedom, and Constante not only claimed the slaves as his own, but denied that the Louisiana Supreme Court or any other state court had jurisdiction over him as a Spanish citizen; he stated that he planned to pursue the matter in the (federal) district court of the United States.[12]

This is an unreported case, and the Louisiana Supreme Court's ruling is unclear. Because of the new law of 1818, the high court decided that the state should relinquish its right in the case, and dismissed the informers' suit. The court authorized the slaves to pursue their claim to freedom in *forma pauperis,* implying that the court would appoint an attorney to represent them. It is difficult to understand the basis for this action when the law clearly intended that confiscated slaves be sold. However, the court also ruled that the five slaves were to pay the court costs of *State, Snipes,* et al. v. *Five African Negroes*. Since the five almost surely were penniless, it must be assumed the court intended that they be sold for the costs of the legal action. Almost certainly the court struggled with this particular decision. It is difficult to assign motives for the judgment, but the issue here was one of federal versus state jurisdiction. The judges may have feared setting a precedent that might have led to many cargoes of confiscated Africans being freed in Louisiana. The Spanish captain ultimately took the case to federal court and proved to the court's satisfaction that the cargo of slaves was originally his property.[13]

In a similar case decided in 1819, *Gomez* v. *Bonneval,* the Louisiana Supreme Court firmly upheld the law of 1818. Candido Gomez sued for his freedom, claiming he had been illegally imported into Louisiana and

12. State, Snipes, et al. v. Five African Negroes, Unreported Louisiana Supreme Court Case No. 61 (1818); Don Juan Constante v. 186 Slaves, the Cargo of the Schooner *Patronilla,* No. 1095 (1817), in Historical Records Survey, Works Progress Administration, *Conspicuous Cases in the United States District Court of Louisiana* (1940–41), Book E, Cases No. 1050–1199. For jurisdiction rules, see John Edwards Leonard, *A Digest of the Decisions of the Supreme Court of the United States in Louisiana Cases* (New Orleans, 1875), 17. Constante's successful attorney was the controversial Edward Livingston.

13. *Louisiana Supreme Court, Minute Book, Western District, 1813–1843,* October 3, 1818, p. 45; State, Snipes et al. v. Five African Negroes, Unreported Louisiana Supreme Court Case No. 61 (1818).

was free because he had been born free in Brazil. He was a seaman aboard the *Falcon* when it was captured by pirates—led, he claimed, by Jean Lafitte. Gomez alleged he was taken to New Orleans as the slave of Alexander Bonneval, who planned to sell him. The mulatto man admitted that his mother was a slave owned by his (white) father, but stated that he had been treated as a son, not a slave. However, shipmates testified that Gomez was a slave. The lower court ruled that Gomez was born in bondage of a slave mother, and as there was no proof he had become free, he was to remain in bondage as the property of Bonneval. The Louisiana Supreme Court ruled that although Gomez was illegally imported into the United States, he was to remain a slave and be sold according to law: "individuals thus imported acquire no personal rights." Judge Pierre Dérbigny, writing for the court, declared that illegally imported slaves were "mere passive beings" to be sold. The court seems to have resolved whatever problems it had in making such a judgment in *Snipes* et al. six months earlier. Dérbigny never considered the legal presumption of *Adéle* v. *Beauregard* (1810) that mulattoes were free, since evidence that Gomez was the son of a slave mother destroyed the presumption arising from his color.[14]

During the remainder of the antebellum period, only a few cases appeared before the Supreme Court of Louisiana that involved the illegal importation of slaves. Federal courts handled the majority of violations because the parties involved were usually from different states or countries, which indicated federal jurisdiction under diversity of citizenship. After 1820, state cases involving actual smuggling were rare, although rumors of illegal importations were common.[15]

14. Gomez v. Bonneval, No. 364, 6 Mart. (o.s.) 656 (La. 1819); Adéle v. Beauregard, 1 Mart (o.s.) 183 (La. 1810); Randolph B. Campbell, *An Empire for Slavery: The Peculiar Institution in Texas, 1821–1865* (Baton Rouge, 1989), 11–12. It is doubtful that Jean Lafitte himself was involved in Gomez's abduction. By 1819 he had moved his operation to Galveston. Perhaps some of his men remained at the old Grand Terre base on Barataria Bay. *Dictionary of American Biography* (1933), X, 540.

15. Taylor, "Foreign Slave Trade in Louisiana," 39, 43. One such case was a suit on a security bond given for the hire of African slaves (number not specified). When it was proved that the slaves had been illegally imported, the Louisiana Supreme Court declared the bond to be void. Montgomery v. Russell, 2 La. 67 (1830). Three cases from federal courts involving violation of the law of 1808 were brought to the United States Supreme Court during the antebellum period (during this era the normal route to the United States Supreme Court was via the federal court system; the Louisiana Supreme Court was the highest appellate court of the state court system): United States v. *Joseph Segunda,* 18 U.S. (5 Wheat.) 338 (1820), 23

In 1841 the high court heard *Penalta* v. *Borges' Executor,* a case involving a confiscated Portuguese vessel. The ship, loaded with slaves, was captured by pirates and recaptured by an American vessel, which brought it and its cargo to Charleston in 1820. A South Carolina court condemned the ship and its cargo to be sold, but the Portuguese consulate intervened, claiming the vessel belonged to Portuguese subjects. Unable to find a ship in Charleston bound for Portugal, its owner hired one Captain Penalta to take the slaves to New Orleans to await a Portuguese voyage. The captain delivered nine of the slaves to New Orleanian Manuel Borges, who allegedly agreed to hire them and send the proceeds to Penalta in Rio de Janeiro. Borges never remitted any money, and twenty years later Penalta sued Borges' estate for $63,634 in wages. Borges' heirs could not plead prescription—here, a means of acquiring title to property through possession as owner—because of *Civil Code* article 3476: "Those who possess for others, and not in their own name, cannot prescribe, whatever may be the time of their possession." The lower court dismissed the suit for lack of evidence, but Judge Martin, presiding in the supreme court, remanded the case to admit evidence ruled inadmissible by the lower court. The plaintiff had attempted to use "parole evidence" to prove that Borges acknowledged that he had received and held the slaves as the agent of Penalta; the lower-court judge had refused to admit the testimony as evidence because Louisiana law prohibited the use of parole evidence to prove title to a slave. Martin stated that the lower-court judge erred in this ruling, as the plaintiff was using parole evidence to establish agency, not title. The ultimate outcome of the case is unknown.[16]

An African-born bondswoman named Isabella attempted to use the law of 1807 to claim her freedom in *Isabella* v. *Pecot* (1847). Her attorney used two legal arguments. The first was that she had been brought to Louisiana from Texas when it was still a part of Mexico, where "by the constitution and laws . . . slavery is not tolerated, but is prohibited." (Mexico had outlawed the institution in 1810 as a way of discouraging American immigration; the Texas slaveowners "freed" their slaves, then

U.S. (10 Wheat.) 312 (1825); United States v. *Mary Ann,* 21 U.S. (8 Wheat.) 380 (1823); and United States v. *Preston,* 28 U.S. (3 Pet.) 57 (1830). For a federal district court case, see United States v. *Ohio,* Federal Case No. 15,914 (1849).

16. Penalta v. Borges' Executor, No. 4266, 18 La. 348 (1841); *Civil Code,* Art. 3476, p. 526.

signed them to contracts as servants for life). The second argument was that if Isabella were indeed a slave, she had been imported illegally into Louisiana, and was therefore free: "that by the laws of the United States no one can hold her in slavery." Witnesses testified that she was an African, "black, fat, chunky," who spoke an African dialect and stuttered when speaking English. At the time of the suit she had a mulatto child, age five. Isabella had been part of a cargo of Africans brought to Texas in the early 1830s—before the Republic of Texas outlawed the African slave trade in 1836. After three or four quick sales, a blacksmith named Gates purchased her in 1834, when she was twelve or thirteen. Two years later Gates brought her to Louisiana: "Gates and his wife went off by land with the Girl [Isabella] towards the United States in 1836, at the time of what is generally called in Texas 'the runaway scrape'—wen [*sic*] General Houston retreated to San Jacinto, the inhabitants who did not join the army generally retreated to the United States—Gates and his family were with the crowd—the last time I saw them, the Girl was with him."

Gates remained in Louisiana and by 1837 was insolvent; he sold Isabella to Milton Johnson to pay some of his debts. Johnson sold her three years later, but the next buyer paid only the first installment of her purchase price ($700) because he feared she was free. Johnson repossessed her for nonpayment and then sold her again to St. Mary Parish planter Peter Pecot, whom she sued for her liberty. The St. Mary District Court ruled against her, and she appealed. The Supreme Court of Louisiana affirmed the judgment. Justice Thomas Slidell reasoned that slavery did exist on Texas plantations in fact, and therefore Isabella was a slave, as she had "failed to establish that she had been unlawfully held to slavery in Texas." The case turned on a technical point in the law of evidence. A witness for Isabella was not allowed to introduce oral evidence that a law forbidding slavery in Mexico existed, and he was unable to produce written evidence of such a law at trial (the judge denied Isabella's request for a continuance so she could send to Mexico City for a copy of the law). The high court apparently found no flaw in this procedure, and as for the question of illegal importation, Slidell held that the Texas refugees who fled to Louisiana were not violating the act of 1807, and furthermore that even if Isabella were illegally imported, there was no provision in federal or state law that would free her: "Slaves unlawfully imported were to remain subject to such regulations as the State legislature might establish and the statutes of Louisiana provided that such slaves should be sold by the sheriff as slaves for life. . . . There is nothing in our State legislation which recognizes the freedom of the slave as acquired by the illegal importation."[17]

Another provision of the act of 1807 was designed to prevent smuggling of foreign slaves from Florida or the West Indies; it limited the interstate coastal slave trade to vessels of over forty tons. An early case decided by the Louisiana Supreme Court dealt with a violation of this law. John B. Dupré attempted to hide two of his slaves aboard the ship *Clara* on an 1809 voyage from New York to New Orleans. When the ship passed Hog Island in New York harbor, a small boat carrying the slave women came alongside the *Clara* and Dupré took them on board, presumably to avoid having their names appear on the passenger list or cargo manifest. The women were hidden in the hold until the ship was safely out to sea. They were permitted on deck until the *Clara* arrived at the mouth of the Mississippi River, when they were again concealed below decks. An unknown informant warned the port authorities of their presence, and the ship was condemned as forfeited to the United States because the *Clara* weighed less than forty tons. The shipowners spent $1,149.75 defending the suit and sent an express (which cost $150) to Washington to obtain a remission of the forfeiture; they sued Dupré in a state court in a tort action to recover their expenses. Judge Martin ruled that since the captain of the *Clara* had allowed Dupré to conceal the slaves, the shipowners could not recover.[18]

17. Isabella, f.w.c., v. Pecot, No. 373, 2 La. Ann. 387 (1847); Campbell, *Empire for Slavery*, 46. Either sympathetic whites or free blacks must have helped Isabella institute her lawsuit, but the record is silent as to how she was able to hire an attorney and afford an appeal. For a discussion of the roles of free blacks in emancipations, see Lawrence J. Kotlikoff and Anton J. Rupert, "The Manumission of Slaves in New Orleans, 1827–1846," *Southern Studies*, XVIX (Summer, 1980), 172–81. See also Carson v. Dwight, 5 Rob. 484 (1843). In a case similar to Isabella's, the slave Lewis sued for his freedom on the grounds that he had been taken to Texas in 1826, when it was a foreign country in which slavery did not exist. In 1832 someone stole him and brought him to Louisiana. When his Texas master found him, he seized him in preparation for taking him back to Texas. Lewis' suit was unsuccessful because the Texas constitution that outlawed slavery (theoretically) did not go into effect until 1827, whereas Lewis was in Texas in 1826. Lewis v. Cartwright, No. 4621, 7 Rob. 186 (La. 1844); Cartwright v. McMillen and Nichols, No. 906, 3 La. Ann. 685 (1848).

18. Davis, *Slavery in the Age of Revolution*, 137; Foster and Giraud v. Dupré, No. 219, 5 Mart. (o.s.) 6 (La. 1817). The *Clara* was almost certainly the same ship mentioned earlier in this chapter, with at least one of the same New York owners, Giraud. Two cases appeared before the Louisiana Supreme Court involving illegal importation of slaves into Mississippi because one of the parties involved was a citizen of Louisiana (the Mississippi state constitution of 1832 prohibited the importation of any slave into Mississippi for sale by a nonresident). One

The Louisiana Supreme Court ruled on many more cases involving the legal domestic slave trade than the illegal foreign importation. Although the cases do not give a complete picture of the interstate and intrastate trade, they suggest the origin and some of the practices peculiar to this commerce.

Most slaves brought into Louisiana through the domestic slave trade came from Virginia. The New Orleans *Bee* stated that 1,011 slaves entered Louisiana in only one month in 1831, and most were from Virginia. Although the court had no reason to interfere with this perfectly legal activity, several cases demonstrate that Virginia's reputation as a slave-exporting state was well deserved in Louisiana. Often legal actions involving the domestic trade were caused by one partner in the Virginia trade failing to split profits as agreed or becoming insolvent and leaving the state. For example, in *Spraggins* v. *White* (1825), two men sold seventy-three Virginia slaves in Louisiana for $41,237. Both claimed the proceeds were not divided fairly, and they sued each other. Judge Alexander Porter decided that two unsold slaves should be disposed of and the purchase price divided equally between the claimants. In *Gourjon* v. *Cucullu* (1832), ninety-four Virginia slaves were brought to Louisiana in 1831; within three months sixty-one had been sold for $22,175. Other cases involved slave traders who traveled to Virginia annually to purchase slaves, transported them to Louisiana, and sold them in the state.[19]

In some instances slaves from Virginia were ill, injured, diseased, or "bad"; possibly they were sold to protect the owner's investment, the owner knowing they would be resold in an area where no one was familiar with their vices of body or character. In these instances the court used Louisiana's laws of redhibition to protect Louisiana purchasers from unscrupulous and dishonest slave dealers. For example, in *Nelson* v. *Lilliard* (1840), the plaintiff purchased five Virginia slaves for $5,000. Within a short time he claimed that all were worthless and sued for a

---

was Cotton v. Brien, No. 1029, 6 Rob. 115 (La. 1843); see also Charles S. Sydnor, *Slavery in Mississippi* (New York, 1933), 161–65. The other was fought to the United States Supreme Court: Groves and Graham v. Slaughter, 15 Pet. 449 (1841).

19. New Orleans *Bee,* November 18, 1831; Spraggins v. White, No. 1169, 3 Mart. (N.S.) 661 (La. 1825); Gourjon v. Cucullu, No. 2324, 4 La. 115 (1832); Brinigar v. Griffin, No. 302, 2 La. Ann. 154 (1847); Sullivan v. Williams, No. 23, 2 La. Ann. 876 (1847); Bank of Charleston v. Hagan, No. 464, 2 La. Ann. 999 (1847). In this last case John Hagan, a New Orleans slave dealer, traveled annually to Virginia to buy slaves, then to Charleston for the same purpose, then to New Orleans to sell them.

rescission of the sale. Nelson described them as Willis, an "idiot" ($800); Cynthia, with an injured hip, who died soon after sale ($1,000), Solomon, club-footed and epileptic, who also soon died ($1,000); Frank, "diseased" ($1,200); and Moses, consumptive ($1,000). The vendor admitted that "the slaves sold were an old, no account set of negroes, and if he had known what kind they were, they never should have come out from Virginia." Judge Edward Simon rescinded three of the five sales (Nelson had purchased two of the slaves with no guarantee). Simon rescinded the sale of another Virginia slave in 1840 because he was a habitual runaway, a thief, a drunkard, and all in all "a bad negro."[20]

Two years later, in *Palmer* v. *Taylor,* the same slave traders as in the preceding case sold a Virginia slave named Jim to the East Feliciana Parish planter Archibald D. Palmer. This case shows the risk involved in purchasing slaves unaccustomed to the climate of Louisiana. Jim was raised by Captain George Duff in Fauquier County, Virginia, and was described by his former owner as being five feet ten inches tall, "stoutly formed," and a "well looking field hand." When Jim was eighteen years old Duff sold him to J. M. Saunders, a slave trader, who sold him to Humphrey and J. W. Taylor, Saunders' Louisiana partners in trade. The Taylor brothers marched Jim and a group of Virginia slaves twenty-five miles a day until they reached Louisiana. Witnesses testified that Jim ate well on the journey and was so healthy he was able to dance half the night, go to bed, and be ready to march the next day. Jim's owner may have sold him because he was difficult to manage. Witnesses testified that his back was scarred by old whippings and that he was "considered a great rascal in the neighborhood and was once or twice punished for

20. Nelson v. Lilliard, No. 800, 16 La. 336 (1840); Smith v. Taylor, No. 5755, 10 Rob. 133 (La. 1844). Unscrupulous whites sometimes contributed to increasing the criminal population among Louisiana slaves for profit. William H. Williams was convicted of importing slave criminals into the state from Virginia. Apparently he purchased twenty-four slaves who had been sentenced to death for felony offenses, including arson, murder, poisoning, rape, and insurrection. Despite the seriousness of the crimes the governor of Virginia was willing to grant the slaves reprieves if a buyer could be found to transport them out of the United States. Williams agreed but then brought them to New Orleans, allegedly to sell them. He was found guilty and sentenced to be fined $500 for each offense ($12,000 in all) and jailed until the fine was paid. The case came before the Louisiana Supreme Court twice, in 1842 and 1844, and both times the judgment was affirmed. Ironically, the court itself contributed to the state's criminal slave population: the slaves were sold in Louisiana, with half the proceeds going to the state and the other half to the informer. State v. Williams, No. 4671, 7 Rob. 252 (La. 1842, 1844).

stealing pigs and fowls." Jim died in his new master's fields five months after the sale from a "chronic inflammation of the stomach and bowels"—possibly, a physician speculated, because he was unaccustomed to the Louisiana climate and Mississippi River water. Palmer sued to cancel the sale, but the Taylors were able to prove that Palmer failed to provide medical care for Jim, and because of his neglect Chief Judge Martin refused to void the sale: "the slave died in the field, and it does not appear that . . . he had received the attention and care due to a sick slave."[21]

Like other merchants, operators in the interstate slave trade often insured their shipments, and predictably, the Louisiana Supreme Court decided several matters involving insurance on the lives of slaves. Thomas McCargo, a slave dealer, purchased $20,800 in insurance for 26 of the 135 slaves shipped from Norfolk, Virginia, on the brig *Creole,* destined for New Orleans in 1841. The slaves mutinied, took over the ship, and sailed to Nassau, and were totally lost to their owners. In *McCargo* v. *Merchants Insurance Co.* (1845), McCargo sued the insurer for $20,800 and won in the lower court. However, the insurance policy had excepted insurrection as a cause of recovery, and the Supreme Court of Louisiana reversed the judgment. Despite this loss, McCargo was able to recover $14,400 on another policy from a different insurer. The court heard five similar cases pertaining to the *Creole* rebellion immediately following the McCargo case; all but one were won by the insurance companies.[22]

21. Palmer v. Taylor, No. 4755, 1 Rob. 412 (La. 1842). For a similar case, see Miller v. Coffman, No. 1618, 7 Mart. (N.S.) 556 (La. 1829). For other cases pertaining to slave shipments from Virginia, see Armistead v. Bowden, No. 2416, 5 La. 263 (1833), and Mulhollan v. Eaton, No. 3118, 11 La. 291 (1837). William H. Williams was convicted for bringing twenty-four Virginia slave criminals into Louisiana; State v. Williams, No. 4671, 7 Rob. 252 (1844). For an example of a slave shipment from Mississippi, see Offutt v. Morancy, No. 1108, 12 Rob. 92 (La. 1845). According to Sydnor, *Slavery in Mississippi,* 152, Warren Offutt was a slave trader in Mississippi who claimed he sold $6,500 in bondsmen for tax purposes in 1833. For cases involving slaves shipped from Georgia, Kentucky, and Tennessee (respectively) for sale in Louisiana, see Chew v. Keene, No. 2316, 4 La. 144 (1832); Rudy v. Harding, No. 1074, 6 Rob. 70 (La. 1843); and Back v. Meeks, No. 1941, 1 La. 309 (1830).

22. Sydnor, *Slavery in Mississippi,* 152; McCargo v. New Orleans Insurance Co., No. 5146, 10 Rob. 202 (La. 1845); McCargo v. Merchants Insurance Co., No. 5123, 10 Rob. 334 (La. 1845); Andrews v. Ocean Insurance Co., and Lockett v. Fireman's Insurance Co. (consolidated cases), 10 Rob. 332 (La. 1845); Hagan v. Ocean Insurance Co., 10 Rob. 333 (La. 1845); Johnson v. Ocean Insurance Co., No. 5123, 10 Rob. 334 (La. 1845); Lockett v. Merchants Insurance Co., No. 5164, 10 Rob. 339 (La. 1845); Howard Jones, "The Peculiar Institution and National Honor: The Case of the *Creole* Slave Revolt," *Civil War History,* XXI

In *Hunter, Murphy, and Talbot* v. *General Mutual Insurance Company of New York* (1856), Virginia slave dealers shipped fourteen slaves by sea from Richmond to New Orleans, insuring the group for $7,075 for loss in the event of shipwreck or drowning. The vessel became stranded in the Bahamas, and a portion of the nonhuman cargo had to be jettisoned to save the crew and the slaves. The slave dealers sued the insurance company to recover what they were obliged to pay as their assessment of the value of the lost cargo. The Louisiana Supreme Court affirmed the judgment of the lower court that ordered the insurance company to reimburse the slave traders, reasoning that the insurers actually benefited from the jettison because the slaves were saved.[23]

A complicating factor for interstate slave traders was an 1829 Louisiana law that prohibited a slave child under the age of ten from being brought into the state unaccompanied by his or her mother. This statute was consistent with provisions in the *Code Noir* and the *Black Code* prohibiting the sale of mothers and children under ten years of age apart from each other. Slave traders claiming that an unaccompanied young child was an orphan were required to furnish proof that the child's mother was dead. In all trials for violations of this statute, the law required that the burden of proof that the child was an orphan was to fall on the accused. Convicted violators of this act were to be fined no less than $1,000 and no more than $2,000, and were also to be jailed for no less than six months and no more than one year. This statute markedly lowered the number of sales in Louisiana of out-of-state, unaccompanied young slave children. Immediately before passage of this law, 13.5 per-

(March, 1975), 28–50. For an unrelated case in which a master attempted to collect $500 life insurance on his slave described as a "climate risk" (unacclimated), who died of "inflammation of the intestines and ulceration," see Murphy v. Mutual Benefit Life and Fire Insurance Co., No. 2244, 6 La. Ann. 518 (1851). For a similar case in which the deceased slave was washed overboard from a steamboat in a storm on the Mississippi River, see Summers v. United States Insurance Co., No. 5423, 13 La. Ann. 504 (1858).

23. Hunter, Murphy, and Talbot v. General Mutual Insurance Company, No. 3122, 11 La. Ann. 139 (1856). Slaves were usually insured for two-thirds or three-fourths of their value; insurance companies feared that if bondsmen were insured for full value, they might be as valuable dead as alive to their masters. Todd L. Savitt, "Slave Life Insurance in Virginia and North Carolina," *Journal of Southern History,* XLIII (November, 1977), 587–88. See also Eugene D. Genovese, "The Medical and Insurance Costs of Slaveholding in the Cotton Belt," *Journal of Negro History,* XLV (July, 1960), 141–55; and Robert S. Starobin, *Industrial Slavery in the Old South* (New York, 1970), 71–74, 254–55.

cent of the slaves sent from Virginia to New Orleans were under the age of ten years. Immediately following passage of the act, shipments from Virginia of slave children under ten declined to 3.7 percent, and none of these were unaccompanied by their mothers.[24]

As for intrastate, rather than interstate, slave transactions, the Louisiana Supreme Court heard several appeals during the antebellum period concerning violations of the law against selling children under ten away from their mothers. This unique feature of Louisiana slave law did not disappear as the Civil War approached; like redhibition, it never became Americanized. In *Nouret* v. *Bollinger* (1860), a Mr. Balletin gave the seventeen-year-old slave Ellen Shockley and her child, Susan, to a Mrs. Bollinger to defraud Balletin's creditors. Bollinger sold the mother for $700 in 1850 but retained the three-year-old child. The new owner sued for possession of Susan under the law prohibiting separation of slave mothers and children under ten. However, by the time the case reached the Louisiana Supreme Court, Susan had attained that age. In the dictum, Chief Justice Edwin Merrick stated that possibly the sale could have been annulled if legal action had been taken sooner, but now that the child was ten, it was "idle" to consider it.[25]

In *Kellar* v. *Fink and Baos, f.w.c.* (1848) the court ruled that selling a five-year-old girl away from her mother was not a violation of the law because of the unusual circumstances of the case. Nathan Nichols owned the slave woman Aimée and her daughter, Lucinda, who had been born in 1837 or 1838. In 1841 Aimée ran away to Illinois, and then to Canada. Nichols never expected to recover her when he sold Lucinda to a free woman of color named Emily Baos. The act of sale described the child as the "orphan" child of Aimée, who had fled to Canada. However, Nichols somehow recovered Aimée and subsequently sold her in 1843 at a sheriff's sale when he became insolvent. Her purchaser, Bedilia G. Kellar, sued Baos for possession of the child on the grounds that since children under ten could not be sold away from their mother, "the child is the accessory of the mother, and becomes the property of any pur-

24. *Black Code,* Secs. 9, 8, p. 154; Schafer, "New Orleans Slavery in 1850 as Seen in Advertisements," 37; Donald M. Sweig, "Reassessing the Human Dimension of the Interstate Slave Trade," *Prologue,* XII (Spring, 1980), 11–14; Stampp, *Peculiar Institution,* 252–53; "An Act Relative to the Introduction of Slaves in this State . . . ," Act of February 2, 1829, *Louisiana Acts, 1829,* Secs. 15–16, p. 48.

25. Nouret v. Bollinger, No. 6313, 15 La. Ann. 293 (1860).

chaser of the latter." Testimony showed that Nichols never expected to recover the mother and had not intended to break the law when he sold the child. Indeed, he seems to have acted in the interest of the child, as he selected her purchaser because "the person to whom she was sold was a good mistress and took good care of her." Chief Justice George Eustis affirmed the judgment of the lower court that allowed Baos to retain the child: "We are at a loss to conceive what right of property the plaintiff [Kellar] ever acquired in the subject of this suit."[26]

Cases reflecting obedience to the nonseparation law appeared before the Louisiana Supreme Court more often than cases reflecting violation of it. William Underwood sold the slave Peggy in 1848 for $800 to Firmin Lacapère. Her mulatto infant, William, was not listed in the act of sale but went with her "because of his tender age." In *Underwood* v. *Lacapère* (1859), Underwood's executor sued Lacapère for possession of William, now eleven. Justice Alexander Buchanan ruled that William had been "of no appreciable value" at the time of the sale and that he had accompanied his mother because of the law prohibiting their separation: "[He] was necessarily included in the conveyance, however, because [under] the humane provision of our law [it] is imperative, that the slave mother cannot be sold separately from her offspring of tender age." The court reasoned that since Lacapère had paid no price for William, Underwood's estate owned him, and since he was now older than ten, could reclaim him. In *Terrebonne* v. *Walsh* (1852), Justice Slidell ruled that the slave child Fanny should stay with her mother, Polly, until she attained the age of ten, when she should be returned to her owner.[27]

In two instances, slaves sold with the right of redemption at a later date gave birth to children before the original owner repurchased them, and controversy developed over possession of these children. In both cases the Supreme Court of Louisiana ruled that the young children were the property of whoever owned the mothers. Therefore, if the former owner redeemed the mother, he or she became the owner of the child as well. In another instance the high court ruled that offspring of a slave mother born while she was mortgaged were born subject to the same mortgage. Although some aspects of slave law in Louisiana were brutal,

26. Kellar v. Fink and Baos, f.w.c., No. 598, 3 La. Ann. 17 (1848). Baos is mistakenly reported as Bowyer.

27. Underwood v. Lacapère, No. 5348, 14 La. Ann. 276 (1859); Terrebonne v. Walsh, No. 2460, 7 La. Ann. 61 (1852).

the law and the courts did attempt to keep slave mothers and their young children together, an effort not legally sanctioned in other slave states.[28]

Insolvency proceedings and succession (estate) settlements swelled the number of slave sales within Louisiana. Often insolvency or death necessitated the sale of large communities of slaves. From an examination of cases heard by the Louisiana Supreme Court it is impossible to ascertain whether most of these large groups of slaves were sold as whole lots, small units, or individually, since most of the evidence is found in inventories or lists of slaves for sale, and not records of purchases. One case involved an entire plantation sold as a unit—land, slaves, livestock, tools, and cotton gin.[29]

In one instance a Carroll Parish planter's last-minute effort to keep his slave community in the neighborhood failed. *Jackson and Van Pelt* v. *Moore* (1859) involved a slaveowner, Robert A. Armstrong, who had executed a will in 1857, leaving everything he owned, including his plantation and slaves, to his cousin Minerva Armstrong of Memphis. In 1858 he contracted pneumonia and, fearing he would die, called in his slaves to tell them good-bye and inform them of the terms of his will. The slaves one and all begged him to change the testament to ensure that they would be sold locally, and only the proceeds sent to Armstrong's cousin. They stated "that they had been in the Swamps a good while and wished to stay." One witness testified that Armstrong "was considered a wild young man," but he was apparently a considerate master. Testimony established that he "thought a great deal of his negroes and at the time he made the will, would have made any kind of sacrifice to have pleased his negroes." Samuel W. Moore, Armstrong's neighbor and friend, agreed to purchase the slaves as a unit, and Armstrong changed his will on his deathbed to allow the sale to Moore, who was ordered to send the proceeds to Minerva Armstrong. By the time the

28. Patterson v. Bonner, No. 341, 14 La. 214 (1839); Boner v. Mahle, No. 86, 3 La. Ann. 600 (1848); Solibellas v. Consolidated Association, 11 La. Ann. 682 (1856). For examples of cases where mothers and children are listed as being sold together, see Bruneau v. Michon, Unreported Louisiana Supreme Court Case No. 514 (1821); Heirs of Beale v. Walden, No. 5227, 11 Rob. 67 (La. 1845); Succession of Tete v. Blanchard, Eimer, and Co., No. 2050, 7 La. Ann. 95 (1852); and Neasom v. D'Armond, No. 5624, 13 La. Ann. 294 (1858).

29. Oldham v. Groghan, No. 1133, 3 Mart. (N.S.) 517 (La. 1825). In another case an entire slave community was hired as a unit: Philips v. Fulton's Heirs, No. 83, 7 Mart. (O.S.) 241 (La. 1819).

new will was prepared, Armstrong was delirious and too weak to sign it, although testimony proved that he was lucid when it was read to him and that he stated that it reflected his wishes. After his death, his cousin's agents successfully sued Moore, the executor, to have the deathbed testament declared void on the grounds that Armstrong was "crazy with pneumonia" and the document was unsigned. The Carroll Parish District Court found the 1858 will to be void, and the Supreme Court of Louisiana affirmed the decision on both grounds. In the dictum, Justice Thomas Land commented: "The cause which hinders a testator from signing his name . . . must be a physical cause, and not mental, such as delirium or insanity."[30]

One of the most remarkable and persistent attempts to maintain slave communities intact can be seen in a series of appeals heard by the Louisiana Supreme Court involving the will of the well-known Pointe Coupée planter and philanthropist Julien Poydras. One of the stipulations in his will was that the slaves on his several plantations were to be kept together and not sold away from their respective plantations, and that purchasers of his plantations must agree to honor his wishes. Those who bought Poydras' plantations also had to promise to free the slaves twenty-five years from the date of sale. Poydras died in 1824, and his plantations were sold to different buyers. Although the purchasers agreed to abide by the will, several sales of individual slaves took place between Poydras' death and the Civil War. Poydras had died childless, but his nephew and heir, Benjamin Poydras DeLaLande, styling himself "protector of the slaves," went to court repeatedly to force rescission of these sales and return of the slaves to their communities. In one case the state supreme court commented that Poydras' will was "impracticable and contrary to the spirit of our institutions"; even so, the court did not allow the slaves to be sold away from the land. The justices admitted that "the terms and conditions of the will . . . [are] destructive of the absolute power which sound policy and the laws of the land require the master should exercise over his slaves." However, the court noted that DeLaLande had "the undoubted right to interpose and prevent a violation of the testator's intentions as expressed in his will, and to demand a specific performance of the conditions of the sale made in conformity to it." The court reasoned that the value of the succession had been signifi-

30. Jackson and Van Pelt v. Moore, No. 6062, 14 La. Ann. 213 (1859).

cantly diminished by the "very onerous and burdensome conditions . . . annexed." As a result, DeLaLande had the right "to preserve and protect the intention of the testator and the objects of his benevolence, when by the very fact of the diminution of price, at the sale of his [Poydras'] succession, . . . [DeLaLande] parted with a very valuable consideration." The court never cited *Civil Code* article 1506, which stated, "In all dispositions . . . impossible conditions, those which are contrary to the law or to morals, are reputed not written," meaning that they were null and void. Neither the attorneys, the lower-court judges, nor the judges and justices of the Supreme Court of Louisiana mentioned the common-law rule against perpetuity. If there were such considerations, they do not appear in the record.[31]

Slave families and entire communities of slaves were often split as a result of the insolvency of their owners. The large number of cases pertaining to bondservants being sold as a result of the poor financial management of their owners is evidence that despite the fact that slaves were supposed to be immovable property under Louisiana law, they were in fact an asset that could be converted to cash. By the late antebellum period, at least some slaveowners feared that the practice of seizing slaves for debt was discouraging some poorer Louisianians from becoming slaveholders. In 1856 the New Orleans *Daily True Delta* suggested that the state legislature create "a species of homestead in slave property" that would protect property in slaves from seizure should the owner fall into debt. It was hoped that this practice would lead to a wider distribution of slave property by allowing poorer slaveowners to feel secure in their ownership. The resulting expansion of the slavehold-

31. Poydras v. Mourain, Unreported Louisiana Supreme Court Case No. 1599 (1829) and No. 2871, 9 La. 492 (1836); Poydras v. Taylor, No. 2873, 9 La. 488 (1836) and No. 3204, 3254, 18 La. 17 (1841); DeLaLande v. Bormeau, No. 4197, 1 Rob. 315 (La. 1842); Succession of DeLaLande, Unreported Louisiana Supreme Court Case No. 3197 (1854); *Civil Code,* Art. 1506, p. 229. A perpetuity is any limitation that may take away or suspend the power of alienation of property for a period beyond life or lives being and twenty-one years thereafter. For Poydras' accomplishments, see Mary F. P. Russell. "The Life of Julien Poydras" (M.A. thesis, Louisiana State University, 1940). DeLaLande was born in Nantes, France, in 1778. He arrived in Louisiana in 1804 after being captured by the Spanish en route. He became a citizen of the United States in 1812 and a justice of the peace in Pointe Coupée Parish in 1813. He owned several plantations along the Mississippi River and many slaves. He visited his homeland several times during his life and in 1835 married a French woman (Cécile Richard de la Roulière of Nantes) who never came to Louisiana. He had three children, born in 1837, 1839, and 1844. He died in France in 1851.

ing class, the *Delta* argued, would "enlarge and diffuse the interest of the whites in Negro slavery."[32]

The Louisiana *Code of Practice* stipulated that slaves seized for debt could be "appraised either by the head or by families" and "sold together, or separately, to the best advantage of the debtor, as he may direct." More than likely, selling them separately would have yielded a higher price. Separation must have been common in antebellum Louisiana, judging from the number of cases that the state's highest court heard involving the seizure and sale of slaves for the failure of their owners to prudently manage their financial affairs. In all debt-seizure cases, slaves who were involved suffered to some extent, even if a sale never occurred. As soon as a creditor filed such a suit, the court in which the creditor filed issued an order of sequestration for the slave or slaves involved, which meant imprisonment in the parish jail pending the outcome of the suit. The purpose of sequestration was to prevent debtors from leaving the state with their property. Legal delays to gather testimony and to suit the convenience of the court and attorneys could often extend this period of incarceration for many months. In one instance, eleven slaves were kept in the Ascension Parish jail for over a year. Cases appealed to the state supreme court usually required a period of two years or more between the date of filing of the original lawsuit and the final decision. Of course, this practice was also a further hardship to the debtor, as he would be less able to meet his obligations if deprived of the services of his slaves.[33]

In *Cox* v. *Myers* (1849), the Louisiana Supreme Court found that as slaves were not movable property, they could not be sequestered as security for their masters' rental obligations. David Cox seized Jim, a slave

32. *Black Code,* Sec. 10, p. 154; New Orleans *Daily True Delta* quoted in Thomas D. Morris, "'As If the Injury Was Effected by the Natural Elements of Air, or Fire': Slave Wrongs and the Liability of Masters," *Law and Society Review,* XVI (1981–82), 597. Economic security for slaveholders could be tenuous; see James Oakes, *The Ruling Race: A History of American Slaveholders* (New York, 1982), 123–26.

33. *Code of Practice* (1824), 228; Parkison v. Boyle, No. 5463, 7 Rob. 82 (La. 1844). In this case the sheriff of Ascension Parish sued the owner of eleven slaves for $1,157.01 (about thirty cents per slave per day) for their board while they were sequestered for about one year in the parish prison awaiting the outcome of a debt-seizure lawsuit. One witness stated that thirty cents a day was "unreasonable for negroes" because he was able to board white men for "two bits" a day. Another testified that "one bit" a week for corn and "two bits" for meat was sufficient to maintain a slave. The Ascension Parish jury awarded the sheriff $420 (about ten cents per day per slave), probably a rather accurate estimate of the expense of feeding a slave.

belonging to John Myers, and had him jailed because Myers had failed to pay Cox $307 for rent of land and slaves. The twenty-two-year-old slave died in the unheated jail, and Myers countersued, claiming the seizure illegal and demanding $1,000 for the value of the slave and $200 damage. Justice Pierre Rost ruled that although Cox proved his claim, he was liable for the value of the slave because only movable property could be legally seized in a provisional seizure by a lessor, and slaves were immovables. Citing *Civil Code* article 2675, Rost ruled: "Slaves are not subject to provisional seizure to secure the rent of the premises on which they are found, even when the tenant has no other property. The right of the lessor can only be exercised on the movable effects found on the leased premises. . . . The seizure of the slave in this case was an illegal act." As the slave died in "a damp and unhealthy jail" as a result of the illegal seizure, Myers was entitled to compensation for the slave's value. The Louisiana Supreme Court affirmed the judgment of the lower court awarding Myers $148 (the adjudged value of the slave—$455—minus the $307 Myers owed Cox).[34]

The same year, in *Gaulden* v. *McPhaul,* the supreme court ruled a seizure for debt illegal not because the slaves involved were immovable

34. *Civil Code,* Art. 461, p. 72; Cox v. Myers, No. 1234, 4 La. Ann. 144 (1849); *Civil Code,* Art. 2675, pp. 411–12. Although slaves could not be sequestered as security, as immovables they could be mortgaged: For other seizure-debt-sale cases, see Syndics of Dussuau, f.m.c., v. Bredaux, No. 155, 4 Mart. (o.s.) 450 (La. 1816); Pierce v. Curtis, No. 296, 6 Mart. (o.s.) 418 (La. 1819); Knight v. Hall, No. 417, 7 Mart. (o.s.) 410 (La. 1820); Stewart v. His Creditors, Unreported Louisiana Supreme Court Case (1820); Sterling v. Fusilier, No. 420, 7 Mart. (o.s.) 442 (La. 1820); Camfranc v. Dufour, No. 453, 8 Mart. (o.s.) 144 (La. 1820), and No. 401, 11 Mart. (o.s.) 607 (La. 1822); Montegut v. Dauphin, No. 726, 1 Mart. (n.s.) 258 (La. 1823); Oldham v. Polk, No. 1490, 6 Mart. (n.s.) 465 (La. 1828); Saul v. Creditors, No. 166B, 7 Mart. (n.s.) 425 (La. 1829); Miles v. Oden, 8 Mart. (n.s.) 214 (La. 1829); Armistead v. Bowden, No. 2416, 5 La. 263 (1833); Offut v. Hendsley, 9 La. 1 (1835); Thompson v. Thompson's Heirs, 11 La. 324 (1837); Benoit v. Broussard, 19 La. 387 (1841); Parkison v. Boyle, No. 5463, 7 Rob. 82 (La. 1844); Drummond v. Commissioners of the Clinton and Port Hudson Railroad, No. 5495, 7 Rob. 234 (La. 1844); St. Martin v. Creditors, Unreported Louisiana Supreme Court Case No. 3666, 3722 (1844); Fink and Baume v. Martin, No. 5344, 8 Rob. 256 (La. 1844); Bank of Orleans v. Hodge, No. 5535, 8 Rob. 450 (La. 1844); McFarlane v. Richardson, No. 5217, 11 Rob. 13 (La. 1845); Robinett v. Compton, No. 331, 2 La. Ann. 846, 861 (1847); Palmer v. Moore, No. 565, 3 La. Ann. 208 (1848); Brown v. Glathary, No. 1256, 4 La. Ann. 124 (1849); Macon v. Willson, No. 3010, 9 La. Ann. 178 (1854); Cochran v. Walker, No. 3336, 10 La. Ann. 431 (1855); McAlpin v. Jones, No. 398, 10 La. Ann. 552 (1855); Whann v. Hufty, No. 4982, 12 La. Ann. 280 (1857); Walker v. Sanchez, No. 4485, 13 La. Ann. 505 (1858); Smith v. Taylor, 14 La. Ann. 663 (1859); and Brainard v. Sheriff, 15 La. Ann. 489 (1860).

property, but because the creditor took the law into his own hands. Matthew G. Gaulden alleged that his creditor, Angus McPhaul, with a band of armed men, had entered his East Baton Rouge Parish woodyard and "without any justification and with force and violence" attempted to seize a number of Gaulden's slaves. Five slaves escaped and made their way back to Gaulden's home, thirty miles across the Mississippi state line. Gaulden claimed that on the way "a valuable and favorite negro man raised by your petitioner" was so terrified "by the rude and violent trespass" of McPhaul that he died of fright. Gaulden sued McPhaul for $1,200, the value of the deceased slave, and $600 for loss of wages and damages. McPhaul claimed that Gaulden owed him a large sum of money in Mississippi and had moved the slaves from that state to Louisiana to put them out of McPhaul's reach. A lower-court jury awarded Gaulden $800, but on appeal the supreme court lowered the amount to $100. Chief Justice Eustis, writing for the court, held that no proof existed to establish any violence on the part of McPhaul, and furthermore, that there was no evidence that the deceased slave's flight caused his death, since he had always been healthy and was accustomed to labor. The $100 award was a combination of recompense to Gaulden for the disturbance of his slaves' labor at the woodyard and a penalty for McPhaul's taking the law into his own hands: "No court in Louisiana would permit the defendant to take the slaves . . . until after the default should have been established."[35]

Slaves could be and often were converted into cash to satisfy debts of their owners, adding to the intrastate slave trade. Selling slaves made more economic sense than selling off a piece of the slaveholder's land. If financial good times returned, one could always purchase another slave, but reacquiring contiguous land could be more difficult. If hope of financial equilibrium was dim, the slaveowner might declare insolvency, necessitating the sale of all of his slaves.[36]

In antebellum Louisiana slaves, as property, were also used as collateral to be mortgaged against a debt and sold when their masters fell into financial difficulties. Mortgage foreclosures also contributed to the slave trade within Louisiana. By allowing slaves to be mortgaged, Louisiana law once again placed more emphasis on them as property than as per-

35. Gaulden v. McPhaul, No. 1181, 4 La. Ann. 79 (1849).

36. *Civil Code,* Arts. 1980–89, pp. 308–309.

sons. Two cases that were heard by the Supreme Court of Louisiana are examples of this type of legal action. In *Bank of Louisiana* v. *Stansbury* (1835), W. S. Stansbury borrowed $8,000 from the Bank of Louisiana in 1833. As collateral he listed his Ascension Parish sugar plantation, situated on the west bank of the Mississippi River, and fourteen slave men, women, and children, ranging in age from thirty-five to one year. When Stansbury failed to repay the loan, the bank foreclosed and the court ordered the sheriff to proceed with the sale of the plantation and slaves.[37]

The Civil War interrupted another slave mortgage case, *Déjean* v. *Arnaud* (1873). In 1862 Honoré Déjean received a judgment in his favor to have the sheriff sell a slave belonging to Jacques Arnaud in order to satisfy a mortgage. In the confusion of the war the sale never took place, and the slave became free in the general emancipation following the South's surrender. Undaunted by this development, Déjean sued Arnaud eight years after hostilities ended to enforce the mortgage. The Louisiana Supreme Court dismissed his suit, ruling that since slavery no longer existed, debts secured by slaves could not be honored.[38]

In a number of instances, financially troubled slaveowners pretended to sell their bondservants to a friend or relative to avoid losing them to

37. Bank of Louisiana v. Stansbury, No. 2694, 8 La. 257 (1835). In another instance a man mortgaged slaves belonging to his wife. General William Youngblood came to Louisiana from South Carolina in 1829 with his wife, children, and twenty-three slaves and became a sugar planter. In 1830 he mortgaged his slaves for a loan of an unspecified amount of money. Five years later he defaulted on the loan and his creditor had the slaves seized and sold for the debt. Youngblood's wife was able to prove that the slaves were her separate property and therefore could not be mortgaged or sold to satisfy her husband's financial obligations. Youngblood v. Flagg, McBurney v. Flagg, 11 La. 333 (1837).

38. Déjean v. Arnaud, No. 601, 25 La. Ann. 521 (1873). In one early slave mortgage case, four skilled bondsmen and one bondswoman (soap manufacturers and turpentine distillers) were at issue: Baron v. Phelan, No. 122, 4 Mart. (O.S.) 88 (La. 1816). For other cases involving mortgaged bondsmen, see Piernas v. Blanque's Syndic, No. 309, 6 Mart. (O.S.) 577 (La. 1819); Stafford v. Stafford, No. 209, 1 Mart. (N.S.) 648 (La. 1823); Kimball v. Kimball, Unreported Louisiana Supreme Court Case No. 242 [*ca.* 1830–37]; Cariau v. Reiffel, No. 1022, 2 Mart. (N.S.) 619 (La. 1824); Munday v. Wilson, No. 11, 4 La. 338 (1832), Wilson v. Munday, No. 40, 5 La. 483 (1833); Coquet v. His Creditors, No. 2322, 4 La. 198 (1832); Offutt v. Hendsley, 9 La. 1 (1835); Baker v. Directors of Bank of Louisiana, No. 6071, 2 La. Ann. 371 (1847); Waters v. Grayson, No. 82, 3 La. Ann. 595 (1848); Johnson v. Bloodworth, 12 La. Ann. 699 (1857); Bisland v. Provosty, No. 6030, 14 La. Ann. 169 (1859); and Levy v. Petrovic, Unreported Louisiana Supreme Court Case No. 6031 (1859). The question of whether debts for slaves purchased before the Civil War were valid after slavery ended was a major issue after the war. The Supreme Court of Louisiana handled dozens of cases involving this issue after 1865. See chap. 11.

creditors. *Wilson* v. *Green* (1851) involved the validity of the sale of the slave David, age twenty-one, appraised for $650. David's master, Albert Toby, had died of yellow fever in 1829 at the age of twenty-nine, without a will or heirs. Before he died Toby had placed David in the care of a free black barber in New Orleans named Richard Green; David was to learn barbering, but the move was also intended to protect him from Toby's creditors. After Toby's death one of his lenders, J. C. Wilson, sued Green for possession of David. Green produced a bill of sale for the bondsman for $1,000, but testimony proved that Green had faked it in order to hold on to the slave. A witness testified that Green had stated that "if Toby died, he would retain the boy as his own as he had often been cheated by white persons." Testimony also established that Toby had told Green to free David when Toby died, and a witness had overheard Green telling the young slave "to go and do the best he could for himself" after Toby's death. The lower court awarded David to Toby's creditor, and Green appealed. Green died before the Louisiana Supreme Court could hear the case, and no one pursued the appeal. Presumably the creditor sold David for Toby's debts.[39]

A series of cases involving New Orleans slave dealer Theophilus Freeman dealt with simulated sales and donations intended to defraud creditors. Freeman was an unscrupulous businessman who falsified slave ages, sold young children away from their masters, and whipped and kicked bondsmen in his slave pen. It was Freeman who brought Solomon Northup, later famous for his memoir *Twelve Years a Slave,* from Washington, D.C., and sold him to an Avoyelles Parish planter. Freeman lived with his ex-slave and mistress, a mulatto laundress named Sarah Conner, who had purchased her freedom from him in 1841 for $700. Just after her emancipation Freeman's finances became shaky, and he transferred most of his assets to her to avoid having them seized by his creditors. He was arrested several times in 1845 because authorities feared he would flee the state. Litigation concerning Freeman's fraudulent sales, secret donations, and transactions in Conner's name continued until 1861, when it was interrupted by the Civil War, during which Freeman left New Orleans.[40]

39. Wilson v. Green, f.m.c., Unreported Louisiana Supreme Court Case No. 2372 [filed 1851].

40. Solomon Northup, *Twelve Years a Slave,* ed. Sue Eakin and Joseph Logsdon (Baton Rouge, 1968), 49–51; *Civil Code,* Art. 190, p. 29; Union Bank of Maryland v. Freeman, No. 4938, 3 Rob. 485 (La. 1843); Mielkie v. Freeman, No. 5238, 5 Rob. 524 (La. 1843); Lambeth

Some slaveowners fled the state with their bondservants rather than have them seized and sold for the master's unmet financial obligations. The primary reason for sequestering the slaves of a master unable to pay his debts was the fear that the debtor would remove them from the state. Suspicions that a slaveowner might "abscond" to sell his slaves in another state were well founded; absconding debtors regularly—if illegally—contributed to the interstate slave trade. The Louisiana Supreme Court heard several such cases. For example, in *Wilkins* v. *Bobo* (1858), when the sheriff of Caddo Parish attempted to seize Edy, valued at over $800, for her owner's debts, her master threatened the official and his deputies with physical violence, and they desisted. Immediately thereafter the debtor took the slave out of the state and sold her, probably in Texas.[41]

In *Sandridge* v. *Jones* (1847), a sheriff who went to a plantation to seize the bondservants of a debtor let the plantation owner persuade him to allow the slaves to sleep in their cabins that night, and not take them away until the next morning. The sheriff failed to post a guard; the plantation was six or eight miles from Texas, and the debtor lived in that state. The next morning the slaves were missing. The lower court found the sheriff negligent and ordered him to reimburse the creditor for his

and Thompson v. Freeman, Unreported Louisiana Supreme Court Case No. 5588 (1845); Freeman v. Profilet, Unreported Louisiana Supreme Court Case No. 5829 (1845); Romer v. Woods, No. 1846, 6 La. Ann. 29 (1851); Freeman v. His Creditors, No. 948, 3 La. Ann. 669 (1848); Bank of Kentucky v. Conner, No. 1315, 4 La. Ann. 365 (1849); Dunbar v. Conner, Unreported Louisiana Supreme Court Case No. 1700 (1850, 1851); Freeman v. His Creditors, No. 6473, 15 La. Ann. 397 (1860). In a case with the opposite outcome, the creditors of Achille B. Courcelle (a white man) sued Louise A. Vitry, f.w.c., his mistress of nineteen years, to recover a large amount of property and a number of slaves in her name, but alleged by the lenders to be really his property. The Louisiana Supreme Court found no fraud in her ownership, and the creditors' "pretensions" were rejected. Syndic of Courcelle v. Vitry, f.w.c., No. 6544, 15 La. Ann. 653 (1860). For other simulated sale cases see: Syndics of Dussuau, f.m.c., v. Bredaux, No. 155, 4 Mart. (o.s.) 450 (La. 1816); Tessier v. Hall, No. 416, 7 Mart. (o.s.) 411 (La. 1820); Hawkins v. Vanwickle, No. 1501, 6 Mart. (N.S.) 418 (La. 1828); Verdier v. Leprete, No. 2314, 4 La. 41 (1832); Coquet v. Creditors, No. 2322, 4 La. 198 (1832); Penny v. Toulouse, No. 2996, 11 La. 109 (1837); Taylor v. Rostrop, No. 676, 3 La. Ann. 100 (1848); George v. Marshall and James, Unreported Louisiana Supreme Court Case [filed 1849]; Botts and Pool v. Nichols, No. 2680, 7 La. Ann. 263 (1852); and Barbin v. Gaspard, No. 347, 15 La. Ann. 539 (1860). For a case in which a vendor claimed a sale of two slaves was fraudulently obtained because he was intoxicated at the time of the transfer and agreed to a price much lower than the value of the bondsmen, see Cecile, f.m.c., v. St. Denis, f.w.c., No. 709, 14 La. 184 (1839).

41. Wilkins v. Bobo, No. 687, 13 La. Ann. 430 (1858).

loss. The supreme court affirmed this judgment. Justice King, writing for the court, held the sheriff liable as a result of his laches (a legal term meaning a failure to do a thing at the proper time, laxness).[42]

James R. Bisland, a Mississippi planter and owner of fifty-eight heavily mortgaged slaves, stole away from his plantation near Natchez in the middle of the night just before Christmas, 1855, with his slaves. After placing them aboard a passing steamboat that carried them to the Louisiana side of the Mississippi River, he brought them to his brother-in-law's plantation in Pointe Coupée Parish, where he executed a "pretended" sale to the overseer. The Louisiana Supreme Court voided the sale, ruling that it had been made to defraud his creditors.[43]

In antebellum Louisiana, "gone to Texas" was a phrase used to describe debtors who fled to escape their creditors. Three Louisiana Supreme Court cases are good evidence of the Louisiana meaning of this idiomatic expression. A Mississippi planter in debt for $1,339.62 plus interest fled the state with his family and slaves for Texas. His creditor caught up with him on a schooner docked in New Orleans and seized his twenty slaves. The planter claimed the slaves were not his, but were the separate property of his wife. Since Mississippi was a common-law state that did not honor a wife's separate property, Judge Martin ruled that the slaves could be sold to satisfy the debt; the planter could not avail himself of Louisiana law to protect his slaves: "Marital rights in Mississippi, are shown to be governed by the principles of common law . . . the property of the wife belongs absolutely to her husband . . . the slaves by the laws of Mississippi, became the property of the husband, consequently liable to his debts." In *Smith* v. *Berwick* (1845), an Opelousas, Louisiana, man who was deeply in debt slipped across the Sabine River in the middle of the night with twenty slaves and became a resident of Texas. Similarly, H. Alsbury, who was in debt for $13,300, persuaded the captain of the steamboat *New York* to tow him and his thirty-five slaves in a small vessel from the mouth of the Mississippi River to Galveston to avoid having to surrender the slaves to Alsbury's

42. Sandridge v. Jones, No. 71, 2 La. Ann. 933 (1847).

43. Bowman v. McKleroy and Bradford, No. 5545, 14 La. Ann. 587 (1859). For other cases of removing slaves from the state to protect them from creditors, see Broussard v. Philips, 6 Mart. (N.S.) 309 (La. 1827); Williams v. Hagan, No. 1971, 2 La. 122 (1830); Bronaught v. Neal, No. 793, 1 Rob. 23 (La. 1841); Gaulden v. McPhaul, No. 1181, 4 La. Ann. 79 (1849); and Beebe v. Robbins, 8 La. Ann. 470 (1852).

creditor. It is clear from the ship's log that the debtor was planning a fresh start in Texas; also aboard was a carriage, farm utensils, "Negro baggage," clothing, hams, carpets, and furniture.[44]

Those who profited most from the interstate and intrastate slave trade, the slave dealers, often were a mixed lot. Legal sources show that they sold diseased slaves as healthy with some regularity, and sold habitual fugitives, representing them as being of good character. At least one (other than Freeman) defaulted on a sizable debt, and another was characterized by a reliable witness as being a drunk and a gambler who incurred large monetary losses. One New Orleans slave dealer was caught evading the five-dollars-per-head tax on 114 slaves. At least one New Orleans slave trader was a woman, C. M. Hyams. One professional seller of slaves, Elihu Cresswell, provided for the emancipation of all the slaves who happened to be in his possession at the time of his death. He also manumitted his personal servant, Gabriel, "for his long and faithful service" and left him fifty dollars. The others, except for an orphaned infant who obviously could not care for herself and a slave too ill to make the journey, were eventually taken by Cresswell's executor to New York and set free.[45]

The dual nature of slaves under the law was the reality that as human beings they could be bought and sold, bartered and wagered, mortgaged, seized, and sold for their masters' debts. No matter how much

44. Stampp, *Peculiar Institution,* 203; Rogers, Slocomb and Co. v. Breedlove, No. 2725, 8 La. 143 (1835); Smith v. Berwick, 12 Rob. 20 (La. 1845); Irish v. Wright, Haggerty, and Morgan, No. 5255, 8 Rob. 428 (La. 1844).

45. For other examples of shady dealings by slave traders, see Gibson v. Huie, No. 608, 14 La. 124 (1839); Armor v. Huie, No. 3554, 14 La. 346 (1840); Gay v. Kendig, No. 4804, 2 Rob. 472 (1842); Coulter v. Cresswell, No. 2734, 7 La. Ann. 367 (1852); Riggin v. Kendig, No. 4718, 12 La. Ann. 451 (1857); Buie v. Kendig, No. 6356, 15 La. Ann. 440 (1860); and Palms v. Kendig, No. 6279, 15 La. Ann. 264 (1860). For examples of debt default, see Fazende v. Hagan, No. 4824, 9 Rob. 306 (La. 1844); Rist v. Hagan, No. 4503, 8 Rob. 106 (La. 1844); Gatlin v. Kendig, No. 6894, 18 La. Ann. 118 (1866); Bank of Charleston v. Hagan, No. 464, 2 La. Ann. 999 (1847); Coote v. Cotton, No. 2410, 5 La. 12 (1832); Heres v. Powell, No. 1808, 6 La. Ann. 586 (1851); Hyams v. Smith, No. 2172, 6 La. Ann. 362 (1851); Coulter v. Cresswell, No. 2734, 7 La. Ann. 367 (1852); and Succession of Cresswell, No. 2423, 8 La. Ann. 122 (1853). According to an article in *De Bow's Review,* some of the slaves were so miserable in New York that they begged the executor to return them to Louisiana, even if it meant selling them as slaves, cited in Ulrich B. Phillips, *American Negro Slavery: A Survey of the Supply, Employment, and Control of Negro Labor as Determined by the Plantation Regime* (New York, 1918), 429.

lip service the courts gave to the personage of the individual slave or to the fact that the law defined slaves as immovable property, the underlying truth that they could be disposed of as though they were personal property reduced them to mere things.

It is ironic that Elihu Cresswell, who spent his adult life transferring slave property from one owner to another, would provide for the emancipation of his slaves upon his death, thereby transforming them under the law from property into free persons by means of a relatively simple legal action. This overnight metamorphosis from slavery to freedom was not an uncommon occurrence in antebellum Louisiana, indicating that not only this one slave trader, but many other whites as well, remained unconvinced in their hearts by proslavery rhetoric insisting that blacks were by nature content in slavery. Free persons of color obviously cherished their freedom, even when their physical living conditions were worse than those of slaves. And under Louisiana law, free persons of color could not be reduced to slavery to satisfy their debts, nor could emancipations be revoked or emancipated slaves be reenslaved against their will. The Louisiana legislature passed a law on the eve of the Civil War entitled "An Act to Permit Free Persons of African Descent to Select Their Masters and Become Slaves for Life." This act allowed free people of color to select masters and voluntarily become slaves. Surprisingly, twelve free persons of color attempted to enslave themselves for life under this act. The records of the existing cases are silent as to what might have motivated them.[46]

46. *Civil Code,* Art. 189, p. 29; "An Act to Permit Free Persons of African Descent to Select a Master and Become Slaves for Life," Act of March 17, 1859, *Louisiana Acts, 1859,* pp. 214–15; Donald E. Everett, "Free Persons of Color in New Orleans, 1803–1865" (Ph.D. dissertation, Tulane University, 1954), 160. For voluntary enslavement, see Joseph Thomas, f.m.c., v. State of Louisiana, No. 13318, filed October 1, 1859; William Gray, f.m.c., v. State of Louisiana, No. 13320, October 1, 1859; Mary Walker, f.w.c., v. State of Louisiana, No. 13319, October 1, 1839; Fifth District Court of New Orleans, Emilia Stone, f.w.c., v. State of Louisiana, filed September 6, 1859, trial March 6, 1860. The Sixth District Court cases have vanished: Jane Moore, f.w.c., v. State of Louisiana, No. 7589, January 11, 1859; John Wells, f.m.c., v. State of Louisiana, No. 9593, September 15, 1859; John Clifton, f.m.c., v. State of Louisiana, No. 8647, September 15, 1860 (reported in New Orleans *Daily Delta,* May 18, 1860); Austin Lloyd v. State of Louisiana, No. 8648, September 15, 1860; James Stewart, f.m.c., v. State of Louisiana, No. 9158, February 13, 1861; Amelia Stone, f.w.c., v. State of Louisiana, No. 8465, August 28, 1861; One free man of color, Joseph Jones, enslaved himself by notarial act: James Graham, Notary Public, Vol. 21, No. 4909, May 20, 1861.

7

"OPEN AND NOTORIOUS CONCUBINAGE"

The Emancipation of Slave Mistresses by Will

THROUGHOUT THE ANTEBELLUM PERIOD THE SUPREME Court of Louisiana heard cases involving the emancipation of slaves, and despite ever-tightening restrictions on manumission, slaves continued to be legally transformed from property into free persons each year. Other Deep South slave states during this period prohibited masters from emancipating their slaves without legislative sanction. By 1860, only by a special act of the state legislature could slaves in Deep South states other than Louisiana be freed, and then only for meritorious service, a specific act, such as saving the life of the master or mistress.[1]

One way masters could emancipate their slaves in Louisiana was by executing a will that gave them their liberty upon their owner's death. It was not uncommon for a slaveholder to emancipate his slave mistress in this manner. Emancipation law in Louisiana resisted Americanization and continued to be more beneficial to the slave seeking freedom than any other southern state until shortly before the Civil War. Throughout the period, the supreme court affirmed emancipations of slaves in many of the appeals of manumission suits it heard. The popularly elected state legislature throughout this period sought to restrict and ultimately prohibit manumissions, indicating that the majority view in the state was in line with developments elsewhere in the South. The supreme court, however, was prone to resist major revisions in the state's organic law. Although the Louisiana legislature sought to make emancipation more difficult as the antebellum period went on and, indeed, finally prohibited

1. Stampp, *Peculiar Institution,* 232–34; Ira Berlin, *Slaves Without Masters: The Free Negro in the Antebellum South* (New York, 1974), 139*n*.

it entirely in 1857, the supreme court resisted the legislature's attempt to pattern Louisiana's emancipation regulations after those of other southern states. In this area the court often continued to rule in favor of freedom, rejecting the innovations of the legislature in "Americanizing" emancipation law.

Several aspects of the state's laws concerning manumission were unique to Louisiana, reflecting the legal heritage of the state. In the early decades of the nineteenth century, emancipation procedures in Louisiana seemed relatively simple. There were two qualifications for freedom stipulated in the *Black Code* of 1806: that the slave had been of "honest conduct" for four years before the emancipation—specifically, that he or she had not run away or committed a criminal act—and that he or she had reached the age of thirty years. The age requirement was a remnant of the Roman law of slavery, which held that slaves emancipated before they reached thirty could not be Roman citizens. Both the age and conduct stipulations could be waived if the slave to be freed had saved the life of the slaveowner or a member of the owner's family.[2] The age qualification was a formidable object. Slaves under thirty were without recourse. This restriction prevented an owner from freeing a family with children. It also prevented a free black man who managed to purchase his underage slave wife from freeing her until she achieved the specified age, and the children born before her emancipation were destined to be slaves for at least thirty years. At times these slave children fell into their father's succession and probate court judges ordered them sold away from the family to satisfy debts owed by the father at the time of his death.

In 1827 the Louisiana legislature softened the age requirement. A slave under thirty years of age could be freed if given permission by the judge and police jury of the parish of the owner, providing the slave was a native of the state (younger non-native slaves were probably considered a greater insurrection risk). An act of 1830 required all newly freed

2. "An Act to Regulate the Conditions and Forms of the Emancipation of Slaves," Act of March 9, 1807, *Orleans Territory Acts, 1807,* pp. 82–88; *Civil Code,* Arts. 185–86, p. 29. The Louisiana Supreme Court stated in 1857 that if slave children could be freed, masters would be allowed "to flood the community with a class of persons who are totally incapable of supporting and taking care of themselves": Carmouche v. Cramouche, No. 243, 12 La. Ann. 721 (1857); Watson, *Roman Slave Law,* 29.

slaves to leave the state within thirty days of their emancipation and required that the former owner post $1,000 security bond to ensure the ex-slave's departure. An amendment passed the following year softened this requirement. Parish police juries could, by a three-fourths vote, allow emancipated slaves to remain in the state. And any slave freed for "meritorious conduct" could bypass the restrictions altogether.[3]

Despite these measures, the population of free persons of color continued to increase, and in 1852 the Louisiana legislature added another obstacle to the manumission procedure—slaveowners were to send their freed slaves to Liberia, paying their passage of $150. Former slaves not departing within twelve months following their emancipation risked reenslavement. Slaveholders flooded the state legislature with individual petitions for exceptions, and in 1855 the legislature repealed the requirement of departure for Liberia. However, the new requirements, passed the same year, were no less strict; to free a slave, one had to sue the state in a district court. A jury decided the fate of slaves seeking freedom, and if it chose to free one, it also decided whether he or she could remain in the state. If residence was granted, the ex-slave's former master had to post $1,000 surety bond against the newly freed person's becoming a public charge—for one purpose of much of this legislation was to reduce the likelihood of freed slaves' becoming wards of the state by discouraging owners from emancipating elderly or infirm slaves who were no longer of any use. To that extent, the social policy inherent in such legislation may have been humane in intention, aimed at forcing slaveowners to support elderly or sick slaves, rather than leaving them to shift for themselves or become public charges. The need for such legislation suggests that some owners viewed their slaves as property to be discarded or thrown into the public welfare system when they became too old or too ill to work. Despite, however, this relatively beneficent side to the gradual restriction of emancipation in Louisiana, the driving force

3. "An Act To Determine the Mode of Emancipating Slaves Who Have Not Attained the Age Required by the Civil Code for Their Emancipation," Act of January 31, 1827, *Louisiana Acts, 1827,* pp. 12–14; "An Act to Prevent Free Persons of Color from Entering into This State . . . ," Act of March 16, 1830, *Louisiana Acts, 1830,* pp. 90–94; "An Act to Amend an Act Entitled 'An Act to Prevent Free Persons of Color from Entering into This State . . . ,'" Act of March 25, 1831, *Louisiana Acts, 1831,* pp. 96–98; Taylor, *Negro Slavery in Louisiana,* 156.

behind the tighter requirements was fear of increasing the free black population.[4]

The obstacles to emancipation in the 1855 act seem to have been less than effective, at least in New Orleans. The First District Court in that city heard eight manumission suits in two days late in 1855. The juries granted emancipation in all eight suits and allowed all of the newly freed slaves, seven women and one man, to remain in the state, even though these decisions meant that the former owners had to post $1,000 surety bonds. These cases demonstrate the resistance of not only the courts, but also the jurors, to the legislature's attempt to make Louisiana's law of emancipation similar to that of her sister Deep South states. In this area, apparently, the people wanted to retain some aspects of their French and Spanish heritage, and resist Americanization.[5]

By 1857, however, public sentiment in favor of emancipation had waned, and the legislators—frustrated by continuing emancipations made possible by judges and juries sympathetic to certain individuals seeking their liberty and unconcerned about increasing the free black population—closed the door to freedom in Louisiana. On March 6, 1857, the Louisiana legislature eliminated all loopholes and totally prohibited emancipations: "From and after the passage of this act, no slave

4. "An Act Concerning the Emancipation of Slaves in This State," Act of March 18, 1852, *Louisiana Acts, 1852,* pp. 214–15; "An Act Relative to Slaves and Free Colored Persons," Act of March 15, 1855, *Louisiana Acts, 1855,* p. 387; Taylor, *Negro Slavery in Louisiana,* 156. For some individual acts of legislative emancipation, see "An Act to Enable Baptiste Dupeyre . . . to Emancipate the Slave Zoé, Without Removing Her out of the State," Act of April 28, 1853, *Louisiana Acts, 1853,* pp. 163–64; "An Act to Emancipate the Slaves Belonging to the Estate of the Late J. B. Cajus, of the Parish of Orleans," Act of April 30, 1853, *Louisiana Acts, 1853,* pp. 273–74; "An Act Authorizing W. C. Wilson to Emancipate His Slave David," Act of March 7, 1854, *Louisiana Acts, 1854,* pp. 34–35; and "An Act to Authorize John Cousin, of the Parish of St. Tammany, to Emancipate the Slave Frances and Her Three Children," Act of March 7, 1854, *Louisiana Acts, 1854,* p. 35. Some of these acts stated that the slave was allowed to remain in the state "any law to the contrary not withstanding."

5. First District Court of New Orleans, *Minute Book, 1855–1856,* November 22, 23, 1855. See Murphy v. State (Slave Martha), No. 10,680; Cruzat v. State (Slave Victoire, alias Mamzelle), No. 10,723; Perret v. State (Slave Ellen), No. 10,686; Widow Clay v. State (Slave Justine), No. 10,764; Elizabeth, f.w.c., v. State (Slave Annie, alias Amelia), No. 10,737; Fortier v. State (Slave Menos, alias Aimée), No. 10,736; Fortin v. State (Slave Adeline), No. 10,734; Widow Bourg v. State (Slave Gaston Delille) No. 10,735. Although it cannot be ascertained whether the slaves freed were mistresses, children, or loyal slaves, the important point is that the juries freed all of them with permission to remain in the state.

shall be emancipated in this state." On the morning of March 6, the *Louisiana Courier* printed a fiery editorial condemning the practice of emancipation and cataloging its horrors in an editorial entitled "Results of Negro Emancipation in Jamaica": "Jamaica promises soon to become as pestiferous a sink of vice and corruption as the most libertine enthusiast can desire."[6]

Motives for manumission varied, and are often impossible to ascertain from the case records. Fear of free persons of color as a class was much stronger than fear of individual people of color; fear was often overridden by bonds of love and blood relationships. A number of manumission cases heard by the antebellum Louisiana Supreme Court involved attempts by white men to free their slave mistresses and/or their offspring. One possible explanation for the willingness of police juries and lower courts to grant emancipation in these circumstances was that they were only legalizing what was in some instances already established practice—some owners no doubt treated their slave mistresses and children as though they were free.

Cases heard by the Louisiana Supreme Court in which white masters emancipated their slave mistresses and their children usually arose from squabbles over inheritances and legacies left in the will of the master for his slave or ex-slave mistress and children. Freeing a slave mistress meant not only overcoming legislative restrictions, but also surmounting two additional legal obstacles firmly embedded in the Louisiana *Civil Code*. The first of these was forced heirship. Forced heirship required that legitimate children, which the court called "descending heirs," at a minimum receive a specified portion of the property of the deceased parent or grandparent. Forced heirs could be disinherited for committing serious offenses against a parent, such as striking the parent or, somewhat more exotically, failing to ransom a parent held on the high seas. If an individual died childless but one or both parents survived, they were forced heirs—"ascending heirs"—and entitled to a specified portion of the estate. With either ascending or descending heirs, the forced portion varied according to the number of forced heirs, and the *Code* clearly spelled out every possible configuration of heirship.

6. "An Act to Prohibit the Emancipation of Slaves," Act of March 6, 1857, *Louisiana Acts, 1857,* p. 55; Taylor, *Negro Slavery in Louisiana,* 156–57; *Louisiana Courier* (New Orleans), March 6, 1857.

Under Louisiana law, freeing a slave was considered a monetary donation to that person, and the state's forced heirship doctrine came into play. Article 190 of the *Civil Code* held that "any enfranchisement made in fraud of . . . the portion reserved by law to forced heirs, is null and void . . . [if] it shall appear that at the moment of executing the enfranchisement, the person granting it had not sufficient property . . . to leave to his heirs the portion to them reserved by law."

Even if a man attempting to emancipate a slave mistress had no forced heirs, he encountered the second obstacle in the *Civil Code*. According to article 1468, "Those who have lived together in open concubinage are respectively incapable of making to each other, whether *inter vivos* [during life] or *mortis causa* [after death], any donation of immovables, and if they make a donation of movables, it cannot exceed one-tenth part of the whole value of the estate." In protecting the property rights of the legitimate heirs, article 1468 presented two obstacles to the emancipation of a slave concubine. If the value of the slave mistress exceeded 10 percent of the property of the estate, she could not be freed. The second barrier, ignored by the Louisiana Supreme Court until the 1850s, was more formidable: people living in open concubinage could not donate immovable property of any value to each other while they were alive or by will—and slaves were immovables under Louisiana law. No cases exist at the appellate level challenging an emancipation on the basis of a donation *inter vivos*, but several instances arose in the 1850s of heirs challenging wills emancipating slave concubines on the basis that slaves were immovables.[7]

There is no way of knowing how many masters who attempted to emancipate their slave concubines by will understood the complexities of either Louisiana's law of forced heirship or the 10-percent rule. Although a slaveowner could seek the advice of a notary or an attorney in making a will, handwritten (olographic) wills were legal in Louisiana, as long as the testator wrote the document by hand and signed and dated it; the *Civil Code* required neither witness nor notary. A master attempting to emancipate a slave mistress could therefore easily write a will whose provisions were against Louisiana law, if he were ignorant of its intricacies.[8]

7. *Digest of 1808,* Tit. VI, Chap. III, Art. 26, p. 42; *Civil Code,* Art. 190, p. 29, Art. 1468, p. 223.

8. *Civil Code,* Art. 1581, pp. 241–42.

Judge François-Xavier Martin clarified the interpretation of article 1468 in *Prudence* v. *Bermodi* (1830): "Emancipation is a donation of the value of the slave, and when the donation is attacked as excessive and evidence is given that the donor has insufficient property to justify it, it behooves the donor to prove that he had." Prudence, an elderly, "always well-behaved" slave, had sued for her freedom under an 1828 will that stipulated she was to be freed upon the death of her owner. Apparently she had followed her master to New Orleans from St. Domingue even though she could have remained on that island and been free. Notwithstanding this act of loyalty, Martin ruled against her because she failed to produce any evidence that the succession of the defendant's mother had any other assets but herself. Since her value exceeded the disposable portion of the succession, the court could not rule otherwise.[9]

During the antebellum era the Louisiana Supreme Court followed this formula to the letter, making certain that forced heirs received their correct portion of the succession. For example, in *Maria and Angel* v. *Destrehan* (1831), Jacob Philips, a plantation carpenter, owned a mulatto woman, Maria, and her ten-year-old daughter, Angel. He left a will in which he ordered his executor to free the two and asked his white daughter to see to their emancipation "as a particular favor to her father." He also left Maria and Angel all of his movable property, stating in his will that "they have been purchased out of her own funds and by her labour." The executor inventoried Philips' entire estate at $1,497.25, which included the value of Maria and Angel, appraised at $850. After the carpenter died, Maria and Angel sued Philips' executor for their freedom. The lower court ruled that since Philips had a legitimate daughter, and therefore a forced heir, she must receive her required portion of the estate, and freeing Maria and Angel would alienate too large a portion of the inheritance. Judge Alexander Porter remanded the case on a procedural issue because the parish judge in the case made his judgment "out of the presence of the parties, and without notice to them. It is not shown, the case was tried at term time, nor regularly fixed for trial." However, it is unlikely that Maria and Angel were ever freed, since their value exceeded one-tenth of the estate. It is ironic that the more valuable the slaves in these circumstances, the less likely they were to be freed

9. Prudence v. Bermodi, No. 1888, 1 La. 234 (1830); *Civil Code,* Art. 1462, p. 222.

because of the objections of the legitimate heirs, who stood to lose their value as a portion of the inheritance.[10]

In one concubine-emancipation case, *Vail* v. *Bird* (1851), Henry Clay Vail freed his bondswoman-mistress, Jane, in his will and left her two promissory notes of $100 each. Vail's heirs alleged that, as the *Civil Code* defined slaves as immovable property, emancipating Jane was a disposition of immovable property to a concubine, which Louisiana law prohibited, and they sued to annul the donation. The heirs contended that Vail could only leave Jane one-tenth of the value of his estate in *movable* property, and that the court should have made her a party to the suit, to annul the donation. The executor claimed that as a slave, Jane could not be a party in a civil suit. He further argued that Jane was not a "concubine," since she was a slave and slaves by law were without will; concubinage, under Louisiana law, implied consent. Furthermore, he argued, the heirs should not "enrich themselves . . . [by] proving the turpitude of the deceased." The executor won in the lower court, and the heirs appealed. The Louisiana Supreme Court, although recognizing that female slaves were particularly vulnerable to the power of the master, ruled that the donation of freedom deprived the heirs of their rightful inheritance. The estate was worth only $1,686, of which sum Jane and her child, Louisa, accounted for $900, well over one-tenth of the total value. The court based its decision on the assumption that female slaves generally participated willingly in sexual relations with their masters: "It is true, the female slave is peculiarly exposed . . . to the seductions of an unprincipled master. That is a misfortune; but it is so rare in the case of concubinage that the seduction and temptation are not mutual, that exceptions to the general rule cannot be founded upon it."[11]

This statement suggests that slaves were capable of free will, being able to *choose* to live in concubinage with their masters, and therefore fell under the restrictions of article 1468; an obvious implication is that there were limits to the concept of the slave as property. Citing article 1468's restriction of donations to concubines to one-tenth of the movable property of the estate, Justice Isaac Preston, writing for the court, observed: "It [article 1468] is an explicit provision of law of great im-

10. Maria and Angel v. Destrehan, No. 2228, 3 La. 434 (1831).
11. Vail v. Bird, No. 2129, 6 La. Ann. 223 (1851).

portance to the order, decency and well being of society, and this must be carried into full effect by the courts." Preston accepted the argument that slaves were immovable property: "Slaves are made by our law immovable property. . . . The donation of freedom to a slave deprives the heirs of the slave, and is therefore the donation of an immovable." This is the first instance in which the court treated the emancipation of a slave concubine by will as a donation of immovable property (the value of the slave) to the slave freed by the will.[12]

Undaunted by the unfavorable decision, Vail's executor continued to work for Jane's freedom. In *Bird* v. *Vail* (1854), he claimed that as Vail's heirs were not direct ascendants or descendants, and therefore not forced heirs, according to *Civil Code* article 1491 they had no right to a forced portion of his inheritance. The executor sued for possession of Jane and her daughter in order to free them. The irate heirs concealed the slaves and told the executor that before he "could get possession of said slaves he would be forced to find them . . . or words to this effect." Justice James Campbell acknowledged Jane's right to freedom but ruled for the heirs, stating that slaves did not become absolutely free by the probate of a will, "but only entitled to their freedom, upon compliance with the formalities prescribed by law for the emancipation of slaves; until these formalities were complied with . . . the heirs had a right . . . [to] enjoy their services and labor. The possession of the slave by the heir, will not preclude the executor from taking all steps . . . for her emancipation." Campbell never addressed the issue of donation of immovable property to a concubine in this ruling. He had succeeded Preston on the bench in 1853, following Preston's death in a steamboat accident in 1852. The change in personnel may be responsible for the court's ignoring the issue.[13]

12. *Ibid.; Civil Code,* Art. 1468, p. 223; *Black Code,* Sec. 10, p. 154.

13. Bird v. Vail, No. 3454, 9 La. Ann. 176 (1854); *Civil Code,* Art. 1491, p. 227. See also Nimmo v. Bonney and Bird, No. 5138, 4 Rob. 179 (La. 1843). It is not clear whether Louisa was Vail's daughter. She was born when her mother was thirteen. If so, Jane became Vail's mistress at the age of twelve.

The post-Reconstruction supreme court demonstrated a complete change in attitude toward slave concubines. In an 1878 decision the court stated: "That mother's concubinage, the illegitimacy of her son, were the almost inevitable results of their [the slaves'] condition, and . . . that condition was not of their choice [and the] concubinage can not be invoked as a crime against the emancipated mother." Neel v. Hibard, No. 6737, 30 La. Ann. 808 (1878); Warren M. Billings, *Historic Rules of the Supreme Court of Louisiana,* 44, 48.

The court's stand on the issue of donation of immovable property to a concubine is much clearer in an appeal heard in 1853, *Adams* v. *Routh and Dorsey.* William Adams, Jr., lived in what the courts called "open concubinage" with a slave named Nancy. Adams died in 1851 and left a will ordering his executor to free Nancy and give her his watch and furniture. There were also two legacies of $1,000 each for their children, who were already free. Adams' father inherited as a forced heir because Adams, Jr., had died with no legitimate children. The father sued to prevent the emancipation of Nancy and the awarding of the legacies to her and the children on the grounds that since the entire estate was worth only $4,750, the donation to Nancy of her value and the additional legacies far exceeded the one-tenth disposable portion of the succession; Nancy alone was valued at $1,000. Citing *Prudence* v. *Bermodi,* Justice Pierre Rost addressed the issue of the donation of immovable property to a concubine: "Admitting that . . . emancipating a slave by will should, in favor of liberty, be considered not as the donation of an immovable, but as a donation to the slave of his own value, yet that value must not exceed the disposable portion." Rost ruled that as "the disposition was excessive," Adams could not free Nancy, and therefore she could not receive a legacy, as slaves were unable to inherit anything. Since Adams, Sr., was entitled to only one-fourth of his son's estate, sufficient assets remained in the succession to permit payment of the legacies to the children, as Adams, Sr., "has . . . no interest or standing in court to contest the validity of those legacies."[14]

Two slave concubines lost the freedom left to them in their masters' wills because between the time the master executed the will and the date the court decided the appeals of their suits for freedom, the legislature passed the 1857 act prohibiting emancipation. Both lost their chance for freedom by a matter of days. In the first instance, a white man named John Turnbull went before a notary and two witnesses on December 19, 1855, to formally acknowledge his five mulatto children, born of his twenty-three-year-old slave, Rachel. The purpose of acknowledgment of an illegitimate child was to give that child legal capacity to inherit from the father, provided there were no legitimate heirs. On the same day, Turnbull made a will instructing his executor to free his children

14. Adams v. Routh and Dorsey, No. 3009, 8 La. Ann. 121 (1853); *Civil Code,* Art. 900, p. 135.

and their mother upon his death. He stated that if emancipation were legally impossible, his executor should take them to a country or state of their choice where slavery did not exist and set them free; the costs of transportation were to be paid by the estate. Turnbull also left one-third of his estate to Rachel and the children, to be divided equally. Turnbull died six months later, in June, 1856, but his executor refused to free the slave woman or her children. Her court-appointed curator sued the executor in *Turner* v. *Smith* (1857) to force him to comply with the will. The executor stated that Turnbull's acknowledgment of the children as his own was "contrary to law and good morals." The lower court ruled that Rachel and her children should receive their legacies as soon as they could be emancipated, noting that it could not blame Rachel for "yielding obedience to his wicked desires" because this would be to punish "the weak and helpless for the sins of the strong and powerful." This recognition of the helpless position of slave women is unusual among antebellum Louisiana court decisions of this sort. Blame, when placed at all, was usually assigned to the "seductiveness" of bondswomen.

Unfortunately for Rachel, before the Louisiana Supreme Court rendered a decision on the executor's appeal in this case, the Louisiana legislature passed the act prohibiting emancipation. Justice Alexander Buchanan began his reversal of the decision of the lower court by declaring the act of acknowledgment of Rachel's children null and void because "the object of an acknowledgment of a natural child; is to confer upon the child certain rights, such as . . . inheritance. . . . The same notarial act which declares . . . [them] to be Turnbull's children declares at the same time that they are his slaves. Such an acknowledgment, besides being offensive to morality, is without any . . . effect in law . . . [as] a slave can neither sue for alimony nor inherit." Buchanan further argued that Turnbull took no steps to emancipate Rachel and her children during the six months between the notarial act and his death, and his executor made no attempt to emancipate them after Turnbull's death. In the meantime, the justice stated, the legislature passed the act of 1857. "The enfranchisement of Rachel and her children having thus become legally impossible," Buchanan wrote, "the legacy made to them by the testator of one-third of his estate has lapsed."

In explaining his ruling, Buchanan stated: "The subject of enfranchisement of slaves is one over which the State has always exercised a controlling power . . . which the court cannot permit to be disregarded. This . . . holds good of a legislative prohibition to enfranchise altogether." This ruling, which made the act of 1857 retroactive, seems clearly wrong, as Rachel and her children had acquired the right to their freedom well before March 6, 1857. It is difficult to understand Buchanan's reasoning in light of the court's refusal to make the law of 1857 retroactive in cases involving slave transport (see chapter 10). Nevertheless, the decision was that Rachel and her children could not now be legally freed and, as slaves, could neither inherit nor own property. The court ruled that Turnbull's heirs divide Rachel and her children among them.[15]

Two years later, in *Price* v. *Ray* (1859), the court ruled once more on the emancipation of a slave concubine. Simeon Hyde left a will in which he directed the emancipation of his slave Minnie and her eight children, and left them his entire estate. Hyde died without forced heirs, either ascending or descending; his legal heirs claimed the estate, contending that Minnie could not be freed under the 1857 prohibition of manumission and because she was the concubine of the testator. The heirs won the decision in the District Court of Ouachita Parish, and the executor of the will appealed. Justice Cornelius Voorhies brushed aside the objection that Minnie had lived in concubinage with the deceased and could not therefore be freed: "It is no objection to the slave's right to manumission . . . that she was the concubine of her owner." The second obstacle, that of the 1857 law, could not be ignored, however, and Voorhies also applied it retroactively:

> At the time of the death of *Simeon L. Hyde,* it was lawful for him to manumit his slaves by last will and testament; but the rights acquired by them were inchoate, subject or conditioned to be perfected according to the existing regulations and laws upon this subject-matter. In the meantime the *status* of these parties was that of slavery; and their inchoate right of freedom was subject to be defeated by subsequent legislation, rendering impossible its consummation. Such is the effect of the legislation of the year 1857, by which it is provided, "that from and after the passage of this Act, no slave shall be emancipated in this State."
>
> Unless this law be repealed, and provision made by which the last wills and testaments of *Simeon L. Hyde,* deceased, might be carried into effect, it is evident that the slaves he directed should be

15. Turner v. Smith, No. 5076, 12 La. Ann. 417 (1857); *Civil Code,* Art. 1470, 1473, pp. 223–24.

> manumitted, cannot stand in court for any purpose. They could not, before the Act of 1857, be heard, except with reference to their freedom and emancipation; and now this very privilege is withdrawn from them by legal enactment. . . .
>
> It does not follow, however, that these slaves forfeit absolutely the inchoate right, acquired by them under the will; for if the law should happen to be changed, their remedy might be revived. At the time the will took effect, the right of owners to emancipate their slaves was recognized. The slaves of the deceased have not acquired a vested right to become free at a future period; nevertheless, they have acquired an inchoate right, which may yet be perfected, should a change of legislation permit . . . the question involved is one of State policy.[16]

A few cases heard by the antebellum Louisiana Supreme Court are evidence not only of longstanding relationships between white men and their slave mistresses, but also of careful attempts to free and provide for their children. Generally the supreme court allowed these acts, provided that legitimate heirs did not suffer the loss of their rightful inheritance and the terms of article 1468 respecting concubinage were not violated. The slave Venus was born in 1787 of the slave Nancy, owned by B. Farrar of Pointe Coupée Parish. Her father, Christopher Beard, a white planter, stipulated in his will that at his death Venus was to receive 750 arpents of land (630 acres) on False River, be instructed in the Christian religion, and be apprenticed to a silkmaker to learn the craft at the expense of the estate. Beard died in 1789. Twelve years later Farrar died, leaving a will emancipating Venus, "supposed to be a bastard child of C. Beard, deceased." Farrar also left Venus six of his slaves and instructed his executor to deliver this legacy when Venus became eighteen years. Apparently Farrar wished to be thought a humane master, as he stated in his will that he wanted his bondservants to "be used with the greatest humanity consistent with the state they are in and be made as happy as possible in their situation." After Farrar's death, the land left to Venus by Beard was sold by Beard's heirs to Julien Poydras, and she sued to recover it in *Beard* v. *Poydras* (1816). At issue was whether she was free at the time of Beard's death, since slaves could not inherit under

16. Price v. Ray, No. 697, 14 La. Ann. 697 (1859); "An Act to Prevent the Emancipation of Slaves," Act of March 6, 1857, *Louisiana Acts, 1857,* p. 55.

Louisiana law. (Beard could not have placed the land in trust for her: Louisiana law prohibited trusts; the object of succession law was to put the property of the deceased directly into the hands of heirs. Besides, as a slave, she could not have been a beneficiary of a trust.)

The district court ruled in Venus' favor, despite denying her attempt to present witnesses to prove that she was free. (The court's reasoning was that the *Black Code* allowed only written proof of emancipation, not oral evidence.) On appeal, Judge Pierre Dérbigny ruled that the district court judge erred in this matter. Dérbigny remanded the case with orders to admit "any legal evidence which the plaintiff may offer. Not producing written evidence of emancipation raised a suspicion that she was not able to prove so much. Yet, as it did not exclude all probability [that she could prove her freedom], she ought to have been permitted to introduce her witnesses. . . . Being of the opinion that as the case now stands, she ought not to recover, we are obliged to remand it." No record of the new trial exists.[17]

The daughters of a white man, Jean Baptiste Lagarde, and one of his slaves, Adelaide, were well cared for but not legally freed, possibly because of the enmity of a white wife. After a daughter, Amelia, was born to him and Adelaide, Lagarde—an overseer—purchased mother and daughter in 1829 and treated them as free. Lagarde's second daughter, Cydalize, was born after the sale; Adelaide died shortly thereafter of cholera. Lagarde paid a free woman of color, Marie Louise Audat, to raise his daughters and treat them as her own. Witnesses testified that Lagarde often stated the girls were his, and that when they were older he planned to send them to his sister in France. Lagarde subsequently married a white woman. He died in 1840, and the two girls were included in the inventory of his estate and auctioned off at a probate sale. Audat managed to purchase them, and she brought suit for their freedom in *Audat* v. *Gilly* (1845). The First District Court of New Orleans declared Amelia and Cydalize free by prescription according to *Civil Code* article 3510, since they had lived free—that is, in free, good-faith possession of *themselves*—for more than ten years in the state. Perhaps the reason that Lagarde did not take the legal steps to emancipate them was the resentment of his new wife or his children by his first marriage,

17. Beard v. Poydras, No. 72, 4 Mart. (o.s.) 348 (La. 1816); *Civil Code,* Arts. 1507, 1508, pp. 229–30.

as it is obvious he intended them to be free. Audat won on appeal. Judge Alonzo Morphy declared the girls free, and the funds that Audat used to purchase them were listed as a debt of Lagarde's succession payable to her; in other words, she would be reimbursed.[18]

A wealthy Opelousas man, Douglas Wilkins, died in 1846 and left property worth $62,725.28. In his will, Wilkins emancipated his slave mistress, Leonora, and his acknowledged sons, Joseph Douglas and Charles Douglas. He also left Joseph and Charles $3,000 and $2,000, respectively, and stipulated that his executor send them to a free state to be educated in the "three Rs" and taught a trade. He also provided Leonora with a $150 annuity. Wilkins' will stipulated that his sons receive their legacies when they became twenty-one; the executor was to invest the funds at 8 percent for the maintenance of the children. Joseph Douglas died before reaching twenty-one, and Leonora sued in *Leonora, f.w.c., v. Scott* (1855) to recover her son's legacy, as his forced heir (ascending). The lower court found in her favor, and the executor appealed. Associate Justice Henry Spofford described the issue: "The question is, whether a legacy in favor of the natural child of the plaintiff, who has died since the testator, lapsed by the subsequent death of the child . . . whether the testamentary disposition . . . was conditioned upon an uncertain event [the child's becoming twenty-one]." Leonora's freedom was not at issue; she had been free since 1847, and no one contested her status. The real issue was whether free persons of color deserved equal treatment to whites under the law; in this case, the court upheld the principle that they did. Spofford, writing for the court, ruled that the bequest to Joseph Douglas was not conditioned upon his reaching the age of majority. Ruling in Leonora's favor, Spofford amended the judgment of the lower court to award her the $3,000 as well as 8 percent interest from the date of Wilkins' death in 1847.[19]

The Civil War interrupted several cases involving emancipation and legacies to slave or ex-slave concubines and their children, and often

18. Audat v. Gilly, No. 5337, 12 Rob. 323 (La. 1845); *Civil Code,* Art. 3510, p. 532. For another case that involved a white father providing by will for his illegitimate children by a slave or ex-slave woman, see Brosnaham v. Turner, 16 La. 433 (1839).

19. Leonora, f.w.c., v. Scott, 10 La. Ann. 651 (1855). In a similar case William Weeks left $16,000 to his white son to pay boarding, clothing, and tuition for his four illegitimate children by a slave woman. The Louisiana Supreme Court ruled the donation invalid. O'Hara v. Conrad, 10 La. Ann. 638 (1855).

worked to the benefit of the blacks or mulattoes involved. Bernard Chappel freed his mistress, Ida Hannah, before his death, but could not free his daughter, Clementine, because she was not yet thirty years old. He died in 1854. His will provided for Clementine's manumission as soon as legally possible. It also made both mother and daughter his only heirs. Clementine was still a slave, although a *statu liber*—a legal term meaning a slave for a limited number of years. The act of 1857 prohibiting all emancipations did not mean that Clementine ceased to be a *statu liber;* although the law prohibited her from being emancipated as long as it remained in effect, she remained a *statu liber,* and in the event the legislature repealed the prohibition, she would have been entitled to her freedom. In 1861 Hannah sued in *Succession of Chappel: Hannah, f.w.c.,* v. *Eggleston* (1865), claiming the whole estate, as her daughter was still a slave and could not inherit. She won in the lower court, and a court-appointed curator for Clementine, who was a minor, appealed. The war interrupted the appeal, and the case was one of the first to be decided when the Louisiana Supreme Court was reactivated in June, 1865. The justices reversed the decision of the lower court, ruling that a *statu liber* could legally inherit, and anyway the issue was moot, as Clementine was now free following the general emancipation at the end of the war. The court ordered the estate divided between mother and daughter.[20]

Another post–Civil War decision involved an emancipated slave who was the child of a white man and a slave woman. In 1846 a Mr. Porter of New Orleans died, leaving a will that instructed his executors to purchase from a Mr. Metoyer a child, the son of the slave woman Meme, and to emancipate him. Porter also left $1,000 to be invested for the boy's education and support; the remaining funds were to be given to him when he attained the age of eighteen. Before he had reached that age, the child received his legacy in Confederate notes. After the war was over and his eighteenth birthday had passed, he sued for his inheritance in *Porter* v. *Brown* (1869), claiming that Confederate money was now worthless. The Louisiana Supreme Court ruled that since he was a minor when he first received his legacy, he could not have legally consented to the payment, and furthermore, that the currency was "illicit." The court ordered the executor to pay him in legal tender.[21]

20. Succession of Chappel; Hannah, f.w.c., v. Eggleston, No. 198, 17 La. Ann. 174 (1865).
21. Porter v. Brown, No. 137, 21 La. Ann. 532 (1869).

Even emancipation following the Civil War did not help two ex-slave children fathered by a white planter gain their inheritance. Abram Bird died in 1860, leaving a large estate and three legal, white heirs. After providing for them according to law, Bird provided for the emancipation of two of his slaves as soon as state law permitted (the act of 1857 stood in the way) and left them each a legacy of $8,000. Louisiana law placed another obstacle in Bird's path—he could not place the $16,000 in trust for his slave children, as the *Civil Code* prohibited *fidei commissa,* that is, placing property in the hands of one person for the benefit of a third party; slaves could not be trust beneficiaries even if the trust were legal in Louisiana. After Bird's death the legal heirs ceased to hold the two in slavery but left the bequests unpaid. After the war the ex-slaves sued for their inheritance in *Barrow* v. *Bird* (1870). The legal heirs alleged that as "adulterous bastards" (Bird had a white wife as well as a slave mistress) the two could not inherit: according to *Civil Code* article 1470, illegitimate children could not receive more than bare subsistence from their parents, if legitimate children existed; moreover, article 1475 prohibited donations to "adulterine or incestuous children," other than minimum subsistence. In any case, they could not inherit, as they were what the court termed "adulterous issue" and there were legitimate children. The legitimate heirs further contended that "the plaintiffs are the issue of an adulterous concubinage . . . the mother was his slave," and as such, incapable of inheriting. The court reluctantly ruled for the legitimate heirs: "However barbarous the statute of 1857 may appear, we cannot give the plaintiffs the relief they seek." But the real issue was that they were "adulterous bastards," not that they were slaves. The Louisiana Supreme Court affirmed the judgment of the lower court that they had no right of inheritance.[22]

In a few lawsuits heard by the Louisiana Supreme Court, irate and greedy heirs attempted to revoke legal emancipations of slave mistresses of white owners either to block donations to them by their ex-masters or to claim the freed women or their children as their own property. Laurent Grangé legally emancipated his slave mistress, Marie Fanchonette, in 1836. She subsequently gave birth to a son, John. After

22. Barrow v. Bird, No. 2706, 22 La. Ann. 407 (1870); *Civil Code,* Arts. 1507, 1508, pp. 229–30.

Grangé's death in 1842, the white heirs seized her child as a slave belonging to the succession and claimed Fanchonette had been born a slave and had never been emancipated. Fanchonette sued for her freedom and that of her child in *Fanchonette* v. *Grangé* (1844); she also demanded $1,000 in damages for "the illegal and forcible seizure and detention of her person." Judge Rice Garland affirmed the lower court's decision and declared Fanchonette and her child to be free. In his decision Garland stated that "there is no excuse for him, in aiding to reduce the plaintiff to a state of slavery after she had been declared free by a competent tribunal." Fanchonette received $100 in damages, plus a judgment of 10 percent interest for frivolous appeal against the heirs.[23]

One white man attempted unsuccessfully to arrange for the freedom of a slave woman and his son by her, both of whom belonged to another person. In his will Erasmus R. Avart ordered his executor to buy the slave Marie and her child, Gaston, and free them. Avart died without forced heir, ascending or descending. Marie's master was willing to sell her and the child for a reasonable price, but Avart's brothers and sisters objected to the will, and no sale occurred. Marie sued the executor and heirs in *Marie* v. *Avart* (1819–1821) to have the terms of the will obeyed. Avart had committed suicide; he had executed the testament between the infliction of his fatal wound and his demise. His heirs claimed that he was insane when he wrote the will and mentally incapable of making sound judgments. To prove this assertion they stated that since he was "consumed with passion" for Marie, he must have been of unsound mind! Several witnesses testified that Avart was in full possession of his faculties. The lower-court jury found for the heirs, and Marie requested a new trial on the basis of newly discovered evidence. The lower court refused to grant a new trial, and the plaintiff appealed. Judge Martin ruled that the judge of the Orleans Parish court had erred on three grounds in allowing the insanity claim. The first was that no one had interdicted Avart before his death. Interdiction was a civil-law process by which the family of a person who was incapable of handling his own affairs could have the court appoint a curator to handle them. Since no family member had made any attempt to interdict Avart, the judge refused to admit evidence of insanity. The dead could not be interdicted:

23. Fanchonette v. Grangé, 5 Rob. 510 (La. 1843), 9 Rob. 86 (La. 1844).

according to *Civil Code* article 396, "After the death of a person, the validity of acts done by him cannot be contested for cause of insanity, unless his interdiction was pronounced or petitioned for previous to [his] death." The second reason for rejecting the contention that Avart was insane when he wrote the will was the refuting testimony of the notary who drew up the will and the witnesses to it; all declared he was of sound mind. Third, Martin rejected the heirs' contention that Avart's insanity could be proved by the lack of wisdom he displayed in leaving a legacy to his concubine and two natural children:

> It is true, that Erasmus R. Avart disposes of a portion of his property in favor of two natural children; but, in these dispositions, who is the man, callous enough to all natural sentiments, who instead of seeing feelings natural not only to men, but to animals, will discover an act of insanity? Certainly Avart, in becoming father of such children is not exempt from reproach in the eyes of morality; but he did not infringe the laws of his country, since the framers of our code (more humane than certain stoics who have no indulgence for the frailties of others, because they were lucky enough to be born virtuous, or perhaps because circumstances have favoured them) have impliedly permitted donations *causa mortis* and *inter vivos,* to be made to concubines, . . . and, in several places, not only have permitted dispositions in favor of natural children, but have given them certain rights on the successions of their fathers and mothers. Our legislators knew that they were framing laws for men like themselves. At the time, that they wished to favor marriages, on which the prosperity and good order of society chiefly depend, they knew, also, that *jura sanguinis nullo jure civili dirimi possunt* [the right of blood and kindred cannot be destroyed by any civil law]. . . . It is evident, therefore, that Erasmus R. Avart, not only obeyed the dictates of nature, but, also, acted under the authority of the law.

Martin was inclined to grant Marie a new trial. However, the heirs' attorney also argued that Marie was a slave and, as such, had no right to sue in court for anything but her freedom. She had no capacity, he contended, to sue to force compliance with Avart's will. To this argument Martin acquiesced. The Louisiana Supreme Court ruled that Marie could not bring suit to have the will executed as written, because slaves could institute a legal action only to prove their freedom.[24]

In its decisions pertaining to inheritance cases that involved slave women who had become the mistresses of their white masters, the antebellum Louisiana Supreme Court acted quite predictably, given the restrictions placed on the justices by the *Civil Code* and the Louisiana constitution. The law frowned upon "open and notorious concubinage," restricting *both* partners in such alliances to receiving only one-tenth of each other's movable property. This prohibition, designed to spare other family members the financial consequences of an illicit intimate relationship, was consistent with the intention of the writers of the *Civil Code* to promote family solidarity. It is important to note here that the law was identical for all involved in these liaisons, male and female, black, mulatto, and white. In several antebellum decisions, the court applied the 10-percent rule to white concubines. In this instance Louisiana law was oblivious to gender and color. Theoretically, the supreme court should not have allowed any slave concubine to be freed, as freeing a slave was a donation of immovable property and concubines were restricted to 10 percent of movable property. The conflicting decisions on this in *Prudence* v. *Bermodi* and *Vail* v. *Bird* demonstrate the difficulty of dealing with slaves as persons and simultaneously as property. Even the highest court in Louisiana found it difficult to be consistent in its rulings on this issue.

In cases involving slave concubines, the Louisiana Supreme Court adhered to the letter of the law; slaves could inherit nothing except their freedom, and that only in special circumstances. Ex-slave concubines of white masters were allowed to receive one-tenth of their former master's estate in movable property; their illegitimate children, if formally acknowledged, were allowed their legal one-fourth if no legitimate heirs existed. If the women and children were still slaves, they could not be freed unless their value did not exceed one-tenth or one-fourth, respectively, of the total estate. In these rulings the fact that slaves were valuable property overshadowed their qualities as persons under the law.

24. Marie v. Avart, No. 352, 6 Mart. (o.s.) 731 (La. 1819); No. 488, 8 Mart. (o.s.) 512 (La. 1820); No. 488, 10 Mart. (o.s.) 25 (La. 1821). *Digest of 1808,* Bk. I, Tit. IX, Chap. I, Art. 16, p. 80; *Civil Code,* Art. 396, pp. 57–58.

White concubines were also restricted to inheriting 10 percent, but at least their freedom was not at issue.[25]

Louisiana's continental legal heritage is evident in these rulings. Illicit and illegal liaisons were a threat to the institution of the family. The *Civil Code* ensured that the legitimate family of the free partners in an illegal relationship would not be deprived of their inheritance. Of course, slaves had no legitimate families under the law, could own no property, and were in fact property themselves. These factors operated in most court decisions to make these laws more burdensome on them than on whites.

Concubinage and illegitimacy were not the only causes of avaricious relatives' seeking to void wills freeing bondsmen and leaving them an inheritance. A number of emancipation-by-will cases that were heard by the Supreme Court of Louisiana during the antebellum period did not involve either concubinage or illegitimacy. Rather, resentment by relatives over the testamentary generosity of a deceased slaveowner, along with simple greed, inspired a series of lawsuits designed to thwart such eleemosynary donations.

25. The Louisiana Supreme Court was no more likely to allow donations exceeding 10 percent to white concubines than to those of color. See Lowery v. Kline, No. 2519, 6 La. 380 (1834); Succession of Bosquet, No. 5632, 10 Rob. 143 (La. 1845); and Carmena v. Blaney, No. 116, 16 La. Ann. 245 (1861).

8

"LETTING LOOSE IN OUR MIDST . . . PERSONS OF COLOR"

Further Difficulties in Freeing Slaves by Will

EMANCIPATION BY WILL WAS NOT MOTIVATED ONLY BY concubinage or by the children who were the result of such unions. Other manumissions by will resulted from affection for a particular slave or from humanitarian motives (the latter, perhaps inspired by apprehension concerning the slaveholder's fate in the next world, sometimes led to the emancipation of a whole group of slaves). During the antebellum period, the Supreme Court of Louisiana heard dozens of cases in which slaves sued for freedom bequeathed to them by their late owner's will or legal heirs of the testator contested such manumissions.

The *Digest of 1808* and the 1825 *Civil Code* explicitly permitted masters to emancipate their slaves: "A master may manumit his slave in this State, either by an act *inter vivos* or by a disposition made in prospect of death, provided such manumission be made with the forms and under the conditions prescribed by law; but an enfranchisement, when made by a last will, must be express and formal, and shall not be implied by any other circumstances of the testament, such as a legacy, an institution of heir, testamentary executorship or other dispositions of this nature, which in such case, shall be considered as if they had not been made."[1] The qualifying language in this provision meant that simply ordering the executor of a will to free a slave did not immediately give him or her liberty. The executor had to take the actions prescribed by law to institute and complete emancipation proceedings. Emancipation by will was one of the most common methods used to free slaves, and wills that bequeathed slaves their freedom had to meet the usual requirements of

1. *Digest of 1808,* Bk. I, Tit. VI, Chap. III, Art. 25, p. 40; *Civil Code,* Art. 184, pp. 28–29.

Louisiana succession law, including proper form and consideration of forced heirship. Providing for the emancipation of a slave could substantially reduce the size of the legacies to the decedent's heirs, who often fought to retain what they considered their rightful inheritance.

On several occasions a slaveowner stipulated by will that one or more slaves were to be emancipated after the testator died, and the slaveowner's relatives sued to void the will and prevent manumission. They were sometimes successful because the testator had failed to follow proper forms, either because of ignorance of the law or because the law had changed after the will was written. It is impossible to know whether owners of slaves were oblivious to articles of the *Civil Code* pertaining to emancipation and to the acts of the Louisiana legislature (which were published in antebellum newspapers regularly, as required by law) or simply believed that their survivors would respect their wishes and see to it that the slaves were freed, rather than regarding the slave or slaves involved as property belonging to the estate, and thus part of their own inheritance. Certainly there was a natural obligation to carry out the intent of the testator. However, in the cases heard by the antebellum Supreme Court of Louisiana, the financial interest of relatives often took precedence over the wishes of the deceased.

The *Civil Code* provided for three different types of wills: nuncupative wills, mystic testaments, and olographic wills. The first required the services of a notary, who could be consulted if the testator had doubts concerning the legality of the provisions of the will. A mystic will—in effect a "secret testament," and very rare in Louisiana—also required a notary, to whom the will was to be presented, closed and sealed, in the presence of seven witnesses. Olographic wills required neither attorneys nor notaries, unless the testator sought advice.

Humanitarian motives prompted several slaveowners to free groups of slaves. In a few cases masters stipulated that their slaves were to be freed by their executor, some with legacies to be paid to each freed slave. More often than not, these masters left specific instructions as to how their wishes were to be executed. One of the earliest cases in which heirs attempted to nullify a bequest of freedom for several slaves was *Chardon's Heirs* v. *Bongue* (1836). It is impossible to determine why the first appeals of this nature did not occur until 1836—perhaps there were few large-scale manumissions before that year, or perhaps acceptance of emancipation was eroding by 1836 and heirs felt justified in fighting decedents' wishes.

Chardon involved a slaveowner, Joseph Chardon, who summoned his notary a few days before his death and made a will emancipating all of his slaves; he left two of them, Jenny and Eugene, $3,000 each. He gave the remainder of his estate to Pierre Isaac Bongue, the owner of a gambling house in New Orleans. Chardon had no forced heirs, ascending or descending, but his brothers and nephews, his heirs at law, sued to have the will declared void. If Chardon had died intestate—that is, without a legal will—the heirs would have inherited the entire estate, including the slaves. The heirs based their case on allegations that the will was not properly witnessed, as the witnesses were employees at Bongue's gambling establishment, and that the mere fact that the notary drew up the will at Bongue's residence "alone makes it suspicious." The lower court found for Bongue, dismissing the complaint that the witnesses were Bongue's employees: "Although it be not disputed that there are but few employments less honorable than those of a gambling house, still there is no law in this state, incapacitating persons of that description to appear as witnesses, either to a will or any other act, or in a court of justice; nor is there any law in this state, declaring that a man in the employment of a legatee, cannot be a witness to the will."

To the complaint that Chardon's presence in Bongue's house was evidence of "fraud and violence" to coerce Chardon to write a will disinheriting his brothers and nephews, the judge of the lower court replied:

> The reason of his [Chardon's] not leaving any thing to his relations was, that they had attempted to assassinate him at the Havana [Cuba], speaking of his nephews; and would not leave anything to his brothers, that the nephews should not profit through them. He expressed this opinion six months before his death, and always, for six or eight years had been of the same mind, ever since the nephews attempted to assassinate him . . . from the whole of the testimony, the court has been forced to come to the conclusion, that his sentiments in that respect had undergone a complete change. It appears that . . . he went to France, where he made but a short stay, that he took with him, or was followed by two of his nephews; that being in the Havana he was robbed by those neph-

ews, who even attempted to take his life, and inflicted upon him wounds which kept him lingering until his death, and that since that time he was entirely estranged from his family, and determined not to leave his property to them.

Judge Henry Bullard affirmed the judgment of the lower court, holding that the will was properly witnessed and that there was no evidence of fraud or conspiracy to influence the testator. Bullard cited *Civil Code* article 1479, which prohibited heirs from attacking a testamentary disposition with evidence that it had been made "through hatred, anger, suggestion, or captation."[2]

During the next term the court heard another appeal, *Sarcé* v. *Donoyer's Executor* (1837), involving a testator who wrote a will in 1833 in which he bequeathed freedom to several of his slaves and instituted them as his universal legatees (a civil-law term meaning they would inherit all of his estate after any debts of the succession and particular legacies were satisfied).[3] He also left legacies to his grandnephews and grandnieces of $1,200 and $2,000, respectively. Two years later he made another will, without any clause revoking the first will. The second will also called for emancipation of the slaves but left each one only a small legacy. Donoyer made his executor the universal legatee in the second will and made no mention of any legacies to his grandnephews and -nieces, and when both wills were submitted to probate, these heirs sued the executor to recover their legacies under the first will. The judge of the probate court cited *Civil Code* article 1686 in ruling for the plaintiffs: "Posterior testaments, which do not in an express manner revoke the prior ones, annul in the latter only such of the dispositions therein contained as are incompatible with the new ones, or contrary to them, or entirely different."

The executor appealed the decision. Judge Bullard reasoned that the mere substitution of the executor for the slaves as universal legatee did not demonstrate a change that nullified the legacies to the grandnieces and grandnephews. In ruling for the plaintiffs Bullard wrote: "We are sensible, that to the great mass of the citizens it will appear absurd, that a man can leave two last wills in force. But we are to ascertain the prob-

2. Chardon's Heirs v. Bongue, No. 2931, 9 La. 458 (1836). *Civil Code,* Art. 1479, p. 225. *Captation* is an old word of French origin meaning manipulation.

3. *Civil Code,* Art. 1599, p. 244.

able intentions of testators, not by reference to the common received notions on these subjects, but according to the provisions of law, and must presume, however gross the fiction, that the testator knew the law and even its subtleties as well as, if not better than, a professor of the faculty of Paris." The emancipation of the slaves was never an issue, but this ruling reduced their inheritance to a small bequest rather than the remainder of the estate.[4]

During the next term of the court, fifteen slaves lost their chance for emancipation in *Langley's Heirs* v. *Langley's Executors* (1838) because they became ensnared in the complexities of Louisiana's succession law. In 1836 George Langley of East Baton Rouge Parish made a will in which he gave each of his two named executors a slave, and also emancipated fifteen of his slaves, to whom he left all of his personal property. He had no forced heirs. Relatives of the deceased man sued to have the will nullified on the basis that three witnesses were not present during the dictation of the will to the notary, as required by article 1571 of the *Civil Code*. The executors proved that three witnesses had been present when the notary read the will back to the testator, and all three heard him declare that it was his will. All three signed the will. However, the plaintiffs were able to prove that during Langley's dictation of the will to the notary, only two witnesses were actually in the room. The judge of the probate court found the will to be valid, and Langley's relatives appealed. Judge Henry Carleton reversed the decision because article 1571 required three witnesses to be present at the dictation of the will to the notary. This requirement, Carleton contended, was "a double safeguard for the faithful execution of wills, by requiring they should be dictated in presence of three witnesses, to whom they are then to be read, that it may appear they were truly written as dictated." Ruling that "the will is a mere nullity," the court ordered the executors to turn all of Langley's property over to his relatives, including the slaves.[5]

That was not the end of it. Langley's executors discovered another will written by George Langley, this one an olographic will dated 1835 and valid in form. In it, Langley gave several of his slaves to his execu-

4. Sarcé v. Dunoyer's Executor, No. 3106, 11 La. 220 (1837); *Civil Code*, Art. 1686, p. 256.

5. *Civil Code*, Art. 1571, p. 240; Langley's Heirs v. Langley's Executors, No. 3140, 12 La. 114 (1838). See also Succession of Key, 5 Rob. 482 (La. 1843), and Keller v. McCalop, No. 5814, 12 Rob. 639 (La. 1846).

tors and his heirs to serve them until they could be emancipated at age thirty. Langley also ordered his executors to immediately emancipate six of his slaves. He further ordered that all of his property be divided among five of the named slaves. The supreme court decision in *Langley's Heirs* v. *Langley's Executors* occurred in March, 1838; the executors probated the olographic will in May, 1838, although they took no steps to emancipate the slaves that Langley had ordered emancipated immediately. Langley's nieces sued the executors for possession of the slaves in *Nimmo* v. *Bonney and Bird* (1843), on the grounds that since the executors had made no effort to free the six slaves, they should surrender them to the deceased's legal heirs. The executors won in the lower court, and the heirs appealed. Judge Alonzo Morphy reversed the decision and ruled for the heirs. Morphy accepted the argument that in accordance with an act of 1831, slaves under the age of thirty could be emancipated only if they were natives of Louisiana. Thus, the six slaves could not be freed before they became thirty years of age, as they had been born elsewhere. Since they could not be freed until age thirty, the court ruled, the heirs were entitled to their services until that time. "How then can they [the executors] refuse to surrender to the petitioners property in their hands belonging to the estate of their uncle, and undisposed of by his will? This surrender will not impair the right of the slaves to obtain their emancipation whenever it can legally take place."[6]

In *Succession of Senac* (1842), the court denied two slaves the freedom left to them in their master's will. In 1836 Guillaume Senac made an olographic will that provided for the emancipation of the slaves. Two days after writing the will, he married and left for France, where he remained until his death in 1838. In 1837, Senac's wife gave birth to a son. After Senac's death, his widow sued to have the 1836 will declared null. The basis of her suit was *Civil Code* article 1698, which stated: "The testament falls by the birth of legitimate children of the testator, posterior to its date."[7] Since Louisiana's law of forced heirship required all parents to treat their children equally, the children alive at the time the testament was made would have an unfair advantage over any child born subsequently. Therefore, wills made prior to the birth of a child were null and void. The probate court nullified the will on the basis of article 1698, and the legatees appealed on the grounds that the deceased

6. Nimmo v. Bonney and Bird, No. 5138, 4 Rob. 176 (La. 1843).

7. Succession of Senac, No. 4080, 2 Rob. 258 (La. 1842); *Civil Code,* Art. 1698, p. 257.

was at the time of his death a resident of France, and that French law, which would not invalidate the will, should apply. In considering this appeal, the justices referred to *Civil Code* article 483, which provided that "persons who reside out of the State, cannot dispose of the property they possess here, in a manner different from that prescribed by its laws," and article 10: "The form and effect of public and private written instruments are governed by the laws and usages where they are passed or executed." In ruling to void the will, the justices reasoned:

> In the present instance the will having been made in Louisiana, and the property of the deceased being situated here, we can see no good reason why our law should be superseded by that of France. Article 1698 may in some measure be considered as a tacit resolutory condition, on the happening of which the will was to become void. Of this the testator must have been aware when he left his will behind him, to be carried into effect under our laws. This provision of our Code is founded on the presumption that he would not have made such a will, had he foreseen that he would thereafter have children. If, as has been remarked, the testator did not revoke this will during the sixteen months that he survived the birth of his child, it is fair to presume that it was because he knew that by the law of Louisiana, under which it was made, it had become a nullity on the birth of such child.

The attorney for the legatees under the will had argued that even if the will were null, the bequests of freedom to the slaves should be honored, as they were valid under Roman law. The court denied this request on the basis that the Roman law cited had no application in this case and that as the will was a nullity, it could have no effects: "It could hardly be expected of us to adopt as a rule to be followed the decision of the Emperor Antoninus in relation to a succession, claimed by the Treasury on account of a will that had become void for the want of instituted heirs. He decided in his liberality that certain slaves emancipated by the will should be set free, notwithstanding its nullity; but this decision was obtained from his munificence, and not on principles of strict law. *Quod nullum est nullum producit effectum*."[8]

Stephen Henderson, a penniless Scottish immigrant who became a

8. *Civil Code,* Art. 1698, p. 257, Art. 483, pp. 71–72, Art. 10, pp. 4–5; Succession of Senac, No. 4080, 2 Rob. 258 (La. 1842). "What is null produces no effects."

merchant, planter, and millionaire, wrote a will with a detailed plan of gradual emancipation of his slaves and maintenance of them in the interim. Henderson, known as "Monsieur Croesus" and "the Scottish Marvel" as well as "Old Baggy Pantaloons," died in 1838. His assets included a country home in White Sulphur Springs, Virginia, three plantations valued at upwards of $400,000, 569 slaves, and an elegant residence on Canal Street in New Orleans. He stated in his 1838 will: "My greatest object is to do the greatest quantity of good, and to the greatest number of persons and to the poorest people." He left money to churches, asylums, hospitals, and the firemen of New Orleans (who used it to purchase Cypress Grove Cemetery). The most unusual provisions of the will concerned his slaves. He set up an elaborate scheme that stipulated that his executor was to arrange for some slaves (chosen by lot) to be sent to Africa, and some kept together on one of his plantations, which was to be turned into "an industrial emporium." The remaining slaves were to be taught to make "negro cloth" and "negro shoes" by Scottish weavers and shoemakers imported for that purpose. The slaves were to have as an overseer a "man of humanity" who was to treat them with kindness. They were each to have three pounds of beef or pork a week and to be allowed to keep the proceeds of their gardens, an allotment that Henderson smugly observed was much more than European laborers consumed. Henderson stated, "I have always treated my blacks with much indulgence and even personal kindness."

Beginning five years after Henderson's death, five male and five female slaves were to be chosen by lot each year and offered the option of being transported to Liberia and given $100 plus $75 for transportation. If they chose instead to stay in Louisiana, they were to remain enslaved; should they go and return, they were to be reenslaved. Henderson's will was the subject of many lawsuits and several decisions of the Supreme Court of Louisiana right up to the Civil War. The first suit, *Rost* v. *Henderson* (1846), dealt with the first group of slaves sent to Africa. Following Henderson's death, the heirs had divided the slaves among them. Those who were in possession of the ten slaves chosen by lot to leave for Africa refused to hand them over to the executors, one of whom was Justice Pierre Adolphe Rost. The executors sued for delivery of the slaves and for the $100 for each slave as directed by Henderson's will. The lower court found for the heirs, and the executors appealed. Judge François-Xavier Martin ordered the heirs to deliver the slaves and the money to the executors: "The defendants, by the act for the division of the slaves, and to which the executors were parties, bound themselves, in case that portion of the will which relates to the transportation of the slaves to Africa, should be declared valid by the courts having jurisdiction, to comply therewith, and to support all the charges and expenses attending the execution of the same."[9]

To prevent having to comply with the will the following year, Henderson's brother and sister sued his executor in *Heirs of Henderson* v. *Rost* (1850) to invalidate the will on the basis that it was "an attempt by a testator to perpetuate his succession in violation of the policy of the law . . . to make that inalienable which the policy of all civilized nations had declared . . . to be marketable." The district court found for the heirs, ruling that Henderson's will was contrary to Louisiana law: "Our jurisprudence, as it is well known, [was] to prevent property from being tied up for a length of time in the hands of individuals, and placed out of the reach of Commerce." On appeal, Justice Thomas Slidell affirmed the judgment, stating that Henderson's will violated Louisiana's prohibition of trusts and perpetuities. Slidell cited *Civil Code* article 1507, "Every disposition, by which the . . . heir or legatee is charged to preserve for or return a thing to a third person; is null," and article 1702, "Every portion of a succession remaining undisposed of . . . shall devolve upon the legitimate heirs." No provisions of Henderson's will were executed after this decision except the bequest to the firemen. Much of Henderson's vast fortune disappeared, perhaps consumed by the attorneys involved; what Slidell referred to as Henderson's "socialist scheme" failed.[10]

A master's failure to make a new will deprived the slave Betty of her freedom in *Succession of Dupuy* (1849). George Dupuy died in 1848, leaving a will in which he made his brother, Joseph, his universal legatee

9. Rost v. Henderson, No. 5617, 12 Rob. 549 (La. 1846).

10. Heirs of Henderson v. Rost, Nos. 1469, 5617, 5 La. Ann. 441 (1850); Henderson v. Rost, No. 2255, 11 La. Ann. 541 (1856); Rost and Montgomery v. Doyal, No. 6564, 15 La. Ann. 265 (1860); Henderson v. Rost, No. 6726, 15 La. Ann. 405 (1860); *Civil Code,* Arts. 1507, 1702, pp. 229, 258; John Churchill Chase, *Frenchmen, Desire, Good Children, and Other Streets of New Orleans* (New Orleans, 1949), 107. See also Francis P. Burns, "Stephen Henderson," New Orleans *Times-Picayune Dixie Roto,* September 24, 1950. Henderson's wealth did not entirely vanish. A small trust, dedicated to making charitable grants, exists to this day. The trustees wish that their names and other details about the trust remain secret and unavailable to the public.

and Antoine Michoud his executor. He also attached a codicil in which he ordered Michoud to emancipate the slave Betty. After the testator died, Michoud probated the will and the codicil, and asked to be named executor. One of Dupuy's heirs objected, alleging that the will and the codicil were null and void because Joseph Dupuy had predeceased George Dupuy and now "there was no longer any will to execute." The heirs contended that the succession should be administered as though Dupuy had died intestate. The lower court ruled that the will was invalid and discharged Michoud as executor. He appealed. Justice Rost affirmed the decision: "There being no testamentary dispositions to execute, and no debts to pay, in this case, the appointment of the defendant as executor has become inoperative."[11]

John McDonogh, a New Orleans merchant who died in 1850, successfully freed forty-one of his ninety-four slaves in his will. In 1842 McDonogh had allowed eighty-four of his slaves to purchase their freedom by night and weekend labor, and he had sent them to Liberia. Before his intentions were known, his neighbors gossiped that McDonogh must be a very cruel master to force his slaves to work so enthusiastically for such long hours. After the first group departed for Liberia, McDonogh immediately purchased another gang of slaves from Maryland and Virginia, planning to allow them to earn their freedom in fifteen years. A firm believer in the African colonization movement, which advocated sending blacks back to the land of their origin, McDonogh left one-eighth of his succession to the American Colonization Society in his will, and he freed half of his slaves and provided for their transportation to Africa. Overseers to supervise the remaining slaves were to be chosen with care to lead the slaves to Christianity and teach them an occupation. McDonogh also petitioned the Louisiana legislature to allow his slaves to be taught to read in order that they might benefit by reading the Bible. Those who were not immediately freed were to be emancipated and sent to Liberia fifteen years after his death.

McDonogh died in 1850, and litigation over his will prevented any slaves from departing from Louisiana until 1859, when they finally sailed to Liberia. McDonogh had no forced heirs, but his other relatives sued to have his will annulled because he left the bulk of his money for the establishment of public schools in New Orleans and Baltimore. The

11. Succession of Dupuy, No. 1438, 4 La. Ann. 570 (1849).

heirs argued that this legacy set up a trust in violation of Louisiana law. They cited *Heirs of Henderson* v. *Rost* in support of their position. Chief Justice George Eustis ruled against the heirs, affirming the decision of the lower court: "The distinction between this and *Henderson's* will . . . is obvious. *Henderson* made no disposition of his property in favor of any one, but simply provided that it should forever form part of his succession and be administered by his executors and commissioners to be named after them to the end of time—while *McDonogh* has made a valid disposition of his property, and the perpetuity of the bequest is merely the consequence of the perpetual existence of the legatee" (emphasis in original).[12]

During the same term, the supreme court heard another case in which a testator attempted to free a number of his slaves, *Succession of Cresswell* (1853). Elihu Cresswell, a New Orleans slave dealer, wrote a will in which he bequeathed freedom and $50 to his slave Gabriel "for his long and faithful services, that he may acquire his freedom in the slave States, or be sent to the free United States of America, as he may desire." He also left freedom to all slaves that he happened to own at the time of his death, and transportation to a free state, the expense of which was to come from the succession. The remainder of his succession he left to his mother, or her heirs if she should have predeceased him. One of Cresswell's appointed executors failed to keep the funds of the succession in a bank, as required by law. For this irregularity, the probate court dismissed him and fined him 20 percent of the value of the succession. He sued for his commission on the value of the succession (a fee to compensate executors for their services), including the value of the slaves, whom he had made no attempt to emancipate. The probate court refused to include the slaves in the evaluation. Justice Rost affirmed the decision. A new executor emancipated the slaves and subsequently sent them to New York.[13]

In *Gentile* v. *Plasencia* (1855), the court once more heard an appeal in which heirs of a person who bequeathed freedom to several slaves sued

12. Arthur G. Nuhrah, "John McDonogh: Liberal Slaveholder" (M.A. thesis, Tulane University, 1947), 54, 71–73; States of Louisiana and Maryland v. Executor of John McDonogh and the City of New Orleans, No. 2175, 8 La. Ann. 171 (1853).

13. Succession of Cresswell, No. 2423, 8 La. Ann. 122 (1853); Succession of Cresswell, Unreported Supreme Court Case No. 3521 (1854). Compare this case with Bailey v. Poindexter, 14 Grattan 132 (Va. 1858).

to have his will annulled. Francisco Plasencia had made a will in which he ordered his executors to free four of his slaves and give them a legacy of $2,000. The executor named in the will was one of Plasencia's sons, and the court appointed an attorney to defend the suit to annul the will, as the executor-son, being himself one of the heirs at law, "might be deemed to have an interest opposed to that of the legatees." The lower court judged the will to be valid and ordered the executor to free the slaves and pay them their $2,000. The attorney who had successfully defended the will demanded $500 of the succession as his fee. The executor petitioned the court to allow him to take the $500 from the $2,000 legacy to the slaves. The lower court allowed this action, and the slaves' attorney appealed. Justice Alexander Buchanan reversed the lower-court decision, ruling that the heirs must pay the fee from the succession: "If there be a liability any where [*sic*] to pay the value of the curator's services, it would seem to rest upon the heirs who provoked his appointment in their unsuccessful attack upon the testator's will. It seems just that they, his universal legatees, should bear the burden of any expense incurred in resisting the execution of the declared will of their testator, to-wit: the emancipation of their slaves."[14]

In 1854 Jacques Molaison made a will in which he ordered his executor, Valmont Hébert, to free all of his slaves upon his death. His heirs sued in *Molaison* v. *Hébert* (1857) to annul this part of the will because it was not in accordance with the act of 1852 that required masters freeing slaves to provide $150 for their transportation to Liberia or stipulate that they be hired out until they could earn $150 for their passage. The lower court found the portion of the will ordering the emancipation of the slaves void because it was not in compliance with the 1852 statute. In the trial court, the judge had appointed a curator *ad hoc* for the slaves, and he appealed. Justice Henry Spofford dismissed his appeal: "We have been referred to no law authorizing a curator *ad hoc* to stand in judgment in such a proceeding as this, and we do not think it was contemplated by the lawgiver [the legislature]." This ruling did not, however, preclude an appeal by the executor, Hébert. Spofford dismissed the curator's appeal in March, 1857, the same month as the passage of the 1857 prohibition of all emancipations. There is no record of an appeal by Hébert.[15]

14. Gentile v. Plasencia, No. 3843, 10 La. Ann. 203 (1855).

15. Molaison v. Hébert, No. 5031, 12 La. Ann. 232 (1857); "An Act Concerning the Emancipation of Slaves in This State," Act of March 18, 1852, *Louisiana Acts, 1852,* 214–15.

The 1857 act, rather than Louisiana's succession law, thwarted two other attempts by masters to free their slaves by will. Baker Woodruff's will, drawn up in February, 1855, directed the emancipation of a large number of his slaves. He further ordered his executor to send the freed slaves to Pennsylvania and provide them with bread and meat for one year. After Woodruff's death in May, 1857, the executor applied for a court order to take the slaves to Pennsylvania and free them, and for funds to provide for their transportation and maintenance. The heirs opposed this action, stating that the provisions of the will "relating to the manumission of the slaves and their removal to Pennsylvania, are contrary to the laws of the State of Louisiana, and to public policy, and are absolutely null and void." The judge of the St. Bernard District Court found for the heirs, and the executor appealed. Justice James Cole stated that it was clear that Woodruff had intended his slaves to be freed in Louisiana, and then transported to Pennsylvania:

> In the absence of any provision of the will exhibiting an adverse intention, a testator must be presumed to have intended that the provisions of his will should be executed in accordance with the laws of the State where it is made, where he lives and has his property, rather than in accordance with the laws of a foreign State.
>
> If the law prohibiting emancipation had not been passed, it would have been the duty of the executor under this will to have applied in this State for the emancipation of the slaves, and afterwards for a sufficient sum of money to be taken from the estate to buy for them food for their sustenance in Pennsylvania, where they were to be sent after their emancipation.
>
> If the executor had demanded of the court permission to take the slaves to another State to be emancipated, whilst our laws would have allowed him to have freed them in this State, it is evident that the permission would have been refused, because the intention of the will was, they should be liberated in this State. . . .
>
> The testator lived a sufficiently long time after the enactment of the law prohibiting emancipation to have adopted some other method of enfranchising his negroes, if his intentions, as manifested in the testament, had remained unchanged.[16]

16. Succession of Woodruff, No. 5699, 14 La. Ann. 295 (1859).

During the same term, the court heard *Deshotels* v. *Soileau* (1859). In an 1855 will, André Deshotels had left his nephew and his wife all of his property, personal and real, including all of his slaves, on the condition that as soon as possible after his death the nephew and wife should free thirteen of the slaves. He stipulated that those freed should be permitted to stay in the state. If this were impossible under Louisiana law, the nephew and wife were to free the slaves, give them $150, and transport them out of Louisiana. Failure to comply with these terms would annul the legacy to the nephew and his wife. After Deshotels' death in 1855, the nephew and wife made no attempt to free the slaves, and the executor brought suit to compel compliance with the will. By the time he sued, the 1857 law was in effect, but he claimed the slaves had possessed "a vested and indefeasible right" to freedom since Deshotels' death in 1855. Citing *Succession of Woodruff,* Justice Alexander Buchanan ruled in favor of Deshotels' nephew and his wife:

> We then held, and we adhere to the doctrine, that the right of a slave to freedom under the will of his master, was not vested, until the formalities required by law for consummating the emancipation had been complied with.
>
> The right of the owner of a slave to give the slave his freedom, was always a qualified right in Louisiana, subject to the action of the constituted authorities, and by the Act of the 6th of March, 1857, the right, qualified as it was before, has been annihilated. Dating from the passage of that Act, we understand the policy of this State to be, that the slaves within her borders shall remain slaves.
>
> . . . The legacy of their freedom, . . . be declared to have failed.[17]

The Civil War and the resulting emancipation of all slaves mooted cases involving emancipation by will. However, emancipation by will was practiced often enough during the antebellum period that the Supreme Court of Louisiana heard a few appeals of such cases each year. The court was not reluctant to approve these acts, providing that the testator followed proper forms and did not disinherit forced heirs, until the 1857 prohibition of emancipation. One can only speculate as to why

17. Deshotels v. Soileau, 14 La. Ann. 745 (1859).

masters freeing their slaves by will failed to ensure their free status by liberating them legally before their demise. Perhaps the disapproval of family members, an optimistic belief that survivors would carry out the will of the deceased, or simple ignorance of the legal obstacles to emancipation and the complexities of Louisiana's succession laws were the cause. However, as many of these people had substantial wealth and could have consulted lawyers, a more likely explanation is the slaveholders' desire to control their slaves while alive, perhaps cloaked by a paternalistic concern for the well-being of their freed slaves. Of course, as a practical matter, freed slaves could choose to leave their former owner's service, causing loss of labor and convenience. In any event, lack of foresight annulled several emancipation attempts.

As for the heirs of men or women who emancipated slaves by will, blood may have been thicker than water, but often the reality of alienating a liquid asset from the estate was thicker still. Greed thwarted more manumissions by will than did jealousy or fear of public opinion. And in several cases heard by the Supreme Court of Louisiana, the avarice of free black relatives of slaves emancipated by will and their disregard of succession law matched that of their white counterparts.

Cases involving emancipation of slaves by will when the testator was a free person of color did come before the Supreme Court of Louisiana, although they were not so numerous as those involving whites freeing their bondservants by testament. Considering the fact that many free blacks owned members of their own family, this is surprising. One explanation is that free people of color who owned their relatives tended to emancipate them as soon as possible with *inter vivos* donations, rather than by will. Also, because black slaveowners probably did not treat their husbands, wives, or children as slaves even if they were legally slaves, wills freeing them simply pronounced what was already a fact. Many such manumissions were uncontested and therefore do not appear in trial court records. Also, slaves living as free persons—as must often have been the case when they were owned by free persons of color—could acquire prescriptive title to freedom by ten years' good faith possession of themselves, at least prior to 1857.

Emancipation cases heard by Louisiana's highest court involving free black masters emancipating slaves by will often reflect the same motivations for manumission as with white masters: bonds of conjugal or filial love between slaveowner and slave. Before 1835, 63 percent of slaves emancipated by free blacks were their own family members. In fact, this type of manumission formed a high percentage of all emancipations: between 1827 and 1851, 501 of the 1,353 petitions to free slaves in New Orleans (or 37 percent) involved free blacks attempting to free their relatives by marriage or blood.[18]

Jun, f.m.c., v. *Livaudais* (1827) was one of the earliest appeals of a case involving a contested will of a free black attempting to emancipate his children by will. Mathurin Jun, a free black man, had four children, all of whom he wished to free. As soon as the eldest three children, Josephine, Rosette, and Mathurin, Jr., reached the legal age (thirty) at which Louisiana law permitted emancipation, Jun freed them. In 1823 he executed a will leaving all three free children $500 each. He also left his executor $600 to free his fourth child, Narcisse, as soon as he became thirty years old. Josephine died in 1824; Jun, Sr., in 1825. Mathurin, Jr., sued the executor, with two objectives. First, he claimed that since Josephine had predeceased her father, her $500 should be split between him and Rosette, as his father's only free heirs. The lower court refused this request, as Josephine had a young daughter. Although born to Josephine when she was still a slave, and therefore a slave herself, the child had the right to freedom as soon as she should reach the legal age for emancipation. The judge cited article 196 of *Civil Code:* "The child born of a woman after she has acquired the right of being free at a future time, follows the condition of its mother, and becomes free at the time fixed for her enfranchisement, even if the mother should die before that time." As to her right to inherit even though still a slave, the judge cited article 193: "The slave who has acquired the right of being free at a future time, is from that time, capable of receiving by testament or donation. Property given or devised to him must be preserved for him, in order to be delivered to him in kind, when his emancipation shall take place. In the mean time [*sic*] it must be administered by a curator."

Mathurin, Jr., also contested the $600 given to the executor to free

18. *Civil Code,* Art. 3510, p. 532; Kotlikoff and Rupert, "Manumission of Slaves in New Orleans" 180; John W. Blassingame, *Black New Orleans, 1860–1880* (Chicago, 1973), 11. From May 27, 1846, to June 4, 1850, the First Municipality of New Orleans sanctioned the emancipation of 250 slaves. Of these, 72 were emancipated by free people of color. Jerrye Louise Baehr Martin, "New Orleans Slavery, 1840–1860: Testing the Wade Theory" (M.A. thesis, Tulane University, 1972), 31.

Narcisse, claiming that this provision made the will null and void because the $600 was actually a donation to Narcisse, who, as a slave, was unable to inherit anything. He requested that the $600 be divided between him and Rosette. The probate-court judge brushed aside this argument also, as Narcisse was a *statu liber,* having acquired the right to freedom at a certain time or upon a certain condition. Therefore, his father was entitled to provide for his emancipation, although Narcisse would belong to Mathurin, Jr., Rosette, and Josephine's daughter until he became free. The probate-court judge ruled that Mathurin, Jr., was to inherit only the $500 stipulated in the will, that the executor should preserve Josephine's daughter's legacy for her until her emancipation, and that the $600 provided for Narcisse's emancipation was a valid stipulation of the will. Mathurin, Jr., appealed to the supreme court. Confronted with his attempt to appropriate his niece's inheritance and to prevent the emancipation of his brother, the court affirmed the judgment of the lower court: "This is one of the harshest demands and the most revolting to every principle . . . that has yet fallen under our consideration."[19]

In *Succession of Duplessis, f.m.c.* (1845), the heirs managed to thwart the attempt of their relative, Martin Duplessis, f.m.c., to free the slave Sophie and her children by the terms of his will. Duplessis died in Plaquemines Parish in 1833. He made several specific legacies in his will, including ordering the emancipation of Sophie and her children. His executor, Valfrey Duplessis, a brother of the testator, died in 1834 without having executed any part of the will, and no one was appointed in his place. Martin Duplessis' heirs took possession of his property and slaves; they kept Sophie and her children until 1842, when they requested a partition (a civil-law term meaning division) of the slaves; the district court ordered the slaves appraised and sold, and the proceeds divided among the heirs. Two years after the sale, one Louis Lombard applied to the probate court to be appointed executor of Duplessis' will in order to emancipate Sophie and her children. The heirs opposed this action, alleging that Duplessis' will was invalid and, therefore, he died intestate. The heirs also pleaded that they had been in peaceful possession of the succession for five years. The Probate Court of Plaquemines

19. Jun, f.m.c., v. Livaudais, No. 1292, 5 Mart (N.S.) 301 (La. 1827); *Civil Code,* Arts. 196, 193, p. 30.

Parish rejected Lombard's application, and he appealed. Judge Alonzo Morphy affirmed this decision:

> It is entirely unnecessary for us to enquire into the alleged invalidity of the will, as, upon another ground, we are of opinion that the application for letters testamentary was properly rejected. If Sophie and her children were yet in the possession of the heirs of Martin Duplessis, the fact of their having taken possession of the estate, some years ago, would afford no good ground for rejecting the application of the appellant, the special duty of an executor being to carry into effect the will of the testator, which it may be and is often the interest of the heirs to disregard. . . . In the present case, Sophie and her children are no longer in the possession of the heirs; they have been sold, and have passed into the hands of other persons, in disregard of whose apparent rights, the applicant, were he appointed executor, could not proceed to the emancipation of these slaves under the will. The right of Sophie and of her children to their freedom has not been lessened, nor in any way impaired by the course pursued by the heirs of the testator, but it must be asserted contradictorily with the person who bought them.

Thus the supreme court did not end this matter. The issue of Sophie's right to freedom would confront the court twice more before its final resolution in a special type of lawsuit—the only way the *Civil Code* permitted a slave to be a party in, and actually instigate, a civil lawsuit—a suit for freedom. The outcome of Sophie's two suits for freedom will be discussed in the following chapter.[20]

Illness and legal intricacies prevented the emancipation of the slave Louis in *Michel* v. *Dolliole, f.m.c.* (1846). Joseph Prieto, a free black man, left a will, which his executor, Jean Louis Dolliole, f.m.c., submitted to probate court in 1838. One provision of the will ordered Dolliole to take $500 from the succession to purchase Prieto's nephew, Louis, from his owner, Michel, and free him. Prieto also provided money for the purchase and emancipation of his other slave relatives. Dolliole offered the plaintiff $500, but she refused to sell Louis at that price. She subsequently agreed to sell him for $550, but then Dolliole refused to execute

20. Succession of Duplessis, f.m.c., No. 5598, 10 Rob. 193 (La. 1845); *Civil Code,* Art. 2415, p. 377.

the sale. Michel sued for specific performance. The trial court judge ruled in her favor, and Dolliole appealed. The supreme court reversed the decision on two grounds. Citing *Civil Code* article 2415, Justice Rost ruled the agreement invalid because it was not written:

> All sales of immovable property or slaves, shall be made by authentic act, or under private signature.
>
> All verbal sale of any of these things shall be null, as well for third persons as for the contracting parties themselves, and the testimonial proof of it shall not be admitted.

The second reason for the reversal was the condition of the slave when Michel finally agreed to sell him:

> And as, at the time she gave that notice, the slave was lying dangerously ill, there would have been nothing unreasonable in the defendant's refusal to accept the sale, till he was restored to health. In his condition, he was not worth the price demanded for him.[21]

Each year during the antebellum period the Louisiana Supreme Court heard appeals in which legitimate heirs attempted to annul wills that left certain slaves their freedom upon the death of the testator. The court was not philosophically opposed to the emancipation of slaves by will, so long as such dispositions conformed to Louisiana's laws governing emancipations. As the state's stake in slavery increased, so did the number of restrictions on manumission. Louisiana's unique inheritance laws, especially forced heirship, also made emancipation more difficult. However, Louisiana lawmakers, unlike their colleagues in other Deep South states, never restricted emancipation to a handful of specific legislative acts, and they refused, at least until 1857, to end one of the most important rights that Louisiana slaves possessed. Until that year, a slave not only could be a party to a civil suit, but indeed could initiate such a suit—providing it was a suit for freedom.

21. Michel v. Dolliole, f.m.c., No. 6120, 1 La. Ann. 459 (1846).

9

"AN EMANCIPATION, ONCE PERFECTED, IS IRREVOCABLE"

Suits for Freedom

SUING FOR FREEDOM WAS AN EXCEPTIONAL LEGAL ACtion in antebellum Louisiana. It was the *only* time a slave had the right to initiate a lawsuit. Article 177 of the 1825 *Civil Code* stated: "He [the slave] cannot be a party in any civil action, either as plaintiff or defendant, except when he has to claim or prove his freedom." This provision gave slaves in Louisiana the right to institute a civil suit for freedom directly.

In most common-law slave states, slaves who wished to sue for freedom had to proceed through the use of a legal fiction. Usually, the common-law states prohibited slaves from suing directly for their freedom without the aid of a free person, a court-appointed guardian *ad litem*—a "Near Friend" (as it was called in Tennessee) or "Next Friend" (as some other southern courts termed it). In some states a suit for freedom could not be initiated directly at all, even with the aid of a court-appointed representative. Instead, the guardian of the slave or the slave himself or herself had to begin an action of trespass for an assault against the master or mistress, who would respond by stating that the plaintiff was a slave and could not sue, whereupon the plaintiff would claim to be free. The court would then ignore the assault issue and agree to rule on the issue of freedom.[1]

The ability of a slave to sue for freedom directly was unique to Louisiana. Even in Roman law, slaves suing for freedom had to have a "prisoner's friend" bring the suit for them. The French *Code Noir* deprived slaves of standing or capacity in civil litigation. However, under Spanish

1. Stampp, *Peculiar Institution,* 197; Howington, "Treatment of Slaves and Free Blacks," 17–20; Finkelman, *The Law of Freedom and Bondage: A Casebook* (New York, 1986), 97–99; Watson, *Roman Slave Law,* 24–25.

rule, Louisiana slaves gained the right of self-purchase (*coartación*). To bring self-purchase petitions against their masters, slaves had to possess judicial standing, a right never in doubt in Spanish Louisiana. Although the right of *coartación* did not survive the Spanish period, the capacity of the slave to sue for freedom was incorporated into the *Digest of 1808* and the *Civil Code of 1825*.[2]

Throughout the antebellum period the Louisiana Supreme Court heard appeals of cases in which slaves, on a variety of grounds, sued for their freedom. The court was generally in favor of freedom—at least until the act of 1857 prohibiting emancipation—as long as the slave could prove that he or she was legally entitled to it.

Incidentally, it is clear from the record that slaves suing for their freedom used attorneys to plead their causes. How they hired and paid for counsel is a mystery. Perhaps members of the free black community, possibly blood relatives, contributed toward attorneys' fees, or perhaps attorneys served without compensation.

Although article 177 strictly denied slaves the capacity to sue for anything except their freedom, attorneys for a few slaves attempted unsuccessfully to bring civil suits for other reasons. In *Delphine, f.c.g.*, v. *Segher's Syndics* (1820), the slave woman Delphine sued the creditors of her master to require that whoever purchased her should continue her education as a seamstress; she wanted to ensure that she could support herself. She also sued to force her new master to free her when she attained the legal age of thirty because her old master, before he fell on financial hard times, had promised in writing to free her. She complained that since his creditors had seized her, they had placed her

2. Barry Nicholas, *An Introduction to Roman Law* (New York, 1962), 72–73. The slave Louis petitioned the Louisiana Supreme Court in 1848 to appoint a curator to aid him in pursuing his claim for freedom. His former owner, Antoine General, had died in January, 1836, when Louis was fourteen years of age. General left a will instructing his executor to care for Louis until he reached twenty-one, at which time he was to be freed. He became the specified age in 1847, and the executor made no attempt to free him. The executor claimed that Louis had run away several times, was disobedient, had committed several assaults on whites, and was generally disrespectful toward white people. The court ruled that Louis did not need a curator, that he could sue for his freedom without aid. It is not known whether he brought suit in a subsequent action. Louis, *statu liber,* v. Cousin, No. 972, 3 La. Ann. 467 (1848) [reported as *ex parte* Louis]. See also Rankin, "Tannenbaum Thesis Reconsidered," 19–20; Baade, "Law of Slavery in Spanish Luisiana," in *Louisiana's Legal Heritage,* ed. Haas, 65, 70; *Digest of 1808,* Tit. IV, Chap. 3, p. 30; *Civil Code,* Art. 177, p. 28.

"among the slaves of the worst description, to the manifest injury both of her morals and her instruction." The Supreme Court of Louisiana dismissed her appeal, stating that she had no right to sue to continue her education or improve her living conditions. Citing article 177, the court ruled that she had no standing in court until she attained the legal age required for emancipation; at that time she could sue only for her freedom.[3]

The court made a similar ruling in another appeal. The plaintiff, a free woman of color, brought suit in *Dorothée* v. *Coquillon* (1829), claiming that her daughter, Azélie, who was to be freed at age twenty-one under the terms of her late master's will, was being cruelly treated. She further alleged that her daughter was not being taught a trade to enable her to earn a living when freed, as stipulated in the will, and that even though Azélie had "a cold in her left arm" that disabled her for any other trade than that of a seamstress, the girl had been forced to perform hard labor that aggravated her condition. Moreover, the daughter's new mistress had had her jailed just prior to the filing of the lawsuit, and the girl had been forced to labor in the streets of New Orleans as a member of a chain gang. Azélie's mother petitioned the court to order Azélie's mistress to hire her out to a seamstress until she attained the age specified for manumission. The lower court ruled that the mother personally had no right of action against the slave's mistress, and dismissed the suit. Judge François-Xavier Martin affirmed the decision, ruling that since the daughter was still a slave, she could not sue for ill treatment. Citing article 177, Martin held that she had no right to sue, except for freedom, a right she would not acquire until the age of twenty-one.[4]

Judge Martin also cited article 177 in rejecting a lawsuit initiated by a slave who contested her owner's title to her. In *Trudeau's Executor* v. *Robinette* (1817), the slave Robinette claimed she had been free after her master's death and was about to sail for Cuba with her children when her former master's executor seized her as property of the succession. She produced a certificate of emancipation, dated 1812, which declared her to be a free woman, twenty-four years old when freed, who had lived as free. The executor contested the introduction of the bill of emancipation, as Robinette had not achieved the legal age for emancipation

3. Delphine, f.c.g., v. Segher's Syndics, Unreported Supreme Court Case No. 483 (1820).

4. Dorothée v. Coquillon, No. 1649, 7 Mart. (N.S.) 350 (La. 1829).

François-Xavier Martin, whose service dated back to the Superior Court of the Territory of Orleans, presided as chief judge of the state supreme court from 1836 to 1846 and was a historian of Louisiana.

Photo by Warren Gravois. Courtesy of the Librarian, Law Library of Louisiana

of thirty years at the time the bill was executed. The trial court found for Robinette, and the executor appealed. Martin declared the bill of emancipation to be "illegal, null and void," and declared that the lower-court judge erred in admitting it to evidence. The court further ruled that since she was still a slave, she had no right to contest the executor's title: "A slave, considered as an object of property, is a thing, and as such not entitled to resist the exercise of ownership on him on account of a want of title in the person who claims or uses him as his property." The only proper issue on which a slave could bring suit, Martin held, was "*liber vel non,*" the issue of freedom. "Owners ought not to be subjected to support or exhibit their titles, contradictorily with their slaves." Martin reversed the decision of the lower court and ordered Robinette to return to the executor as a slave.[5]

Besides allowing slaves to sue only for their freedom, Louisiana law recognized the exceptional nature of emancipation in another way: just as slaves could steal themselves, they could also purchase themselves. According to *Civil Code* article 174, "the slave is incapable of making any kind of contract, except those which relate to his own emancipation." This right to contract for freedom was a legacy of Roman law and the Spanish right of *coartación,* although it did not appear in the French *Code Noir.* Antebellum Louisiana law allowed slaves to contract for their freedom but denied them the capacity, as slaves, to own anything without consent of their master. Under Spanish law, slaves could own property in their own right. Article 174, then, was a watered-down version of the Spanish *coartación,* as it did not force the master to sell the slave if the slave got up the purchase price and slaves could accumulate property and money only with the consent of their owner. Although Louisiana slaves who attempted self-purchase were bound by the same rules governing any transfer of immovable property in the state, their right to contract for freedom was unique: no other slave state allowed this practice. Slaves in other states were occasionally able to purchase their freedom if the master allowed it, but only in Louisiana did they have the capacity to enter into a contract for their liberty.[6]

5. Trudeau's Executor v. Robinette, No. 184, 4. Mart. (o.s.) 477 (La. 1817). For similar cases, see Berard, f.w.c., v. Berard, f.p.c., No. 2866, 9 La. 156 (1836), and Dolliole, f.m.c., v. White, No. 1213, 5 La. Ann. 98 (1850).

6. *Civil Code,* Art. 174, p. 27; Baade, "Law of Slavery in Spanish Luisiana," in *Louisiana's Legal Heritage,* ed. Haas, 50–51, 53; Stampp, *Peculiar Institution,* 96–97.

The Louisiana Supreme Court heard several appeals in which slaves were attempting to attain their freedom by enforcing contracts with their owners for purchasing themselves. Unscrupulous owners sometimes used ignorance or inattention to proper legal forms to continue to hold bondservants in slavery even though they had fulfilled the contract and remitted the agreed-upon price. The earliest appeal of this nature was *Victoire* v. *Dussuau* (1816). The slave woman Victoire had sued for her freedom in 1815 after she reimbursed her mistress for her full purchase price but the mistress continued to hold her in slavery. The lower court ruled against her because no written evidence of the contract existed. Chief Judge George Mathews affirmed the decision because Victoire was able to offer only oral evidence to prove the existence of the contract: "Between free persons no valid or binding contract can be made, so as to alter the title to slaves, unless it be in writing: and, if we are correct in the position above taken, that the same rules must govern in covenants to which slaves are allowed to become parties, it is equally clear that parol [*sic*] evidence ought not to be admitted to establish the existence of the contract, on which the plaintiff and appellant founds her action: because it tends to dispose of a slave." Mathews reasoned that although slaves had the right to make contracts for their freedom, a slave was immovable property and the *Civil Code* required transactions involving the disposition of immovable property to be in writing: "no parole [oral] evidence must be admitted."[7]

Two years later, in *Cuffy* v. *Castillon* (1818), the court heard an appeal of a slave woman's suit for freedom based on what closely resembled a self-purchase contract. The contract dated to the Spanish period in Louisiana, when Cuffy—the plaintiff's father, a freedman—and her then-owner reached an agreement by which she and three other of Cuffy's children were to be freed on condition of the owner's receiving $2,400. Apparently this price was set by a Spanish colonial tribunal, the exact proceedings of which were unclear to the 1818 supreme court. Apparently, too, only $316 was ever paid to the owner, and that in behalf of one of the other children, not of the plaintiff. Nevertheless, many years later, she sued for her freedom. Her attorney based the suit on a Roman-law concept that stipulated that if slaves wishing to be free could not pay the whole price of their freedom, they could acquire freedom by their labor from the date of the contract. The attorney cited the Roman-law

7. Victoire v. Dussuau, No. 103, 4 Mart. (o.s.) 212 (La. 1816); *Civil Code,* Art. 174, p. 27.

predisposition *in favorem libertatis* (in favor of liberty), the concept that, when possible, a decision should be given in favor of freedom. The trial court had found for the defendant because only $316 of the agreed-upon amount had been remitted: "Freedom must not be so favored by interpretation, as to depart entirely from the intention of the contracting parties, apparent on the contract itself." Chief Judge Mathews affirmed the judgment. To the Roman-law argument that the slave's labor was compensation for the disparity between the amount paid and the amount agreed upon, Mathews reasoned:

> The law which authorizes the *residue* of the price to be supplied by the labor of the person claiming his freedom, as purchased with his own money, or by the circumstance of acquiring property, is, in our opinion, (and as insisted on by the counsel of the defendant) applicable only to such persons as are made free *instanter,* on condition of paying a certain sum *in futuro*. In such a case, when a part of the price of the person is paid, and the freedman continues to labor for his former master, the value of his labor may be fairly imputed, as a payment. . . .
>
> But, in the case under consideration, the master contracted to give the deed of emancipation of the children of Cuffy, when the latter should have satisfied and paid him 2400 dollars. This mode of expression demonstrates the intention of the master to liberate them *in futuro,* after the fulfillment of the condition, on which alone they were to be freed, viz: the complete payment of the price of their freedom.[8]

Six years later the court heard another appeal involving a contract of self-purchase, *Doubrère* v. *Grillier's Syndic* (1824). Louis Doubrère claimed that in 1819, when he was a slave, Pierre Grillier had purchased him from his master for $1,800. Doubrère then paid Grillier $1,700 for his freedom. A free woman of color testified that the black community had collected money to aid Doubrère and that many people had contributed twenty or thirty dollars; some, including herself, had also lent him money. Grillier gave Doubrère a written act of sale (a Louisiana-law

8. Cuffy v. Castillon, No. 225, 5 Mart. (o.s.) 494 (La. 1818), emphasis in original of Mathews' opinion, which at one point also gives the agreed-upon price for the children's freedom as $3,400, not $2,400; it is unclear which amount is correct. See also Watson, *Roman Slave Law,* 12.

term denoting an official sale that was witnessed, notarized, and recorded) despite the $100 discrepancy. Since that time, the plaintiff had lived and worked as free. When Grillier became insolvent in 1822, his creditors seized Doubrère as a slave, and therefore an asset capable of being used to satisfy his owner's debts. Doubrère sued for his freedom on the basis of a receipt signed by Grillier in 1819 for $1,700 from Doubrère for the purpose of purchasing himself. The trial-court judge summarized the issue: "The cause presents a question of the greatest importance to the petitioner, and of no inconsiderable magnitude to the public, and it is this, whether all *bona fide* contracts, of immoveable property or slaves, made *sous seing privé* [under private signature], are void against creditors, and can be set aside by them, in case of the insolvency of their debtor." The lower court found for the creditors on the grounds that the emancipation defrauded them. Doubrère appealed. Judge Alexander Porter reversed the decision of the trial court. He reasoned that if the contract to sell Doubrère to himself was a fair one, "the object received represents . . . that which was alienated. . . . Supposing this sale [of Doubrère to himself] had never been made, the conditions of the persons now seeking to annul it, would not in any point . . . be at all changed." Porter ruled that the sale was valid but ordered Doubrère to make up the $100 difference between the price Grillier paid to purchase him from his original master ($1,800) and the amount Doubrère paid Grillier for his freedom ($1,700). The court ordered that Grillier's creditors were to "be perpetually enjoined from claiming petitioner as a slave." An important distinction in this case was that the creditors were general creditors, rather than secured creditors. If any of them had had a judgment against Grillier before Doubrère's suit for freedom, Doubrère would have lost.[9]

A fifty-one-year-old slave named Prince Mathews sued for his freedom in *Mathews* v. *Boland and Smith* (1843) after his master attempted to defraud him of his liberty. Mathews had paid Michael Boland $650 to purchase himself, but after Boland accepted the money, he sold Mathews to William Smith for $600. Mathews sued Boland and Smith for his freedom. At the trial, Mathews produced a receipt "in full for his purchase," signed by Boland, for $650, and the New Orleans District Court declared him free. Testimony proved that Smith knew that Mathews

9. Doubrère v. Grillier's Syndics, No. 860, 2 Mart. (N.S.) 171 (La. 1824).

had purchased himself from Boland, and that Smith and Boland were in collusion. A witness testified that Smith had said "*that it mattered not* [that Mathews had purchased his freedom], *he would beat them at law*" [emphasis in original]. Although Judge Henry Bullard knew that Mathews had purchased himself, he declared that Mathews was not entitled to an unconditional ruling for freedom: "Public policy forbids absolute emancipation by simple agreement of this kind, and requires certain formalities, which cannot be dispensed with. These formalities depend upon the age, condition, and conduct of the slave to be emancipated." Insisting on strict adherence to legal forms, Bullard reversed the decision freeing Mathews but ordered the current owner, William Smith, to emancipate him "unless some legal obstacle should be shown to exist, growing out of [his] conduct and character." In this ruling, Bullard was referring to *Civil Code* article 185, which required proof of good conduct for four years prior to an emancipation.[10]

Two years later the court heard another appeal by a slave who claimed he had purchased himself, *François* v. *Lobrano* (1845). In 1835 Louis Pilié had accepted $740 from his slave, François, in partial payment of his freedom. That same year Pilié sold him for the remainder of his value, $300, with the condition that when the slave paid the remaining $300, the new owner would set him free. Eight years later, François sued his current owner, Jacinto Lobrano, for his liberty, claiming he had paid Lobrano the remainder of his purchase price. Lobrano not only refused to free him but alleged that François was a runaway and a drunk and of so bad a character that he was not suited for freedom. At the time of the initiation of the suit, Lobrano put François in the chain gang in the parish prison. François was undoubtedly a very valuable slave. He was a skilled hatter who hired his own time and lived away from his master. He claimed he paid his wages of $30 a month to Lobrano. Lobrano denied that François ever paid him the $300 and alleged that the slave often failed to hand over his monthly wages. On one such occasion Lobrano had struck François, brandished a sword cane, and threatened to kill him. François behaved so well while forced to labor in the chain gang, and was so obviously intelligent, that the sheriff removed him from that work and put him to work in the office of the mayor of New

10. Mathews v. Boland and Smith, No. 5119, 5 Rob. 200 (La. 1843); *Civil Code,* Article 185, p. 29.

Orleans. However, the slave was not able to prove that he had paid Lobrano the $300, and although the supreme court recognized that he had paid some of his purchase price, it ruled that he could not be partially free, nor could he own any property without consent of his master. The difference between this case and *Doubrère* v. *Grillier* is that in *Doubrère,* the master gave the slave a written act of sale to himself, despite the fact that the slave paid him $100 less than his price, and there were no secured creditors of Grillier. Nor did Grillier claim that he still owned Doubrère. In *François,* there was only circumstantial evidence to prove that François had purchased himself. Judge Alonzo Morphy ruled that François was a slave, and denied a requested rehearing.[11]

In *Gaudet* v. *Gourdain* (1848), the supreme court heard an appeal that involved the status of children born to a slave mother after she had acquired the right to be free by making a contract for her freedom. The Louisiana *Civil Code* was quite explicit on this subject. Article 196 stated: "The child born of a woman after she has acquired the right of being free at a future time, follows the condition of its mother, and becomes free at the time fixed for her enfranchisement, even if the mother should die before that time." In 1829 a slave woman named Clarisse contracted with Jean Gourdain for her freedom for $220. She paid the first of two installments in March, 1831, and gave birth to a daughter, Azéla, in November, 1831. She paid the second half of her purchase price in 1832 and lived free with her daughter until Gourdain's death in 1845. Gourdain's son took forcible possession of Azéla shortly after his father's death, meted out "cruel and harsh treatment" to her, and hired her out as a slave. Her employer testified that she had stolen money and other articles of value from him, insulted his wife, and "absconded." Azéla sued for her freedom under article 196. The trial court ruled against her, and she appealed. Citing *Mathews* v. *Boland and Smith,* Justice Pierre Rost declared her free because her mother had acquired the right to freedom before her birth. In *Mathews,* Rost reasoned, the only written proof of the contract was a receipt given to the plaintiff for the price of his freedom, and on this evidence the court had ordered Mathews' owner to emancipate him. The payment had already been proved in *Gaudet,* stated Rost, and although the price was paid before Azéla was born, she acquired by that payment the right to her emancipation. Declaring that

11. François v. Lobrano, No. 5347, 10 Rob. 450 (La. 1845).

"the defendant unjustly withheld that right from her," Rost ordered "that there be judgment in favor of the plaintiff, and that she be forever quieted in the possession, exercise, and enjoyment of her liberty, against all claims and pretensions of the defendants, the said defendant, *Jean Gourdain,* paying the costs in both courts."[12]

In *Baker, f.m.c.,* v. *Tabor* (1852), Justice Rost recognized the validity of a completed contract for freedom between an owner and a slave but refused to allow the former slave to be a party in a civil suit because his former master had never formally emancipated him. Edward Baker, a man of color, sued Susan Tabor for payment he alleged she owed him for services he performed for her as a free person. Tabor denied that Baker had capacity to sue, as he was a slave. The District Court of Caddo Parish ruled in Tabor's favor, and Baker appealed. Rost declared himself "under the painful necessity of affirming the judgment." However, he suggested two avenues of action to compensate for his decision. Baker had the capacity, he noted, to institute a suit for freedom, rather than a suit for wages for services performed. In an extraordinary statement, Rost also suggested a more immediate remedy:

> We deem it our duty to state, the cause of the plantiff [*sic*] appears to us a just one; and, that he is not without a remedy. His master may claim, in his own name, the benefit of the contract entered into by him, and the damages resulting from the breach of it by the defendant, and he will, no doubt, deem it his duty to do so.
>
> The right of the master to claim the services of his slaves may cease, but his duty to protect them, terminates only with their life. Even after emancipation, he is bound, not only to protect, but also to maintain them, when they are no longer able to maintain themselves.[13]

The ruling in this case, stressing responsibility for slaves after emancipation, reflects a primary concern of policy makers in the 1850s, the important social problem of preventing freed slaves from becoming wards of the state in their old age.

12. Gaudet v. Gourdain, No. 364, 3 La. Ann. 136 (1848). See also Catin v. D'Orgenoy's Heirs, No. 459, 8 Mart. (o.s.) 218 (La. 1820).

13. Baker, f.m.c., v. Tabor, No. 328, 7 La. Ann. 556 (1852).

Occasionally masters stipulated in an act of sale of a slave that they wanted the slave to be allowed to purchase his or her freedom. The slave Henriette was sold at auction to settle the estate of her late owner. At the sale the auctioneer announced that as Henriette and her two children wanted to be free, and that as her former master's heirs did not object, her purchaser would have to agree to give her her liberty when reimbursed for her value and that of her children. Oscar Arroyo of Plaquemines Parish purchased her under this condition. Her suit for freedom, *Henriette,* statu liber, v. *Arroyo* (1854), came before the Supreme Court of Louisiana six years later. Henriette proved that she had paid her new master $700 of the $1,000 purchase price and that he had refused to accept the final $300 and free her and her children. Although the parish court ruled against her, the supreme court remanded the case for a new trial, stating that the slave woman had a "clear cause of action."[14]

Sukey Wormley, a former slave who had successfully contracted to purchase her freedom and that of her daughter and six grandchildren, had to defend a suit, *Hardesty* v. *Wormley* (1855), brought against her by the relatives of the white man with whom she had lived until his death in 1853. Moses C. Hardesty had freed Wormley in 1834. Testimony proved that she had purchased herself and the members of her family by her "industry, economy and good character." Wormley earned her freedom by doing laundry for resort hotels across Lake Pontchartrain from New Orleans. According to one witness, she could be seen laboring at her ironing table "day and night." After she became free, she continued to live with Hardesty even though he became "crazy frequently from drink" and incurred large gambling debts, which she occasionally paid. After Hardesty's death, his siblings sued for possession of Wormley and her family as their slaves, claiming that her self-purchase was fraudulent. The heirs based the suit on the claim that Hardesty's freeing Wormley constituted a "disguised donation" *inter vivos,* which defrauded them of their rightful portion of the succession—although they were not forced heirs. Evidence proved that Hardesty had petitioned the police jury in 1834 to allow him to free Wormley and her children, stating that she had already paid half of the purchase price. The police jury gave a decree of emancipation. A character witness stated that the mulatto woman was

14. Henriette, *statu liber,* v. Arroyo, Unreported Louisiana Supreme Court Case No. 3706 (1854).

"an upright honest person and has enjoyed the respect & good opinion of every one here as much as any person of her class." The lower-court jury ruled in Wormley's favor, and the heirs of Hardesty appealed. Chief Justice Thomas Slidell affirmed the decision of the lower court, citing *Gaudet* v. *Gourdain.* Slidell observed that the heirs' lawsuit was a "cruel experiment upon the earnings of an humble and deserving woman."[15]

A slave named Louisiana, who claimed she had purchased herself and her two children for $1,350 in 1856, was unsuccessful in her suit for freedom, *Louisiana, f.w.c.,* v. *Gordon* (1857). Her owner, F. Baillio, had purchased her and the children in 1855 and lived in what the court called "open concubinage" with her until his death in 1857, after which his executor seized her and sold her as part of Baillio's estate; she sued her purchaser for her freedom. She produced in court a notarized act of sale for herself and her children from Baillio to herself. Although the Rapides Parish District Court declared her free in 1857, the Supreme Court of Louisiana ruled that she should sue Baillio's estate for her liberty, not the purchaser. She did, and the Louisiana Supreme Court heard *Louisiana, f.w.c.,* v. *Baillio* in 1860. Justice Thomas Land ruled that the sale of Louisiana to herself was a fraud because no money changed hands, and that it was also a disguised donation to a slave woman who was a concubine by law, as after the alleged sale Louisiana continued to live with Baillio: "Where the vendor remains in possession, the law raises a presumption that the sale is simulated and requires the parties to produce proof of . . . the reality of the sale." The justices declared Louisiana and her children to be the property of the succession, and ordered them to be sold to satisfy its debts.[16]

Between Louisiana's two suits for freedom, the supreme court heard an appeal of *Pauline, f.w.c.,* v. *Hubert* (1859), in which a justice, in an unusual dissenting opinion, questioned the power of the 1857 legislative prohibition to preclude a slave from suing for freedom. In 1851 a slave named Arsène contracted with her master, Onil Bourgeat, for the emancipation of herself and her daughter, Pauline, for $1,500. Arsène was only able to raise $600, her own price, and Bourgeat executed an act of

15. Hardesty v. Wormley, No. 3056, 10 La. Ann. 239 (1855); *Civil Code,* Art, 1482, p. 225.

16. Louisiana, f.w.c., v. Gordon, Unreported Louisiana Supreme Court Case No. 267 (1857); Louisiana f.w.c., v. Estate of Baillio, No. 362, 15 La. Ann. 555 (1860); *Civil Code,* Art. 2456, p. 383.

emancipation for Arsène alone. Some time later Arsène gave Bourgeat $900 for Pauline, who had just given birth to a daughter, Julie. Bourgeat demanded an additional $100 for Julie, which Pauline subsequently paid. Bourgeat emancipated Pauline, but the act of emancipation omitted mention of Julie. After Bourgeat's death, his executor listed Julie in the inventory of his succession as a slave. Pauline brought suit to prevent Julie's sale to satisfy debts of the succession and to have the court affirm Julie's freedom. Pauline won in the Pointe Coupée District Court, and the executor appealed. The plaintiff's attorney argued that Julie was free by the terms of *Civil Code* article 196—the provision that the child of a woman who has acquired the right of being free follows the condition of its mother. Chief Justice Edwin Merrick agreed that article 196 gave Julie the *right* to freedom, but as she had not been emancipated according to Louisiana law, she was not free, but a *statu liber.* Since the act of 1857 denied slaves the right to sue for freedom, she could not be legally emancipated. The majority opinion ordered the judgment of the lower court reversed as to the freedom of Julie but granted a perpetual injunction to stop the executor from selling her, and ordered her delivered to her mother. Justice James Cole wrote a dissenting opinion in which he differed with the majority interpretation of article 196:

> This Article plainly declares, that at the moment the mother is entitled to be enfranchised, the child becomes free. The child being free, no ratification of it by a court of justice is necessary. It is different as to the mother, for the Article says, "after she has acquired the right of being free." The Article distinguishes between the two, giving to the mother a "*right* of being free," which implies a *right* of *action* to have her freedom judicially pronounced, and giving to the child freedom at the moment the right of action of her mother commences.
>
> Besides, the Article, as to the mother, speaks of her "enfranchisement," which implies some action for becoming free; whereas, as to the child, it says it "*becomes free,*" even if the mother should die before the time fixed for her enfranchisement.
>
> If my interpretation of Article 196 be incorrect, another serious question would arise, whether the plaintiff had not acquired under this Article, even as interpreted by the majority of the court, such a vested right to her liberty as she could not be divested of by

> subsequent legislation, prohibiting the emancipation of slaves. Sess. Acts, 1857, p. 55. Art. 174 of the Civil Code declares, "that a slave is incapable of making any kind of contract, except those which relate to his own emancipation."
>
> This Article, then, so far as emancipation is concerned, treats slaves as persons capable of contracting, and they are vested with the same right of contracting as to their emancipation, as freemen are as to any other species of contract.

Pauline, f.w.c., v. *Hubert* was one of only two decisions of the supreme court in which a dissent questioned the denial of a slave's right to be free that had been acquired before the passage of the act of 1857.[17]

According to article 3510 of the Louisiana *Civil Code,* a slaveowner who allowed a slave to live as free for ten years within the state or twenty years outside its borders could not recover possession of the slave. This was manumission by prescription, and the slaveowner's permission was essential to it; fugitives could not gain their freedom this way no matter how long they lived away from their owners. A few blacks in antebellum Louisiana successfully defended their freedom acquired through prescription using article 3510.

A slave under the age of thirty could not gain freedom by prescription. In *Meilleur* v. *Coupry* (1829), the heirs of Marguerite Meilleur Rilieux, f.w.c., alleged that Joseph Coupry, the named testamentary executor for the succession of Rilieux, was legally incompetent to serve in that capacity, as he was a slave. Coupry claimed that he was free and petitioned the court to declare him competent to serve. The heirs alleged that Coupry had never been legally emancipated. Judge Martin ruled that even though Coupry had lived as free for fourteen years, a slave under the age of thirty—as Coupry still was—could not be presumed to have been freed.[18]

Sixty-five-year-old Eulalie sued to confirm her freedom and that of her six children and ten grandchildren in *Eulalie* v. *Long and Mabry*

17. Pauline, f.w.c., v. Hubert, No. 6012, 14 La. Ann. 161 (1859); emphasis in original of Cole's opinion. The other case in which such a dissent was filed was *Marshall* v. *Watrigant* (1856), discussed in the next chapter.

18. Meilleur v. Coupry, No. 1726, 8 Mart. (N.S.) 128 (La. 1829). See also Carmouche v. Carmouche, No. 243, 12 La. Ann. 721 (1857).

(1854). Eulalie and her children and grandchildren were forcibly taken from their homes in Pointe Coupée Parish at gunpoint in the night, brought to a New Orleans slave market, and sold at auction for $12,000. Eulalie had been the slave of Simon Porché, a white man, who had allowed her to marry his wife's free half-black half brother forty-five years earlier. Eulalie's master had never officially emancipated her, but she had lived as though free since her marriage. The seizure and sale of the sixteen people of color was precipitated by the death of Porché's widow; the heirs claimed them as property of the succession. Eulalie's case was first heard by the Supreme Court of Louisiana in 1854 and was remanded to the lower court because of a technicality. The high court heard the appeal a second time in 1856. Justice Henry Spofford declared Eulalie and her descendants to be free and observed the suspicious circumstances surrounding the sale:

> There is no doubt from the evidence that the heirs of *Mrs. Porché* were privy to this abduction of the plaintiffs from Pointe Coupée, yet they do not figure in the conveyance to defendants; neither, although the defendants ostensibly paid twelve thousand dollars in cash for the plaintiffs, do they make any call in warranty.
>
> Their bill of sale gives no origin to the vendor's title. The production of a certificate of mortgages is dispensed with; and their vendor is declared by defendants to be dead and insolvent. These are circumstances calculated to inspire a suspicion that the true parties in interest are keeping out of sight. And if so, the reason may be easily imagined.

Justices Spofford and James Lea concurred in this opinion but noted that Porché had never formally emancipated Eulalie and her children and grandchildren. Spofford, writing for the court, cited *Meilleur* v. *Coupry* and *Baker* v. *Tabor* and raised the very pertinent issue of the public policy regarding the possibility that freed slaves could become wards of the state:

> I concur in the judgment, but I do not think the Article 3510 of the Code was intended to introduce a mode of emancipating slaves, or of changing their *status*. Its cautious phraseology shows that such a result was not contemplated. "If a master suffer a slave

> to enjoy his liberty for ten years, during his residence in the State, or for twenty years while out of it, he shall lose all right of action to recover possession of the *slave,* unless the slave be a runaway or fugitive." The Article treats of the slave as being still a slave after the ten years' enjoyment of his freedom. But it prohibits the master from restraining him. The public has an overruling interest in the question of his *status;* and the laws by which the manumission of slaves has always been so sedulously guarded from abuse are all in vain if the State can be compelled to recognize as unconditionally free, with liberty to remain in the State, and without regard to age, character, or other legal qualifications, all such slaves as their masters may choose to turn loose for the space of ten years.[19]

The Louisiana Supreme Court also refused to allow a free black woman to reenslave her sister-in-law and the sister-in-law's seven children, all of whom had lived free for over twenty years. Just before the beginning of the Civil War, Juliette Maran, a free woman of color, had her recently deceased brother's wife, Euphrémie, and Euphrémie's children seized and handed over to a New Orleans auctioneer to be sold as part of the brother's estate. Ephrémie and her offspring were advertised for sale and appraised at $3,500. Euphrémie sued in the Third District Court of New Orleans in *Euphrémie, f.w.c,* v. *Maran, f.w.c., and Noble (alias Jourdan)* for her freedom and $5,000 in damages. Several witnesses testified in her behalf, stating that no one had ever treated her as a slave. The lower court ruled in her favor, and Maran appealed. Maran's attorney had warned the lower-court judge of the danger of "letting loose in our midst . . . persons of color." He also reminded the court "of the dreadful events which have lately taken place at Harper's Ferry." Infuriated at this attempt to intimidate him, the trial-court judge declared to Maran's attorney that his court constituted a "Court of Law, and not a Court of Expediency." The judge also reminded the attorney that the free blacks of Louisiana were part of "the gallant army, who defended our soil and the honor of our mothers, under the illustrious Jackson in 1814 and 1815 in the plains of Chalmette." This unreported case was one of those in progress when the Union army captured New Orleans in the

19. Eulalie v. Long and Mabry, No. 3237, 9 La. Ann. 9 (1854) and No. 3979, 11 La. Ann. 463 (1856); emphasis in original of Spofford's opinion.

spring of 1862, and it was not decided until just after the end of the war, when the reconstituted court ruled that Euphrémie was free.[20]

Article 189 of the Louisiana *Civil Code* stated: "An emancipation, once perfected, is irrevocable." In *Maples* v. *Mitty and Sarah, f.w.c.* (1857), John Maples sued to have his deceased father's emancipation of a black woman, Mitty Broxton, and her children revoked. Maples alleged that his father's sale of Broxton to herself was simulated, that no money changed hands, and that the sale was therefore a disguised donation to Broxton, which deprived Maples' father's forced heirs of their portion of the succession designated by law. On this basis, Maples demanded that Broxton's emancipation and that of her children be revoked. The trial court found for Maples, and Broxton appealed. The supreme court reversed the decision. Maples' father died possessed of $3,138. He had no debts. Broxton and her children were worth $1,000—one-third of the succession, and less than its disposable portion. Maples had kept Broxton and her children incarcerated pending the outcome of the suit. Following the ruling in her favor, Broxton sued for damages in *Broxton* v. *Bloom* (1860). Justice Thomas Land rejected her appeal, stating that before Broxton and her children were imprisoned they were "indolent, lazy and thriftless" and that during their confinement in jail they were well fed and clothed. On this basis the high court denied that the sequestration was malicious or that the freed slaves had suffered damages. Thus, although the court refused to revoke Broxton's emancipation, it also refused to allow a freed slave to recover damages for being temporarily denied that freedom.[21]

Under Louisiana law one requirement for emancipation was that a slave be well behaved for at least four years before being manumitted. Poor conduct deprived the slave woman Nolé of her freedom. Nolé's mistress died, leaving a will that instructed her son-in-law and executor, Charles de St. Romes, to free Nolé and her two children. He made no attempt to emancipate Nolé, and she sued for her liberty in *Nolé* v. *St. Romes*

20. Euphrémie, f.w.c., v. Maran, f.w.c., and Noble, alias Jourdan, Unreported Louisiana Supreme Court Case Nos. 6740, 6741 [filed 1860, decided 1865].

21. Maples v. Mitty and Sarah, f.w.c., No. 4985, 12 La. Ann. 759 (1857); Broxton v. Bloom, No. 6664, 15 La. Ann. 618 (1860).

(1843), alleging he had put her in jail for two years to prevent her from suing for her freedom. De St. Romes claimed that he could not manumit her, as she had a "bad reputation" and was "thievish and insolent." Witnesses testified that Nolé was known to be a runaway and on one occasion had been a fugitive for eight months. One witness claimed she was in the habit of stealing and kept the other slaves in "a continued state of disorder" by "giving bad advice." She also allegedly spoke to her mistress as though they were equals. A prison physician testified that she was "addicted to drinking." The First District Court of New Orleans ruled against Nolé on the grounds that her behavior prevented her emancipation and that she had not proved she was thirty years old. The court reserved the right of Nolé's children to sue for their freedom at the age of thirty but denied Nolé's petition for freedom. Chief Judge Martin upheld this judgment, reiterating the rights of the children and denying Nolé's emancipation: "The mother's behavior during the four years preceding her application, would alone have prevented her emancipation."[22]

The most outrageous case involving denial of emancipation because of bad conduct involved the slave women Carmelite, who sued for her freedom in *Carmelite* v. *Lacaze* (1852). Jean Lacaze had purchased Carmelite for $800 on the condition that he would free her seven years from the date of sale—her former mistress had sold her with this stipulation as a reward for her faithfulness in nursing one of the mistress' children through a serious illness. Lacaze claimed he could not emancipate Carmelite even though the seven years had elapsed because she was guilty of offenses that made her unfit to live in freedom. When she requested that he free her, he put her in prison and "detain[ed] her in irons." Carmelite testified that Lacaze refused to free her because she would not "comply with and obey to certain immoral purposes of Jean Lacaze." She further asserted that she feared being sent out of the state and sold elsewhere to remove her from the jurisdiction of the court. Carmelite sued for her freedom and $1,000 damages, plus wages of $25 a month from the date of the filing of the suit.

Lacaze answered the suit by alleging that Carmelite had embezzled

22. Nolé attempted to prove her age by claiming that she had a daughter who had already become pregnant and had an abortion, which supposedly showed that the daughter was at least fifteen years old and that Nolé herself must therefore be older than thirty. Nolé v. St. Romes, No. 4950, 3 Rob. 484 (La. 1843).

some of his goods, had struck him and one of his white servants, was insubordinate and insolent, and was therefore totally unfit for freedom. Her former mistress, a free woman of color named Françoise E. Doubrère, intervened in the suit, alleging that she had sold Carmelite for her services for seven years only, and that if Lacaze refused to free her, the court should order Lacaze to return her to her original mistress. Witnesses stated that Lacaze had purchased Carmelite "to make his wife of her." They had lived together for some time, after which Lacaze placed her in a house of prostitution that he owned and took another woman of color into his home as his "wife." Another witness testified that Carmelite "used to be dancing till midnight with other people in her room in a complete state of nudity. There were both negroes and white people there." Further testimony established that Lacaze had put her in the brothel "for profit" and corrupted her mind and character.

Despite the overwhelming evidence that Lacaze had led Carmelite into a life of immorality, Chief Justice Eustis ruled that she remain his slave because her conduct rendered her unfit for freedom: "It seems that the misconduct of the slave . . . was the necessary result of the vile and profligate employment and associations to which Lacaze subjected her, and it is strongly pressed upon us, that we cannot permit a man to falsify his title by his own infamy. It is a matter of regret that we are not permitted to act upon this suggestion and to visit upon the party [Lacaze] the consequences of his iniquity. But the question before us is one exclusively of property, and must be determined according to the rules of law." Eustis held: "If her right of emancipation should be defeated or terminate, from any cause . . . she remains absolutely his slave." Under Spanish law, forcing a slave to work in a brothel entitled her to freedom. The court's ruling in Carmelite's case shows how far the development of Louisiana slave law had departed from the liberalizing influence of Spanish law. Rather than freeing her because her master forced her to work in a brothel, Eustis held that she was no longer fit for freedom and therefore must remain enslaved. By the 1850s the real issue had become the right of the state to regulate manumission. Although Carmelite should have been freed, her manumission flew in the face of the public policy of restricting emancipation to model slaves.[23]

23. Carmelite, Slave, v. Lacaze, No. 2506, 7 La. Ann. 629 (1852); Henry E. Sterkx, *The Free Negro in Antebellum Louisiana* (Rutherford, N.J., 1972), 37–38.

This same policy appears to have played a part in denying a slave her liberty until the general emancipation following the Civil War. The slaveowner Aimé Guillet left a will in which he instructed his wife to free the slave girl Delphine as soon as possible following his death. Guillet died in 1847. Delphine sued for her freedom in *Delphine* v. *Guillet* (1856), claiming that although she had repeatedly asked Guillet's widow to set her free, the widow continued to hold her in slavery. Delphine also claimed freedom for her daughter, Josephine, who was born after Guillet's death. Mrs. Guillet answered that Delphine was under the legal age for emancipation and had not "behaved well any four years since" Guillet's death. She also asserted that since Delphine was only six or seven when Guillet died, she had not been freed for long and faithful service. A witness stated that Delphine was "familiar and pretty bold"; a local pharmacist had warned her "not to take my apothecary shop for a brothel," and she had threatened to slap him if he refused to stop "joking" with her. He claimed she did touch him "in the face" in an insolent manner. Delphine offered to prove that she was "of good character & sober habits, and had always behaved well & conducted herself respectfully towards white persons." The widow objected, stating that Delphine had not claimed proof of good character in the petition instituting the lawsuit. The lower court found that Delphine was entitled to her freedom and instructed the widow to institute proceedings to emancipate her. Guillet appealed to the Louisiana Supreme Court, which reversed the decision and remanded the case for a new trial. Justice Henry Spofford held: "Were this an ordinary case of private right, we might have perhaps presumed that the plaintiff was able to establish the facts . . . but as it concerns the public that none but worthy persons should be admitted to the *status* of freemen; it is our duty to exact the proof."

Once again Delphine sued for manumission in a lower court, this time including evidence of good character in her petition, and once again the lower court ruled that she was entitled to her freedom and instructed the widow to commence emancipation proceedings immediately. The lower court's judgment was rendered in February, 1857. The widow Guillet appealed to the supreme court for a suspension of the judgment. On March 6, 1857, the Louisiana legislature passed the law forbidding all emancipations in the state. The Louisiana Supreme Court rendered the final decision in Delphine's appeal in April, 1858. Justice Spofford, writing for the court, stated:

> The judgment was probably correct, at the date of its rendition. But, at that time, there were lawful modes of enfranchising slaves within this State. Since then the Act of March 6, 1857, (p. 55), entitled "an Act to prohibit the emancipation of slaves," has been passed, declaring that from and after the passage of that Act, no slave shall be emancipated *in this State.*"
>
> In our former opinion we declared that the plaintiff was not free, but had acquired, under the will, a right to be emancipated so soon as she should show that it had become lawful to emancipate her. The laws respecting the manumission of slaves fluctuate with the legislative will. It is now impossible to affirm a decree ordering the defendants to emancipate *Delphine* in this State, because the lawgiver has forbidden them to do so. If the law should be changed, her remedy might be revived.[24]

In several other instances the supreme court heard suits from slaves who claimed that they had acquired the right to freedom, but that their masters continued to hold them in slavery. In 1826 Thomas Simmons won his suit for freedom, *Simmons, f.m.c,* v. *Holland and Parker.* Simmons was born the slave of Lewis and Mary Rose of Kentucky. In 1804 his owner executed a deed of emancipation that would have freed him on May 1, 1823, and recorded the act in the Mercer County court. Simmons' master sold the slave's remaining time to a physician, Joseph McMurty, sometime after executing the manumission papers, and Simmons came to New Orleans with McMurty. McMurty later claimed he sold Simmons as a slave for a term of years, rather than for life, to William and Nathaniel Wyer, New Orleans slave dealers. One more transaction followed, and then Edward E. Parker purchased Simmons, who was represented as a slave for life. It is not clear in which transaction Simmons lost his status as a *statu liber* and became a perpetual bondsman. In the last transaction, however, his price dropped from $1,000 to $600, perhaps an indication that his title was unsound. A witness testified that Parker knew of Simmons' claim to be free; in fact, he purchased Simmons *pendente lite,* with knowledge of Simmons' suit for freedom. In 1824 Simmons sued for his freedom in a New Orleans court. His original master, Lewis Rose, testified to being "sensibly im-

24. *Civil Code,* Art. 185, p. 31; Delphine, f.w.c., v. Guillet, No. 4249, 11 La. Ann. 424 (1856), and No. 5145, 13 La. Ann. 248 (1858), emphasis in original of Spofford's opinion.

pressed with the belief that all men and women ought at a suitable age to be free." He admitted that he had emancipated Simmons and stated that he had not regretted the act. The lower-court jury declared Simmons to be free and ordered the slave dealers to reimburse Parker for Simmons' purchase price. The Louisiana Supreme Court reaffirmed the judgment. In his decision, Judge Porter ordered Simmons to "enjoy his freedom in the same manner as if born free."[25]

A number of slaves sued for their freedom in Louisiana courts because their former owners' legal heirs or executors refused to emancipate them despite being directed to do so in the owner's will. The plaintiff in *Bernardine* v. *L'Espinasse* (1827) was a Marie Louise Bernardine, born a slave in 1781 in St. Domingue. During the slave revolts on that island in the 1790s, her white owners fled the country for their lives. Had she remained behind she would have been free, but when Bernardine saw her master and mistress leaving, she jumped into the sea and swam to their boat. She accompanied them to Cuba, where she served them until 1809, when they took her to Louisiana. (Her importation did not violate the 1808 prohibition of the foreign slave trade; a special act of Congress in 1809 allowed the St. Domingue refugees to enter Louisiana with their slaves.) Soon afterward, her mistress died intestate but on her deathbed told her husband not to forget Bernardine's faithful service; she requested that her husband set the slave free. He died a few years later, leaving a will ordering his executor to free Bernardine and her two children. When she demanded her freedom, the executor stalled, saying she owed him money and would have to work to repay him. After several years of continuing to refuse to liberate her, he set up title to her in himself and sold her. In 1826 Bernardine successfully sued her purchaser for her freedom; he in turn won a lawsuit against the executor for selling her without a clear title, and the executor appealed this judgment. Judge Porter ruled against the executor and affirmed the ruling in Bernardine's favor, stating that "the justice and equity of it [her claim to freedom] are most emphatically on her side."[26]

In 1847 the supreme court heard the second appeal of a case involving the freedom claim of the slave Sophie. In 1845 the court had decided *Succession of Duplessis, f.m.c.,* in which Sophie's master's heirs sold her

25. Simmons, f.m.c., v. Holland and Parker, No. 1145, 4 Mart. (N.S.) 200 (La. 1826).

26. Bernadine v. L'Espinasse, No. 1422, 6 Mart. (N.S.) 94 (La. 1827); LaChance, "1809 Emigration of Saint-Domingue Refugees," 118–21.

and her children as slaves for life despite her late master's will, in which he ordered them freed upon his death. In *Sophie,* statu liber, v. *Heirs of Duplessis* (1847), Sophie sued her master's heirs for her freedom under his 1833 will. The heirs contended that Martin Duplessis had not executed his will according to the forms prescribed by law, and that it was therefore void. The specific flaw alleged by the heirs was that the will was improperly witnessed. According to *Civil Code* article 1574, three witnesses who resided in the parish in which the testator executed the will, or five witnesses who lived outside the parish, were necessary to witness a nuncupative will. Sophie failed to prove the will had been witnessed according to law. Although Justice George Rogers King ruled against Sophie, she was not without remedy: "The plaintiff may still be able to supply the present defects of proof, by showing that the witnesses all resided in the parish in which the will was made; or, if they did not, that a greater number could not be procured by the exercise of reasonable diligence. Until proof is administered of every fact necessary to establish the validity of the will, its execution can not legally be ordered; and until such order, the plaintiff can not avail herself of the will as a title to her freedom."

Justice King ruled on an appeal in the same matter the following year in *Sophie,* statu liber, v. *Duplessis* (1848). This time Sophie's attorney was able to prove that Duplessis' will satisfied *Civil Code* article 1576: "In the country it suffices for the validity of nuncupative testaments under private signature, if the testament be passed in the presence of three witnesses residing in the place where the testament is received, or of five witnesses residing out of that place, provided that in this case a greater number of witnesses cannot be had." Since Duplessis was dying of cholera, a delay to procure the proper number of witnesses would probably have resulted in his dying before making any will. King ruled in Sophie's favor: "A necessity more urgent could not well be presented for dispensing with the attendance of the full number of competent witnesses; and, in our opinion, it excuses the failure to procure them." There is no indication why Sophie's attorney did not make this argument in the 1847 case. Perhaps he had no need to do so in the trial court, as the issue of the defective will came up only on appeal.[27]

27. Succession of Duplessis, f.m.c., No. 5598, 10 Rob. 193 (La. 1845); Sophie, *statu liber,* v. Heirs of Duplessis, No. 424, 2 La. Ann. 724 (1847); Sophie, *statu liber,* v. Duplessis, No. 919, 3 La. Ann. 658 (1848); *Civil Code,* Arts. 1571, 1574, 1576, pp. 240–42, Arts. 1214–17, pp. 185–86.

During the same term, the supreme court heard another appeal, *Angelina* v. *Whitehead* (1848), involving a person who claimed to be illegally held in slavery. Angelina's master had sold her to one Philander Campbell in 1820 with the express condition that Campbell emancipate her. When Angelina reached the legal age at which she could be freed (1841), Campbell failed to emancipate her. He died soon after, and his heirs seized Angelina and her three children as slaves, and therefore property of the succession. Angelina sued for her freedom. She lost in the District Court of Lafayette Parish and appealed. The supreme court reversed the decision. In the dictum, Chief Justice Eustis stated that the purpose of the original sale had been to ensure the eventual emancipation of Angelina, "an essential condition of the contract, without which it would not have been made." When she reached the age of thirty, the legal age for emancipation in Louisiana, "her right to be emancipated then became complete . . . the right of the plaintiff to have her condition adjudicated upon, and her emancipation ordered, we think, is unquestionable." Citing the *Partidas,* portions of which were still in force in 1820, Eustis reasoned that the conditions in the act of sale, the agreement to free Angelina, were valid because the *Civil Code* recognized the right of slaves to contract with their owners for freedom. This right implicitly gave slaves a cause of action to enforce such contracts. Citing *Cuffy* v. *Castillon,* the supreme court declared Angelina and her three children, ages seventeen, fifteen, and two, to be *statu liberi* and not slaves for life, and ordered the heirs to institute emancipation proceedings for Angelina "without delay." The court could not simply declare her free until the heirs followed the legal procedure to free her, because the issue litigated here was one of private law—namely, contracts—and the regulation of manumission was a matter of public law.[28]

In *Maranthe, Genie,* et al. v. *Hunter* (1856), the supreme court heard an appeal of a lawsuit that represented the culmination of a series of suits occasioned by the will of Julien Poydras, the Pointe Coupée planter and philanthropist. As was discussed in chapter 6, Poydras had devised that each of his plantations was to be sold; however, purchasers had to agree to keep the slaves on their respective plantations and free them twenty-five years after his death. After Poydras died in 1824, his nephew, Benjamin Poydras DeLaLande, went to court repeatedly to prevent the new

28. Angelina v. Whitehead, 3 La. Ann. 556 (1848); *Code of Practice,* Art. 103, p. 120.

owners of Poydras' former slaves from selling them away from their plantations. In an 1842 appeal, *DeLaLande* v. *Bormeau,* the Pointe Coupée District Court judge ruled against DeLaLande, stating that there had been so many decisions on the Poydras will that its meaning was an "open question." This will, the trial-court judge contended, had been as prolific as "the dragon's teeth of Cadmus," and he expressed his disgust with it as "impracticable and contrary to the spirit of our institutions. . . . To plant *in perpetua* a colony of ignorant dysolute [*sic*] free Blacks in the heart of a slave holding population . . . might lead to scenes of bloodshed and murder, the extent where of can scarcely be imagined." However, in this case and in the others, the supreme court upheld the conditions of the contracts under which the new owners had purchased the slaves.[29]

DeLaLande died in 1851 in France. None of the new owners afterward instituted emancipation proceedings, and in 1856 fifty of Poydras' former slaves sued their current owner, Charles G. Hunter, for their freedom in *Maranthe.* They lost in the Pointe Coupée court, and their attorney appealed, asking the supreme court to declare them free and to order Hunter to pay them wages from the date of filing of the original suit, 1854. On the issue of wages, the supreme court cited article 177 and *Delphine* v. *Guillet* to the effect that slaves could instigate civil suits only to claim their freedom. As to the claim of freedom, Hunter used as a defense the legislative act of 1855 concerning emancipation. He alleged that this act imposed additional burdens and charges on persons wishing to emancipate their slaves, including the expense of suing the state in court before a jury to effect an emancipation. He claimed that conditions of the contract he signed when purchasing the slaves did not include these additional obligations, and therefore he was not bound to emancipate the slaves. The supreme court rejected this reasoning:

> Undoubtedly, no mere act of legislation can change a contract, or impair its obligation. But the question in this case is, what was the contract? An obligation to emancipate a slave twenty-five

29. DeLaLande v. Bormeau, No. 4197, 1 Rob. 315 (La. 1842). See also Moussa v. Allain, No. 123, 4 Mart. (N.S.) 99 (La. 1825); Poydras v. Taylor, 9 La. 488 (1836); Poydras v. Mourain, No. 2871, 9 La. 492 (1836); Poulard v. Délamare, No. 3101, 12 La. 267 (1838); DeLaLande v. Taylor, Nos. 3204, 3254, 18 La. 12, 17 (1841); Succession of DeLaLande, Unreported Louisiana Supreme Court Case No. 3197 (1854); DeLaLande v. DeLaLande, No. 2941, 10 La. Ann. 220 (1855); and DeLaLande v. Poydras, No. 3228, 25 La. Ann. 405 (1873).

> years hence, and to take all legal steps, and to incur all necessary charges incident to such emancipation has reference, we think, not to such legislation as was in force at the date of the contract, but to such as might be in force when the contract is to be carried into execution. We cannot suppose that it was contemplated by the parties, that a change in the form, or even the legal charges incident to an emancipation, might deprive the plaintiffs of their ultimate right to freedom.

The court remanded the case for further action in December, 1856. There is no evidence that Hunter took steps to free the slaves before the 1857 legislative prohibition of all emancipation proceedings.[30]

Two years later the supreme court heard an appeal of an emancipation suit, *Julienne, f.w.c.,* v. *Touriac* (1858), based on a condition in the sale of a slave. Julienne alleged that her mistress had sold her to the defendant's father in 1837 with the express agreement that he would emancipate her. He died before he fulfilled the condition, and his son took possession of Julienne as property of his father's succession. She brought suit for her freedom in April, 1857. The judge of the district court of St. Landry Parish ruled for the defendant, citing the March 6, 1857, legislative prohibition of emancipation. The supreme court changed that judgment from a final one against her to one of nonsuit, leaving open the possibility that Julienne might sue at a subsequent time for her emancipation should the legislative prohibition be lifted, but Justice Spofford agreed with the trial-court judge's reasoning that Julienne had not acquired a vested right to freedom: "It [the act of 1857] does not divest a vested right, for the condition upon which the defendant's ancestor acquired title to the plaintiff was, 'que la dite dame veuve *Don Louis Touriac* donnera la liberté a la dite negritte *Julienne, sitot que faire se pourra.*' If it should hereafter become possible, the plaintiff will have a remedy. At present she has none. The time for her to acquire freedom has not arrived. The judgment, we think, should be changed from a final judgment in favor of the defendant to one of nonsuit."[31]

In 1859 the supreme court heard an appeal of a suit for freedom based on prescription. In this case, *George* v. *Demouy* (1859), Benjamin Poydras DeLaLande was once more a key figure. The issue was the freedom

30. Maranthe, Genie, et al. v. Hunter, No. 4328, 11 La. Ann., 735 (1856).

31. Julienne, f.w.c., v. Touriac, 13 La. Ann. 599 (1858); emphasis in original of Spofford's opinion.

of Leon George, whose mother, a slave named Olive George, was the property of Guy Richard, a plantation owner in Pointe Coupée Parish. Leon George was born in 1833; in 1834 Richard decided to place him in the charge of the wife of DeLaLande's overseer because of the "bad behavior" of the slave child's mother. Richard died suddenly of cholera in 1834. DeLaLande, Richard's executor, sent the child to his overseer's wife to comply with Richard's wishes. In 1838 DeLaLande sold Olive George and her other children to the defendant, Demouy. The act of sale of Olive George and her children specifically exempted Leon George from the sale. In 1843, while DeLaLande was on a visit to France, Demouy asked the overseer's wife to send Leon to see his mother. He said he wanted to give Leon some gifts and would send him back within one week. Demouy defaulted on this promise and kept Leon in his service until he filed suit for freedom in 1857, after which he ran away. A witness claimed that Demouy treated Leon as free and admitted he was free. This witness said that Demouy, seeing Leon outside the courthouse, had asked him to "ne parle pas trop" (don't talk too much). Other witnesses, however, stated that Demouy treated Leon as he did his other slaves.

Leon George won in the Pointe Coupée Parish District Court, and Demouy appealed. Chief Justice George Eustis reversed the decision and found that Leon was still a slave: "The only question which we can consider is, whether the plaintiff had acquired the *status* of a free person of color prior to the promulgation of the Act of 1857, which now prohibits emancipation." Once more, the court did not inquire whether the person suing for freedom had acquired the *right* of being free, but whether he had actually been emancipated. The court concluded that since Leon could not prove he had been emancipated and since the act of 1857 removed his right to sue for freedom, the appropriate judgment was one in favor of the defendant. As in *Pauline* v. *Hubert,* decided the same month, Justice Cole dissented, questioning whether the act of 1857 destroyed a vested right to freedom acquired before its passage. Cole contended that the prohibition of emancipation in Louisiana did not apply to freedom acquired by prescription. Article 3510, he argued, was not repealed by the act of 1857. "The former provides for the loss of action of the master to recover possession of the slave after he has been permitted to enjoy his liberty for a certain time; the latter forbids the enfranchisement of slaves by the technical mode of emancipation." Cole reasoned that Leon George was a free person through the operation of prescription:

> According to Article 3510, if a master suffer a slave to enjoy his liberty for a certain time, he loses all right to recover possession of him. . . . The slave after that time must then be free, and he becomes subject to the laws relative to free persons of color, for if the master cannot claim him, certainly no other person could. If the slave were not then free, there would be no sense in the Article, for if the master could not assert title to him, no other person ought to be allowed to do so, and if no one can claim him he is free. . . .
>
> The control exercised over plaintiff during the greater part of his life by defendant, was not that of a master and owner, for defendant cannot, by his own will, change the nature of his tenure of plaintiff. He got possession of him under false pretences, and he ought not to be allowed to derive any benefit from a possession obtained by treachery, and from a control over the plaintiff, exercised without any permission from his master or heirs. . . .
>
> If there were any doubt as to the right of plaintiff to recover his freedom as against the defendant, the doubt ought to be decided in favor of plaintiff.[32]

In 1859 the supreme court handed down several decisions in appeals of suits for freedom and always with the same result: denial of freedom. The basis of these decisions was always that before 1857 slaves could initiate a legal action for one purpose only—to claim their freedom—and that the act of 1857 closed that one avenue. Neither the *Civil Code* nor the legislature empowered Louisiana justices to make decisions based on what they considered to be good public policy. One possible explanation is that the justices chose to implement the act of 1857 as they did because of their own predilection to limit the growth of the free black population of Louisiana. In this instance they acted more as common-law judges, and in that sense became more like judges in the common-law slave states.

Just as they could initiate lawsuits only for their freedom, Louisiana bondservants were allowed by state law to enter into only one kind of contract—to purchase their freedom (here again the law emphasized the exceptional nature of emancipation). The latter sometimes led to the

32. George v. Demouy, No. 5969, 14 La. Ann. 175 (1859). See also *Civil Code,* Art. 3510, p. 532.

former, for if such a contract were violated, a subsequent suit for freedom was the slave's only legal recourse. Suits involving contracts for freedom were often successful if the contract had been drawn up in the correct legal form for the disposition of immovable property and could be properly proved. The Supreme Court of Louisiana was especially unsympathetic to those who made a profit from such contracts by accepting the agreed-upon purchase price from slaves and then either refusing to free them or, worse, selling them as slaves for life. However, strict proof of these questionable transactions was required by the court to satisfy compliance with the letter of the law.

Provisions and laws concerning emancipation were quite detailed, and the Louisiana Supreme Court on most occasions dutifully ruled in accordance with these laws. Slave children born after their mother had acquired the right to be free were judged free, as required by law, at the time the mother became free *if* strict proof existed that the children were born *after* the mother became a *statu liber.* Similarly, the court usually refused to revoke emancipations already effected and often upheld emancipations by prescription. Strict proof of good behavior was required by law for manumission, and the court refused to free slaves of proved "bad" character. Executors and heirs who refused to free slaves as instructed by will usually lost in court if all conditions could have been met to legally free the designated slave.

The supreme court interpreted the law of 1857 prohibiting emancipations within Louisiana as eliminating the only legal action that could be initiated by a slave. After that date a Louisiana slave could not bring any form of lawsuit and could be a principal party in court only as an accused criminal. When, however, a slave was transported to an area where slavery was prohibited, the Louisiana Supreme Court refused to apply the law of 1857, provided the slave had been on free soil before the legislative prohibition of emancipation.

10

"AS SHE WAS A FREE WOMAN THERE, SHE MUST BE HELD SO EVERY WHERE"

Comity, Conflict of Laws, and Suits for Freedom

PROBLEMS CAUSED BY CONFLICTS OF LAW BETWEEN states during the antebellum period were as old as the nation itself. United States Supreme Court justice Joseph Story wrote one of the first treatises on the subject, in 1834. In *Commentaries on the Conflict of Laws,* he argued that the concept of comity required that laws of nations and states should "have the same force every where" unless they "prejudice the power or rights of other governments, or of their citizens." Comity, or the respect that one state or nation accords to the laws of another, became a thorny issue as the laws of free states and slave states diverged. Was the status of Louisiana slaves affected by brief sojourns with their owners in states where the law prohibited slavery? What if a slaveowner changed residence to a free state? Could slaves from other jurisdictions use Louisiana courts to attempt to gain their freedom?

The Supreme Court of Louisiana struggled with these conflicts throughout the antebellum period, as did the courts of other states, free and slave. The United States Supreme Court also confronted the issue several times, culminating in the famous decision of *Dred Scott* v. *Sandford* (1857). The issues generated by conflict-of-law cases sharpened as courts of the North and South refused to grant each other comity in the increasingly divisive debate over slavery.[1]

In Louisiana, as well as in other states, the concept of *lex loci domicilii,* the law of the legal domicile of the parties in a case, was of vital importance in resolving disputes involving conflict of laws. *Civil Code* article 10 incorporated this concept and defined the limits of comity in Louisiana law:

1. Joseph Story, *Commentaries on the Conflict of Laws* (Boston, 1834), 30; Finkelman, *Imperfect Union,* 14–16; Dred Scott v. Sandford, 19 Howard (U.S.) 393 (1857).

> The form and effect of public and private written instruments are governed by the laws and usages of the places where they are passed or executed.
>
> But the effect of acts passed in one country, to have effect in another country, is regulated by the laws of the country where they are to have effect.[2]

An 1827 decision of the Supreme Court of Louisiana, *Saul* v. *His Creditors,* illustrates the court's interpretation of article 10. Judge Alexander Porter, writing for the court, held: "Contracts are governed by the country where they are made, but they cannot be enforced to the injury of a state whose aid is required to carry them into effect. Nor where they are in opposition to the positive laws of that state. In the conflict of laws, where it is doubtful which should prevail, the court that decides should prefer the law of its own country to that of the stranger."[3]

On many occasions the Louisiana Supreme Court had to confront the issue of conflict of law in appeals of slave suits for freedom involving laws of other states or countries. Suits of this nature fell into two categories: those in which the conflict of law was between Louisiana and another slave state, and those in which the comity issue resulted from a conflict between Louisiana law and the law either of a free state or of a foreign nation in which slavery did not exist. In both instances the rulings of the court reflect careful attention to substantive and procedural due process.

Although Louisiana's emancipation laws were more favorable to slaves seeking their freedom than the laws of other Deep South slaveholding states throughout much of the antebellum period, the Supreme Court of Louisiana refused to allow slaves from other states to use Louisiana's courts to gain freedom where the laws of their owners' domiciles denied it to them. In most freedom suits involving out-of-state bondservants, the trial courts ruled in favor of the slave; however, the Supreme Court of Louisiana reversed the judgment, denying jurisdiction.

2. *Civil Code,* Art. 10, p. 4. For a thorough discussion of comity, see Paul Finkelman, *Imperfect Union.*

3. Saul v. His Creditors, 5 Mart. (N.S.) 569 (La. 1827). The issue in *Saul* generated an important legal treatise, Samuel Livermore, *Dissertations on the Questions Which Arise from the Contrariety of the Positive Laws of Different States and Nations* (New Orleans, 1828).

In 1833 the bondswoman Mary sued for her liberty in *Mary, f.w.c., v. Morris* under the 1809 will of her late master, John Marshall, of Columbia County, Georgia. "Conscientiously believing that civil and religious liberty is the natural right of all men," as he put it, Marshall willed that his slave Jude and her two children, Mary and Ellender, were to be given to his daughter to serve her for five years, after which "they are hereby declared free." In her petition Mary claimed that Marshall's daughter never informed her of the terms of the will but instead brought her to Louisiana and continued to hold her and her (by then) five children in slavery. The Baton Rouge District Court held that Mary and her five children were free, although the judge denied Mary's request for $2,000 for her services while illegally held as a slave because slaves could only sue for freedom, not for wages. Chief Judge George Mathews reversed the decision because, under Georgia law, slaves could be freed only by legislative act, not by will. Mathews stated that the Georgia law restricting manumission to a special act of the legislature was made for "the peace and good order of the community," and Mary could not circumvent that law simply by coming to Louisiana:

> The only question which the cause presents, arises out of a conflict between the laws of the state where the testator resided before his death, and where his succession was opened by probate of the will, and the bequest of freedom in favor of certain slaves named in said will, amongst which was the plaintiff.
>
> These laws are prohibitory, and had relation to the peace and good order of the community, for the government of which they were enacted. They inhibit absolutely all owners of slaves within the limits of the state, from doing any act giving liberty to their slaves, and prohibit them from granting freedom in any manner whatsoever, except by application to the legislature for that purpose. . . . This bequest was made in contravention of a prohibitory law; it was in derogation of a law made in relation to the peace and good order of the community, and was, consequently, absolutely null and void in the state where the law was in force. The plaintiff remained a slave so long as her owner kept her in that state, and certainly could not *ipso facto* become free by being removed to this, wherein slavery is also tolerated.[4]

4. Mary, f.w.c., v. Morris, No. 78, 7 La. 135 (1834).

Mississippi slaves suing for their liberty in Louisiana fared no better than Mary. In 1840 the Supreme Court of Louisiana heard an appeal of a lawsuit in which the slaves Bob, Milly, and their seven children claimed their freedom under the will of their late master, Timothy O'Hara of Mississippi. O'Hara had requested his executor to free the slave family in Mississippi if possible, and if not, he was to take them to Ohio for that purpose, after which they were to return to Mississippi. Each slave was to receive $100 at the time of his or her emancipation. The unscrupulous executor transported the slave family to Louisiana and mortgaged them. The family successfully sued for their freedom in the District Court of Iberville Parish in *Bob, Milly and Their Children* v. *Syndic of Nugent*. Chief Judge François-Xavier Martin reversed the decision of the lower court and rendered a verdict of nonsuit, reasoning that the family could not be freed because Mississippi law stipulated that slaves in that state could be freed only by a legislative act as a reward for meritorious service. Although Martin failed to note that Mississippi law did not prohibit taking a slave to Ohio in 1840, he observed that his decision did not preclude the slaves from suing the executor in Mississippi to compel him to petition the Mississippi legislature to consent to their freedom or take them to Ohio. A judgment of nonsuit was not final in Louisiana and did not preclude the slaves' taking further action, possibly even in federal court, although there is no record that they did so.[5]

Two years later, the Louisiana Supreme Court upheld the laws of Tennessee, although the issue involved a trust, which was absolutely prohibited by Louisiana law. On the day of her marriage to Hambright Black, Elizabeth Morgan of Tennessee created a trust in which she gave title of several of her slaves to Lewis Jordan on the condition that she retain the use of the slaves during her lifetime. It is clear that Morgan was attempting to preserve the separate character of her property (a problem she would not have faced in Louisiana, which honored the separate property of married women). Upon her death, Jordan was to emancipate the slaves. After Morgan's marriage, Black attempted to sell some of the slaves, and Jordan sued him in a Tennessee court to prevent the sale. Although Jordan lost in the lower court, the Supreme Court of Tennessee perpetually enjoined Black from selling the slaves and forbade

5. Bob, Milly and Their Children v. Syndic of Nugent, No. 3779, 15 La. 63 (1840).

him to remove any of them from the state. Black defied the ruling of the court and brought several of the slaves to Louisiana with the intention of selling them. Jordan sued him in the District Court of West Feliciana Parish, which ordered the slaves restored to Jordan in order that he could execute the trust according to the laws of Tennessee. Black appealed to the Louisiana Supreme Court in *Jordan* v. *Black* (1842), contending that the trust was "a fraud upon his marital rights." Judge Rice Garland affirmed the decision of the lower court, upholding the trust and the ruling of the Supreme Court of Tennessee:

> One, and the main purpose of this suit, is to prevent an evasion of the decree of the Supreme Court of Tennessee: and, as a reason why this should not be prevented, the defendant says that that decree is erroneous, and that we ought to revise it. Whether the judgment was in accordance with the allegations and prayers contained in the bill in chancery, is not for us to enquire. We look to the judgment, which forbids the defendant from removing the negroes out of the state, whereby the execution of the trusts may be entirely defeated, or so much embarrassed, as to injure materially those interested. . . . We have the authority of the highest legal tribunal in Tennessee, for saying, that the laws of that state did not, under the circumstances, vest the title to the slaves in the defendant; and we know that his marriage would not have given him any title, had it taken place in this state. The use of the slaves is vested in the defendant's wife, during her life, and he is, under the laws of Tennessee, entitled to the benefit of that use; but that does not authorize a removal of the slaves beyond the limits of the state, in defiance of the commands of her courts, and without the consent of all parties interested.

Although Garland did not specifically mention the "full faith and credit" clause of the United States Constitution, he upheld it in spirit: "a question decided by a competent tribunal of another state, after due proceedings, will not be examined into by the courts of this State." Had the Supreme Court of Louisiana declared the trust invalid, the outcome would have been identical because the state's laws regarding the separate property of married women would have been in effect.[6]

6. Jordan v. Black, No. 4768, 1 Rob. 575 (La. 1842); *Civil Code,* Arts. 1507, 2314, pp. 229–30, 362.

Another Mississippi slave, Mary, sued in a Louisiana court for her freedom in *Mary, f.w.c.,* v. *Brown* (1850). She claimed that James Read, a Mississippi planter, had liberated her for "her faithfulness and fidelity" in Ohio in 1846. Mary stated that although she could have remained in Ohio, "her friend and former master" was in poor health, and she returned to Mississippi and nursed him until he died. The executrix of Read's estate claimed her as a slave and hired her out to a Concordia Parish planter. The Concordia Parish court declared Mary to be free, but the Louisiana Supreme Court reversed the judgment. Although Mary's attorney argued that "the right to freedom is a vested personal right which exists and may be asserted wherever the person is, or wherever he goes," Chief Justice Eustis ruled that Mary's status could only be decided in the domicile of her master, which was Mississippi:

> The domicil [*sic*] of *James Read* was in Adams county, Mississippi, where his succession was opened, and the status of the plaintiffs under the state of facts exhibited, can be determined under no other laws than those of Mississippi. They were born slaves, and it is in evidence that *Read* took them from his domicil in Mississippi to Ohio, for the purpose of liberating them from slavery, and, after having executed the act of emancipation in Ohio, returned with them to his place of residence in Mississippi. Was the status of the plaintiffs changed by this fact, according to the laws of Mississippi? . . . the deed of emancipation was void, being a contract made in Ohio, in violation and fraud of the laws of Mississippi, and calculated to injure the State and its citizens, and set a dangerous example, since no owner could emancipate his slave, except by proper deed or will, and proof of meritorious services to the Legislature, which must ratify the emancipation.[7]

Three years later the court heard another appeal involving a slave from Mississippi claiming freedom, *Haynes, alias Mielkie,* v. *Hutchinson and Forno* (1853). Sarah Haynes was a slave, the property of Edward C. Mielkie of Vicksburg. In 1843 Haynes traveled from Vicksburg with a permit signed by Mielkie granting her permission "to pass unmolested

7. Mary, f.w.c., v. Brown, No. 1640, 5 La. Ann. 269 (1850). *Executrix,* in Louisiana legal terminology, signified a female executor. A well-known Mississippi case decided just before the Civil War used exactly the same reasoning: Mitchell v. Wells, 37 Miss. 235 (1859). See also Finkelman, *Imperfect Union,* 287–95.

to Cincinnati, in Ohio, generally, or any other free State she may choose." Mielkie paid Haynes's travel expenses to Cincinnati. She remained in Cincinnati for a few days, then went to New Orleans, where she remained for nearly ten years until Mielkie's executor (Mielkie having died in 1851) attempted to seize her as the property of Mielkie's minor daughter. Haynes unsuccessfully sued for her freedom in the First District Court of New Orleans, and she appealed the decision to the state supreme court. Chief Justice George Eustis held that her status could only be determined by the operation of Mississippi law because Mississippi was the domicile of her master. Citing *Mary, f.w.c.,* v. *Brown,* Eustis wrote:

> But the *status* of the slave must be tested by the law of Mississippi, where the owner resided, and where the writing under which she claims her freedom, was executed. The law of that State forbids the emancipation of slaves otherwise than by an instrument in writing duly proved or acknowledged, and proof to the General Assembly of some meritorious act by the slave, followed by an Act of the General Assembly, sanctioning the emancipation, and a compliance by the owner with the conditions imposed by that Act.
>
> It has been decided by the Supreme Court of Mississippi, that a deed of emancipation, executed in Ohio by the master, who went there with his slaves for that purpose, and afterwards returned to Mississippi with the slaves, was in fraud of the laws of Mississippi, and totally void, although the master recited in his will the fact that he had executed such a deed, and declared his intention to ratify it, and acknowledged one of the slaves to be his son. *Hinds* et al. v. *Brazealle* et al., 2 Howard's Miss. Rep. 841, 42, 43. If all these solemnities were in vain because they were in contravention of a law established for wise purposes of public policy, surely a mere *permit* to go to a free State, cannot be more effectual.

As to the issue of whether Haynes's brief sojourn in Ohio operated to free her, Eustis stated:

> The true rule is laid down in the case of the *Slave Grace* 2 Hagg, Adm. Rep. 94, and, although more liberal views once prevailed in Louisiana, we have been compelled to return to the English

> doctrine. The slave who goes, by the permission of his master, to a free State, does not thereby become free. He merely ceases to be subject to the coercion of his master, so long as he remains in free territory; but the moment he returns *voluntarily* to his master's domicil he is again subject to his authority, and resumes his former condition.[8]

An Alabama slave fared no better in his attempt to gain his freedom before the Louisiana Supreme Court. In his 1850 will, Francis Gay of Alabama left his bondsman Albert Young to his friend Stephen Charpentier, a Mobile barber, with instructions to take Albert to a free state and give him his liberty. However, Charpentier sold Albert to McRae, Coffman, and Company, New Orleans slave traders, who promptly sold him as a slave for life. In 1853 he sued for his freedom and $500 in damages in *Young, f.m.c.,* v. *Egan*. The Orleans Parish District Court declared him to be free, but the Supreme Court of Louisiana reversed the decision, reasoning that since Alabama law prohibited emancipation by will, he could not be freed. Justice Alexander Buchanan noted that since Gay and Charpentier were both residents of Alabama, "the respective rights of Charpentier and of the plaintiff [Young] under this will, are to be governed by the laws of Alabama":

> In that State, the emancipation of a slave by last will, is forbidden by law. But a devise of a slave to an executor, coupled with a trust to convey him out of the State, with a view to his emancipation, has been held by the Supreme Court of Alabama, not to be illegal.
>
> The case last quoted, however, only went the length of declaring that the Courts of Alabama would not interfere, at the instance of the next of kin of the testator, to prevent the executor from executing such a trust.

However, Buchanan did not believe that the request to take Young to a free state and liberate him constituted a command, and therefore, Young could claim no right to freedom from the request:

> The testator commences by devising the ownership of the slave, *Albert,* absolutely to *Stephen Charpentier;* and concludes by *request-*

8. Haynes, alias Mielkie, v. Hutchinson and Forno, No. 2850, 8 La. Ann. 35 (1853); emphasis in original of Eustis' opinion.

> *ing Charpentier* to have the slave transferred into some other State or country where slavery is not recognized by law. The devise is absolute, depending on no contingency. The request is addressed to the discretion, or, to use words of the Supreme Court of Alabama, "to the conscience" of the devisee. . . . Lastly, supposing the words of request in this devise to have the effect of a command, they clearly did not import a command to give to the plaintiff his freedom within the limits of a slave holding State. The policy of Alabama, as we gather from her legislation, is to prevent the multiplication of the class of free persons of color, by restricting the power of emancipation. The testator, aware of this policy of his State, has endeavored to conform to it. He did not contemplate that the plaintiff should have his freedom in Alabama, or in any other slave holding State. It does not seem to be carrying out the intentions of this will, to set the plaintiff free in Louisiana.[9]

During the same term, the court heard an appeal involving another issue of comity between two slave states, *Mathilda, f.w.c.,* v. *Autrey* (1855). In 1853 Mathilda sued for her freedom, alleging that the defendants "illegally held her in servitude." She had originally been the slave of Richard Baker of Kentucky. In his will, Baker left Mathilda to his wife during her lifetime; at the wife's death, Mathilda was "to be free to all intents and purposes as if she were born free." Shortly after Baker's death, his wife moved to Alabama, where she died in 1835. Rather than returning Mathilda to Kentucky and setting her free, the defendants brought her to Louisiana, where they kept her as a slave. The defendants' answer to Mathilda's suit for freedom was a claim of prescription, that she belonged to them without need of "exhibiting further title" because they had peaceably possessed her for fifteen years. The District Court of Monroe declared Mathilda to be free, and Autrey appealed. The supreme court upheld the district court's decision. In denying the defense of prescription, Justice Spofford cited *Civil Code* article 3457: "A possession by violence, not being legal, does not confer the right of prescribing. That right only commences when the violence has ceased." Justice Spofford ruled that Mathilda was *de jure* free when she came to

9. Young, f.m.c., v. Egan, No. 4075, 10 La. Ann. 415 (1855); emphasis in original of Buchanan's opinion.

Louisiana, having been freed by the operation of the laws of Kentucky and Alabama:

> No attempt was made by the defendants to show that there was anything illegal in this bequest, under the laws of Kentucky. On the other hand, the decision quoted from the judicial reports of that State, would seem to indicate that the disposition was valid.
>
> We have no reason to doubt the proposition that the courts of Alabama would have recognised the vested rights of the plaintiff. No prohibitory statutes of that State have been offered in evidence derogating from the power of a master to manumit his slave, or restricting the rights of a *statu liber* introduced from another State.
>
> The conduct of the defendants in hurrying away the plaintiff from Alabama immediately after she became free by the death of Mrs. *Baker,* in 1835, and detaining her for so many years in Louisiana, in violation of the trust imposed upon them by Mrs. *Baker,* who told them to carry her back to Kentucky to be free, indicates a desire on the part of the defendants to avoid the tribunals of those States.[10]

In 1857 the Supreme Court blocked a suit for freedom based on a decision of a Kentucky court. Louisa Marshall was born in 1822 in Mercer County, Kentucky, the slave of George Belcher. When she was only two years of age, her master died, leaving a will that granted her freedom when she should become thirty years old. Belcher's nephew sold her to a Louisiana slave dealer as a slave for life, and Anna Watrigant purchased her in 1854. Shortly after the sale, Marshall escaped from her owner in New Orleans, fled to Mercer County, and procured a judgment from a Mercer County court declaring her to be free. Armed with this decree she returned to New Orleans and filed suit for her freedom in Louisiana in 1856 in *Marshall* v. *Watrigant.* The Louisiana legislature passed the act of 1857 before the Louisiana Supreme Court could rule on the case. The trial court ruled in her favor, but the Louisiana Supreme Court reversed the decision to one of nonsuit. The basis for the rejection of her claim to freedom was the issue of domicile, and Justice Buchanan

10. Mathilda, f.w.c., v. Autrey, No. 411, 10 La. Ann. 555 (1855); *Civil Code,* Art. 3457, p. 524.

cited the recent United States Supreme Court decision on the issues of transportation and domicile:

> The first question which the record presents is the effect which must be given to the Kentucky decree. Does it bind the defendant?
>
> We are of the opinion it does not, for two reasons, viz: 1st, the domicil of *Louisa Marshall* was Louisiana, and the laws and courts of Louisiana alone had jurisdiction over her *status,* and, 2d, because the domicil of the defendant was also in Louisiana, and a foreign court could not assume jurisdiction over them in such a manner as to bind them in the absence of notice.
>
> The decree of the court of Mercer County and State of Kentucky could not then bind the defendants, because it was not vested with jurisdiction over the subject-matter, (the *status* depending upon the domicil of the slave,) nor over the person of the pretended parties to the decree. See *Dred Scott's* case, 19 Howard, 452. . . .
>
> The decree which the plaintiff presents, (obtained whilst she was a fugitive,) must, therefore, be looked upon as in fraud of defendant's rights and obtained under the supposition that it would confer upon the plaintiff some undue advantage. It cannot be enforced here.

Justice Henry Spofford dissented from this decision. The issue, he stated, was not a suit to procure an emancipation, but an action by a woman alleging to be free but "fortuitously restrained of her liberty." The Kentucky decree of freedom did not operate to emancipate Marshall, Spofford argued; it simply confirmed that she was a free person. "It did not create her status; it only acknowledged it." Under the terms of Belcher's will, "the mere lapse of time transformed her into a free person, without any further formality, under the Kentucky law." Citing *Mathilda* v. *Autrey,* Spofford wrote: "The wrongful act of a usurper in carrying her out of Kentucky and selling her as a slave for life, could not destroy her vested rights. She would still be free at the age of thirty years, leaving purchasers to their recourse against their warrantors."[11]

11. Marshall v. Watrigant, No. 5220, 13 La. Ann. 619 (1858).

Pelagie Brown, a Mississippi slave, sued for her freedom in 1859 in *Brown, f.w.c.,* v. *Raby.* Brown alleged that the defendant had brought her to New Orleans against her will. When she ran away, he had the sheriff arrest her as a fugitive slave. She claimed that Mary Walker, her former mistress, had sold her to a Pascagoula, Mississippi, man with the condition of emancipating her. Both the defendant and Walker were residents of Mississippi. The lower court found in favor of the defendant, and Brown appealed. Citing *Marshall* v. *Watrigant,* Justice Cole maintained that the supreme court had no jurisdiction in the matter. "We are of the opinion that she ought not, under such circumstances, be permitted to have her rights judicially investigated in this State, but ought to resort to the courts of Mississippi, where her master resides."[12]

One of the last two appeals involving a conflict of laws between slave states was *Bateman* v. *Frisby and Kendig* (1860). Isaac Bateman's master, an Arkansas planter, had died in 1850, leaving Bateman to serve his wife until her death, after which he and all of his master's other slaves were to be appraised and hired out until they earned two-thirds of their value, after which they were to be free. The wife died in 1851; Bateman was appraised at $600, and his hire in Arkansas was worth $150 per year. Four years later, instead of setting him free, the administrator of the estate sold Bateman to Bernard Kendig, a New Orleans slave dealer, as a slave for life (this is the same Kendig who engaged in the practice of buying diseased slaves at a low price and selling them fully guaranteed). Bateman sued, claiming his freedom under his late master's will. He won in the lower court, and Kendig appealed. Justice Thomas Land summarized the laws of Arkansas concerning emancipation:

> Sec. 1. Any person may emancipate his slaves by last will and testament, or by any other instrument in writing, under hand and seal, attested by two witnesses, and proved in the Circuit Court of the county where he resides, or acknowledged by the party in the same court.
>
> Sec. 2. Such emancipation shall have the effect to discharge the slave from the performance of any contract entered into during servitude, and shall make such slave as fully and perfectly free as if such slave had been born free.

12. Brown, f.w.c., v. Raby, No. 5797, 14 La. Ann. 41 (1859).

Affirming the action of the lower court, Land ruled that Bateman had been free since 1856 by the operation of the laws of Arkansas, and approved the lower-court jury's award of $300 in damages.[13]

During the same term the court issued its last ruling on the issue, *Foster* v. *Mish* (1860). Andy Foster sued for his freedom in the Fourth District Court of New Orleans, claiming he had been born free in Clark County, Kentucky, his mother, an ex-slave, having been manumitted by his white father, John Foster, before his birth. He further claimed that his father had always recognized him as his son and had taken him to Ohio to attend school and learn a trade. Sometime after his father's death, he was kidnapped in St. Louis, brought to New Orleans, and sold as a slave for life to William Mish. He offered into evidence the deed of emancipation of his mother, which the court found was "signed, sealed and delivered by John Foster." The trial court ruled against Andy Foster because of the act of 1857 that prohibited emancipation, but the Supreme Court of Louisiana reversed the decision. In a strong statement, Justice Land declared: "If no right of action existed in such cases, then free negroes might be kidnapped . . . and sold into slavery in this State with impunity—a species of slave-trade, which our Legislature never intended to legalize by the Act of 1857, prohibiting emancipation." Furthermore, Land recognized that Foster had been legally free under the operation of the laws of Kentucky. Land cited article 10 of the *Civil Code* in his ruling: "The form and effect of public and private written instruments are governed by the laws and usages of the places where they are passed or executed." Article 10, he argued, meant that the effect of the act of manumission was governed by the laws of Kentucky, where it was intended to have its legal effect, and not by the laws of Louisiana: "We judicially take cognizance of the fact, the common law prevails in the State of Kentucky, and that a deed is one of the most solemn and authentic instruments known to that system of laws, by which the rights of property can be alienated, and that it is sufficient in form and content in the common law States of this Union, in the absence of statutory enactments to the contrary, to transfer to and vest in a slave a full and perfect title to freedom."[14]

The Supreme Court of Louisiana consistently honored the laws of the

13. Bateman v. Frisby and Kendig, No. 6242, 15 La. Ann. 58 (1860). See chap. 5 for more on Kendig's fraudulent dealings.

14. Foster v. Mish, No. 6344, 15 La. Ann. 199 (1860); *Civil Code,* Art. 10, 183, pp. 4, 28.

other southern states in appeals based on conflicts of law and, with few exceptions, granted comity to the laws of northern states in suits for freedom based on transportation to a free state or country, despite the attempt of the Louisiana legislature to restrain the scope of these rulings. If the legislature had intended to close any opportunity to sue for freedom, the law of 1857 would have meant that no legal redress was available to kidnapped persons of color to establish their freedom.

The Supreme Court of Louisiana's handling of cases involving whether a slave taken to a territory, state, or country in which slavery did not exist would thereby become free by the operation of the laws of the free state must be seen in the context of the state's legal heritage. Under Roman law, slavery was considered a creation of the state that was contrary to natural law. Because the justices were trained in the common law, they were no doubt aware of the similar philosophy of a famous English case, *Somerset* v. *Stewart* (1772). The slave in this case, James Somerset, had traveled to England with his master, Charles Stewart. When Stewart arranged to return him to Jamaica, Somerset applied for relief under a writ of *habeas corpus.* The chief justice of the Court of King's Bench, Lord Mansfield, ruled that the master could not forcibly remove Somerset from England and that Somerset was within his rights in applying for *habeas corpus.* Furthermore, Mansfield ruled, Somerset was free because no positive law existed in England to hold him in slavery. This holding—that slavery could not exist without a body of positive law—was one of the most important opinions on slavery in Anglo-American law.[15] In most emancipation cases decided by the Supreme Court of Louisiana involving transportation to a free state or country, the rulings favored the slave suing for freedom and demonstrate the court's concern with substantive and procedural due process.

From 1791 on, French law held that as soon as a slave's foot touched the free soil of France, he or she was instantly free.[16] During the antebellum period the Supreme Court of Louisiana followed this rule in

15. Daniel Chamier, *A Manual of Roman Law* (New York, 1893), 16–17; Finkelman, *Law of Freedom and Bondage,* 31–35; Somerset v. Stewart, Loft 1 (1772); 20 Howell St. Tr. 1 (1772). See also William M. Wiecek, "*Somerset:* Lord Mansfield and the Legitimacy of Slavery in the Anglo-American World," *University of Chicago Law Review,* XLII (Fall, 1974), 86–146.

16. "Tout individu est libre aussitôt qu'il est en France." Finkelman, *Imperfect Union,* 206. Finkelman has an excellent discussion of cases on this point, 206–16. However, he had nothing but the printed reports with which to work.

most emancipation cases based on transportation to free soil, even after the Louisiana legislature in 1846 specifically enacted a law to the contrary, stating that "from the passage of this act, no slave shall be entitled to his or her freedom, under the pretence that he or she has been, with or without the consent of his or her owner, in a country where slavery does not exist, or in any of the States where slavery is prohibited."[17] Despite this law, the court continued to grant freedom to slaves who had been in a free territory before 1846, and granted the 1846 act only prospective application. In refusing to make legislative acts retroactive, the court granted freedom to several slaves. In only one case decided on this basis in the 1850s did the court refuse to free a slave. The court's overall record in these cases was thus clearly more often in favor of the slave than not. Only in the one ruling, in 1852, did the court begin to approach a closer conformity not only to legislative wishes but to slave law in other Deep South states.[18]

In one of the earliest cases of this kind to come before the Supreme Court of Louisiana, William Forsyth in 1816 claimed to own a slave named Jeffries Nash. To prove ownership, Forsyth produced a bill of sale for Nash that had been executed in Detroit. Louisiana's high court ruled in *Forsyth* v. *Nash* (1816) that since the Northwest Ordinance of 1787 prohibited slavery in Michigan, Nash's presence in Michigan created the presumption that he was free. Judge Martin commented that only by proving Nash was a fugitive who had run away to the Northwest Territory could Forsyth's suit have been successful. Since Forsyth presented no evidence to prove that Nash's residence had ever been in a slave state, or that he had ever been a fugitive, Martin affirmed his freedom.[19]

The landmark case in suits for freedom based on transportation to a free area was *Lunsford* v. *Coquillon* (1824). The slave Rebecca Lunsford

17. "An Act to Protect the Rights of Slaveholders in the State of Louisiana," Act of May 30, 1846, *Louisiana Acts, 1846,* p. 163.

18. Dargo, *Jefferson's Louisiana,* 171; Finkelman, *Imperfect Union,* 188–89.

19. Forsyth v. Nash, No. 150, 4 Mart. (o.s.) 385 (La. 1816); Finkelman, *Imperfect Union,* 207; U.S. Censuses of 1810, 1820. In 1810 the Supreme Court of Louisiana heard a freedom suit brought by Adéle, who had been brought from the West Indies and boarded in a New York school before being taken to New Orleans. Although she could have won her freedom on this basis, she claimed that because she was a mulatto she was legally presumed free, and won that way. Adéle v. Beauregard, 1 Mart. (o.s.) 183 (La. 1810).

claimed her freedom on the basis that her master had "effectually emancipated" her by taking her from his residence in Kentucky to Ohio. In 1816 she had sued for freedom in Ohio; her master had thwarted the suit by forcibly returning her to Kentucky and subsequently selling her to Michel Fortier of Louisiana. Witnesses testified that she had lived in Ohio for more than three years. The Supreme Court of Louisiana affirmed a lower-court judgment in her favor, noting that her sale to Louisiana was "a species of kidnapping worse than was ever practiced by the Turks against Grecian captives." As Chief Judge Martin expressed it, "as she was a free woman there [Ohio], she must be held so every where." The court based its ruling not only on Roman law but also on public law, specifically the Constitution of the United States, which permitted "a state to pass laws dissolving the relation of master and servant." Martin gave an extraordinary interpretation to the fugitive-slave clause of the United States Constitution, which held that a fugitive slave could not become free by escaping to a free state or territory. Martin interpreted this clause to mean, by implication, that slaves whose masters voluntarily took them to free territory were freed by the operation of the laws of the free state. No law, of course, would operate to free slaves who escaped into free states as opposed to those voluntarily taken. Martin also used the reasoning of *Somerset* in ruling that slavery was "a creature of the municipal [public] law" in states where it existed. Therefore, Martin concluded, the constitution of Ohio *ipso facto* emancipated slaves voluntarily brought into Ohio by their masters. If it did not, prohibiting slavery within its borders would be useless. In addition, article 189 of the *Civil Code* stated that "an emancipation, once perfected, is irrevocable."[20]

In a few instances the court heard cases involving white masters who traveled to a free state with their slave mistresses and children expressly for the purpose of freeing them, or who happened to free them when there. This practice was legal until the Louisiana legislature attempted to close this avenue to freedom in 1842. M. C. McWalker of New Orleans took his slave Isabella, a Negro, and her daughter, a "bright mu-

20. Lunsford v. Coquillon, No. 815, 2 Mart. (N.S.) 401 (La. 1824); *Civil Code*, Art, 189, p. 29. Chief Justice Lemuel Shaw of the Massachusetts Supreme Judicial Court cited *Lunsford* in his famous decision freeing the slave girl, Med; Commonwealth v. Aves, 18 Pick. 193 (Mass. 1836).

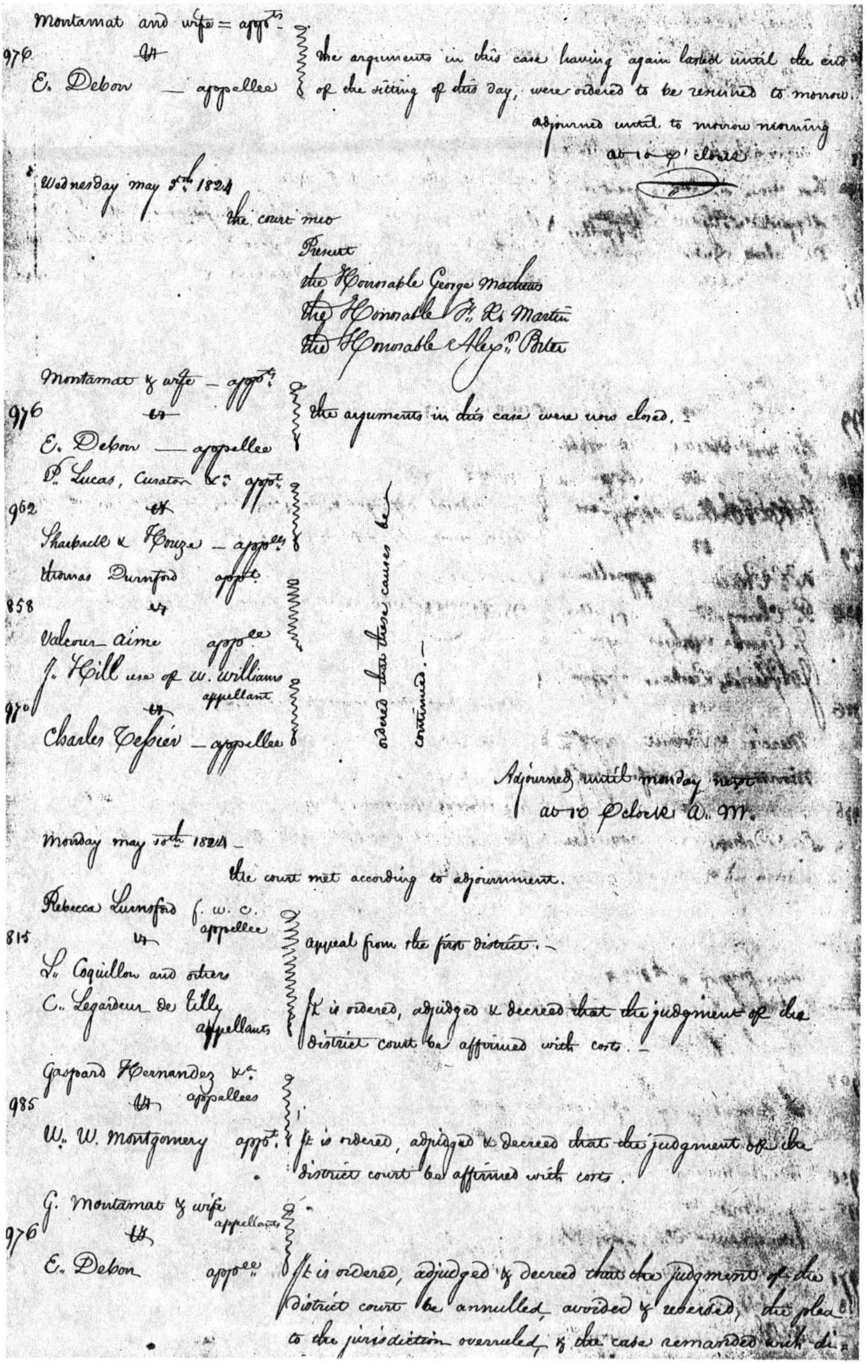
Montamat and wife = app^{ts}.
976 vs
E. Debon — appellee

The arguments in this case having again lasted until the end of the sitting of this day, were ordered to be resumed to morrow.

Adjourned until to morrow morning at 10 o' clock

Wednesday may 5th 1824

the court met
Present
the Honorable George Mathews
the Honorable F. X. Martin
the Honorable Alex^{r}. Porter

Montamat & wife — app^{ts}.
976 vs
E. Debon — appellee

the arguments in this case were now closed. —

P. Lucas, Curator &c. app^{t}.
962 vs
Shackell & Houze — app^{ees}
Thomas Durnford app^{t}.
858 vs
Valcour aime app^{ee}
J. Hill use of W. Williams appellant
970 vs
Charles Tessier — appellee

ordered that these causes be continued. —

Adjourned until monday next at 10 o'clock A. M.

Monday may 10th 1824 —

the court met according to adjournment.

Rebecca Lunsford f. w. c. appellee
815 vs
L. Coquillon and others
C. Legardeur De Tilly appellants

appeal from the first district. —

It is ordered, adjudged & decreed that the judgment of the district court be affirmed with costs. —

Gaspard Hernandez &c. appellees
985 vs
W. W. Montgomery app^{t}.

It is ordered, adjudged & decreed that the judgment of the district court be affirmed with costs.

G. Montamat & wife appellants
976 vs
E. Debon app^{ee}

It is ordered, adjudged & decreed that the judgment of the district court be annulled, avoided & reversed, the plea to the jurisdiction overruled, & the case remanded with di-

Minutes of the Supreme Court of Louisiana, Book 3, p. 108. Notice the entry for *Lunsford, f.w.c., v. Coquillon,* in which the court affirmed the freedom of Rebecca Lunsford.

Courtesy of the Supreme Court of Louisiana Collection of Legal Archives

latto," to Cincinnati in 1822 and executed an act of emancipation to free them. All three returned to Louisiana and continued to live together until 1827, when McWalker became insolvent and his creditors seized Isabella, her child, two slaves, four horses, and two cows (all acquired since her emancipation) to sell them for McWalker's debts. Isabella sued for her freedom in *Hawkins* v. *Vanwickle* (1828). The creditors, citing an 1810 ruling of the Superior Court of the Territory of Orleans, *Adéle* v. *Beauregard,* which held that Negroes were presumed to be slaves, argued that since Isabella was black, she could not be presumed free. (This was an incorrect reading of *Adéle,* which held only that blacks were presumed to be slaves unless they could produce proof to the contrary, not that blacks could not be free.) McWalker admitted that Isabella was "Black and her head is Black and covered with negro wool." The creditors also contended that McWalker had given her the slaves and livestock to defraud his creditors, and that since she was a slave herself, she could own nothing.

The lower court held that Isabella and her child were slaves. The crucial question was the admissibility into evidence of the Ohio deed of emancipation, as the burden of proof was on Isabella because she was black. The trial court had refused to admit the act of emancipation on the ground that Isabella had not proved a compliance with the formalities required by Ohio in its laws regarding the emancipation of slaves. The supreme court not only ruled that the lower-court judge had erred in refusing to admit the document, but in a remarkable opinion, shifted the burden of proof to the creditors. Justice Alexander Porter, writing for the court, saw no reason why Isabella could not have introduced the act of emancipation and subsequently proved that it was valid by the laws of Ohio:

> But the whole proceeding was in fact irregular. This was not the case of a slave suing for her freedom, but of a woman in the enjoyment of it, suing another for property which she alleged belonged to her. In such case the burthen of proving the fact of slavery was on the party making the allegation. By a law of the Partidas where a man claims another who is in the actual possession of liberty as his slave, the necessity of proving him such is thrown on the claimant—*a fortiori,* where the question arises collaterally with a third party; and the former master by his not interfering in the suit, furnishes a violent presumption that the state

and condition of the plaintiff is that which she represents it to be. *Partidas* 3, *Tit.* 15, *Law.* 5.[21]

Two years later the court addressed a variation on the question of whether a slave was freed by touching free soil when it ruled on the status of a person born in an area where slavery was prohibited. John Merry sued for his freedom in a New Orleans court in *Merry, f.m.c.,* v. *Chexnaider* (1830) on the basis that he was born in the Northwest Territory after passage of the Ordinance of 1787, which prohibited slavery. André Chexnaider, the man who claimed Merry as his slave, stated that his real name was Jean Marie and that he was "addicted to running away." Merry alleged that he had been living free in Illinois when he was arrested by agents of Chexnaider in 1826 and brought to St. Louis. He had successfully sued for his freedom in a Missouri court; however, Chexnaider seized him, brought him to New Orleans, and "reduced him to slavery" in 1828. Merry again sued for his freedom, this time in a New Orleans court. The lower court declared Merry a free man and Judge Porter affirmed the judgment, saying that Merry was "clearly entitled" to his freedom because he had been born on free soil.[22]

Four years later the court heard an appeal of a more complex issue in *Louis, f.m.c.,* v. *Cabarrus* (1834). Louis Richardson claimed his freedom on the grounds that although he had been born a slave, he had resided in Ohio for between two and three years, and that since the Ohio constitution prohibited slavery, he was entitled to his freedom. The defendant, who had purchased Louis as a slave for life, contended that Louis had been born of a slave mother and was therefore a slave, and his property. The lower-court jury found for Louis, declaring him free. The defendant appealed to the supreme court, alleging error in the charge to the jury. Cabarrus' attorney argued that mere residence in Ohio, unconnected with any other proof, did not establish Louis' freedom. Judge Martin agreed with this reasoning and reversed the judgment for freedom, remanding the case for further action. The crucial issue was whether Louis' master had given his *consent* to Louis' residing in Ohio: "The residence of a slave in Ohio, contrary to the will, or without the knowledge of his master or owner, does not deprive the latter to his

21. "An Act More Effectively to Prevent Free Persons of Color from Entering into This State," Act of March 16, 1842, *Louisiana Acts, 1842,* p. 314; Hawkins v. Vanwickle, No. 1501, 6 Mart. (N.S.) 418 (La. 1828); Adéle v. Beauregard, 1 Mart. (O.S.) 183 (La. 1810).

22. Merry, f.m.c., v. Chexnaider, No. 1877, 8 Mart. (N.S.) 699 (La. 1830).

right of property." Martin ordered the district court "to charge the jury that proof of a slave's having resided in the state of Ohio, or any free state during the period of two or three years, unconnected with any other proof, does not authorise or entitle him to his freedom; and to abstain from charging or stating to the jury, that the permission given by the master to his slave, to go and labor in the state of Ohio, had the effect to emancipate him."[23]

In *Phillis, f.w.c.,* v. *Gentin* (1836), the Louisiana Supreme Court once again faced the question of whether birth on free soil conferred liberty. Phillis, a Negro woman, claimed to have been born free in Pennsylvania. Testimony proved that in 1814, when Phillis was fifteen years old, she was bound as an indentured servant for thirteen years to one Benjamin Page of Philadelphia. Several transfers later, she disappeared in St. Louis in 1822. One witness testified that she had run away and had allegedly stolen $100 from one of her masters. Testimony established that she had lived in Cincinnati with one of her owners for some time. She reappeared in an 1823 sale in St. Louis and then was sold several more times. At some point she was fraudulently sold (along with her two children) as a slave for life for $925. Phillis sued for her freedom in the First Judicial District Court of New Orleans in 1834 and asked for $500 damages. Gentin petitioned the court to award him $750 in damages from his vendor if it ruled in her favor. The lower court judged her free and awarded her damages. Citing *Forsyth* v. *Nash,* the Supreme Court of Louisiana affirmed the judgment, noting that if Phillis were not free by her place of birth, she would have been automatically freed by her residence in Ohio with the consent of her master. However, Chief Judge Mathews refused to grant her damages from Gentin because he claimed that Gentin had honestly believed she was a slave for life when he purchased her and had therefore acted in good faith. Mathews noted that damages could only be allowed against the unknown vendor who first sold her as a slave for life.[24]

In a suit for freedom that confronted the supreme court twice, *Marie Louise, f.w.c.,* v. *Marot* (1835, 1836), the court actually *suggested* using transportation to free soil as a potentially successful tactic for a slave seeking her freedom. Marie Louise, a free woman of color, sued Marie Marot, the alleged owner of her daughter Josephine, for the daughter's

23. Louis, f.m.c., v. Cabarrus, 7 La. 170 (1834).
24. Phillis, f.w.c., v. Gentin, No. 2889, 9 La. 208 (1836).

freedom on the basis of a document promising to free her when she had attained the age of twenty. The First Judicial Court of New Orleans ruled in Marie Louise's favor, but the supreme court reversed the decision, declaring the document void because of an error in form. While the appeal was in process, it became known that Josephine had traveled with her mistress to France to learn hairdressing. Obviously distressed by having to deny Josephine her freedom, Chief Judge Mathews, writing for the court, made this remarkable statement:

> It is really painful, in applying rules of law . . . to be obliged to violate . . . feelings of humanity: but this pain is sometimes felt by judges. . . . Yet . . . we do not consider ourselves bound to leave the wretched victim of present affliction without hope . . . the facts . . . have convinced us that it is a case in which we ought to exercise the general power granted by law to remand causes . . . whenever justice, in our opinion, requires such a proceeding. It is, perhaps, true, as a general rule, that the supreme court . . . should be influenced alone by . . . the record; . . . but it is an action brought to redeem a helpless female from slavery; and every thing which may properly be done *in favorum* [*sic*] *libertatis,* should be done, even to notice facts *dehors* the record. It was stated at the bar, and not denied, that . . . [she] was taken by her owners to France . . . and was placed by them under the direction of a hairdresser, to learn his art. Did she not become free in France? Being brought . . . in to the United States, is she not free, according to . . . laws enacted by Congress? . . . questions which we will not solve; but . . . remand the cause, in order that they may be put in a train for solution.

In other words, Mathews suggested a legal avenue to freedom and declared that the court felt an obligation to do "every thing which may properly be done" *in favorem libertatis.* Symbolic of the court's tendency to favor the petitioner in freedom suits is the fact that the plaintiff in such suits was allowed to use the initials f.w.c. or f.m.c. when initiating an action for freedom. This practice was a custom of courtesy, not an official rule of the court.[25]

25. Marie Louise, f.w.c., v. Marot, No. 2748, 8 La. 475 (1835); "An Act to Prescribe Certain Formalities Respecting Free Persons of Color," Act of March 31, 1808, *Orleans Terri-*

After this verdict Marot imprisoned Josephine, who sued for her freedom on the basis of her sojourn in France; she also asked for $500 in damages. *Marie Louise, f.w.c.,* v. *Marot* (1836) reached the Supreme Court of Louisiana one year later, and this time the court affirmed the lower court's judgment in Josephine's favor, although it denied damages. Chief Judge Mathews, writing again for the court, noted that the issue was whether being taken to France produced an "immediate emancipation"; he concluded that "such is the benign and liberal effect of the laws and customs of that State [France]." Mathews reasoned: "Being free for one moment in France, it was not in the power of her former owner to reduce her again to slavery"; as in *Lunsford* v. *Coquillon,* he also cited article 189 of the Louisiana *Civil Code,* which held that an emancipation, once perfected, was irrevocable.[26]

Two years later the supreme court ruled again on a slave transportation case, *Frank, f.m.c.,* v. *Powell* (1838). The slave Frank had sued for his freedom in a New Orleans court, claiming he had been born of a slave mother while her master was traveling through Pennsylvania en route from Maryland to Kentucky. The supreme court did not have to attack the thorny question of whether a child who happened to be born to a slave mother while passing through free territory was free or slave, although Chief Judge Martin cited *Merry* v. *Chexnaider.* Testimony proved Frank had been hired out with his owner's consent in the free state of Ohio. The court declared him free on the basis of the Ohio residence because his master, according to the reasoning of the court, was presumed to have consented to the legal consequences of his actions; therefore, since his master brought him to Ohio, he must have consented to his emancipation. In this decision Chief Judge Martin, writing for the court, cited *Lunsford* v. *Coquillon* to the effect that Frank's owner had consented to his being in Ohio and therefore "had submitted him-

tory Acts, 1808, pp. 138–40. Justice McLean cited *Marie Louise* in his dissent in the *Dred Scott* decision: Scott v. Sandford, 19 Howard (U.S.) 393 (1857) at 561. Although the law required that the initials *f.m.c.* or *f.w.c.* be placed after the names of free persons of color in court records, trial courts were not always so generous. The First District Court of New Orleans consistently used the initials *c.w.* or *c.m.* (colored woman or man) for slaves suing for freedom. For example, Arsène, c.w., v. Pignéguy, No. 395, No. 434 was the title of a case in this court. When Arsène appealed to the Supreme Court of Louisiana, the title was Arsène, alias Cora, f.w.c., v. Pignéguy, No. 459, 2 La. Ann. 620 (1847).

26. Marie Louise, f.w.c., v. Marot, No. 2914, 9 La. 473 (1836); *Civil Code,* Art. 189, p. 29.

self and the property he brought with him, to the operation of the constitution and laws of that state:" Martin elaborated: "Every man is presumed to have consented to all the necessary legal consequences of his actions. The emancipation of a slave brought into the state of Ohio, is the necessary legal consequences of his removal thither; and his former owner, by whose agency his removal is effected, must have presumed to have consented to that emancipation." Martin also commented on a recent decision of the United States Supreme Court on the issue of transportation:

> Our attention has been drawn to the case of the United States *vs.* the ship Garonne, (11 *Peters*), in which the Supreme Court of the United States held, that the ship was not forfeited, in consequence of a slave who had followed her mistress on a voyage from New-Orleans to France, having been brought back in her with the intention of retaining the slave in her service. From this decision the inference has been drawn, that the court considered that the slave had not acquired her freedom on her being landed in France. It has appeared to us, from a close examination of the opinion of the court, that the court decided only, that the return of a slave from a voyage from New-Orleans to France, could not be considered as the importation of a negro from a foreign country, in violation of the acts of Congress. The object of these acts was to put an end to the slave trade from foreign countries, and to prevent the increase of the slave population of the United States. A lady, visiting France, attended by one of her slaves, and returning with her, could not be considered as having been engaged in the slave trade, or as having added to the slave population of the United States.[27]

A comparison of the United States Supreme Court case Martin mentioned in *Frank* with its Louisiana counterpart demonstrates how Louisiana could be markedly kinder to the slave seeking freedom on the grounds of having touched free soil than were some states with an English common-law foundation. In *U.S.* v. Garonne (1837) and *Smith* v. *Smith* (1839), the slave involved was Pricilla Smith. In 1837 the United States Supreme Court had held that Pricilla Smith was still a slave even

27. Frank, f.m.c., v. Powell, No. 3280, 11 La. 501 (1838).

though she had accompanied her mistress and the mistress' daughter to Havre, France, in 1835. The case was a prosecution under the act to prohibit the foreign slave trade. Although Pricilla's status was not an issue, Chief Justice Roger Taney determined that French law was not applicable to this case: "even assuming that by the French law . . . [Pricilla] was entitled to freedom, the Court is of opinion that there is nothing in the act of Congress [the act of 1807, prohibiting foreign importation of slaves] . . . to prevent her mistress from . . . continuing to hold her as before, in her service." In other words, the United States Supreme Court refused to recognize a French law that held that touching the free soil conferred freedom on a slave because it was irrelevant to the issue of the violation of the slave trade. The question of whether federal courts have to recognize the law of a foreign jurisdiction, especially when they are in conflict with stated public policy, is not the same as the question of whether state courts were required to give full faith and credit to each other's laws and judgments, which is mandated in the federal Constitution. However, the issue of Pricilla Smith's freedom was ultimately decided by the Supreme Court of Louisiana.[28]

In *Smith, f.w.c.,* v. *Smith* (1839), Pricilla unsuccessfully sued for her freedom in a New Orleans court after her return from France. She appealed the unfavorable decision, and the Supreme Court of Louisiana heard her appeal in 1839. The slaveowner's attorney argued that the owner could not evade the laws of Louisiana by taking slaves out of the state. He was referring to the law that required slaves to be thirty years of age at the time of the emancipation; Pricilla was under that age. To this assertion Chief Judge Martin replied that if such an emancipation were to be void, "it cannot be so on the application of a party [Pricilla's mistress] to the . . . fraud." The slaveowner's attorney also argued that under an 1830 act of the Louisiana legislature, emancipated slaves were required to leave the state, and therefore Pricilla had no right to be heard. Martin also refused this line of argument, on the basis of the sixteenth section of the act of 1830, which specifically exempted Loui-

28. U.S. v. *Garonne,* U.S. v. *Fortune,* 11 Peters (U.S.) 73, January, 1837. This is a consolidated case, as the title suggests. It also involved a Mr. Pecquet, who took two female slaves to France for the purpose of emancipation and then returned with them to New Orleans, where the two women lived as free. The United States Supreme Court noted that as "no deed of emancipation for either of them had been executed," they were still slaves. See also Catterall, *Judicial Cases Concerning American Slavery,* III, 513.

siana slaves emancipated in any other state and returned to Louisiana with consent of their owner from having to leave the state. The purpose of this exception, Martin noted, was "that they have their relations . . . and friends here, whom it would be cruel to prevent them from rejoining." Since the legislature had in effect recognized the rights of owners to emancipate their slaves in other states, the court reversed the decision of the lower court, set Pricilla free, and ordered her former mistress to pay court costs. Martin stated that the issue in *Smith, f.w.c.,* v. *Smith* was indistinguishable from *Marie Louise, f.w.c.,* v. *Marot.* Martin never mentioned the United States Supreme Court's 1837 decision concerning Pricilla, although he had commented on it in *Frank, f.m.c.,* v. *Powell.* It is ironic that in differing rulings in the high court of a southern slave state and in the highest national court, the slave received a more favorable decision from the judicial system of the slave state. Both decisions, of course, can be rationalized in terms of the interests involved. The United States Supreme Court was concerned mainly with interpreting the 1808 prohibition of the international slave trade, rather than with Pricilla's status; the Louisiana Supreme Court was more concerned with status of a Louisiana slave, the property of a citizen of the state.[29]

In 1840 yet another slave came before the Supreme Court of Louisiana to sue for freedom on the basis of transportation to a free state. In *Thomas* v. *Generis,* Elizabeth Thomas claimed she had been born free in Virginia and that one O. C. Vanlandingham "by some means" got possession of her when she was a child, conveyed her to Kentucky, and then in 1833 took her to Shawneetown, Illinois. Four years later he brought her to Louisiana and sold her to L. F. Generis as a slave for life for $1,000. She sued Generis for her freedom on the basis of her Illinois residence. Generis petitioned the court for a reimbursement of the $1,000 under the title warranty if Thomas were successful. In his defense

29. "An Act to Prevent the Emigration of Free Negroes and Mulattoes into the Territory of Orleans," Act of April 14, 1807, *Orleans Territory Acts, 1807,* pp. 82–89; *Civil Code,* Art. 185, p. 29; "An Act to Prevent Free People of Color From Entering into This State," Act of March 16, 1830, *Louisiana Acts, 1830,* pp. 90–94; *Black Code,* Secs. 9, 8, p. 154; Smith, f.w.c., v. Smith, No. 3314, 13 La. 441 (1839); Finkelman, *Imperfect Union,* 339–43.

Considering the composition of the 1837 United States Supreme Court, the ruling in the *Garonne* case is hardly surprising. A majority of the court, five justices, were appointed by President Andrew Jackson between 1835 and 1837; Chief Justice Taney and several of the others were decidedly proslavery. See Harold M. Hyman and William M. Wiecek, *Equal Justice Under Law: Constitutional Development, 1835–1875* (New York, 1982), 58–63, and Don E. Fehrenbacher, *Slavery, Law, and Politics: The Dred Scott Case in Historical Perspective* (New York, 1981), 118–19.

Generis presented the testimony of an Illinois Supreme Court justice, Walter B. Scates, which established that Thomas had been ill and had requested Vanlandingham to send her to a physician in Illinois, and that her removal to a free state with her master's consent did not act to free her. Scates testified that the crucial issue was the consent of the slave: "the consent or non-consent of the owner is immaterial; if the slave be held in *involuntary* servitude in Illinois, she becomes immediately free by the [Illinois] constitution, but that cannot be involuntary to which she *consents* [emphasis in original]. Louisiana Supreme Court judge Edward Simon rejected this argument, stating that it must be recognized that "a slave has no will." Instead, Simon ruled that her residence on free soil made her free, and "being once free, she could not be again made a slave by removing her to a slave state." In this decision he cited *Lunsford* v. *Coquillon; Frank, f.m.c.,* v. *Powell; Marie Louise, f.w.c.,* v. *Marot;* and *Smith, f.w.c.,* v. *Smith* as to the liberating effect of free soil. Again the Louisiana high court's ruling was more beneficent to the litigant than the law of the "free" state of Illinois.[30]

In 1842 the Louisiana legislature tried to close this avenue to freedom by prohibiting slaveowners from taking their slaves to free soil and then returning to Louisiana with them. This was an attempt to limit the free black population of the state; there was nothing to prevent a slaveowner from emancipating slaves in a free state and leaving them there. Violators could be sued for up to $1,000 per slave removed and returned. In effect, this law meant that the Louisiana legislature recognized that slaves who trod upon free soil were free.[31] No reported cases testing this law were ever brought to the Supreme Court of Louisiana.

It was not until 1846 that the Louisiana legislature attempted to repudiate the supreme court's jurisprudence favoring slaves who used transportation to a free territory, state, or country as a basis for freedom. In that year the legislature passed a law that firmly rejected the court's recent precedent-making decisions. The law stated that no slave should be declared free under the "pretence" that he had been on free soil with or without (in the case of fugitives) the consent of his master.[32] The new

30. Thomas v. Generis, No. 4234, 16 La. 483 (1840); *Civil Code,* Art. 189, p. 29.

31. "An Act More Effectually to Prevent Free Persons of Color from Entering into This State," Act of March 16, 1842, *Louisiana Acts, 1841,* p. 314. The session began in 1841, but this act was actually passed in 1842.

32. "An Act to Protect the Rights of Slaveowners in the State of Louisiana," Act of May 30, 1846, *Louisiana Acts, 1846,* p. 163.

law was silent as to whether it applied to slaves who had touched free soil *before* its passage but sued for their liberty after 1846; however, its wording implied a firm purpose of stopping this avenue to freedom. It is not remarkable, given the long history of strict judicial interpretation of statutes, that the state supreme court refused to recognize the law's retroactive application and continued to free slaves who sued for freedom, provided they could prove that they had been on free soil before passage of the law.

Immediately after passage of this law, in *Josephine, f.w.c.,* v. *Poultney* (1846), the supreme court rendered a decision on yet another appeal concerning a slave suing for freedom on the ground of transport to free soil. The slave Josephine had accompanied her mistress to New York and Philadelphia in 1841, and had remained on free soil for three years. Upon her return to New Orleans, she sued for her freedom. The trial court ruled in her favor, and her mistress appealed. Chief Justice Eustis, writing for the court, affirmed the judgment for her freedom: "Her condition being once fixed [meaning free on free soil], *under the decisions of the late Supreme Court,* she cannot be reduced to the condition of the slave" [emphasis added]. In this decision, Eustis cited *Lunsford; Louis, f.m.c.,* v. *Cabarrus;* and *Smith, f.w.c.,* v. *Smith,* as well as *The Slave, Grace.* The latter was an English case, decided in 1827, that held that slave status would reattach to a slave who left England and returned to a slave jurisdiction: "It is understood that this decision relates only to the right of *ownership* of the plaintiff, as the slave of the defendant" (emphasis in original).[33]

The following year the Supreme Court of Louisiana heard two transport cases. In the first, *Eugénie, f.w.c.,* v. *Préval* (1847), the court explicitly recognized the new law regarding the potentially liberating effect of free soil, and stated openly its refusal to make the law retroactive. Chief Justice Eustis wrote: "A law can prescribe only for the future; it can have no retrospective operation." The slave Eugénie Smith had accompanied her master's daughter to France in 1830 and remained there until 1838. After her return to New Orleans, she sued for her freedom and won in the lower court. Her owner appealed unsuccessfully to the supreme court, which declared her to be free, awarded her $146 in wages (from

33. Josephine, f.w.c., v. Poultney, No. 5935, 1 La. Ann. 329 (1846); The Slave, Grace, 2 Haggard Admiralty 94 (1827); Finkelman, *Imperfect Union,* 185–87.

the date of the filing of the lawsuit to the day of its final judgment), and denied her former mistress a rehearing.[34]

In the same term, in a nearly identical case, *Arsène, alias Cora, f.w.c.,* v. *Pignéguy* (1847), the slave woman Arsène had accompanied her master to France in 1836 and did not return to New Orleans until 1838. She apparently was motivated to file suit for her freedom because her owner threatened to sell her for $650 in 1845. In response to her suit for freedom, her owner argued that he had only visited France, had never acquired domicile in that country, and was therefore unaffected by French law. Eustis brushed this argument aside: "We cannot expect that foreign nations will consent to the suspension of the operation of their fundamental laws, as to persons voluntarily sojourning . . . for such a length of time." The court concluded that French law had not been suspended, and Arsène was therefore free; she also won wages of eight dollars per month from the date of the lawsuit's initiation.[35]

In 1850 a clearly reluctant state supreme court, in *Couvent, f.m.c.,* v. *Guesnard,* finally handed down a ruling that was consistent with the act of the Louisiana legislature of 1846 declaring that the act of touching free soil did not free a slave. Mary, the slave of Mr. and Mrs. William Guesnard, accompanied her mistress and master to France one year *after* passage of the law. The Guesnards decided to remain permanently in France and sent Mary back to New Orleans to be sold as a slave for life

34. Eugénie v. Préval, No. 99, 2 La. Ann. 180 (1847).

35. Arsène, alias Cora, f.w.c., v. Pignéguy, No. 459, 2 La. Ann. 620 (1847). The same year, the Supreme Court of Louisiana again tacitly recognized the freeing effect of free soil. Samuel Miller had sold his plantation in Louisiana and moved to St. Louis. He left with his slave concubine, a mulatto named Patsy, whom he freed in Indiana in May, 1844. He died about a year later, and Patsy claimed eight promissory notes of $3,000 each that she alleged Miller left to her and that she had in her possession after his death. The notes were also claimed by Miller's succession, and Patsy sued to have them declared her property. She won in the lower court, but the supreme court reversed the judgment on three grounds: that as his concubine she could receive only one-tenth of the estate; that if he gave her the notes before she was freed, as a slave she could not own anything; and that Miller had purposely sold all that he owned to convert his property to a disposable (movable) form to enable him to evade Louisiana law (immovable property could not be left to a concubine). The court was obviously convinced that the relationship between Patsy and Miller was such that Miller as a dying man would sell all that he owned and move to another state to provide for her. Noting that Miller's concubinage with Patsy was "open and notorious," the court reasoned that she could not inherit more than one-tenth of the estate, and since there was no proof of when she acquired the notes (before or after she was freed), she could recover nothing. Her freedom was never an issue. Cole v. Lucas, No. 53, 2 La. Ann. 946 (1847).

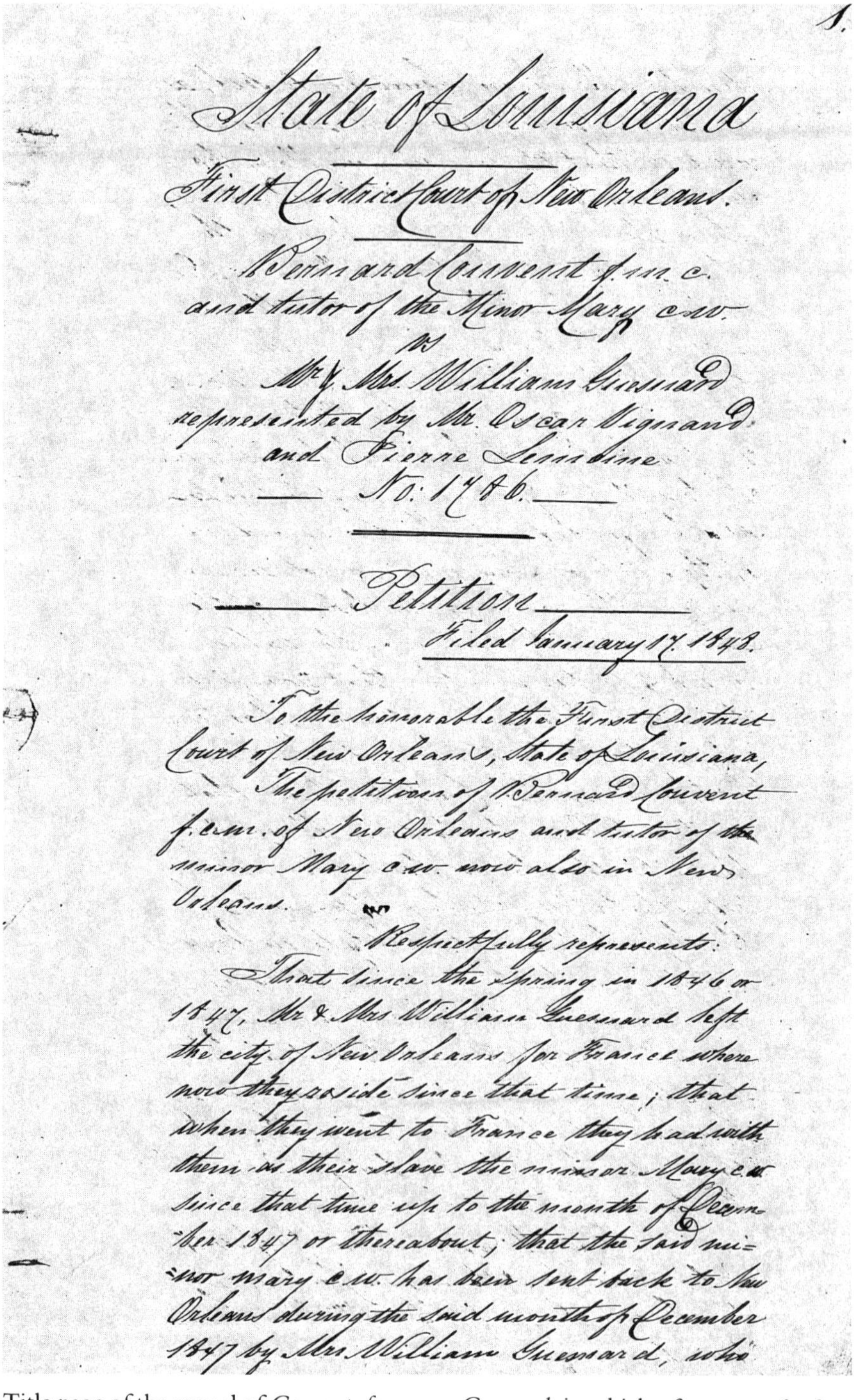

1.

State of Louisiana

First District Court of New Orleans.

Bernard Couvent f.m.c.
and tutor of the Minor Mary c.w.
vs
Mr & Mrs William Guesnard
represented by Mr. Oscar Vignaud
and Pierre Lemoine
No: 1786.

Petition
Filed January 17. 1848.

To the honorable the First District Court of New Orleans, State of Louisiana,

The petition of Bernard Couvent f.c.m. of New Orleans and tutor of the minor Mary c.w. now also in New Orleans.

Respectfully represents:

That since the Spring in 1846 or 1847, Mr & Mrs William Guesnard left the city of New Orleans for France where now they reside since that time; that when they went to France they had with them as their slave the minor Mary c.w. since that time up to the month of December 1847 or thereabout, that the said minor mary c.w. has been sent back to New Orleans during the said month of December 1847 by Mrs. William Guesnard, who

Title page of the appeal of *Couvent, f.m.c.*, v. *Guesnard*, in which a free man of color, acting as "tutor" for the slave Mary, sued unsuccessfully for her freedom.

Courtesy of the Supreme Court of Louisiana Collection of Legal Archives

in December, 1847. She sued for her freedom on the basis that being on French soil had freed her and that return to Louisiana could not reenslave her. The supreme court affirmed the decision of the lower court, which based its decision on the act of 1846, and dismissed Mary's suit. Chief Justice Eustis commented that he was not prepared to say that the legislature was not within its rights to pass such a law, and he felt inhibited in passing upon the merits of such claims. An obviously disgruntled court stated that under the circumstances it could do nothing but dismiss Mary's claim:

> Whatever may have been the rights of slaves acquired by the fact of going, with the consent of their masters, to countries where slavery did not exist, under the jurisprudence of this State previous to that statute we have already determined its provisions to be imperative in all cases occurring since its passage. *Eugénie* v. *Préval,* 2d Ann. 181. The statute merely enacts and establishes as law the rule laid down by Lord Stowell, in the case of the slave *Grace,* determined in the High Court of Admiralty of England. . . . This rule he deduces from general principles, and a review of all the cases that had occurred in England previous to his decision. There can be no question as to the legislative power to regulate the condition of this class of persons within its jurisdiction, and to prescribe in what form and by what facts such condition shall be changed. *Mary,* f.w.c., v. *D. L. Brown.*[36]

Two years later the court finally applied the law of 1846 retroactively, in the case of *Liza* v. *Puissant* (1852). One possible explanation for this change of interpretation of the act of 1846 may have been a pending change of personnel on the court. The court ruled on *Liza* in February, 1852, and an associate justice, Pierre Adolphe Rost, who had been a member of the court since 1846, wrote the decision. Chief Justice Eustis would resign his position in May, 1853. During the 1852 term he wrote significantly fewer decisions than in previous terms. We cannot know whether the impending change in personnel affected the decision in *Liza,* but we do know that by 1852 a majority of the justices had come

36. Couvent, f.m.c., v. Guesnard, No. 1063, 5 La. Ann. 69 (1850). Couvent, a free man of color, was Mary's "tutor," a Louisiana law term for the guardian of a minor child, which Mary was. In Louisiana, slaves could sue directly for their freedom, without need of a guardian *ad litem,* unless they were minors, in which case the tutor sued in their behalf.

to believe that a brief sojourn in a free state or country did not operate to free a slave, a concept in harmony with the United States Supreme Court's ruling in *Strader* v. *Graham* (1850).

In *Liza* v. *Puissant,* the slave woman Liza claimed that in 1821 her owner, Hardi Boisblanc, had traveled to Bordeaux with Liza for the purpose of collecting his family there and moving them to Louisiana. Since her return Liza had given birth to seven children. In 1850 she sued for her freedom, claiming she had become free by virtue of her journey to France. In a decision difficult to reconcile with the court's earlier rulings, Justice Rost denied Liza's claim for freedom on the basis that only a change of *residence* to free soil by the master (not a brief sojourn) could free a slave, and Boisblanc's stay in France had only been a visit. Citing several precedents from other states and the United States Supreme Court, Rost stated: "The principle, that the temporary residence of a slave in a country in which slavery is not tolerated, does not, of itself, work such a permanent change in his *status* as to make him free after his voluntary return to the domicil of his master, by the laws of which slavery exist, is supported by high authority. Case of slave *Grace,* 2d Haggard's Admiralty R. 94 *Commonwealth of Mass.* v. *Aves,* 18 Pickering, 193. Story Conflict of Laws, No. 96. *Strader et al.* v. *Graham,* 10 Howard, 82." The court's reluctance to render rulings consistent with the act of 1846 temporarily disappeared in this case, and the wording of the judgment in Liza's case implies full judicial acceptance of the act.

In his decision, Rost cited *The Slave, Grace* and a decision of the United States Supreme Court on the issue of transportation, *Strader* v. *Graham* (1850). The latter case involved slave musicians who had traveled to free states to perform, with the consent of their master. Chief Justice Taney had ruled that temporary presence in a state in which slavery was prohibited did not operate to free the musicians. In Rost's ruling the issue of domicile, or residence of the owner, as opposed to a temporary visit to a free state was the central issue.

In a concurring opinion, Chief Justice Eustis felt compelled to vent his dissent from the opinion expressed in *Marie Louise, f.w.c.,* v. *Marot,* wherein the court had held that Marie Louise's daughter had been freed by the operation of French law and therefore could not be reenslaved once she returned to Louisiana. Eustis stated that he disagreed with Chief Judge Martin's ruling in *Marie Louise:* "I do not concur in the opinion, that on the voluntary return of the slave to the country of his domicil, from one in which slavery did not exist, the dominion of the master can in no case be exercised." The issue of the residence of the slaveowner was crucial. Finally, Eustis commented on the precedents Rost cited, precedents directly contrary to the holding in *Marie Louise* v. *Marot,* especially the United States Supreme Court's ruling in *Strader* v. *Graham:*

> The courts of Kentucky held, that they [the slave musicians] did not acquire their freedom by this temporary presence in a State where slavery was prohibited. This is the only practical doctrine which can be maintained in a State whose frontier for hundreds of miles, is bounded by free States, where the communication is open, and the intercourse between the inhabitants constant and uninterrupted. It rests with each State to establish and regulate the domestic relations of its inhabitants. A State may prohibit slavery within its limits, may abolish the paternal power; but this imposes no obligation on other States to hold the condition of persons domiciled there, as extinguished by reason of a presence in the State in which the relation is not recognized. This court has held the *status* of a slave to be changed by a residence in a country in which slavery did not exist, when the residence, with the consent of the master, had a character of permanency, but not that the *status* was affected by a transit for a temporary purpose. Cases of this kind, resting mainly on the intention of parties, are attended with great difficulties in their solution; but in this respect, they resemble all cases of contested or questionable domicil.

Moreover, Eustis wrote: "In all cases of this kind . . . we have avoided anything which could be considered as an affirmance of the principle laid down in the case of *Marot.* . . . The jurisprudence, independent of that statute [of 1846], has been far from being settled on principles on which questions of this gravity ought to have rested." The act of 1846 presupposed that the master was a Louisiana domiciliary, and it simply prevented slaves from ever initiating an action to establish freedom on this basis. The slave's domicile was always presumed to be that of his owner: "*Be it enacted by the Senate and House of Representatives of the State of Louisiana in General Assembly convened,* That from the passage of this act, no slave shall be entitled to his or her freedom, under the pretence that he or she has been, with or without the consent of his or her owner, in a country where slavery does not exist, or in any of the States where slavery is prohibited."[37]

One year later, in his last decision on this issue as chief justice, Eustis once again ruled to free slaves on the basis that they had been taken to free soil before 1846. The decision was nevertheless consistent with *Liza* v. *Puissant* in that the slave in question proved his master's *residence* in a free state. In *Brown, f.w.c.,* v. *Smith* (1853), Elijah Mix had purchased Lucy Brown on May 1, 1823, and two days later had executed an "act of enfranchisement" that freed her (it was signed by the mayor of Washington, D.C., and a local justice of the peace). Brown's parents, who were already free, then signed an act indenturing their daughter to Mix, after which he and Brown moved to New York and lived there from 1823 to 1832, when he sold her apprenticeship to one Captain Wells of the United States Army. The crucial issue in the appeal was domicile. Details are sketchy, but several transfers later, a New Orleans slave dealer sold Brown as a slave for life. Although her attorney somehow lost her certificate of emancipation, Chief Justice Eustis ruled that her master had intended to become a resident of New York, and therefore Brown was free. Eustis also noted that Brown was free under New York's nine-month law, a statute in effect between 1817 and 1841. The nine-month law allowed masters to sojourn with their slaves in New York for as long as nine months without changing the status of the slaves. After nine months, slaves in New York with their masters became free. Therefore, Eustis held, Mix's intention to reside in New York, and his actual residence of more than one year, operated to free Brown. Eustis also awarded Lucy Brown five dollars a month wages from the date of institution of her suit to the date of the judgment.[38]

The following year, in *Virginie and Celésie, f.p.c.,* v. *Himel* (1855), the court heard an appeal in which five slaves sued for their freedom on the basis that their mother-grandmother had been taken to a free state and legally emancipated. In 1835 Joseph Bernard, who kept "a public House of entertainment," moved to Cincinnati and by a public act before the

37. Liza v. Puissant, No. 2326, 7 La. Ann. 81 (1852); Finkelman, *Imperfect Union,* 213; "An Act to Protect the Rights of Slaveholders in the State of Louisiana," Act of May 30, 1846, *Louisiana Acts, 1846,* 163; Strader v. Graham, 10 Howard (U.S.) 82 (1850).

38. Brown, f.w.c., v. Smith and Taylor, No. 2761, 8 La. Ann. 59 (1853); Finkelman, *Imperfect Union,* 46–76.

George Eustis, chief justice from 1846 to 1853, whose departure from the Louisiana Supreme Court coincided with a turn toward less leniency in granting freedom to slaves who had sojourned on free soil.

Photo by Warren Gravois. Courtesy of the Librarian, Law Library of Louisiana

mayor of that city manumitted his mulatto slave mistress Mélite and her children Virginie and Celésie. He moved to St. Louis shortly after, and perhaps fearing that they would be reenslaved in Missouri (a slave state), he went to court in that city and acknowledged the act of liberation, after which he returned to Louisiana with Mélite and her children. Mélite died there, and after Bernard's death his white heirs seized Virginie and her daughter Philomene, and Celésie and her children Victorine and Gustave, and sold them to Drausin and Clairville Himel at public auction at a succession sale in New Orleans in 1847. In 1853 the sisters and their children sued for their freedom and for wages for their services from 1847 to 1853. In 1855 the Supreme Court of Louisiana declared them all free. Freedom came too late for Celésie, who died of consumption while the appeal was pending; no physician was called to attend her until she had been ill for three months and was moribund. Associate Justice Abner N. Ogden wrote the decision for the court, which ruled for the plaintiffs. Ogden did not question the validity of the emancipation of Virginia and Celésie in either Ohio or Missouri. The only question he considered involved forced heirship—whether their emancipations were in fraud of the portion reserved by law for forced heirs. Virginie's attorney was able to prove that although Bernard died possessed of only $1,368, at the time of the emancipation he had sufficient means to free the slave women without defrauding his legitimate heirs of their forced portion. The Himels had alleged that Mélite was Bernard's concubine and "that the emancipation was a gift of so much of his estate, which by law is prohibited to be made to one standing in that relation." On this issue Ogden held, "The law has declared what causes shall be sufficient to render the enfranchisement of a slave null and void, and this is not one of them."[39]

The Supreme Court of Louisiana tackled the transportation issue once again in 1856 in *Henriette, alias Mary,* v. *Heirs of Barnes*. In 1849 Charles Barnes had left New Orleans to reside in California, taking with him two of his slaves, Henriette and her daughter, Marietta. About 1854 Barnes died in California; Henriette and Marietta nursed him in his last illness. He left a will in which he freed them both and left them $1,000 and $500 respectively. Barnes's heirs submitted his will to probate in

39. Virginie and Celésie, f.p.c., v. Himel, No. 3842, 10 La. Ann. 185 (1855). In a sidelight to this case, a witness testified that one Jacob Lambert accompanied Bernard to Cincinnatti with three of his female slaves for the purpose of setting them free.

Louisiana but never paid Henriette's and Marietta's legacies. The two women sued for their freedom and their legacies. Although the district court declared them free and rendered a judgment in their favor for $1,500, the supreme court reversed the decision. Justice Buchanan, writing for the court, contended that although enfranchising a slave by will was legal in Louisiana, Barnes had never formally freed Henriette and Marietta according to the forms required by Louisiana law. Buchanan further noted that the district-court judge had erred in assuming that since Barnes had taken Henriette and Marietta to the free state of California, they were now free by the operation of the laws of that state. Although Henriette and Marietta never returned to Louisiana, Barnes's residence, Buchanan asserted, had always been in Louisiana:

> *Barnes*' will was made in Louisiana, of which State he was at the time a resident; where his property is situated; and where his succession is in course of administration. It is evident from the language of the will, made two years before his departure for California, that the intention of the testator was that the emancipation should be effected according to the law of Louisiana. It is the policy of this State, as evinced by its legislation, to restrict the power of masters to emancipate their slaves. Emancipation is considered to be a matter which concerns the State, inasmuch as its tendency is to substitute a free colored population for the system of compulsory labor, which involves to such a vast extent the fortunes of our citizens and the production of our agricultural staples.

Chief Justice Merrick and Associate Justice Spofford both concurred in separate opinions. Merrick was concerned with the implications of granting the legacies to Henriette and Marietta. "Were we to decree to the plaintiff the legacies bequeathed to her in the will of *Charles Barnes,* we should recognize her freedom by a judgment which would be final between the parties to this suit. What then would prevent her return to Louisiana?" Spofford agreed, noting that the status of Henriette and Marietta in Louisiana was not affected by the operation of California law:

> Although, by the law of California, where she now resides, she possesses the *status* of a free person, and although she cannot now be reclaimed by the heirs of *Barnes,* because she is not a fugitive from labor or service, having been carried hence to California by

> her master, with intent to remain permanently, still the policy of our local statutes forbids that she should stand in judgment in the courts of Louisiana for any other cause than to sue for her freedom. Act of May 30th, 1846, p. 163; C. C., 177. As, if she returned hither, she would be a slave until duly enfranchised according to our laws, so, until she is thus enfranchised, she cannot be heard in our courts to sue for a legacy left her in Louisiana by the will of *Barnes,* executed here when she was his slave.[40]

This decision is not inconsistent with *Brown* v. *Smith* because the slaves were taken to a free state *after* the laws of 1842 and 1846 were passed.

In April, 1857, just after the passage of the legislative act totally prohibiting emancipation in Louisiana, the state supreme court once again ruled on an appeal of a freedom suit based on transportation to free soil, *Barclay, f.w.c.,* v. *Sewell.* In 1839 a New Orleans slave dealer, G. A. Botts, had taken his sixteen-year-old slave mistress, Ann Maria Barclay, to Ohio for the expressed purpose of freeing her. After her emancipation she returned to New Orleans and resided there with Botts as a free woman of color. Following Botts's death in 1855, his executor seized Barclay's property (including real estate and a piano) on the basis that she was a slave and could therefore not hold property. She filed suit for her freedom and won in the lower court. The supreme court affirmed the decision, noting that in 1839 it was not illegal to transport slaves out of the state for the purpose of freeing them. In the decision Justice Spofford stated: "The general policy of the Louisiana Legislature . . . was undoubtedly always adverse to the indiscriminate manumission . . . and now it has become altogether prohibitive of emancipations in the State, probably in consequence of injudicious and impertinent assaults from without upon an institution thoroughly interwoven with our interior lives. But in 1830, the Legislature recognized the validity of such emancipations." Spofford reasoned that since Barclay had been freed, her return to Louisiana could not cost her "a forfeiture of her freedom." Thus, even after passage of the law prohibiting *all* emancipations in Louisiana, the state's supreme court continued to uphold the rights of slaves who

40. "An Act More Effectively to Prevent Free Persons of Color from Entering into This State," Act of March 16, 1842, *Louisiana Acts, 1842,* 314; Henriette, alias Mary, v. Heirs of Barnes, No. 3751, 11 La. Ann. 453 (1856). Under Roman law, willing a legacy to a slave implied a direct gift of freedom; Buckland, *Roman Law of Slavery,* 552.

had been transported to free soil before the passage of prohibitory legislation that attempted to close this avenue to freedom. Barclay, Spofford wrote, had become free by the operation of the laws of Ohio:

> There is no question but that it was lawful in Ohio for a master resident in Louisiana, to disfranchise his slave who had been carried thither.
>
> There is no question but that the emancipation in this instance was complete and formal under the laws of Ohio.
>
> *There* the slave became free by the formal act and consent of her master. Her *status* was changed.
>
> Upon her subsequent return hither, did she relapse into her original condition? Not unless some law of Louisiana in force at the time entailed such a penalty upon her for her return.
>
> We have been referred to no such law; we think there was none [emphasis in original].

Spofford also commented on the reasoning of the Louisiana legislature in passing the law of 1846: "We may also remark that this enactment was probably called out by a series of decisions in the Supreme Court of this State, which were incorrect in principle, because they held that the *status* of a slave whose master resided in-Louisiana [*sic*], could be changed by even a transient presence upon free territory; a doctrine which was overruled in *Liza* v. *Paissant* [Puissant], 5 An. 80, where the whole subject is treated and the true doctrine announced as flowing from general principles of law and supported by the highest English and American authorities."[41]

During the antebellum period, the judges and justices of the Supreme Court of Louisiana grappled with conflict-of-laws issues and comity between states whose laws regarding slavery differed from Louisiana's in varying degrees. In appeals involving conflict of laws, the court consistently honored other slave states' laws. In this area, the court was consistent in its rulings throughout the antebellum period and showed a careful regard for due process. However, in appeals based on the laws of free states and their effect on Louisiana domiciliaries, the court tended to narrow its definition of the liberating effect of free soil as the Civil

41. Barclay v. Sewell, No. 4622, 12 La. Ann. 262 (1857); Finkelman, *Imperfect Union,* 216.

War approached, no doubt in response to the successful attempts of the Louisiana legislature to narrow the opportunities for slave emancipations as well as to the jurisprudence of the nation's highest court, which expanded the power of slaveowners to carry their chattels into free states without losing them. Following a series of rulings in which the Louisiana Supreme Court held that a moment upon free soil effectively freed a slave, it began increasingly to focus on the issue of residence or domicile rather than simple transport, as evidenced by the ruling in *Liza* v. *Puissant*. In *Barclay* the court stated that previous rulings on this issue had been "incorrect in principle" because they had held that mere transient presence could change the status of a slave to a free person. By the eve of the Civil War, Louisiana law was no longer as predisposed to freedom as it once had been, although it was still more generous to the slave seeking freedom than emancipation laws in several other Deep South slave states.

11

"TO CLING TO THE DESPERATE FORTUNES OF THE CONFEDERACY"

Appeals Concerning Slavery Heard After the Civil War

FEARING THAT THE INVASION OF NEW ORLEANS WAS close at hand, the Supreme Court of Louisiana adjourned on February 24, 1862. Its scheduled reopening on May 5 never occurred, as four of the five justices fled the city during the approach of the Union forces.[1]

Although the Civil War destroyed slavery in Louisiana, the state's newly reconstituted courts continued to be occupied with cases involving slaves and slavery for many years following the general emancipation. Some postwar lawsuits reflect the upheaval and dislocation of the "peculiar institution" during the war, including desperate attempts by planters to relocate their slaves to Texas as Union armies threatened their plantations. Some slaveholders tried to protect themselves financially when the inevitability of the Union victory became apparent, and they sold their slaves just before the war's end. Of course, accepting payment in Confederate money would not have protected them from a monetary loss should the South be defeated. The three most important categories of cases the Reconstruction supreme court faced concerning the demise of slavery were those arising out of the chaos of the war, those in which the question was whether slave marriages had any civil effect after emancipation, and those in which the court had to decide whether debts incurred for the purchase of slaves on credit before the Civil War were still valid following emancipation.

Chaotic conditions on one Louisiana plantation during the war were reflected in an appeal heard by the Supreme Court of Louisiana in 1867. The heirs of a succession accused the curator of mismanagement.

1. Thomas W. Helis, "Of Generals and Jurists: The Judicial System of New Orleans Under Union Occupation, May, 1862–April, 1865," *Louisiana History,* XXIX (Spring, 1988), 147.

Thomas B. Poindexter had died in 1861, and his executor took an inventory of his property in October of that year. His slaves became free on January 1, 1863, by operation of the Emancipation Proclamation. Many of them left his plantation, carrying off most of its movable property. A few months later, Confederate cavalry burned all of the cotton stored on the property, to keep it out of enemy hands, and confiscated the plantation's corn to feed their horses. The executor had valued the slaves at $171,000, the movables at $17,199, the cotton at $31,240, and the corn at $25,000. In 1862 he joined the Confederate army and left Louisiana. Upon his return, he sued the heirs in *Succession of Poindexter* (1867) for his commission, a percentage of the succession's value, based on his 1861 inventory. The lower court allowed the commission to be based on the value of the slaves, cotton, and plantation movables, and the heirs appealed. Justice Rufus K. Howell, writing for the supreme court, observed that there was no evidence that the executor had spent any money to preserve the property, and in fact his absence (in the Confederate army) was evidence of "official delinquency." Howell ordered the executor's commission reduced from $6,464 to $1,210.50, which was 2.5 percent of the value of the succession after much of the property had been confiscated.[2]

A few appeals heard by the Supreme Court of Louisiana in the years following the Civil War pertained to Louisiana planters' removing their slaves from the path of the Union army, transporting them to Texas, and attempting to work them there. Removing slaves as Federal troops approached was called "running the negroes." One witness observed a train of fifty or sixty wagons of refugees on the road to Texas in 1864, and according to the historian C. Peter Ripley, the movement in total involved "hundreds of whites and thousands of blacks." In 1871 the state high court heard *Powell* v. *Daniell* (1871), an appeal of a suit for $3,634.47 concerning a contract for services rendered by one James J. Powell in carrying Catherine S. Daniell's 160 slaves and forty horses and mules from Tensas Parish to Texas and overseeing and managing them in making salt. Powell began the journey with the slaves and livestock on July 5, 1863, the day after Vicksburg surrendered to Union forces. He returned with "what was left of them" on November 5, 1865. Powell

2. Taylor, *Louisiana, A History*, 90–91; Succession of Poindexter, No. 805, 19 La. Ann. 22 (1867). For an excellent discussion of the effect of the approach of the Union army on Louisiana plantation life, see C. Peter Ripley, *Slaves and Freedmen in Civil War Louisiana* (Baton Rouge, 1976), 14–23.

stated that he had agreed to take all of Daniell's slaves, except the superannuated and the very young children, to Texas if Vicksburg surrendered to the Union army. Powell asserted that the slaves had been willing to go with him, and as a result he had paid off a man hired to accompany him to ensure that the slaves would not attempt to escape before the journey was complete. The hired man was named Menasco; his occupation was to catch runaway slaves with dogs.

Daniell alleged that since slavery no longer existed, the contract was not only illegal, but was also "immoral." She further alleged that Powell had hired out her slaves for $1,200 a month for fourteen months ($16,800 total) and that they had made 1,500 sacks of salt in 1865, which Powell had sold for three to five dollars in silver per sack without sending her any of the proceeds. Powell had converted the hire money and the silver from the salt sale into Confederate bonds. For this and for the loss of a few mules, Daniell sued in reconvention (countersued) Powell for $27,300.

Testimony established that Powell had cared for the slaves in his charge. By the end of September, 1863, none had been lost as a result of the journey, and one baby had been born. Powell testified that many Louisiana slaveowners were living as refugees in Texas and that most had lost several slaves in similar circumstances. Daniell's attorney put a great deal of emphasis on the argument that Powell's contract was "illegal" and "immoral," and that his service to Daniell was a "wicked job" performed with as much zeal as if Powell were spreading the gospel among the heathen. He further expressed amazement that "with a complacent face and unblushing cheeks he enters the portals of a Louisiana Court." This astonishment seems somewhat out of place for the attorney of a woman so lately a slaveholder. However, the Tensas District Court ruled in favor of Daniell. Powell successfully appealed to the Louisiana Supreme Court; Chief Justice John Ludeling ruled that the contract was legal when it was made and that Powell had faithfully executed it.[3]

In 1869 the supreme court heard another case that demonstrated the

3. Ripley, *Slaves and Freedmen,* 15, 152; Josephine Luke, "From Slavery to Freedom in Louisiana, 1862–1865" (M.A. thesis, Tulane University, 1939); Powell v. Daniell, No. 3186, 23 La. Ann. 289 (1871). In a case involving debts owed for the purchase of slaves, the purchaser stated that holding slaves was "contrary to good morals." Holding slaves did not seem to have bothered him when he made the purchase in 1859. Seely v. Blanchard, No. 2581, 22 La. Ann. 409 (1870).

John T. Ludeling, chief justice of the Louisiana Supreme Court from 1868 to 1877, presided over many Reconstruction-era decisions.

Photo by Warren Gravois. Courtesy of the Librarian, Law Library of Louisiana

disruptive effect of the war on Louisiana plantation life and was the only instance in which the Reconstruction court held that a debt for slaves was valid. In 1857 Edward H. Satterfield sold his Avoyelles Parish plantation and sixty slaves to Thomas Jefferson Spurlock for $165,600, to be paid in ten annual installments beginning in 1859. After paying two of the notes, Spurlock defaulted on the debt. During the winter of 1862–1863, Confederate soldiers burned all of the cotton on his plantation to keep it from falling into enemy hands. The fact that no cotton was grown on Spurlock's plantation after 1862 undoubtedly contributed to his continued inability to meet his financial obligations. Fearful of losing the debt owed him as the fortunes of the Confederacy declined, Satterfield repurchased thirty-eight of the slaves for $37,385 on April 12, 1865, planning to move them to Texas "still to cling to the desperate fortunes of the Confederacy." One of the thirty-eight, Bill Collins, was listed in the act of sale as being in the Confederate service: the document stated that Satterfield had the right to collect Collins' wages.

Spurlock testified that he had warned Satterfield not to move the slaves because some would run away: "I am fearful that an effort to move them, will cause trouble and loss," as "they are all satisfied and doing well." It is obvious that Satterfield planned to take the slaves to Texas; he purchased wagons, oxen, mules, pork, and corn for the journey. When Satterfield realized the war was over and the slaves were free, he abruptly changed his tactics to attempt to recoup his losses. He instituted a lawsuit, *Satterfield* v. *Spurlock* (1869), claiming that the slaves had been free at the time of the sale; he alleged that the sale was null and void, and that Spurlock's debt was therefore not reduced by $37,385. The Louisiana Supreme Court refused to "relieve him from the consequences of his own immoral transaction" and declared Spurlock's debt reduced by $37,385.[4] The court's decision in the case is unique; it is the only instance in which a contract with a slave consideration was enforced by the court.

Sales of slaves on credit in Louisiana before and during the Civil War presented a troublesome issue for the state's high court after the war. Often the transactions involved widows and orphans because many sales

4. Satterfield v. Spurlock; Spurlock v. Satterfield (consolidated) No. 2495, 21 La. Ann. 771 (1869).

of slaves on credit were the result of probate sales. After the war and the abolition of slavery, the supreme court was flooded with cases in which people who owed debts for the purchase price or hire of slaves refused to pay and their creditors sued to collect. The court repeatedly refused to honor such debts, although it faced some perplexing issues in dealing with individual cases. One of these problems appeared in a case heard by the court in 1866, *Henderson* v. *Montgomery*. In October, 1861, Mrs. A. E. Henderson Vanwickle had obtained an order of seizure and sale of a number of slaves mortgaged to her by her debtor, R. M. Montgomery. The slaves had been mortgaged as consideration for the debt sued upon, or the plaintiff could have been allowed to execute on other property belonging to Montgomery. Montgomery appealed to the Supreme Court of Louisiana, but the court did not decide the case before it ceased to function in April, 1862. After the war Henderson sued Montgomery for the debt, claiming that if he had not appealed, the slaves would have been sold and she would have recovered her money. In 1866 Associate Justice Howell dismissed the appeal. Obviously he felt that this was the only decision he could choose. Writing for the court, Howell stated that he could not affirm the judgment of the lower court ordering the seizure and sale of the slaves, since there were no slaves, and he could not reverse it because it was legal when it was made.[5]

In January, 1865, Nancy Ann Fenn sold the slave woman Lestenia to Frederick W. Carr in exchange for a future payment of five bales of cotton worth $200 each. After the surrender Carr defaulted on the debt, and Fenn sued him. Carr claimed that Lestenia had been warranted as a slave for life and demanded cancellation of the debt. Fenn successfully defended herself by alleging that she had not warranted the slave woman in the event of the failure of the Confederacy, and that Carr knew that if the South lost the war, property in slaves would no longer exist. Associate Justice Zenon Labauve ruled in *Fenn* v. *Carr* (1867) that since the Louisiana constitution of 1864 had freed slaves in the state on January 1, 1865, the sale was null: free people could not be sold.[6]

5. Henderson v. Montgomery, No. 388, 18 La. Ann. 211 (1866).

6. Fenn. v. Carr, No. 884, 19 La. Ann. 106 (1867). In a similar case the court denied a debt incurred through the purchase of a family of slaves sold on March 3, 1865. They included Hillary (age thirty-two), Catherine (age twenty-three), and their four children, who ranged in age from five years to eight months. This family was sold for the extremely low price of $960, probably because of uncertainty over the future of slavery as the South's fortunes fell. Gosselin

In 1870 the Louisiana Supreme Court heard several cases pertaining to the collection of debts incurred for the hire of slaves before the abolition of slavery. For example, in *Rodriguez* v. *Bienvenu,* Agnes Rodriguez sued Charles Gueriniere Bienvenu for $808, the amount of a note, "fixed according to the standard of Confederate money in 1864," that Bienvenu had given her for the hire of four slaves. Associate Justice James G. Taliaferro, writing for the court, declared the note void, reasoning that if slavery did not exist, the services of slaves could not be hired. There was dissent in this case. Associate Justice W. G. Wyly felt that since the contract was legal when it was executed, the debt should be paid. He was overruled by the majority on the Reconstruction court.[7]

Another problem the Louisiana Supreme Court had to solve was what to do in the case of notes executed before the Civil War for the purchase of slaves and land. Occasionally these appeals also included farm implements and the crop growing in the field. Clever debtors who had paid some of the notes before and during the war claimed afterward that they had been paying the land portion of the debt and not the slave portion, and since debts for slaves could not now be enforced, they owed nothing. In these cases the Supreme Court refused to allow the debtor to use the abolition of slavery to escape his obligation for debts owed on property other than slaves. The justices instead decided that each note paid was payment on all of the land and slaves purchased, determined what portion of the debt was for the slaves, and voided only that portion. For example, John Chastant purchased a sugar plantation and its slaves in 1860 for $200,000. He paid $50,000 to the vendor and defaulted on the remainder, claiming that as the slaves were now free he would not pay any more of the debt. Associate Justice Wyly ruled in *Hebert* v. *Chastant* (1870) that the land portion of the debt must be paid. Chief Justice Ludeling and Associate Justice Howell dissented from this decision. Both observed that there was no direct proof that the payments

v. Womack and Thompson, No. 2129, 21 La. Ann. 193 (1869). For similar cases involving slaves sold during the war, see Halley v. Hoeffner, No. 1071, 19 La. Ann. 518 (1867), Posey v. Driggs, No. 1266, 20 La. Ann. 199 (1868); and Haden v. Phillips and Foster, No. 163, 21 La. Ann. 517 (1869).

7. Rodriguez v. Bienvenu, No. 2829, 22 La. Ann. 300 (1870). For other cases involving the attempt to collect debts for hire of slaves, see Succession of Woodward, No. 1649, 22 La. Ann. 305 (1870); Wise v. Hill, No. 65, 22 La. Ann. 469 (1870); and Succession of Ross, No. 173, 22 La. Ann. 480 (1870).

made before the war were on the price of the slaves, and no such presumption should be made.[8]

An early historian of the Louisiana Supreme Court, Henry Plauché Dart, paints a bleak picture of the Reconstruction high court, asserting that the court of 1868–1877 was "one of the chief instruments in the overwhelming and subjugation of Louisiana by the Republican Party, . . . the bulwark of the wicked government under which they served." Four of the five justices were Unionists who had lived in Louisiana prior to the Civil War. The other was a former Union soldier who had come to New Orleans in 1862. Dart states that despite the fact that they "were contemporaries of the men they now rode with whip and spur . . . they were vindictive, unyielding partisans who abated not one jot or tittle in favor of their ancient fellowship," and that their jurisprudence "on racial and public questions was specious and unsound."[9]

Dart's assessment of the Reconstruction court is overly severe; however, it may help to explain the rulings of the postbellum Supreme Court of Louisiana on a large body of similar cases concerning the collection of debts owed for purchases of slaves before the war began. The overwhelming majority of cases involving slavery heard by the postbellum court dealt with debts of this kind. Persons who had bought slaves on credit refused to pay after the slaves were free, and creditors naturally

8. Hebert v. Chastant, No. 2590, 22 La. Ann. 152 (1870). For other cases involving debts for slaves and land, see Sandidge v. Sanderson, No. 2473, 21 La. Ann. 757 (1869); Walker v. Ducros, No. 1804, 22 La. Ann. 214 (1870); Merritt v. Merle, No. 1379, 22 La. Ann. 257 (1870); Allen v. Tarlton, No. 697, 22 La. Ann. 427 (1870); Conrad v. Callery, No. 710, 22 La. Ann. 428 (1870); Castille v. Offutt, No. 676, 22 La. Ann. 430 (1870); Smith v. McWaters, No. 708, 22 La. Ann. 431 (1870); Thompson v. Simmons, No. 91, 22 La. Ann. 451 (1870); Osborn v. Osborn, No. 2534, 23 La. Ann. 496 (1871); Rabun v. Pierson, No. 205, 23 La. Ann. 696 (1871); Winter v. Tounoir, No. 4584, 25 La. Ann. 611 (1873); and Brusle v. Hamilton, No. 5081, 26 La. Ann. 144 (1874).

9. Henry Plauché Dart, "History of the Supreme Court of Louisiana," in *The Celebration of the Centenary of the Supreme Court of Louisiana* (New Orleans, 1913), 28–29. The most famous justice was James G. Taliaferro, a Catahoula Parish planter and thoroughgoing Unionist. He was also the editor of a small antebellum newspaper, significantly called the *Independent*. The paper's masthead carried this motto (from Cicero): "I defended the republic in my youth, I shall not stop as an old man." He had two sons, named after Daniel Webster and John Quincy Adams. In Louisiana's secession convention he was one of the 9 (of 129) who voted against disunion, "the one wise man in an age of madness." John Rose Ficklen, *History of Reconstruction in Louisiana (Through 1868)* (Baltimore, 1910), 18, 198; Peyton McCrarey, *Abraham Lincoln and Reconstruction: The Louisiana Experiment* (Princeton, N.J., 1978), 59–60; Ted Tunnell, *Crucible of Reconstruction: War, Radicalism, and Race in Louisiana, 1862–1877* (Baton Rouge, 1984), 24; Joe Gray Taylor, *Louisiana Reconstructed, 1863–1877* (Baton Rouge, 1974), 148.

wanted the debts honored. The court held repeatedly that debts with slave consideration were illegal and could not be collected. That the slaves had been guaranteed as slaves for life at the time of sale failed to impress the majority of the justices, as did the argument that notes given for the price of slaves were executed before the Civil War, when slavery and sales of slaves were perfectly legal.

Emancipation destroyed the consideration, but at whose expense, the purchaser's or the seller's? The Supreme Court of Louisiana ruled repeatedly that emancipation destroyed the contract between the buyer and the seller of slaves. The issue was complicated because neither the seller nor the buyer could recover his or her loss because emancipation left the court without power to enforce. The landmark Louisiana case on this issue was *Wainwright* v. *Bridges* (1867). The plaintiff sued to force payment of three promissory notes of $895.50 each, dated December 8, 1860, and payable twelve, twenty-four, and thirty-six months after their issue. The defendants contended that the emancipation of slaves by act of the United States government produced "a failure of consideration," which effectively released them from any obligation to honor the notes, as the slaves were warranted as slaves for life. On the issue of the vendor's warranty in title to the slaves, the defense was that defendants could not be held liable for events no one could foresee: *res periit domino*.[10]

The defendants further contended that emancipation did not destroy the objects of the contract, the slaves, but changed their status: "That the law, making this change of condition, having ceased to secure to the buyer the rights he acquired by the purchase, no longer requires him to comply with his obligation to give the equivalent stipulated for those rights." Associate Justice Taliaferro concurred with this argument, maintaining that no positive law established slavery in the United States, that slavery was tolerated, rather than confirmed, by the Constitution. He observed that the words *slave* and *slavery* did not appear in the federal Constitution. The founding fathers, he contended, purposely avoided the use of those words because they "never entertained the idea of the perpetuity of slavery. They viewed it as an entailed evil upon the country, which it was their desire to be rid of as soon as that object could be effected."

10. Wainwright v. Bridges, No. 1305, 19 La. Ann. 234 (1867). *Res periit domino* means that when a thing is lost or destroyed, it is lost to the person who was the owner of it at the time.

Resorting to natural law and the emancipation itself, Taliaferro concluded that emancipation nullified all laws concerning slavery:

> The sovereign power, the paramount law, puts an end to the ownership. The effect of the act which terminates the owner's right to the slave is not limited merely to that result. It necessarily involves the entire contract, and annuls it throughout. A mortgage of the slave, to secure the payment of the price at which he was purchased, is part of the same transaction. It is a contract made in aid of, and to fulfil an important condition of the contract of sale.
>
> That the mortgage becomes extinct by emancipation is clear. It is evident, then, that the *contract* of mortgage is annulled by the same cause [emphasis in original].

Chief Justice William Hyman and Justice Howell concurred with Taliaferro's opinion. Hyman wrote: "Property in slaves being prohibited, all contracts based upon such property are, necessarily, stricken with nullity."

Justice John Isley dissented from the majority opinion. Isley took issue with Taliaferro's constitutional interpretation: "Slaves were property in the strictest sense of the term. They were deemed so to be by the constitution of the United States, up to the time when, by an amendment to that instrument, slavery was abolished. See the case of *Scott* v. *Sandford,* 19 Howard, page 411; . . . They were introduced into Louisiana as property by the treaty of cession of 1803, and the laws of the United States and of the State of Louisiana, recognized slaves as property until the time of the rebellion." Isley cited an 1866 Missouri Supreme Court decision that had upheld the validity of contracts for slaves made before the Civil War, when such contracts were legal:

> I consider the abolition of slavery by the sovereign people, as the mere enunciation of one great fact, that the status of slavery was extinct, and that slaves became, on the instant libertini or freedmen.
>
> It had no retroactive bearing whatever on contracts which had been entered into, in relation to that species of property. It was an act of sovereignty, which affected only the owner of slaves, and was in contemplation of law to them, *damnum absque injuria* [loss without injury in the legal sense].

William B. Hyman, chief justice in 1867, when the Louisiana Supreme Court decided the landmark case of *Wainright* v. *Bridges*.

Photo by Warren Gravois. Courtesy of the Librarian, Law Library of Louisiana

> It had no more effect upon contracts for slaves than would have a legislative enactment passed after their date, making some act committed by slaves not *malum in se* [a wrong in itself, from the very nature of the transaction], an offence punishable with death or perpetual imprisonment; and it would not be seriously contended that a loss of a slave from such a cause, would be deemed a breach of warranty. . . .
>
> I am satisfied that the right of the plaintiff to recover the price of the slaves sold by him to the defendants, is founded in law, notwithstanding the ingenious and plausible theories submitted to us to sustain the pretensions of the defendants. They soar too high for the judicial mind to contemplate.

Justice Labauve concurred in Justice Isley's dissent, and the court split 3–2. All other appeals of cases involving debts for slaves met with the same result until 1873. These decisions were reinforced by the passage of a new state constitution in 1868. Article 128 of that constitution prohibited the courts of Louisiana from enforcing debts owed on slaves.[11]

Two years later the court extended the *Wainwright* logic to include innocent third-party holders of notes given for the purchase of slaves. In *Groves* v. *Clark and Carnal* (1869), Justice Taliaferro held that the holder-in-due-course was barred from recovering from the maker of a note in

11. *Ibid.;* Benjamin Wall Dart, ed., *Constitutions of the State of Louisiana,* Tit. VI, Art. 128, p. 565. The Missouri case was Phelps v. Evans, 38 Mo. 305 (1866). For other postbellum Louisiana Supreme Court cases involving debts for slave purchases, see Austin v. Sandell, No. 1317, 19 La. Ann. 309 (1867); Tate v. Fletcher, No. 1299, 19 La. Ann. 371 (1867); Gremillon v. Crousillac, No. 1204, 19 La. Ann. 377 (1867); Courtney v. Shelton, No. 1271, 19 La. Ann. 380 (1867); Addison v. Seltoon, No. 1263, 19 La. Ann. 352 (1867); Posey v. Martingley, No. 1265, 19 La. Ann. 384 (1867); Halley v. Hoeffner, No. 1071, 19 La. Ann. 518 (1867); Dickinson v. Maynard, No. 6760, 20 La. Ann. 66 (1868); Delaporte v. Bourg, No. 1173, 20 La. Ann. 152 (1868); Bourgeois v. Billin and Perkins, No. 1560, 20 La. Ann. 153 (1868); Lapice v. Bowman, No. 1658, 20 La. Ann. 234 (1868); Joffrion v. Wilson, No. 1334, 20 La. Ann. 412 (1868); Thomas v. Hackett, No. 2086, 21 La. Ann. 164 (1869); Lytle v. Whicher and Henshaw, No. 430, 21 La. Ann. 182 (1869); Armstrong v. Lecomte, No. 129, 21 La. Ann. 527 (1869); Dranguet v. Rost, No. 174, 21 La. Ann 538 (1869); Levy v. Gremillion, No. 687, 21 La. Ann. 635 (1869); Heirs of Bedell v. Hayes, No. 703, 21 La. Ann. 643 (1869); Succession of Patin, No. 723, 21 La. Ann. 661 (1869); Nunez v. Winston, No. 706, 21 La. Ann. 666 (1869); Seely v. Blanchard, No. 2581, 22 La. Ann. 409 (1870); Smith v. Henderson, No. 197, 23 La. Ann. 649 (1871); Heirs of Brown v. Jacobs, No. 170, 24 La. Ann. 526 (1872); Consolidated Association v. Blanc, No. 2676, 25 La. Ann. 226 (1873); Dupérier v. Darby, No. 771, 25 La. Ann. 477 (1873); and Bruin v. Sasser, No. 3210, 25 La. Ann. 224 (1873).

1859 because a slave had been the consideration in the underlying transaction. Kenneth M. Clark purchased five slaves at a succession sale in 1859 for $8,900, of which he paid $2,225 in cash and executed three promissory notes for $2,225 each. Edward Groves acquired one of these notes from the heirs of the succession in partial payment for a drugstore. When Clark defaulted on the payment to Groves, now the holder of the note, Groves sued. He lost in the trial court, and he appealed. Taliaferro argued that article 128 of the Louisiana Constitution of 1868 forbade the enforcement of obligations incurred for the purchase of slaves. Giving article 128 the broadest possible interpretation, he extended it to include holders-in-due-course: "If an obligation for the payment of the price of slaves in the hands of a third holder can be enforced, then there are some contracts for the sale of persons that are not null and void. Where is the logic of such a conclusion?" Justice Howe dissented: "Suppose A, desiring the death of his neighbor, makes a note to the order of B, a hired assassin, and B transferred the note to C, who endorses it . . . to D for a pew in church. The innocent endorsee brings suit against A. It is clear that contracts to . . . commit murder are 'null and void and shall not be enforced.' . . . But I must confess my inability to see how . . . it [article 128] forbids the enforcement of a bill drawn in favor of the plaintiff . . . in consideration of the sale of half a drug store."[12]

Four years later the United States Supreme Court settled the issue and overturned the *Wainwright* principle. In *Boyce* v. *Tabb* (1873), the high court ruled that a note given for the price of slaves in 1861—before what the Court called "the late rebellion"—was valid, and that the note was not impaired by the passage of the Thirteenth Amendment. In deciding this appeal from Louisiana, the Court ruled that the debtor could not be released by the action of the state in freeing slaves *after* the note was executed. The national Supreme Court noted that the Supreme Court of Louisiana had consistently refused to enforce contracts for slave debts, and further stated that its knowledge of the Louisiana court's holdings in this matter would not stop the federal Supreme Court from holding that the note was valid. The Court based its ruling on its own previous decision in *White* v. *Hart* (1871), in which the issue was whether debts

12. Groves v. Clark and Carnal, No. 139, 21 La. Ann. 567 (1869); Bennett Wall Dart, ed., *Constitutions of the State of Louisiana,* Tit. VI, Art. 128, p. 565.

for slaves were enforceable. The Supreme Court of Georgia had held they were not, basing its decision on the 1868 constitution of Georgia, which forbade Georgia courts to enforce debts for slaves. The federal Supreme Court held that this provision of the Georgia constitution was void, and upheld the debt. Following the decision of the United States Supreme Court in *Boyce,* the Supreme Court of Louisiana heard three more cases involving the issue of the collection of debts for slave purchases incurred before the war. In one case the court followed the federal Supreme Court's 1873 ruling and ordered the debt paid. In two others it restated its previous position that debts for slaves could not be enforced. Since neither of these two rulings was appealed, they were allowed to stand.[13]

Another major issue that the postwar Louisiana Supreme Court had to confront was whether slave marriages that had occurred while the parties were held in bondage became legal unions if the parties continued to live together as husband and wife after the abolition of slavery. The *Digest of 1808* and the *Civil Code* held that slave marriages did not produce any civil effects. Usually these cases were initiated because of a question as to whether community property existed, or whether children born of such unions were legitimate and could therefore inherit from their parents. Cases of this kind extended well into the twentieth century. In all of them the court consistently followed the logic of an early case in which the question was whether slaves who married with the consent of their master remained married if their master subsequently freed them and they then continued to live together. In *Girod* v. *Lewis* (1819), the court had ruled that after emancipation the marriage of slaves had civil effects that had been dormant (because slaves had no civil rights) while the parties remained in bondage. Thus, voluntary cohabitation after freedom was essential to the validation of the marriage.[14]

Eighty-five years after *Girod,* the court heard the appeal of *Johnson's Heirs* v. *Raphael* (1906). In 1851 at Natchitoches, Louisiana, William Johnson and Elizabeth Lee, both slaves, had married with the consent of their mistress, although unions between slaves were not legally binding.

13. Boyce v. Tabb, 18 Wallace (U.S.) 546 (1873); White v. Hart, 13 Wallace (80 U.S.) 646 (1871); Succession of Hebert, No. 5674, 27 La. Ann. 300 (1875); Winter v. Tournoir, No. 4584, 25 La. Ann. 611 (1873); Brusle v. Hamilton, No. 5081, 26 La. Ann. 144 (1874).

14. Girod v. Lewis, No. 350, 6 Mart. (o.s.) 559 (La. 1819).

They had four children, the last of whom was born in 1855. In 1864, during Union general Nathaniel Banks's Red River campaign, William and some other slaves were sent by their mistress to Texas for safekeeping; Elizabeth and the children remained on the plantation. When the Union army neared, Elizabeth and the children ran away, following the Federal forces on their retreat after the battle of Mansfield. Somehow Elizabeth made her way to New Orleans just after the war's end. She returned to Natchitoches in 1868 and found William living with a woman of color named Neonie. In 1869 Elizabeth married Baptiste, an ex-slave formerly owned by Elizabeth's old mistress. Their marriage lasted until 1906, when Baptiste died. William had lived with Neonie until his death in 1894. He died possessed of 120 arpents of land. William and Elizabeth's children sued in 1906 to be declared legitimate children capable of inheriting a portion of William's estate. The case hinged on the question of whether Elizabeth and William could be considered ever to have been legally married. The Louisiana Supreme Court ruled that since the two had not lived together since 1864, and since neither had ever claimed the other as a spouse, they had never been married; their children, therefore, could not inherit.[15]

In similar cases the court consistently held that slaves who married during the existence of slavery, and who continued to live together as man and wife after the Civil War, were legally married, and that such marriages produced all the results of a contract between free people. Well into the twentieth century, the Louisiana Supreme Court ruled that the civil effects of slave marriage came into being as of the date the marriage was contracted if the parties cohabited after emancipation.[16]

In 1873 the court ruled in *Picone* v. *Fontenette* that slaves who married before the war, but who died before they would have been emancipated, were not legally married because the marriage did not exist at the time of emancipation. Since the marriage did not exist at that time,

15. *Digest of 1808,* Tit. VI, Chap. III, Art. 23, p. 40; *Civil Code,* Art. 182, p. 28; Johnson's Heirs v. Raphael, No. 16,241, 117 La. 967 (42 So. 470), 1906. Reiterating the fact that cohabitation after emancipation was essential to validation of the marriage, the Louisiana Supreme Court in 1874 ruled that an ex-slave's marriage while still a slave in Mississippi did not prohibit his marriage in Louisiana to another woman after his emancipation; Succession of Randell, No. 5057, 26 La. Ann. 163 (1874). Former slaves were quite concerned with validating their marriages after emancipation; Ripley, *Slaves and Freedmen,* 156–57.

16. Succession of Young, No. 28,403, 166 La. 285 (117 So. 150) (1928); Pierre v. Fontenette, No. 4757, 25 La. Ann. 617 (1873).

the court ruled the parties' rights in the marriage to be not dormant, but nonexistent.[17]

The number of Louisiana Supreme Court cases that dealt with slavery continued to diminish as the immediate post-war period passed. Although race relations continued to occupy the court's attention, the unique legal problems of slave law no longer existed once the slaves of Louisiana had become free. Slavery's demise meant that Louisiana courts ceased to treat a large portion of the state's population as property. Equality before the law, however, would not become a reality for another century. There was a long, frustrating, and sometimes violent struggle for equal justice under the law in Louisiana, as elsewhere in the United States. But that is another story.

17. Other twentieth-century rulings on this issue include Briggs v. McLaughlin, No. 19,587, 134 La. 133 (63 So. 851) (1913); Succession of Rebecca Robinson, No. 6325, 12 Orleans App. 246 (1915); Marzette v. Cronk, No. 20,880, 141 La. 437 (75 So. 107) (1917); and Anderson v. Thomas, No. 31,645, 174 La. 721 (1412 So. 441) (1932).

BIBLIOGRAPHY

CASES

Cases without docket numbers could not be located in original manuscript form. Some, especially in the Western District, disappeared in the chaos during and following the Civil War. A summary of lost cases can be found in the printed *Louisiana Reports*. Dates are dates of judgment unless otherwise noted.

Superior Court of the Territory of Orleans

Paul v. Succession of Carrière, not reported. New Orleans [?], 1806.
Dewessee v. Morgan, No. 2351, 1 Mart. (o.s.) 1. New Orleans, Fall, 1809.
Brown v. Fort and Giraud, No. 2288, 1 Mart. (o.s.) 34. New Orleans, Fall, 1809.
Debora v. Caffin, No. 2397, 1 Mart. (o.s.) 40. New Orleans, Fall, 1809.
Dormenon's Case, 1 Mart. (o.s.) 129. New Orleans, Spring, 1810.
Mitchell v. Comyns, 1 Mart. (o.s.) 133. New Orleans, Spring, 1810.
McCarty v. Bagnieres, No. 2320, 1 Mart. (o.s.) 149. New Orleans, Fall, 1810.
Adéle v. Beauregard, 1 Mart. (o.s.) 183. New Orleans, Fall, 1810.
Daublin v. Mayor of New Orleans, No. 2347, 1 Mart. (o.s.) 185. New Orleans, Fall, 1810.
Territory v. 153 Negroes, not reported No. 2585. New Orleans, Fall, 1810.
Territory v. Seventy Negroes, not reported No. 2610. Filed New Orleans, Fall, 1810.
Territory v. Five Slaves, not reported No. 2613. Filed New Orleans, Fall, 1810.
Graham v. Forker and Elan, 1 Mart. (o.s.) 197. New Orleans, Spring, 1811.

Territory v. McFarlane, 1 Mart. (o.s.) 221. New Orleans, Spring, 1811.
Orleans Navigation Co. v. Mayor, 1 Mart. (o.s.) 269. New Orleans, Spring, 1811.
Beauregard v. Piernas, No. 2385, 1 Mart. (o.s.) 281. New Orleans, Spring, 1811.
Territory v. Mather, 2 Mart. (o.s.) 48. New Orleans, Fall, 1811.
Meunier v. Couet, No. 2348, 2 Mart. (o.s.) 56. New Orleans, Fall, 1811.
Read v. Bailey, No. 2697, 2 Mart. (o.s.) 60. New Orleans, Fall, 1811.
Delahaye v. Pellerini, 2 Mart. (o.s.) 142. New Orleans, Spring, 1812.
Hayes v. Berwick, 2 Mart. (o.s.) 138. New Orleans, Spring, 1812.
Watkins v. McDonogh, 2 Mart. (o.s.) 154. New Orleans, Spring, 1812.
Tonnelier v. Mauren, 2 Mart. (o.s.) 206. New Orleans, Spring, 1812.
State v. Cecil, 2 Mart. (o.s.) 208. New Orleans, Spring, 1812.
Jacob v. Ursulines, 2 Mart. (o.s.) 269. New Orleans, Fall, 1812.
McCarty's Case, No. 2236, 2 Mart. (o.s.) 279. New Orleans, Fall, 1812.

Louisiana Supreme Court

Laverty v. Duplessis, 3 Mart. (o.s.) 42. New Orleans, May, 1813.
Durnford v. Syndics of Brooks, 3 Mart. (o.s.) 222. New Orleans, January, 1814.
Meunier v. Dupérron, No. 38, 3 Mart. (o.s.) 285. New Orleans, April, 1814.
Dufau v. Massicot, No. 21, 3 Mart. (o.s.) 289. New Orleans, May, 1814.
Ogden v. Blackman, 3 Mart. (o.s.) 305. New Orleans, June, 1814.
Vernought (also Vernot) v. Yokum, No. 14, 3 Mart. (o.s.) 406. Western District, September, 1814.
Yocum v. Raper's Heirs, No. 15, 3 Mart. (o.s.) 424. Western District, September, 1814.
Cloutier v. Lecompte, No. 21, 3 Mart. (o.s.) 481. Western District, October, 1814.
Mayhew v. Bujac, 3 Mart. (o.s.) 613. New Orleans, June, 1815.
Bayon v. Prévost, No. 115, 4 Mart. (o.s.) 58. New Orleans, December, 1815.
Bayon v. Mollere, No. 116, 4 Mart. (o.s.) 66. New Orleans, December, 1815.
Baron v. Phelan, No. 122, 4 Mart. (o.s.) 88. New Orleans, February, 1816.
Williams v. Turner, not reported No. 35. New Orleans, *ca.* 1816.
Dossat v. Guillotte, No. 81, 4 Mart. (o.s.) 203. New Orleans, March, 1816.

Morgan v. McGowan, No. 98, 4 Mart. (o.s.) 209. New Orleans, March, 1816.
Victoire v. Dussuau, No. 103, 4 Mart. (o.s.) 212. New Orleans, March, 1816.
Duvernay v. Pijeaux, No. 147, 4 Mart. (o.s.) 265. New Orleans, April, 1816.
Beard v. Poydras, No. 72, 4 Mart. (o.s.) 348. New Orleans, December, 1814, and May, 1816.
Boon's Heirs v. Johnson, No. 140, 4 Mart. (o.s.) 38. New Orleans, May, 1816.
Labranche v. Watkins, No. 159, 4 Mart. (o.s.) 391. New Orleans, May, 1816.
Forsyth v. Nash, No. 150, 4 Mart. (o.s.) 385. New Orleans, June, 1816.
Syndics of Dussuau, f.m.c., v. Bredaux, No. 155, 4 Mart. (o.s.) 450. New Orleans, June, 1816.
Boré's Executor v. Quierry's Executor, No. 189, 4 Mart. (o.s.) 545. New Orleans, December, 1816.
Duncan v. Cevallos, No. 185, 4 Mart. (o.s.) 571. New Orleans, December, 1816.
Bayon v. Mollere, No. 183, 4 Mart. (o.s.) 621. New Orleans, January, 1817.
Trudeau's Executor v. Robinette, No. 184, 4 Mart. (o.s.) 577. New Orleans, January, 1817.
Sierra v. Llort, No. 336, 4 Mart. (o.s.) 587. New Orleans, February, 1817.
Gale v. Davis' Heirs, No. 163, 4 Mart. (o.s.) 645. New Orleans, March, 1817.
Fortier v. McDonogh, No. 203, 4 Mart. (o.s.) 718. New Orleans, May, 1817.
Petit v. Gillet, No. 213, 5 Mart. (o.s.) 19. New Orleans, June, 1817.
Foster and Giraud v. Dupré, No. 219, 5 Mart. (o.s.) 6. New Orleans, June, 1817.
Seville v. Chrétien, No. 21, 5 Mart. (o.s.) 275. Western District, September, 1817.
Cottin v. Cottin, No. 226, 5 Mart. (o.s.) 93. New Orleans, July, 1817.
Perril v. Terry, No. 252, 5 Mart. (o.s.) 367. New Orleans, February, 1818.
Zanico v. Habine, No. 238, 5 Mart. (o.s.) 372. New Orleans, March, 1818.
Langlishe, f.m.c., v. Schons, No. 270, 5 Mart. (o.s.) 405. New Orleans, March, 1818.

Maurin v. Martinez, No. 259, 5 Mart. (o.s.) 432. New Orleans, March, 1818.
Augustin v. Lafontaine, No. 272, 5 Mart. (o.s.) 464. New Orleans, April, 1818.
State v. Edward, No. 276, 5 Mart. (o.s.) 474. New Orleans, April, 1818.
Noret v. Metayer, No. 288, 5 Mart. (o.s.) 566. New Orleans, April, 1818.
Cuffy v. Castillon, No. 255, 5 Mart. (o.s.) 494. New Orleans, May, 1818.
Delacroix v. Navigation Co., No. 282, 5 Mart (o.s.) 507. New Orleans, May, 1818.
Lucile, f.w.c., v. Touston, f.w.c., No. 275, 5 Mart. (o.s.) 611. New Orleans, July, 1818.
Jourdan v. Patton, No. 304, 5 Mart. (o.s.) 615. New Orleans, July, 1818.
Martineau v. Hooper, No. 49, 5 Mart. (o.s.) 668. Western District, September, 1818.
State, Snipes, et al. v. Five African Negroes, not reported No. 61. Western District, October, 1818.
Mayes v. Calvit, No. 58, 5 Mart. (o.s.) 669. Western District, October, 1818.
Holmes v. Patterson, No. 51, 5 Mart. (o.s.) 693. Western District, October, 1818.
Metayer v. Metayer, No. 318, 6 Mart. (o.s.) 16. New Orleans, January, 1819.
Donaldson v. Rust, No. 308, 6 Mart. (o.s.) 260. New Orleans, February, 1819.
Pierce v. Curtis, No. 296, 6 Mart. (o.s.) 418. New Orleans, March, 1819.
Maurin v. Tousten, No. 338, 6 Mart. (o.s.) 496. New Orleans, April, 1819.
Saulet v. Loiseau, No. 300, 6 Mart. (o.s.) 512. New Orleans, April, 1819.
Girod v. Lewis, No. 350, 6 Mart. (o.s.) 559. New Orleans, May, 1819.
Piernas v. Blanque's Syndic, No. 309, 6 Mart. (o.s.) 577. New Orleans, May, 1819.
Jourdan v. Williams, No. 329, 6 Mart. (o.s.) 659. New Orleans, May, 1819.
Gomez v. Bonneval, No. 364, 6 Mart. (o.s.) 656. New Orleans, June, 1819.
Nadaud v. Mitchell, No. 361, 6 Mart. (o.s.) 688. New Orleans, June, 1819.
Andry v. Foy, No. 342, 6 Mart. (o.s.) 689. New Orleans, June, 1819.
Rouville v. Rouville, No. 358, 6 Mart. (o.s.) 702. New Orleans, June, 1819.
Marie v. Avart, No. 352, 7 Mart. (o.s.) 731. New Orleans, June, 1819.
Police Jury v. McDonogh, No. 370, 7 Mart. (o.s.) 8. New Orleans, July, 1819.

Andry v. Foy, No. 342, 7 Mart. (o.s.) 33. New Orleans, July, 1819.
Philips v. Fulton's Heirs, No. 83, 7 Mart. (o.s.) 241. Western District, September, 1819.
Palfrey v. Rivas, No. 381, 7 Mart. (o.s.) 371. New Orleans, January, 1820.
Knight v. Hall, No. 417, 7 Mart. (o.s.) 410. New Orleans, January, 1820.
Tessier v. Hall, No. 416, 7 Mart. (o.s.) 411. New Orleans, January, 1820.
Dunn v. Vail, No. 375, 7 Mart. (o.s.) 416. New Orleans, January, 1820.
Sterling v. Fuselier, No. 420, 7 Mart. (o.s.) 442. New Orleans, February, 1820.
Stewart v. His Creditors, not reported. New Orleans, February, 1820.
Fox v. Dawson's Curator, No. 470, 8 Mart. (o.s.) 94. New Orleans, May, 1820.
Bazy v. Rose, No. 466, 8 Mart. (o.s.) 149. New Orleans, May, 1820.
Ulzere v. Poeyfarré, No. 468, 8 Mart. (o.s.) 155. New Orleans, May, 1820.
Livaudais v. Fon, No. 475, 8 Mart. (o.s.) 161. New Orleans, May, 1820.
Camfranc v. Dufour, No. 453, 8 Mart. (o.s.) 144. New Orleans, May, 1820; No. 401, 8 Mart. (o.s.) 235. New Orleans, June, 1820.
Catin v. D'Orgenoy's Heirs, No. 459, 8 Mart. (o.s.) 218. New Orleans, June, 1820.
Blondeau v. Galez, No. 484, 8 Mart. (o.s.) 313. New Orleans, June, 1820.
Steel v. Cazeau, No. 402, 8 Mart. (o.s.) 318. New Orleans, June, 1820.
Rachel, alias Betsy, v. St. Armand, No. 478, 8 Mart. (o.s.) 363. New Orleans, June, 1820.
Delphine, f.c.g., v. Seghers' Syndics, not reported No. 483. New Orleans, June, 1820.
Marie v. Avart, No. 488, 8 Mart. (o.s.) 512. New Orleans, June, 1820.
Martineau v. Hooper, No. 49, 8 Mart. (o.s.) 699. Alexandria, September, 1820.
Calvit v. Haynes, No. 108, 8 Mart. (o.s.) 712. Alexandria, September, 1820.
Richardson v. Terrill, No. 71, 9 Mart. (o.s.) 1. Alexandria, September, 1820.
Hicks v. Martin, No. 98, 9 Mart. (o.s.) 47. Alexandria, September, 1820.
Mitchel v. Jewel, No. 406, 9 Mart. (o.s.) 185. New Orleans, December, 1820.
Julien v. Langlish, No. 492, 9 Mart. (o.s.) 205. New Orleans, January, 1821.
Allain, f.m.c., v. Young, No. 537, 9 Mart. (o.s.) 221. New Orleans, January, 1821.

Peabody v. Carrol, No. 511, 9 Mart. (o.s.) 295. New Orleans, February, 1821.
Broh v. Jenkins, No. 509, 9 Mart. (o.s.) 526. New Orleans, April, 1821.
Lazare v. Peytavin, No. 519, 9 Mart. (o.s.) 566. New Orleans, April, 1821.
Mitchell v. Armitage, No. 573, 10 Mart. (o.s.) 38. New Orleans, April, 1821.
St. Romes v. Poré, No. 583, 10 Mart. (o.s.) 30,203. New Orleans, May, 1821.
Bouthemy v. Dreaux, No. 539, 10 Mart. (o.s.) 1. New Orleans, May, 1821.
Marie, a Slave, v. Avart's Heirs, No. 488, 10 Mart (o.s.) 25. New Orleans, May, 1821.
Bruneau v. Michon, not reported No. 514. New Orleans, June, 1821.
Bayon v. Vavasseur, No. 570, 10 Mart. (o.s.) 61. New Orleans, June, 1821.
Miltenburger v. Canon, No. 590, 10 Mart. (o.s.) 85. New Orleans, June, 1821.
Dunbar v. Nichols, No. 522, 10 Mart. (o.s.) 184. New Orleans, July, 1821.
Fleming v. Loccard, No. 123, 10 Mart. (o.s.) 308. Alexandria, September, 1821.
Compton v. Brown, 10 Mart. (o.s.) 425. Alexandria, September, 1821.
Mitchel v. Jewel, No. 499, 10 Mart. (o.s.) 645. New Orleans, January, 1822.
Succession of Wickoff, No. 676, 10 Mart. (o.s.) 667. Alexandria, February, 1822.
Watts v. Wickoff, not reported No. 696. Alexandria, February, 1822.
Delery v. Mornet, No. 616, 11 Mart. (o.s.) 4. New Orleans, February, 1822.
Chrétien v. Théard, No. 612, 11 Mart. (o.s.) 11. New Orleans, February, 1822.
Nicholls v. Roland, No. 649, 11 Mart. (o.s.) 190. New Orleans, March, 1822.
Marie Louise, f.w.c., v. Cauchoix, No. 635, 11 Mart. (o.s.) 243. New Orleans, April, 1822.
D'Aunoy v. Clyma, No. 639, 11 Mart. (o.s.) 557. New Orleans, May, 1822.
Dufour v. Camfranc, No. 401, 11 Mart. (o.s.) 607. New Orleans, May, 1822.
Copelly v. Deverges, No. 682, 11 Mart. (o.s.) 641. New Orleans, June, 1822.
Johnson v. Sprigg, No. 181, 12 Mart. (o.s.) 328. Opelousas, September, 1822.

Surget v. Potter, No. 193, 12 Mart. (o.s.) 365. Alexandria, September, 1822.

Mayes v. Calvit, No. 23, 12 Mart. (o.s.) 373. Alexandria, September, 1822.

Lafariere v. Sanglair, 12 Mart. (o.s.) 399. Alexandria, September, 1822.

Skillman v. Lacy, No. 163, 165, 12 Mart. (o.s.) 404. Alexandria, September, 1822.

State v. Judge (Seghers), No. 773, 12 Mart. (o.s.) 485. New Orleans, December, 1822.

Seghers v. Executor of André, No. 786, 1 Mart. (n.s.) 73. New Orleans, March, 1823.

Seghers v. Executor of André, No. 787, 1 Mart. (n.s.) 84. New Orleans, March, 1823.

Reynaud and Sucko v. Guillotte and Boisfontaine, No. 804, 1 Mart. (n.s.) 227. New Orleans, May, 1823.

Montegut v. Dauphin, No. 726, 1 Mart. (n.s.) 258. New Orleans, May, 1823.

Potter v. Richardson, No. 774, 1 Mart. (n.s.) 276. New Orleans, May, 1823.

Thompson v. Milburn, 1 Mart. (n.s.) 468. Alexandria, August, 1823.

Campbell v. Henderson, No. 223, 1 Mart. (n.s.) 510. Alexandria, September, 1823.

Campbell v. Miller, No. 225, 1 Mart. (n.s.) 514. Alexandria, September, 1823.

Smoot v. Baldwin, Nos. 247, 273, 1 Mart. (n.s.) 528. Alexandria, September, 1823.

Campbell v. Armstrong, No. 224, 1 Mart. (n.s.) 574. Alexandria, September, 1823.

Mulhollan v. Johnson, No. 246, 1 Mart. (n.s.) 579. Alexandria, September, 1823.

McNeely v. McNeely, No. 205, 1 Mart. (n.s.) 646. Alexandria, September, 1823.

Stafford v. Stafford, No. 209, 1 Mart. (n.s.) 648. Alexandria, September, 1823.

McGrew v. Browder, No. 863, 2 Mart. (n.s.) 17. New Orleans, December, 1823.

Desdunes v. Miller, No. 290, 2 Mart. (n.s.) 53. New Orleans, January, 1824.

Doubrère v. Grillier's Syndic, No. 860, 2 Mart. (n.s.) 171. New Orleans, February, 1824.

Wall v. Hampton, No. 935, 2 Mart. (N.S.) 361. New Orleans, April, 1824.
Harper v. Destrehan, No. 965, 2 Mart. (N.S.) 389. New Orleans, April, 1824.
Castellano v. Peillon, No. 944, 2 Mart. (N.S.) 466. New Orleans, May, 1824.
Ulzere v. Poeyfarré, No. 989, 2 Mart. (N.S.) 504. New Orleans, May, 1824.
Lunsford v. Coquillon, No. 815, 2 Mart. (N.S.) 401. New Orleans, June, 1824.
Cariau v. Reiffel, No. 1022, 2 Mart. (N.S.) 619. New Orleans, June, 1824.
Sikes v. Allen, No. 1016, 2 Mart. (N.S.) 622. New Orleans, June, 1824.
Driessen v. Cox, No. 807, 2 Mart. (N.S.) 631. New Orleans, June, 1824.
Delphine, f.w.c., v. Deveze, No. 996, 2 Mart. (N.S.) 650. New Orleans, June, 1824.
State v. Bell, 2 Mart. (N.S.) 683. Alexandria, August, 1824.
Calvit v. Compton, not reported. Alexandria, September, 1824.
English v. Latham, No. 289, 3 Mart. (N.S.) 88. Alexandria, September, 1824.
Crawford v. Chaney, 3 Mart. (N.S.) 142. Alexandria, September, 1824.
Dreux v. Dreux's Syndic, No. 1040, 3 Mart. (N.S.) 239. New Orleans, January, 1825.
Labarré v. Lambert, No. 1033, 3 Mart. (N.S.) 300. New Orleans, January, 1825.
Aubert v. Buhler, No. 1103, 3 Mart. (N.S.) 489. New Orleans, April, 1825.
Oldham v. Groghan, No. 1133, 3 Mart. (N.S.) 517. New Orleans, April, 1825.
Morgan v. Mitchell, No. 1131, 3 Mart. (N.S.) 576. New Orleans, May, 1825.
Richey v. Wilson, No. 1143, 3 Mart. (N.S.) 585. New Orleans, May, 1825.
Saulet v. Dreux's Syndic, No. 1015, 3 Mart. (N.S.) 615. New Orleans, May, 1825.
Spraggins v. White, No. 1169, 3 Mart. (N.S.) 661. New Orleans, June, 1825.
Lewis v. Petayrin, No. 1152, 4 Mart. (N.S.) 3. New Orleans, June, 1825.
Moosa v. Allain, No. 1231, 4 Mart. (N.S.) 99. New Orleans, December, 1825.
Simmons, f.w.c., v. Holland and Parker, No. 1145, 4 Mart. (N.S.) 200. New Orleans, January, 1826.
Wall v. Hampton, No. 1196, 4 Mart. (N.S.) 310. New Orleans, March, 1826.

Beard v. Poydras, No. 72, 4 Mart. (N.S.) 348. New Orleans, March, 1826.
Duncan v. Poydras' Executor, No. 1260-1, 4 Mart. (N.S.) 359. New Orleans, March, 1826.
Spraggins v. White, No. 1237, 4 Mart. (N.S.) 497. New Orleans, March, 1826.
Williams v. Horton, No. 1269, 4 Mart. (N.S.) 464. New Orleans, May, 1826.
Bayon v. Towles, 5 Mart. (N.S.) 1. Opelousas, August, 1826.
White v. Cumming, No. 357, 5 Mart. (N.S.) 199. Alexandria, October, 1826.
Wright v. Harman, 5 Mart. (N.S.) 235. Alexandria, October, 1826.
Adams v. Gaynard, 5 Mart. (N.S.) 248. Alexandria, October, 1826.
Bray v. Cumming, 5 Mart. (N.S.) 252. Alexandria, October, 1826.
Jun, f.m.c., v. Livaudais, No. 1292, 5 Mart. (N.S.) 301. New Orleans, January, 1827.
Thatcher v. Walden, No. 1400, 5 Mart. (N.S.) 496. New Orleans, March, 1827.
Duncan's Exec. v. Poydras' Exec., No. 1206-1, 5 Mart. (N.S.) 492. New Orleans, April, 1827.
Johnson v. Field, No. 1412, 5 Mart. (N.S.) 635. New Orleans, April, 1827.
Overton v. Gervais, No. 1413-1, 5 Mart. (N.S.) 682. New Orleans, April, 1827.
Perrie v. Williams and Adams, No. 1444, 5 Mart. (N.S.) 694. New Orleans, May, 1827.
Saul v. His Creditors, 5 Mart. (N.S.) 569 (La. 1827).
Borie, f.m.c., v. Bush, No. 3039, 6 Mart. (N.S.) 1. New Orleans, May, 1827.
Bernardine v. L'Espinesse, No. 1422, 6 Mart. (N.S.) 94. New Orleans, June, 1827.
Donnet v. Ramsay, No. 1468, 6 Mart. (N.S.) 129. New Orleans, June, 1827.
Gill v. Phillips, 6 Mart. (N.S.) 298. Alexandria, October, 1827.
Broussard v. Philips, 6 Mart. (N.S.) 309. Alexandria, October, 1827.
Fowler v. Griffith, No. 1419, 6 Mart. (N.S.) 89. New Orleans, June, 1827.
Hawkins v. Vanwickle, No. 1501, 6 Mart. (N.S.) 418. New Orleans, January, 1828.
Oldham v. Polk, No. 1490, 1550, 6 Mart. (N.S.) 465. New Orleans, February, 1828.
Dunbar v. Skillman, No. 1575, 6 Mart. (N.S.) 539. New Orleans, March, 1828.

Labarré v. Lambert, No. 1549, 6 Mart. (N.S.) 555. New Orleans, March, 1828.
Hewes v. Barron, No. 1641, 7 Mart. (N.S.) 134. New Orleans, June, 1828.
Sterling v. Luckett, 7 Mart. (N.S.) 198. Opelousas, September, 1828.
Adams v. Gainard, No. 433, 7 Mart. (N.S.) 244. Alexandria, October, 1828.
Dorothée v. Coquillon, No. 1649, 7 Mart. (N.S.) 350. New Orleans, January, 1829.
Morgan's Syndics v. Fiveash, No. 1700, 7 Mart. (N.S.) 410. New Orleans, February, 1829.
Heirs of Cole v. Cole's Executor, No. 2-1702, 7 Mart. (N.S.) 414. New Orleans, February, 1829.
Saul v. His Creditors, No. 166-B, 7 Mart. (N.S.) 425. New Orleans, February, 1829.
Beale v. Grymes, No. 1690, 7 Mart. (N.S.) 457. New Orleans, February, 1829.
Tate v. Penn, No. 1636, 7 Mart. (N.S.) 548. New Orleans, March, 1829.
Miller v. Coffman, No. 1618, 7 Mart. (N.S.) 556. New Orleans, March, 1829.
Lawrence v. McFarlane, No. 1722, 7 Mart. (N.S.) 558. New Orleans, March, 1829.
Pilié v. Férrière, No. 1724, 7 Mart. (N.S.) 648. New Orleans, April, 1829.
Xenes v. Taquino, No. 1748, 7 Mart. (N.S.) 678. New Orleans, April, 1829.
Poydras v. Mourain, not reported No. 1599. New Orleans, June, 1829.
Jordela, f.p.c., v. Abat, No. 1758, 8 Mart. (N.S.) 126. New Orleans, June, 1829.
Meilleur v. Coupry, No. 1726, 8 Mart. (N.S.) 128. New Orleans, June, 1829.
Livaudais v. Scott and *America*, No. 1754, 8 Mart. (N.S.) 166. New Orleans, June, 1829.
Ducrest's Heirs v. Bijeau, 8 Mart. (N.S.) 192. Opelousas, September, 1829.
Miles v. Oden, 8 Mart. (N.S.) 214. Opelousas, September, 1829.
Wells v. Wells, 8 Mart. (N.S.) 307. Alexandria, October, 1829.
Rounds v. Cowand and Field, not reported No. 5127. Alexandria[?], October[?], 1829.
Hepp v. Parker, No. 1788, 8 Mart. (N.S.) 473. New Orleans, January, 1830.
Landreaux v. Campbell, No. 1822, 8 Mart. (N.S.) 478. New Orleans, January, 1830.
Hébert v. Esnard, No. 1818, 8 Mart. (N.S.) 498. New Orleans, January, 1830.

Palfrey v. Kerr, No. 1783, 8 Mart. (N.S.) 503. New Orleans, January, 1830.
Merry, f.m.c., v. Chexnaider, No. 1877, 8 Mart. (N.S.) 699. New Orleans, March, 1830.
Prudence v. Bermodi, No. 1888, 1 La. 234, New Orleans, April, 1830.
Back v. Meeks, No. 1941, 1 La. 309. New Orleans, May, 1830.
Hitchcock v. Harris, No. 1935, 1 La. 311. New Orleans, May, 1830.
Desfages v. Desfages, f.p.c., No. 1785, 1 La. 365. New Orleans, May, 1830.
Dugat v. Markham, 2 La. 29. Opelousas, September, 1830.
Montgomery v. Russell, 2 La. 67. Alexandria, October, 1830.
Madry v. Young, No. 496, 2 La. 104. Alexandria, October, 1830.
Solibellas v. Syndic of McWaters, not reported No. 378. Alexandria, *ca.* 1830.
Kimball v. Kimball, not reported No. 242. Western District, 1830–37[?].
Williams v. Hagan, No. 1971, 2 La. 122. New Orleans, December, 1830.
Preston v. Zabrisky, f.m.c., No. 2040, 2 La. 226. New Orleans, January, 1831.
Dismukes v. Musgrove, No. 1962, 2 La. 335. New Orleans, January, 1831.
Ails v. Bowman, No. 2062, 2 La. 251. New Orleans, March, 1831.
Kemp v. Womack, No. 2020, 2 La. 272. New Orleans, March, 1831.
McMaster v. Beckwith, No. 2017, 2 La. 329. New Orleans, April, 1831.
Beale v. DeGruy, No. 2135, 2 La. 468. New Orleans, April, 1831.
Bocod v. Jacobs, No. 2101, 2 La. 408. New Orleans, June, 1831.
Goodloe v. Hart, No. 2154, 2 La. 446. New Orleans, June, 1831.
Markham v. Close, 2 La. 581. Opelousas, September, 1831.
Labbé v. Abat, 2 La. 553. Opelousas, September, 1831.
Borel v. Fusillier, 2 La. 570. Opelousas, September, 1831.
Jeanne v. Heirs of Joffrion, not reported No. 474. Alexandria, October, 1831.
Harrison v. Faulk, No. 497, 3 La. 68. Alexandria, October, 1831.
Madry v. Young, No. 496, 3 La. 160. Alexandria, October, 1831.
Valsin v. Cloutier, No. 517, 3 La. 170. Alexandria, October, 1831.
Cauchoix v. Dupuy, No. 2125, 3 La. 206. New Orleans, December, 1831.
Maria and Angel v. Destrehan, No. 2228, 3 La. 434. New Orleans, December, 1831.
Hynes v. Kirkman, No. 2039, 4 La. 47. New Orleans, January, 1832.
Cowand v. Reynolds, No. 2220, 3 La. 378. New Orleans, February, 1832.
Roquet v. Richardson, No. 2252, 3 La. 452. New Orleans, March, 1832.
Verdier v. Leprete, No. 2314, 4 La. 41. New Orleans, May, 1832.

Rowlett v. Shepherd, No. 2278, 4 La. 86. New Orleans, May, 1832.
Gourjon v. Cucullu, No. 2324, 4 La. 115. New Orleans, June, 1832.
Barfield v. Hewlett, No. 2335, 4 La. 118. New Orleans, June, 1832.
Reed v. Palfrey, No. 2287, 4 La. 161. New Orleans, June, 1832.
Chew v. Keene, No. 2316, 4 La. 144. New Orleans, June, 1832.
Jung v. Doriocourt, No. 2196, 4 La. 175. New Orleans, June, 1832.
Coquet v. His Creditors, No. 2322, 4 La. 198. New Orleans, July, 1832.
Devine v. Kelly, No. 2363, 4 La. 206. New Orleans, July, 1832.
Armand v. Lizardi, not reported No. 2376. New Orleans, July, 1832.
Munday v. Wilson, No. 11, 4 La. 338. Baton Rouge, August, 1832.
Fuselier v. Masse, 4 La. 423. Opelousas, September, 1832.
Prévost, f.p.c., v. Simeon, f.p.c., 4 La. 472. Opelousas, September, 1832.
McPherson, f.m.c., v. Robinson, No. 528, 4 La. 563. Alexandria, October, 1832.
Bruce v. Stone, No. 2389, 5 La. 1. New Orleans, December, 1832.
Coote v. Cotton, No. 2410, 5 La. 12. New Orleans, December, 1832.
Myers v. Slack, No. 2401, 5 La. 53. New Orleans, January, 1833.
Déslonde, f.m.c., v. LeBéret, No. 2300, 5 La. 96. New Orleans, February, 1833.
Hurst v. Wallace, No. 2402, 5 La. 98. New Orleans, February, 1833.
Borie, f.w.c., v. Borie, f.m.c., No. 2435, 5 La. 87. New Orleans, February, 1833.
Adams v. Ryder, No. 2417, 5 La. 261. New Orleans, March, 1833.
Armistead v. Bowden, No. 2416, 5 La. 263. New Orleans, March, 1833.
Versailles v. Hall, No. 1906, 5 La. 281. New Orleans, March, 1833.
Brabo v. Martin, No. 2458, 5 La. 275. New Orleans, March, 1833.
Moffat v. Vion, No. 2357, 5 La. 346. New Orleans, March, 1833.
Déslondes v. Wilson, No. 2496, 5 La. 397. New Orleans, May, 1833.
Carter v. Cooper, No. 2470, 5 La. 446. New Orleans, May, 1833.
Lange v. Richoux, No. 2491, 6 La. 590. New Orleans, May, 1833.
Wilson v. Munday, No. 40, 5 La. 483. Baton Rouge, August, 1833.
Executor of Hart v. Boni, No. 2526, 6 La. 97. New Orleans, December, 1833.
Lowery v. Klein, No. 2519, 6 La. 380. New Orleans, April, 1834.
Cavelier, f.w.c., v. Germain, No. 2522, 6 La. 215. New Orleans, March, 1834.
Gottchalk v. Delarosa, No. 2520, 6 La. 219. New Orleans, March, 1834.
Hiligsberg v. New Orleans Canal Co., No. 2555, 6 La. 228. New Orleans, March, 1834.

Compton v. Woolfolk, No. 2583, 6 La. 272. New Orleans, March, 1834.
Joyce v. Delalande, No. 2544, 6 La. 277. New Orleans, March, 1834.
Salnave v. Hyde, No. 2587, 6 La. 357. New Orleans, April, 1834.
Psyche v. Paradol, No. 2504, 6 La. 366. New Orleans, April, 1834.
Hyde v. Jenkins, 6 La. 427. New Orleans, May, 1834.
Lewis' Executor v. Casanave, No. 2559, 6 La. 437. New Orleans, May, 1834.
Grounx v. Abat's Executors, No. 2521, 7 La. 17. New Orleans, June, 1834.
Vidal's Heirs v. Duplentier, No. 81, 7 La. 37. Baton Rouge, August, 1834.
Hewet v. Wilson, No. 65, 7 La. 71. Baton Rouge, August, 1834.
Mary, f.w.c., v. Morris, No. 78, 7 La. 135. Baton Rouge, August, 1834.
Keys v. Powell, No. 64, 7 La. 143. Baton Rouge, August, 1834.
Bradford's Heirs v. Clark, No. 41, 7 La. 147. Baton Rouge, August, 1834.
Louis, f.m.c., v. Carbarrus, 7 La. 170. Baton Rouge, August, 1834.
Heirs of Kimball v. Heirs of Lopez, No. 1845, 7 La. 173. Baton Rouge, August, 1834.
McDaniel v. Insall, 7 La. 241. Opelousas, September, 1834.
Niblett v. White's Heirs, 7 La. 253. Opelousas, September, 1834.
Dunlap v. Bailey, No. 577, 7 La. 368. Alexandria, October, 1834.
Hall v. Mulhollan, 7 La. 383. Alexandria, October, 1834.
Stoker v. Leavenworth, No. 567, 7 La. 390. Alexandria, October, 1834.
Hawkins v. Brown, No. 573, 7 La. 417. Alexandria, October, 1834.
Icar v. Suares, No. 2649, 7 La. 517. New Orleans, December, 1834.
Guillet v. Erwin, No. 2687, 7 La. 580. New Orleans, December, 1834.
Borée v. Kellar, No. 2634, 7 La. 500. New Orleans, January, 1835.
Hart v. St. Romes and Dubuys, No. 2663, 7 La. 586. New Orleans, February, 1835.
Hudson v. Perry, No. 2699, 8 La. 121. New Orleans, March, 1835.
Rogers, Slocomb and Co. v. Breedlove, No. 2725, 8 La. 143. New Orleans, March, 1835.
Marie Louise, f.w.c., v. Marot, No. 2748, 8 La. 475. New Orleans, March, 1835.
Bank of Louisiana v. Stansbury, No. 2694, 8 La. 257. New Orleans, April, 1835.
Strawbridge v. Turner, No. 2803, 8 La. 537. New Orleans, June, 1835.
Harris v. Denison, No. 2742, 8 La. 543. New Orleans, June, 1835.
Offut v. Hendsley, 9 La. 1. New Orleans, November, 1835.
Gaillard v. Labat, No. 2824, 9 La. 17. New Orleans, December, 1835.
Ory's Syndic v. David, No. 2787, 9 La. 59. New Orleans, January, 1836.

Bérard, f.w.c., v. Bérard, f.p.c., No. 2866, 9 La. 156. New Orleans, February, 1836.
Noirette v. Diggs, No. 2853, 9 La. 172. New Orleans, February, 1836.
Montreuil v. Pierre; Devilliers v. Carriere, Nos. 2845, 2846, 9 La. 356. New Orleans, February, 1836.
Poydras v. Taylor, No. 2873, 9 La. 488. New Orleans, March, 1836.
Phillis, f.w.c., v. Gentin, No. 2889, 9 La. 208. New Orleans, March, 1836.
Adams v. Hurst, No. 2860, 9 La. 243. New Orleans, March, 1836.
Guerrier v. Lambeth, No. 2899, 9 La. 339. New Orleans, April, 1836.
Chase v. Mayor, No. 2876, 9 La. 343. New Orleans, April, 1836.
Marie Louise, f.w.c., v. Marot, No. 2914, 9 La. 473. New Orleans, April, 1836.
Chardon's Heirs v. Bongue, No. 2931, 9 La. 458. New Orleans, April, 1836.
Winn v. Twogood, No. 2920, 9 La. 422. New Orleans, May, 1836.
Poydras v. Mourain, No. 2871, 9 La. 492. New Orleans, May, 1836.
Boidere and Goule, f.p.c., v. Bank, No. 2956, 9 La. 506. New Orleans, May, 1836.
Keys v. Powell, No. 101, 9 La. 572. Baton Rouge, May, 1836.
Anderson's Executors v. Anderson's Heirs, No. 70, 10 La. 29. Baton Rouge, June, 1836.
Saul v. Magee, No. 2950, 10 La. 39. New Orleans, June, 1836.
Banks v. Botts, No. 2905, 10 La. 42. New Orleans, June, 1836.
Rice v. Cade, 10 La. 228. Opelousas, September, 1836.
Cooper v. Cooper, 10 La. 245. Opelousas, September, 1836.
Nichols v. Alsop, No. 595, 10 La. 407. Alexandria, October, 1836.
Mourain v. Beauvais, No. 3001, 10 La. 477. New Orleans, February, 1837.
Penny v. Toulouse, No. 2996, 11 La. 109. New Orleans, May, 1837.
Thomassin v. Raphael's Executor, No. 3040, 11 La. 128. New Orleans, May, 1837.
Rodriguez v. Vassant, No. 2989, 11 La. 165. New Orleans, May, 1837.
Laclotte's Heirs v. Labarré, No. 3092, 11 La. 179. New Orleans, May, 1837.
Burke, f.w.c., v. Clarke, No. 3112, 11 La. 206. New Orleans, May, 1837.
Sarcé v. Dunoyer's Executor, No. 3106, 11 La. 220. New Orleans, June, 1837.
Mulhollan v. Eaton, No. 3118, 11 La. 291. New Orleans, June, 1837.
Nathan v. Gardère, not reported No. 3119. New Orleans, June, 1837.
Thompson v. Thompson's Heirs, 11 La. 324. Opelousas, September, 1837.

McBurney v. Flagg; Youngblood v. Flagg, 11 La. 333. Opelousas, September, 1837.
Frank, f.m.c., v. Powell, No. 3280, 11 La. 501. New Orleans, February, 1838.
Noe v. Taylor, No. 3255, 11 La. 551. New Orleans, February, 1838.
Tournoir v. Tournoir, No. 3201, 12 La. 19. New Orleans, February, 1838.
Langley's Heirs v. Langley's Executor, No. 3140, 12 La. 114. New Orleans, March, 1838.
Lopez's Heirs v. Bergel, No. 3031, 12 La. 197. New Orleans, April, 1838.
Behan v. Freeland and Faures, No. 3187, 12 La. 211. New Orleans, April, 1838.
Patterson v. Behan, No. 3141, 12 La. 227. New Orleans, April, 1838.
Mulhollan v. Huie, No. 3200, 12 La. 241. New Orleans, April, 1838.
Poulard v. Délamare, No. 3101, 12 La. 267. New Orleans, May, 1838.
Conolly v. Bertrand, No. 3224, 12 La. 313. New Orleans, May, 1838.
Cuny v. Robert, No. 682, 12 La. 474. Alexandria, October, 1838.
Hood v. McCorkle, No. 629, 12 La. 573. Alexandria, October, 1838.
Terrell v. Chambers, No. 648, 12 La. 582. Alexandria, October, 1838.
George v. Fitzgerald, No. 636, 12 La. 604. Alexandria, October, 1838.
Peire v. Martin, not reported No. 2949. New Orleans, December, 1838.
Zimmer v. Thompson, No. 3238, 13 La. 22. New Orleans, January, 1839.
Mathews v. Pascal's Executor, No. 3287, 13 La. 47. New Orleans, January, 1839.
Lesassier v. Dashel, No. 3776, 13 La. 151. New Orleans, March, 1839.
Reynolds v. Swain, No. 3244, 13 La. 193. New Orleans, April, 1839.
Nott v. Bott, No. 3123, 13 La. 202. New Orleans, March, 1839.
Baptiste v. Soulie, No. 3128, 13 La. 268. New Orleans, April, 1839.
Lobdell v. *James Monroe,* No. 3316, 13 La. 348. New Orleans, April, 1839.
Fortier v. Labranche, No. 3289, 13 La. 355. New Orleans, April, 1839.
Goldenbow v. Wright (*Lady Washington*), No. 3108, 13 La. 371. New Orleans, April, 1839.
Smith v. Smith, No. 3314, 13 La. 441. New Orleans, April, 1839.
Peyroux v. Chayat, No. 3432, 13 La. 459. New Orleans, May, 1839.
Johnston's Heirs v. Cox's Syndic, No. 3405, 13 La. 536. New Orleans, May, 1839.
Scott's Executor v. Gorton's Executor, No. 686, 14 La. 111. Alexandria, October, 1839.
Gibson v. Huie, No. 608, 14 La. 124. Alexandria, October, 1839.

Cecile, f.w.c., v. St. Denis, f.w.c., No. 709, 14 La. 184. Alexandria, October, 1839.
Patterson v. Bonner, No. 341, 14 La. 214. Alexandria, October, 1839.
Brosnaham v. Turner, No. 712, 14 La. 433. Alexandria, October, 1839.
Herries v. Botts, No. 3635, 14 La. 432. New Orleans, January, 1840.
Robinette v. Verdun's Vendees, No. 3546, 14 La. 542. New Orleans, January, 1840.
King v. Forsyth, not reported No. 3856. New Orleans, filed January, 1840.
Dunbar v. Thomas, No. 3706, 14 La. 332. New Orleans, February, 1840.
Armor v. Huie, No. 3554, 14 La. 346. New Orleans, February, 1840.
Barnett v. Macoin, No. 3591, 14 La. 428. New Orleans, February, 1840.
Williams v. Duer, No. 3780, 14 La. 523, 531. New Orleans, March, 1840.
Bob, Milly and Their Children v. Syndic of Nugent, No. 3779, 15 La. 63. New Orleans, March, 1840.
Stevens (for Heirs of Mix) v. Miller, No. 4023, 15 La. 66. New Orleans, March, 1840.
Hart v. Winchester (Executor of Thompson), No. 4019, 15 La. 88. New Orleans, March, 1840.
Bernard v. Pyburn, No. 4028, 15 La. 126. New Orleans, March, 1840.
Ware v. Barataria, No. 3434, 15 La. 169. New Orleans, March, 1840.
State v. Judge of the Commercial Court (Stiles), No. 4073, 15 La. 192. New Orleans, April, 1840.
Forsyth v. Despierras, No. 3426, 15 La. 215. New Orleans, April, 1840.
Emmerling v. Beebe, No. 3642, 15 La. 251. New Orleans, April, 1840.
Mulloney v. Doane, No. 3325, 15 La. 278. New Orleans, April, 1840.
Serapuru v. Bousquet, No. 4092, 15 La. 509. New Orleans, June, 1840.
Taylor v. Andrus, 16 La. 15. Opelousas, September, 1840.
Kemper's Heirs v. Hulick, 16 La. 44. Opelousas, September, 1840.
Loussade v. Hartman, 16 La. 117. Opelousas, September, 1840.
Cuny v. Robert, No. 703, 16 La. 175. Alexandria, October, 1840.
Nelson v. Lilliard, No. 800, 16 La. 336. Alexandria, October, 1840.
Miller v. Holstein, No. 665, 16 La. 395. Alexandria, October, 1840.
Brosnaham v. Turner, 16 La. 433. New Orleans, October, 1840.
Thomas v. Generis, No. 4234, 16 La. 483. New Orleans, December, 1840.
Nelson v. Botts, No. 4208, 16 La. 596. New Orleans, January, 1841.
Robert v. Allier, No. 4185, 17 La. 4. New Orleans, January, 1841.
Barrier, f.w.c., v. Gladding, No. 4187, 17 La. 144. New Orleans, February, 1841.

Canty v. Beal, No. 4047, 17 La. 282. New Orleans, March, 1841.
Buel v. *New York,* No. 3689, 17 La. 541. New Orleans, March, 1841.
Lesseps v. Pontchartrain Railroad Co., No. 3698, 17 La. 361. New Orleans, April, 1841.
DeLaLande v. Taylor, Nos. 3204, 3254, 18 La. 12, 17. New Orleans, April, 1841.
Turner v. Renshaw and Wheaton, No. 4245, 18 La. 37. New Orleans, April, 1841.
Fleytas v. Pontchartrain Railroad Co., No. 3772, 18 La. 339. New Orleans, May, 1841.
Penalta v. Borges Executor, No. 4266, 18 La. 348. New Orleans, May, 1841.
State v. Judge (Girod), No. 4260, 18 La. 392. New Orleans, May, 1841.
Hermann and Briggs v. Hootsell, No. 4449, 18 La. 419. New Orleans, May, 1841.
Olivier v. Cannon, No. 3794, 18 La. 474. New Orleans, May, 1841.
Gaillardet v. Demaries, No. 3584, 18 La. 490. New Orleans, May, 1841.
Duncan v. Hawks (*Molaeska*), No. 3912, 18 La. 548. New Orleans, May, 1841.
Russell v. Farier, No. 3840, 18 La. 585. New Orleans, June, 1841.
Bowman v. Ware, No. 3929, 18 La. 597. New Orleans, June, 1841.
Slatter v. Holton, No. 3894, 19 La. 39. New Orleans, June, 1841.
Barrett v. Bullard, 19 La. 281. Opelousas, September, 1841.
Edwards v. Martin's Heirs, 19 La. 284. Opelousas, September, 1841.
Miller v. Lelen, 19 La. 331. Opelousas, September, 1841.
Kemper's Heirs v. Hulick, 19 La. 349. Opelousas, September, 1841.
Blanchard v. Castille, 19 La. 362. Opelousas, September, 1841.
Benoit v. Broussard, 19 La. 387. Opelousas, September, 1841.
Briant v. Marsh, 19 La. 391. Opelousas, September, 1841.
Riggs v. Dupérrier, 19 La. 418. Opelousas, September, 1841.
Brownson v. Fenwick, 19 La. 431. Opelousas, September, 1841.
Smart v. Lecompte, No. 721, 19 La. 484. Alexandria, October, 1841.
Patterson v. Bonner, No. 641, 19 La. 508. Alexandria, October, 1841.
Rowley v. Rowley, No. 810, 19 La. 557. Alexandria, October, 1841.
Heirs of Grubb v. Henderson, No. 728, 1 Rob. 4. Alexandria, October, 1841.
Bronaught v. Neal, No. 793, 1 Rob. 23. Alexandria, October, 1841.
Klady v. McGuire, No. 799, 1 Rob. 25. Alexandria, October, 1841.

Kiper v. Nutall, No. 850, 1 Rob. 46. Alexandria, October, 1841.
Cawthorn v. McDonald, Nos. 834, 835, 1 Rob. 55. Alexandria, October, 1841.
Hooper v. Hyams, No. 856, 1 Rob. 90. Alexandria, October, 1841.
Griffin v. Waters, No. 634, 1 Rob. 149. Alexandria, October, 1841.
Armstrong v. Mooney, No. 3547, 1 Rob. 167. New Orleans, November, 1841.
Jackson v. Bridges, No. 3989, 1 Rob. 172. New Orleans, November, 1841.
Dussin v. Charles, No. 4514, 1 Rob. 195. New Orleans, December, 1841.
DeLaLande v. Bormeau, No. 4197, 1 Rob. 315. New Orleans, February, 1842.
Nolan v. Danks, No. 4676, 1 Rob. 332. New Orleans, February, 1842.
Borne v. Perret, No. 4718, 1 Rob. 342. New Orleans, February, 1842.
Mariah v. Edwards, No. 4536, 1 Rob. 359. New Orleans, February, 1842.
Porché v. L'Admirault, No. 4613, 1 Rob. 365. New Orleans, February, 1842.
Palmer v. Taylor, No. 4755, 1 Rob. 412. New Orleans, March, 1842.
Thomas v. Selser, No. 4774, 1 Rob. 425. New Orleans, March, 1842.
Bertie v. Walker, No. 4764, 1 Rob. 431. New Orleans, March, 1842.
Jordan v. Black, No. 4768, 1 Rob. 575. New Orleans, March, 1842.
Garner v. Poydras, No. 4254, 2 Rob. 1. New Orleans, March, 1842.
Lyons v. Kenner, No. 4770, 2 Rob. 50. New Orleans, April, 1842.
Bank of the United States v. Merle, No. 4699, 2 Rob. 117. New Orleans, April, 1842.
Stanislas v. Doret, not reported No. 4782. New Orleans, April, 1841.
Succession of Senac, No. 4080, 2 Rob. 258. New Orleans, May, 1842.
Menifee v. Johnson, No. 4303, 2 Rob. 274. New Orleans, May, 1842.
Jourdain v. Boissiere, No. 4302, 2 Rob. 289. New Orleans, May, 1842.
Boullemer v. Philips, No. 4219, 2 Rob. 365. New Orleans, June, 1842.
Gay v. Kendig, No. 4804, 2 Rob. 472. New Orleans, June, 1842.
Hollander v. Nicholas, 3 Rob. 7. Opelousas, September, 1842.
Lebesque v. Bonin, 3 Rob. 12. Opelousas, September, 1842.
State v. Linton, 3 Rob. 55. Opelousas, September, 1842.
Galpin v. Jessup, No. 912, 3 Rob. 90. Alexandria, October, 1842.
Harlin v. Leglise, No. 889, 3 Rob. 194. Alexandria, October, 1842.
Womack v. Nicholson, No. 949, 3 Rob. 248. Alexandria, October, 1842.
Hawkins v. Brown, No. 651, 3 Rob. 310. Alexandria, October, 1842.
Hivert v. Lacaze, No. 4250, 3 Rob. 357. New Orleans, December, 1842.

Hazard v. Lambeth, No. 4951, 3 Rob. 378. New Orleans, January, 1843.
Gros v. Bienvenu, No. 5001, 3 Rob. 396. New Orleans, January, 1843.
Smith v. McDowell, No. 4431, 3 Rob. 430. New Orleans, January, 1843.
Nolé v. St. Romes, No. 4950, 3 Rob. 484. New Orleans, January, 1843.
Union Bank of Maryland v. Freeman, No. 4938, 3 Rob. 485. New Orleans, January, 1843.
White v. Guyot, No. 5068, 4 Rob. 108. New Orleans, February, 1843.
Ogden v. Michel, No. 5127, 4 Rob. 154. New Orleans, March, 1843.
Nimmo v. Bonney and Bird, No. 5138, 4 Rob. 176. New Orleans, March, 1843.
Succession of Ducloslange, No. 5033, 4 Rob. 409. New Orleans, May, 1843.
Bertholi v. Deverges, No. 4521, 4 Rob. 431. New Orleans, May, 1843.
Felters v. Anders (*Swallow*), No. 4576, 5 Rob. 7. New Orleans, May, 1843.
Bell v. Dowly, No. 4603, 5 Rob. 18. New Orleans, May, 1843.
Lobdell v. Burke, No. 4580, 5 Rob. 93. New Orleans, June, 1843.
Winston v. Foster, No. 4617, 5 Rob. 113. New Orleans, June, 1843.
Petit v. Laville, No. 4660, 5 Rob. 117. New Orleans, June, 1843.
Ricard, f.m.c., v. Kimball (*John Linton*), No. 4717, 5 Rob. 142. New Orleans, June, 1843.
Soubie v. Sougeron, No. 4728, 5 Rob. 148. New Orleans, June, 1843.
Rosine v. Bonnabel, No. 3638, 5 Rob. 163. New Orleans, June, 1843.
Mathews v. Boland and Smith, No. 5119, 5 Rob. 200. New Orleans, June, 1843.
Fox v. Walsh, No. 4733, 5 Rob. 222. New Orleans, June, 1843.
Forsyth v. Wilkinson, No. 5291, 5 Rob. 263. New Orleans, June, 1843.
Mielkie v. Freeman, No. 5238, 5 Rob. 524. New Orleans, June, 1843.
Hitchcock v. North, No. 5659, 5 Rob. 328. New Orleans, July, 1843.
Succession of Key, 5 Rob. 482. Opelousas, September, 1843.
Carson v. Dwight, 5 Rob. 484. Opelousas, September, 1843.
Re Kershaw, 5 Rob. 488. Opelousas, September, 1843.
Hudson v. Grout, 5 Rob. 499. Opelousas, September, 1843.
Fanchonette v. Grangé, 5 Rob. 510. Opelousas, September, 1843.
Rudy v. Harding, No. 1074, 6 Rob. 70. Alexandria, October, 1843.
Cotton v. Brien, No. 1029, 6 Rob. 115. Alexandria, October, 1843.
Estate of Desormes, not reported No. 5396, New Orleans, February, 1844.
Haydel v. Betts, No. 5420, 6 Rob. 438. New Orleans, February, 1844.
Gardiner v. Cross, No. 5435, 6 Rob. 454. New Orleans, February, 1844.

Arbonneau v. Letorey, No. 5436, 6 Rob. 456. New Orleans, February, 1844.
Verdun v. Splane, No. 5425, 6 Rob. 530. New Orleans, March, 1844.
Parkison v. Boyle, No. 5463, 7 Rob. 82. New Orleans, March, 1844.
Mishon v. Bein, No. 5520, 7 Rob. 146. New Orleans, March, 1844.
Lewis v. Cartwright, No. 4621, 7 Rob. 186. New Orleans, April, 1844.
Villere v. Graeter, No. 5021, 7 Rob. 203. New Orleans, April, 1844.
Drummond v. Commissioners, No. 5495, 7 Rob. 234. New Orleans, April, 1844.
State v. Williams, No. 4671, 7 Rob. 252. New Orleans, April, 1844.
St. Martin v. His Creditors, not reported Nos. 3666, 3722. New Orleans, May, 1844.
Rist v. Hagan, No. 4503, 8 Rob. 106. New Orleans, June, 1844.
Lemos v. Daubert, No. 4198, 8 Rob. 224. New Orleans, June, 1844.
Fink and Baume v. Martin, No. 5344, 8 Rob. 256. New Orleans, June, 1844.
Bank of Orleans v. Hodge, No. 5535, 8 Rob. 450. New Orleans, June, 1844.
Guerin v. Rivarde, No. 5486, 8 Rob. 457. New Orleans, June, 1844.
Irish v. Wright, Haggarty, and Morgan, No. 5255, 8 Rob. 428. New Orleans, July, 1844.
Jenkins v. Thenet, 9 Rob. 34. Opelousas, September, 1844.
Jenkins v. Dutel, 9 Rob. 36. Opelousas, September, 1844.
Fanchonette v. Grangé, 9 Rob. 86. Opelousas, September, 1844.
Milo v. Lynch, 9 Rob. 98. Opelousas, September, 1844.
Lewis v. Gibson, No. 1053, 9 Rob. 146. Alexandria, October, 1844.
Bailey v. Stevens, No. 1185, 9 Rob. 158. Alexandria, October, 1844.
Cecile v. St. Denis, No. 1172, 9 Rob. 231. Alexandria, October, 1844.
New Orleans Gaslight and Banking Co. v. Botts, No. 4545, 9 Rob. 305. New Orleans, December, 1844.
Fazende v. Hagan, No. 4824, 9 Rob. 306. New Orleans, December, 1844.
Farmer v. Fisk, No. 5248, 9 Rob. 351. New Orleans, December, 1844.
Knight v. Heinnes, No. 4851, 9 Rob. 377. New Orleans, December, 1844.
Maserolle v. Françoise, No. 5718, 9 Rob. 528. New Orleans, February, 1845.
Smith v. Taylor, No. 5755, 10 Rob. 133. New Orleans, March, 1845.
Turner v. Parker and Mitchell, No. 5655, 10 Rob. 154. New Orleans, March, 1845.

Succession of Bosquet, No. 5632, 10 Rob. 143. New Orleans, March, 1845.
Succession of Duplessis, f.m.c., No. 5598, 10 Rob. 193. New Orleans, March, 1845.
McCargo v. New Orleans Insurance Co., No. 5146, 10 Rob. 202. New Orleans, March, 1845.
Andrews v. Ocean Insurance Co., No. 5123, 10 Rob. 332. New Orleans, March, 1845.
Lockett v. Fireman's Insurance Co., No. 5123, 10 Rob. 332. New Orleans, March, 1845.
Hagan v. Ocean Insurance Co., No. 5123, 10 Rob. 333. New Orleans, March, 1845.
Johnson v. Ocean Insurance Co., No. 5123, 10 Rob. 334. New Orleans, March, 1845.
McCargo v. Merchants Insurance Co., No. 5123, 10 Rob. 334. New Orleans, March, 1845.
Lockett v. Merchants Insurance Co., No. 5164, 10 Rob. 339. New Orleans, March, 1845.
François v. Lobrano, No. 5347, 10 Rob. 450. New Orleans, April, 1845.
Casimir v. Blanc, 10 Rob. 448. New Orleans, April, 1845.
Lambeth v. Freeman and Thompson, not reported No. 5588. New Orleans, April, 1845.
Freeman v. Profilet, not reported No. 5829. New Orleans, April, 1845.
Stanislaus v. Dorel, not reported No. 4782. New Orleans, May, 1845.
Henderson v. Henderson, not reported No. 5617. New Orleans, May, 1845.
Prévost v. Martel, No. 5345, 10 Rob. 512. New Orleans, May, 1845.
McFarlane v. Richardson, No. 5217, 11 Rob. 13. New Orleans, May, 1845.
Heirs of Beale v. Walden, No. 5227, 11 Rob. 67. New Orleans, May, 1845.
Miller v. Belmonti, No. 5623, 11 Rob. 339. New Orleans, May, 1845.
Milliken v. Andrews, No. 5795, 11 Rob. 241. New Orleans, June, 1845.
Thomson v. Myline, No. 5807, 11 Rob. 349. New Orleans, July, 1845.
Gonor v. Gonor, 11 Rob. 526. Opelousas, September, 1845.
Sandoz v. Gary, 11 Rob. 529. Opelousas, September, 1845.
Smith v. Berwick, 12 Rob. 20. Opelousas, September, 1845.
State v. Thomas; State v. Neal, 12 Rob. 48. Alexandria, October, 1845.
Offut v. Morancy, No. 1108, 12 Rob. 92. Alexandria, October, 1845.
Graves v. Hemken, No. 1125, 12 Rob. 103. Alexandria, October, 1845.
Audat v. Gilly, No. 5337, 12 Rob. 323. New Orleans, December, 1845.

Webb v. Goodbee, No. 6010, 12 Rob. 539. New Orleans, February, 1846.
Rost v. Henderson, No. 5617, 12 Rob. 549. New Orleans, February, 1846.
Keller v. McCalop, No. 5814, 12 Rob. 639. New Orleans, February, 1846.
Cottle v. Wilson, No. 5803, 1 La. Ann. 4. New Orleans, April, 1846.
Fuentes v. Caballero, No. 5802, 1 La. Ann. 27. New Orleans, April, 1846.
Fernandez v. Bein, No. 5894, 1 La. Ann. 32. New Orleans, April, 1846.
Bernard v. Auguste, No. 5715, 1 La. Ann. 69. New Orleans, May, 1846.
Stevens v. Wellington, No. 5840, 1 La. Ann. 72. New Orleans, May, 1846.
Musson v. Clayton, No. 5888, 1 La. Ann. 122. New Orleans, May, 1846.
Holmes v. *Chieftain,* No. 5837, 1 La. Ann. 136. New Orleans, June, 1846.
Bertin v. Phillips, No. 5728, 1 La. Ann. 173. New Orleans, June, 1846.
Spalding v. Taylor (*St. Missouri*), No. 5628, 1 La. Ann. 195. New Orleans, June, 1846.
Josephine v. Poultney, No. 5935, 1 La. Ann. 329. New Orleans, November, 1846.
Lacoste v. Sellick, No. 6101, 1 La. Ann. 336. New Orleans, November, 1846.
Bornet v. Davis, No. 6106, 1 La. Ann. 339. New Orleans, November, 1846.
Richardson v. Johnson, No. 5985, 1 La. Ann. 389. New Orleans, November, 1846.
Downey v. Stacy, No. 5969, 1 La. Ann. 426. New Orleans, December, 1846.
Egerton v. Third Municipality, 1 La. Ann. 435, 437. New Orleans, December, 1846.
Michel v. Dolliole, f.m.c., No. 6120, 1 La. Ann. 459. New Orleans, December, 1846.
Johnson v. Johnson, No. 59, 2 La. Ann. 67. New Orleans, January, 1847.
Robert v. St. Romes, No. 71, 2 La. Ann. 135. New Orleans, January, 1847.
Brinegar v. Griffin, No. 302, 2 La. Ann. 154. New Orleans, February, 1847.
Eugénie, f.w.c., v. Préval, No. 99, 2 La. Ann. 180. New Orleans, February, 1847.
Dunlap v. Hundley, No. 212, 2 La. Ann. 212. New Orleans, February, 1847.
State v. Gilbert, No. 343, 2 La. Ann. 244. New Orleans, March, 1847.
Baker v. Directors of the Bank of Louisiana, No. 6071, 2 La. Ann. 371. New Orleans, April, 1847.

Isabella v. Pecot, No. 373, 2 La. Ann. 387. New Orleans, April, 1847.
Collingsworth v. Covington, No. 469, 2 La. Ann. 406. New Orleans, April, 1847.
Cavelier v. Davenport and Moss, No. 6099, 2 La. Ann. 584. New Orleans, May; 1847.
Arsène, alias Cora, f.w.c., v. Pignéguy, No. 459, 2 La. Ann. 620. New Orleans, June, 1847.
Pahnvitz v. Fassman, No. 512, 2 La. Ann. 625. New Orleans, June, 1847.
Sophie, *statu liber,* v. Heirs of Duplessis, No. 424, 2 La. Ann. 724. New Orleans, June, 1847.
State v. Dubord, No. 563, 2 La. Ann. 732. New Orleans, June, 1847.
Harvey v. Kendall, No. 450, 2 La. Ann. 748. New Orleans, June, 1847.
Hynson v. Meuillon, f.m.c., No. 98, 2 La. Ann. 798. Alexandria, September, 1847.
State v. Fant, No. 121, 2 La. Ann. 837. Alexandria, September, 1847.
State v. Bogan, No. 122, 2 La. Ann. 838. Alexandria, September, 1847.
Robinett v. Compton, No. 331, 2 La. Ann. 846, 861. Alexandria, September, 1847.
Sullivan v. Williams, No. 23, 2 La. Ann. 876. Alexandria, September, 1847.
Morgan v. Estate of Baptist, not reported No. 45. Alexandria, September, 1847.
Girard v. City of New Orleans, No. 18, 2 La. Ann. 897. Monroe, October, 1847.
Cole v. Lucas, No. 53, 2 La. Ann. 946. Monroe, October, 1847.
Sandridge v. Jones, No. 71, 2 La. Ann. 993. Monroe, October, 1847.
Bach v. Barrett, No. 3576, 2 La. Ann. 955. New Orleans, November, 1847.
Roebuck v. Curry, No. 458, 2 La. Ann. 998. New Orleans, December, 1847.
Bank of Charleston v. Hagan, No. 464, 2 La. Ann. 999. New Orleans, December, 1847.
Stachlin v. Destrehan, No. 539, 2 La. Ann. 1019. New Orleans, December, 1847.
Kellar v. Fink and Baos, f.w.c., No. 598, 3. La. Ann. 17. New Orleans, January, 1848.
Taylor v. Rostrop, No. 676, 3 La. Ann. 100. New Orleans, January, 1848.
Segond v. Remy, f.w.c., Nos. 737, 738, 3 La. Ann. 126. New Orleans, January, 1848.
Bibb v. Hebert, No. 753, 3 La. Ann. 132. New Orleans, January, 1848.

State v. Nelson, Edwin, and Henry, Slaves, No. 741, 3 La. Ann. 497. New Orleans, January, 1848.
Gaudet v. Gourdain, No. 364, 3 La. Ann. 136. New Orleans, February, 1848.
Succession of Sinnott, No. 696, 3 La. Ann. 175. New Orleans, February, 1848.
Palmer v. Moore, No. 565, 3 La. Ann. 208. New Orleans, February, 1848.
State v. Lyons, No. 767, 3 La. Ann. 486. New Orleans, February, 1848.
McCarty v. Mandeville, No. 626, 3 La. Ann. 239. New Orleans, March, 1848.
Oates v. Caffin, No. 627, 3 La. Ann. 339. New Orleans, March, 1848.
State v. Slave Isaac, No. 828, 3 La. Ann. 359. New Orleans, March, 1848.
State v. Lewis, No. 584, 3 La. Ann. 398. New Orleans, April, 1848.
Coby v. Kock, No. 520, 3 La. Ann. 439. New Orleans, May, 1848.
Stewart v. Sowles, No. 725, 3 La. Ann. 464. New Orleans, May, 1848.
Louis, *statu liber,* v. Cousin, No. 972, 3 La. Ann. 467. New Orleans, May, 1848.
State v. Ritchie, No. 971, 3 La. Ann. 511, 715. New Orleans, June, 1848.
State v. Patza, No. 983, 3 La. Ann. 512. New Orleans, June, 1848.
Angelina v. Whitehead, 3 La. Ann. 556. Opelousas, August, 1848.
State v. Jerry, No. 129, 3 La. Ann. 576. Alexandria, September, 1848.
Waters v. Grayson, No. 82, 3 La. Ann. 595. Monroe, October, 1848.
Boner v. Mahle, No. 86, 3 La. Ann. 600. Monroe, October, 1848.
Hendricks v. Phillips, No. 98, 3 La. Ann. 618. Monroe, October, 1848.
Peterson v. Burn, No. 912, 3 La. Ann. 655. New Orleans, November, 1848.
Sophie, *statu liber,* v. Duplessis, No. 919, 3 La. Ann. 658. New Orleans, November, 1848.
DePontalba v. New Orleans, No. 707, 3 La. Ann. 660. New Orleans, November, 1848.
Freeman v. His Creditors, No. 948, 3 La. Ann. 699. New Orleans, November, 1848.
Cartwright v. McMillen and Nichols, No. 906, 3 La. Ann. 685. New Orleans, November, 1848.
Davis v. Panin, No. 1034, 3 La. Ann. 712. New Orleans, December, 1848.
State v. Barton, alias Bennet, alias Angel, No. 928, 4 La. Ann. 31. New Orleans, January, 1849.
Botts v. Cochrane, No. 1013, 4 La. Ann. 35. New Orleans, January, 1849.

Amoult v. Deschapelles, No. 1057, 4 La. Ann. 41. New Orleans, January, 1849.
Blanchard v. Dixon, No. 1135, 4 La. Ann. 57. New Orleans, January, 1849.
Frierson v. Irwin, No. 1050, 4 La. Ann. 277. New Orleans, January, 1849.
Gaulden v. McPhaul, No. 1811, 4 La. Ann. 79. New Orleans, February, 1849.
George v. Marshall and James, not reported. New Orleans, filed 1849.
Louis v. Ricard, No. 1211, 4 La. Ann. 87. New Orleans, February, 1849.
Landry v. Peterson, No. 1025, 4 La. Ann. 96. New Orleans, February, 1849.
Brown v. Glathary, No. 1256, 4 La. Ann. 124. New Orleans, February, 1849.
Anderson v. Dacosta, No. 996, 4 La. Ann. 136. New Orleans, February, 1849.
Solomon v. Cavelier, No. 998, 4 La. Ann. 136. New Orleans, February, 1849.
Cox v. Meyers, No. 1234, 4 La. Ann. 144. New Orleans, February, 1849.
State v. Morris, No. 1293, 4 La. Ann. 177. New Orleans, March, 1849.
Johnson v. Campbell and Imboden, No. 1295, 4 La. Ann. 178. New Orleans, March, 1849.
State v. Dick, No. 1224, 4 La. Ann. 182. New Orleans, March, 1849.
State v. Jerry, No. 1302, 4 La. Ann. 190. New Orleans, March, 1849.
Armour v. Downes, No. 1306, 4 La. Ann. 192. New Orleans, March, 1849.
Frierson v. Irvin, No. 1050, 4 La. Ann. 277. New Orleans, March, 1849.
Nott v. Marchesseau, No. 1083, 4 La. Ann. 344. New Orleans, May, 1849.
Miller v. Miller, Nos. 1024, 1114, 4 La. Ann. 354. New Orleans, May, 1849.
Bank of Kentucky v. Conner, No. 1315, 4 La. Ann. 365. New Orleans, May, 1849.
Rost v. Livaudais, not reported No. 1170. New Orleans, May, 1849.
Arbuckle v. Bouny, not reported No. 1380. New Orleans, May, 1849.
State v. Monasterio, No. 1386, 4 La. Ann. 380. New Orleans, June, 1849.
Bertrand v. Arcueil, No. 142, 4 La. Ann. 430. New Orleans, June, 1849.
Edmonds v. Husband, 4 La. Ann. 489. Opelousas, September, 1849.
Wells v. Hardwick, not reported No. 144. Monroe, filed October, 1849.
Beirne and Burnside v. Gilmer, not reported No. 149. Monroe, filed October, 1849.

Fisk v. Proctor, No. 927, 4 La. Ann. 562. New Orleans, November, 1849.
Augustin v. Abell, not reported No. 1335. New Orleans, November, 1849.
Succession of Dupuy, No. 1438, 4 La. Ann. 570. New Orleans, December, 1849.
White v. Slatter, No. 943, 5 La. Ann. 29. New Orleans, January, 1850.
State v. Levy and Dreyfous, Nos. 1414, 1416, 5 La. Ann. 64. New Orleans, January, 1850.
Moore v. Waddell and Lambeth, No. 1570, 5 La. Ann. 66. New Orleans, January, 1850.
Dolliole v. White, No. 1213, 5 La. Ann. 98. New Orleans, January, 1850.
Johnson v. Municipality #1, No. 1444, 5 La. Ann. 100. New Orleans, January, 1850.
O'Blennis v. Corri, No. 1455, 5 La. Ann. 101. New Orleans, January, 1850.
Campbell v. Botts, No. 1436, 5 La. Ann. 106. New Orleans, January, 1850.
McCarthy v. Sheriff (Lewis), Nos. 1355, 1377, 5 La. Ann. 115. New Orleans, February, 1850.
Amandez v. Lawes, No. 1572, 5 La. Ann. 127. New Orleans, February, 1850.
LeDuff, f.m.c., v. Porché and Carmouche, No. 1587, 5 La. Ann. 148. New Orleans, February, 1850.
Marcos v. Bacas, No. 946, 5 La. Ann. 265. New Orleans, February, 1850.
Mary, f.w.c., v. Brown, No. 1640, 5 La. Ann. 269. New Orleans, February, 1850.
State v. Cummings, No. 794, 5 La. Ann. 330. New Orleans, April, 1850.
State v. Fuentes, No. 1529, 5 La. Ann. 427. New Orleans, May, 1850.
State v. Chandler, No. 1536, 5 La. Ann. 489. New Orleans, May, 1850.
Dunbar v. Conner, not reported No. 1700. New Orleans, May, 1850.
Heirs of Henderson v. Rost, Nos. 1469, 5617, 5 La. Ann. 441. New Orleans, June, 1850.
Frierson v. Irwin, No. 1696, 5 La. Ann. 525. New Orleans, June, 1850.
Dugas v. Estiletts, 5 La. Ann. 559. Opelousas, September, 1850.
Dupré v. Désmaret, 5 La. Ann. 591. Opelousas, September, 1850.
Dupré v. Prescott, 5 La. Ann. 592. Opelousas, September, 1850.
Young v. Young, 5 La. Ann. 611. Opelousas, September, 1850.
Adle v. Auty, No. 138, 5 La. Ann. 622. Alexandria, September, 1850.
Bartlett v. Peck, No. 213, 5 La. Ann. 669. Monroe, October, 1850.
Matthews v. Wilson, No. 221, 5 La. Ann. 691. Monroe, October, 1850.

Couvent, f.m.c., v. Guesnard, No. 1063, 5 La. Ann. 696. New Orleans, November, 1850.
Arbuckle v. Bouny, No. 1632, 5 La. Ann. 699. New Orleans, November, 1850.
Roca v. Slawson, No. 1781, 5 La. Ann. 708. New Orleans, November, 1850.
Villars v. Kennedy, 5 La. Ann. 724. New Orleans, December, 1850.
Koch v. McCall and Slater, No. 1748, 5 La. Ann. 739. New Orleans, December, 1850.
Allen v. Campbell, No. 1849, 5 La. Ann. 755. New Orleans, December, 1850.
Dunbar v. Conner, not reported No. 1700. New Orleans, January, 1851.
Bernard v. Auguste, No. 1857, 6 La. Ann. 24. New Orleans, January, 1851.
Romer v. Woods, No. 1846, 6 La. Ann. 29. New Orleans, January, 1851.
Buddy v. *Vanleer,* No. 1901, 6 La. Ann. 34. New Orleans, January, 1851.
Sargent v. Slater, No. 1884, 6 La. Ann. 72. New Orleans, February, 1851.
Carmouche v. Bouis, No. 2032, 6 La. Ann. 95. New Orleans, February, 1851.
Aubert v. Aubert, No. 1985, 6 La. Ann. 104. New Orleans, February, 1851.
Badillo v. Tio, No. 1745, 6 La. Ann. 129. New Orleans, February, 1851.
State v. Capers, No. 2146, 6 La. Ann. 267, 269. New Orleans, February, 1851.
State v. Jerry, not reported No. 2097. New Orleans, filed February, 1851.
Childers v. Johnson, No. 2078, 6 La. Ann. 634. New Orleans, February, 1851.
Vail v. Bird, No. 2129, 6 La. Ann. 223. New Orleans, March, 1851.
State v. Reed, No. 2148, 6 La. Ann. 227. New Orleans, March, 1851.
Wingate v. Wheat, No. 2080, 6 La. Ann. 238. New Orleans, March, 1851.
Walker v. Ferrure, No. 1877, 6 La. Ann. 278. New Orleans, March, 1851.
Dupre v. Uzee, No. 2101, 6 La. Ann. 280. New Orleans, March, 1851.
Dobard v. Nunez, No. 1944, 6 La. Ann. 294. New Orleans, April, 1851.
Hyams v. Smith, No. 2172, 6 La. Ann. 362. New Orleans, April, 1851.
McDowell v. Couch, No. 2093, 6 La. Ann. 365. New Orleans, April, 1851.
Lombard v. Jacobs, No. 2185, 6 La. Ann. 396. New Orleans, April, 1851.
Stackhouse v. Kendall, No. 1851, 7 La. Ann. 670. New Orleans, April, 1851.
Nichols v. Grice, No. 2086, 6 La. Ann. 446. New Orleans, May, 1851.

State v. Powell, No. 1988, 6 La. Ann. 449. New Orleans, May, 1851.
Benjamin v. Davis, No. 2141, 6 La. Ann. 472. New Orleans, May, 1851.
Vinot v. Bertrand, No. 2171, 6 La. Ann. 474. New Orleans, May, 1851.
Leigh v. Meurice, f.m.c., No. 2191, 6 La. Ann. 476. New Orleans, May, 1851.
Nicholson v. Ogden, No. 2229, 6 La. Ann. 486. New Orleans, May, 1851.
Murphy v. Mutual Benefit Life and Fire Insurance Co., No. 2244, 6 La. Ann. 518. New Orleans, May, 1851.
Haggerty v. Powell, No. 2215, 6 La. Ann. 533. New Orleans, June, 1851.
State v. Bradley, No. 1509, 6 La. Ann. 554. New Orleans, June, 1851.
Heres v. Powell, No. 1808, 6 La. Ann. 586. New Orleans, June, 1851.
State v. Jackson, a Slave, No. 2124, 6 La. Ann. 593. New Orleans, June, 1851.
Rawls v. Rawls, 6 La. Ann. 665. Opelousas, September, 1851.
State v. Price, No. 159, 6 La. Ann. 691. Opelousas, September, 1851.
State v. Jonas and Sam, Slaves, No. 279, 6 La. Ann. 695. Monroe, October, 1851.
Dwyer v. Cane, No. 222, 6 La. Ann. 707. Monroe, October, 1851.
Hough v. Vickers, No. 246, 6 La. Ann. 724. Monroe, October, 1851.
Hall v. Hill and McLean, No. 287, 6 La. Ann. 745. Monroe, October, 1851.
Wilson v. Green, f.m.c., not reported No. 2372. New Orleans, filed November, 1851.
Rhinehart v. Doswell, No. 2352, 6 La. Ann. 766. New Orleans, December, 1851.
Bacon v. Leeds, No. 2295, 6 La. Ann. 804. New Orleans, December, 1851.
Huntington v. Ricard, No. 2288, 6 La. Ann. 806. New Orleans, December, 1851.
Stiles v. Cook, not reported No. 2365. New Orleans, December, 1851.
Demoruelle v. Sugg, No. 2500, 7 La. Ann. 42. New Orleans, February, 1852.
State v. Benjamin, No. 2512, 7 La. Ann. 47. New Orleans, February, 1852.
Terrebonne v. Walsh, No. 2460, 7 La. Ann. 61. New Orleans, February, 1852.
Liza v. Puissant, No. 2326, 7 La. Ann. 81. New Orleans, February, 1852.
State v. Parker, No. 2392, 7 La. Ann. 83. New Orleans, February, 1852.
Ross v. Carson, not reported No. 2576. New Orleans, March, 1852.
State v. Harris, not reported No. 2400. New Orleans, April, 1852.

Hooper v. Owens, No. 2405, 7 La. Ann. 206. New Orleans, April, 1852.
Succession of Tete v. Blanchard, Eimer and Co., No. 2050, 7 La. Ann. 95. New Orleans, May, 1852.
Botts and Pool v. Nichols, No. 2680, 7 La. Ann. 263. New Orleans, May, 1852.
Cornelson v. Insurance Co., No. 2626, 7 La. Ann. 345. New Orleans, June, 1852.
Coulter v. Cresswell, No. 2734, 7 La. Ann. 367. New Orleans, June, 1852.
Williamson v. Norton (*Western World*), No. 2417, 7 La. Ann. 393. New Orleans, June, 1852.
Succession of Franklin, No. 2619, 7 La. Ann. 395. New Orleans, June, 1852.
Badillo v. Tio, No. 2410, 7 La. Ann. 487. New Orleans, June, 1852.
State v. Green, No. 2748, 7 La. Ann. 518. New Orleans, June, 1852.
Heirs of Henderson v. Rost, No. 2255, 7 La. Ann. 697. New Orleans, June, 1852.
Winfield v. Little, No. 170, 7 La. Ann. 536. Alexandria, September, 1852.
Gandy v. Taintor, No. 255, 7 La. Ann. 540. Monroe, October, 1852.
Baker, f.m.c., v. Tabor, No. 328, 7 La. Ann. 556. Monroe, October, 1852.
Temple v. Smith, No. 343, 7 La. Ann. 562. Monroe, October, 1852.
Baldree v. Davenport, No. 295, 7 La. Ann. 587. Monroe, October, 1852.
Succession of Pipkin, No. 2809, 7 La. Ann. 617. New Orleans, November, 1852.
Carmelite v. Lacaze, No. 2506, 7 La. Ann. 629. New Orleans, November, 1852.
State v. Barnes, not reported. New Orleans, November[?], 1852.
Hudnall v. Watts, DeSaulles, and Jones, No. 2776, 8 La. Ann. 5. New Orleans, January, 1853.
Haynes, alias Mielkie, v. Hutchinson and Forno, No. 2850, 8 La. Ann. 35. New Orleans, January, 1853.
State v. Geze, No. 2951, 8 La. Ann. 52. New Orleans, February, 1853.
Brown, f.w.c., v. Smith and Taylor, No. 2761, 8 La. Ann. 59. New Orleans, February, 1853.
Audige v. Gaillard, No. 2865, 8 La. Ann. 71. New Orleans, February, 1853.
O'Neal v. Oates, No. 3049, 8 La. Ann. 78. New Orleans, March, 1853.
Simon v. Burnett, No. 3047, 8 La. Ann. 84. New Orleans, March, 1853.
Adams v. Routh and Dorsey, No. 3009, 8 La. Ann. 121. New Orleans, April, 1853.

Succession of Cresswell, No. 2423, 8 La. Ann. 122. New Orleans, April, 1853.

Cooley and Lacoste v. Cecile, f.w.c., No. 2939, 8 La. Ann. 142. New Orleans, April, 1853.

State of Louisiana, State of Maryland intervening, v. Executors of McDonogh, No. 2175, 8 La. Ann. 171. New Orleans, April, 1853.

Simonds v. Byrne, not reported No. 2855. New Orleans, April, 1853.

DeLaLande v. Poydras, not reported No. 2941. New Orleans, April, 1853.

Roundtree v. *Brilliant,* No. 2804, 8 La. Ann. 289. New Orleans, May, 1853.

State v. Kentuck, a Slave, No. 3039, 8 La. Ann. 308. New Orleans, June, 1853.

Heirs of Trahan v. Trahan, 8 La. Ann. 455. Opelousas, September, 1853.

Beebe v. Robbins, 8 La. Ann. 470. Opelousas, September, 1853.

Eulalie v. Long and Mabry, No. 3237, 9 La. Ann. 9. New Orleans, January, 1854.

State v. DeAngelo, No. 3135, 9 La. Ann. 46. New Orleans, January, 1854.

Simonds v. Byrne, No. 2855, 9 La. Ann. 93. New Orleans, February, 1854.

State v. Porte, No. 3384, 9 La. Ann. 105. New Orleans, February, 1854.

Bird v. Vail, No. 3454, 9 La. Ann. 176. New Orleans, March, 1854.

Macon v. Willson, No. 3010, 9 La. Ann. 178. New Orleans, March, 1854.

State v. Lethe, Biner, Hal, and Chloe, Slaves, No. 3083, 9 La. Ann. 182. New Orleans, March, 1854.

Buhler v. McHatton, No. 3448, 9 La. Ann. 192. New Orleans, March, 1854.

Succession of DeLaLande, not reported No. 3197. New Orleans, April, 1854.

Wooten, f.w.c., v. Harrison, No. 3476, 9 La. Ann. 234. New Orleans, April, 1854.

Stephens v. Graves, No. 3449, 9 La. Ann. 239. New Orleans, April, 1854.

Taylor v. Patterson, No. 3473, 9 La. Ann. 251. New Orleans, April, 1854.

Thompson v. Womack, No. 2973, 9 La. Ann. 555. New Orleans, May, 1854.

Lusk v. Swon, No. 2852, 9 La. Ann. 367. New Orleans, June, 1854.

Stewart v. New Orleans, No. 3043, 9 La. Ann. 461. New Orleans, June, 1854.

Succession of Cresswell, not reported No. 3521. New Orleans, June, 1854.

Sherrod v. Calleghan, No. 162, 9 La. Ann. 510. Alexandria, September, 1854.

Sherrod v. Berlin, not reported No. 163. Alexandria, September, 1854.

State v. Martinez, No. 3668, 9 La. Ann. 530. New Orleans, November, 1854.

Dowty v. Templeton, No. 3131, 9 La. Ann. 549. New Orleans, December, 1854.

Henriette, *statu liber,* v. Arroyo, not reported No. 3706. New Orleans, December, 1854.

Hirsh v. Lynch, not reported No. 3805. New Orleans, filed January, 1855.

Berret v. Adams, No. 3806, 10 La. Ann. 77. New Orleans, January, 1855.

Roussell v. Phipps, No. 3810, 10 La. Ann. 119. New Orleans, February, 1855.

State v. Thompson, No. 3804, 10 La. Ann. 122. New Orleans, February, 1855.

Foley and Townsend v. Bourg, 10 La. Ann. 129. New Orleans, February, 1855.

Ryder v. Wright and Marshall, No. 3837, 10 La. Ann. 127. New Orleans, February, 1855.

State v. Hannah, No. 3829, 10 La. Ann. 131. New Orleans, February, 1855.

Lebeau v. Thideau, No. 3847, 10 La. Ann. 164. New Orleans, February, 1855.

Virginie and Celésie, f.p.c., v. Himel, No. 3842, 10 La. Ann. 185. New Orleans, February, 1855.

White v. Hall, No. 3958, 10 La. Ann. 189. New Orleans, March, 1855.

State v. Heas, No. 3830, 10 La. Ann. 195. New Orleans, March, 1855.

Gentile v. Plasencia, No. 3843, 10 La. Ann. 203. New Orleans, March, 1855.

Robertson v. Wallis, No. 3809, 10 La. Ann. 214. New Orleans, March, 1855.

DeLaLande v. DeLaLande, No. 2941, 10 La. Ann. 220. New Orleans, March, 1855.

Hardesty v. Wormley, No. 3956, 10 La. Ann. 239. New Orleans, April, 1855.

Stoppenhagen v. Verdelet, No. 3271, 10 La. Ann. 263. New Orleans, April, 1855.

Fellowes v. Young, No. 3951, 10 La. Ann. 267. New Orleans, April, 1855.

Bloodgood v. Wilson, No. 3272, 10 La. Ann. 302. New Orleans, April, 1855.
Dupré v. Executor of Boulard, No. 3743, 10 La. Ann. 411. New Orleans, May, 1855.
Cochran v. Walker, No. 3336, 10 La. Ann. 431. New Orleans, June, 1855.
State v. Chopin, No. 4113, 10 La. Ann. 458. New Orleans, June, 1855.
State v. Dick, No. 3647, 10 La. Ann. 461. New Orleans, June, 1855.
State v. Sam, not reported No. 4041. New Orleans, June, 1855.
State v. Brien, No. 4061, 10 La. Ann. 454. New Orleans, June, 1855.
Lewis v. Peets, No. 350, 10 La. Ann. 489. Monroe, July, 1855.
Klein v. Emily, a coon [*sic*], not reported No. 431. Monroe, July, 1855.
Kemp v. Hutchinson, No. 452, 10 La. Ann. 494. Monroe, July, 1855.
Kennedy v. Mason, No. 362, 10 La. Ann. 519. Monroe, July, 1855.
Talbert v. Stone, No. 402, 10 La. Ann. 537. Monroe, July, 1855.
Henderson v. Trousdale, No. 413, 10 La. Ann. 548. Monroe, July, 1855.
McAlpin v. Jones, No. 398, 10 La. Ann. 552. Monroe, July, 1855.
Mathilda, f.w.c., v. Autrey, No. 411, 10 La. Ann. 555. Monroe, July, 1855.
Murphey v. Cook, No. 419, 10 La. Ann. 572. Monroe, July, 1855.
Buie v. Doyal, No. 370, 10 La. Ann. 575. Monroe, July, 1855.
O'Hara v. Conrad, 10 La. Ann. 638. Opelousas, September, 1855.
Leonora, f.w.c., v. Scott, 10 La. Ann. 651. Opelousas, September, 1855.
Smith's Executors v. Dwight, 10 La. Ann. 691. Opelousas, September, 1855.
Semère v. Semère, f.m.c., 10 La. Ann. 704. Opelousas, September, 1855.
State v. Maxent and Gueson, No. 4110, 10 La. Ann. 743. New Orleans, November, 1855.
Barry v. Kimball, No. 3500, 10 La. Ann. 787. New Orleans, December, 1855.
Gerard v. Pasgoud, not reported No. 4216. New Orleans, December, 1855.
Succession of Fletcher v. Découdreau, No. 4289, 11 La. Ann. 59. New Orleans, January, 1856.
Peyton v. Richards, No. 3523, 11 La. Ann. 62. New Orleans, January, 1856.
Humphreys v. Utz, not reported No. 3910. New Orleans, February, 1856.
Griffing v. Routh, No. 3921, 11 La. Ann. 135. New Orleans, February, 1856.
Hunter, Murphy, and Talbot v. General Mutual Insurance Co., No. 3122, 11 La. Ann. 139. New Orleans, February, 1856.
Bush v. Decuir, No. 4339, 11 La. Ann. 503. New Orleans, February, 1856.

Hill v. White, No. 4489, 11 La. Ann. 170. New Orleans, March, 1856.
State v. Slaves Bob, Joe, and Catherine, No. 4411, 11 La. Ann. 192. New Orleans, March, 1856.
McCall v. Herndon and DeCamp, No. 4327, 11 La. Ann. 209. New Orleans, March, 1856.
Dixon v. Chadwick, No. 4388, 11 La. Ann. 215. New Orleans, March, 1856.
George v. Greenwood, No. 3687, 11 La. Ann. 299. New Orleans, April, 1856.
State v. Shields, No. 4171, 11 La. Ann. 395. New Orleans, May, 1856.
Fitzgerald v. Ferguson, No. 4007, 11 La. Ann. 396. New Orleans, May, 1856.
Delphine, f.w.c., v. Guillet, No. 4249, 11 La. Ann. 424. New Orleans, May, 1856.
State v. Taylor, f.m.c., No. 4132, 11 La. Ann. 430. New Orleans, May, 1856.
Henriette, alias Mary, v. Heirs of Barnes, No. 3751, 11 La. Ann. 453. New Orleans, June, 1856.
Eulalie v. Long and Mabry, No. 3979, 11 La. Ann. 463. New Orleans, June, 1856.
State v. Bass and McNabb, No. 4603, 11 La. Ann. 478. New Orleans, June, 1856.
Crane v. Allen, No. 4424, 11 La. Ann. 493. New Orleans, May, 1856.
Brack v. Wood, 11 La. Ann. 512. New Orleans, May, 1856.
Dorwin v. Wiltz, 11 La. Ann. 514. New Orleans, May, 1856.
State v. Ned, not reported No. 4629. New Orleans, June, 1856.
Person v. Rutherford, 11 La. Ann. 527. New Orleans, June, 1856.
Henderson v. Rost, No. 2255, 11 La. Ann. 541. New Orleans, June, 1856.
Brien v. Bartlett and Day, Nos. 219, 225, 11 La. Ann. 601. Monroe, July, 1856.
Wilson v. Bossier, No. 571, 11 La. Ann. 640. Monroe, July, 1856.
Wood v. Hardy, No. 520, 11 La. Ann. 760. Monroe, July, 1856.
State v. Munce, No. 499, 12 La. Ann. 625. Monroe, July, 1856.
Solibellas v. Consolidated Association, 11 La. Ann. 682. Alexandria, August, 1856.
Figaras v. Benoist, No. 209, 11 La. Ann. 683. Alexandria, August, 1856.
Templet v. Baker, 12 La. Ann. 658. Opelousas, August, 1856.
Lambert v. King, 12 La. Ann. 662. Opelousas, August, 1856.

State v. Jackson, 12 La. Ann. 679. Opelousas, August, 1856.

Dupérrier v. Dautrive, 12 La. Ann. 664. Opelousas, August, 1856.

Collins v. Administrator, 12 La. Ann. 678. Opelousas, August, 1856.

Semère v. Semère, 12 La. Ann. 681. Opelousas, August, 1856.

Louis v. Richard, 12 La. Ann. 684. Opelousas, August, 1856.

McLellan and Kelty v. Williams, No. 4299, 11 La. Ann. 721. New Orleans, December, 1856.

State v. Harrison, a Slave, No. 4464, 1 La. Ann. 722. New Orleans, December, 1856.

Reynolds v. Brenford; Reynolds v. Batson, No. 4291, 11 La. Ann. 729. New Orleans, December, 1856.

Maranthe, Genie, et al. v. Hunter, No. 4328, 11 La. Ann. 735. New Orleans, December, 1856.

State v. Adeline, a Slave, No. 4503, 11 La. Ann. 736. New Orleans, December, 1856.

Nixon v. Bozeman and Bushy, No. 3485, 11 La. Ann. 750. New Orleans, December, 1856.

Farwell v. Harris and Morgan, No. 4490, 12 La. Ann. 50. New Orleans, January, 1857.

Barrow v. McDonald, No. 4854, 12 La. Ann. 110. New Orleans, February, 1857.

Phipps v. Berger, No. 4852, 12 La. Ann. 111. New Orleans, February, 1857.

Miller v. Stewart, No. 4946, 12 La. Ann. 170. New Orleans, March, 1857.

Owen v. Brown, No. 4927, 12 La. Ann. 172. New Orleans, March, 1857.

Montan v. Whitley, No. 4994, 12 La. Ann. 175. New Orleans, March, 1857.

Lewis v. City of New Orleans, No. 4679, 12 La. Ann. 190. New Orleans, March, 1857.

Mahur v. LeBlanc, No. 5000, 12 La. Ann. 207. New Orleans, March, 1857.

Gil v. Williams and Davis, No. 4999, 12 La. Ann. 219. New Orleans, March, 1857.

Molaison v. Hébert, No. 5031, 12 La. Ann. 232. New Orleans, March, 1857.

McGowan v. Laughlan, No. 4938, 12 La. Ann. 242. New Orleans, March, 1857.

Bennett v. Bennett, No. 5057, 12 La. Ann. 253. New Orleans, April, 1857.

Barclay, f.w.c., v. Sewell, No. 4622, 12 La. Ann. 262. New Orleans, April, 1857.
State v. Scott, No. 4964, 12 La. Ann. 274. New Orleans, April, 1857.
Freeman v. Anis, not reported No. 4934. New Orleans, April, 1857.
Whann v. Hufty, No. 4982, 12 La. Ann. 280. New Orleans, April, 1857.
Knight v. Knight, No. 4576, 12 La. Ann. 59. New Orleans, May, 1857.
Barry v. Kimball, No. 4648, 12 La. Ann. 372. New Orleans, May, 1857.
Daret v. Gray (*El Dorado*), No. 4681, 12 La. Ann. 394. New Orleans, May, 1857.
Williams v. Talbot, No. 4628, 12 La. Ann. 407. New Orleans, May, 1857.
McCay v. Chambliss, No. 4882, 12 La. Ann. 412. New Orleans, June, 1857.
Cornish v. Shelton, No. 4642, 12 La. Ann. 415. New Orleans, June, 1857.
Turner v. Smith, No. 5076, 12 La. Ann. 417. New Orleans, June, 1857.
State v. Clay, No. 5158, 12 La. Ann. 431. New Orleans, June, 1857.
Reed v. Crocker, No. 4708, 12 La. Ann. 436. New Orleans, June, 1857.
Riggin v. Kendig, No. 4718, 12 La. Ann. 451. New Orleans, June, 1857.
State v. Judge (Perkins), No. 5222, 12 La. Ann. 455. New Orleans, June, 1857.
Ogbourne v. Brown, not reported No. 587. Monroe, July, 1857.
State v. King, No. 597, 12 La. Ann. 593. Monroe, July, 1857.
Lawson's Heirs v. Lawson's Executors, No. 567, 12 La. Ann. 603. Monroe, July, 1857.
Johnson v. Bloodworth, 12 La. Ann. 699. Alexandria, August, 1857.
State v. Populus, f.m.c., No. 250, 12 La. Ann. 710. Alexandria, August, 1857.
State v. Morgan, No. 249, 12 La. Ann. 712. Alexandria, August, 1857.
Carmouche v. Carmouche, No. 243, 12 La. Ann. 721. Alexandria, August, 1857.
Oreline v. Heirs of Haggarty, 12 La. Ann. 880. Alexandria, August, 1857.
Louisiana, f.w.c., v. Gordon, not reported No. 267. Alexandria, August, 1857.
Trowbridge v. Carlin, 12 La. Ann. 882. Opelousas, August, 1857.
Bain v. Adams, No. 4634, 12 La. Ann. 753. New Orleans, November, 1857.
Maples v. Mitty and Sarah, f.w.c., No. 4985, 12 La. Ann. 759. New Orleans, November, 1857.

Girod v. Belknap, No. 4831, 12 La. Ann. 791. New Orleans, December, 1857.
State v. Kitty, No. 5154, 12 La. Ann. 805. New Orleans, December, 1857.
Mariacq v. *Wright,* No. 4645, 13 La. Ann. 27. New Orleans, January, 1858.
State v. Brunetto, No. 5376, 13 La. Ann. 45. New Orleans, January, 1858.
Nolasco v. Lurty, No. 5472, 13 La. Ann. 100. New Orleans, February, 1858.
McClure v. King, No. 4975, 13 La. Ann. 141. New Orleans, March, 1858.
Laycock v. Bird, No. 5617, 13 La. Ann. 173. New Orleans, March, 1858.
State v. Peter, No. 5692, 13 La. Ann. 232. New Orleans, April, 1858.
Delphine v. Guillet, No. 5145, 13 La. Ann. 248. New Orleans, April, 1858.
Dickason v. Bell, No. 5582, 13 La. Ann. 249. New Orleans, April, 1858.
Marshall v. Watrigant, No. 5220, 13 La. Ann. 619. New Orleans, April, 1858.
Clague v. City of New Orleans, No. 5658, 13 La. Ann. 275. New Orleans, May, 1858.
Neasom v. D'Armond, No. 5624, 13 La. Ann. 294. New Orleans, May, 1858.
State v. Oscar, No. 5407, 13 La. Ann. 297. New Orleans, May, 1858.
Alexander v. Hundley, No. 5276, 13 La. Ann. 327. New Orleans, May, 1858.
Harper v. Pierce, No. 5380, 13 La. Ann. 340. New Orleans, June, 1858.
Landry v. Klopman, No. 5272, 13 La. Ann. 345. New Orleans, June, 1858.
Lusk v. Church, No. 5332, 13 La. Ann. 360. New Orleans, June, 1858.
State v. Whetstone, No. 668, 13 La. Ann. 376. Monroe, July, 1858.
Ford v. Simmons, No. 636, 13 La. Ann. 397. Monroe, July, 1858.
Jones v. State of Louisiana, No. 568, 13 La. Ann. 406. Monroe, July, 1858.
McAlpine v. Jones, No. 660, 13 La. Ann. 409. Monroe, July, 1858.
Chaffe v. *St. Charles,* No. 646, 13 La. Ann. 415. Monroe, July, 1858.
Wilkins v. Bobo, No. 687, 13 La. Ann. 430. Monroe, July, 1858.
Boulard v. Calhoun, No. 295, 13 La. Ann. 445. Alexandria, August, 1858.
Mackie v. Davis, No. 281, 13 La. Ann. 475. Alexandria, August, 1858.
Laparouse v. Rice, 13 La. Ann. 567. Opelousas, August, 1858.
State v. White and Ward, 13 La. Ann. 573. Opelousas, August, 1858.
Julienne v. Touriac, 13 La. Ann. 599. Opelousas, August, 1858.
Thompson v. Touriac, 13 La. Ann. 605. Opelousas, August, 1858.
State v. Thompson, alias Robinson, and Baer, No. 5799, 13 La. Ann. 515. New Orleans, November, 1858.

State v. O'Connor, No. 5053, 13 La. Ann. 486. New Orleans, December, 1858.
State v. Henderson, No. 5621, 13 La. Ann. 489. New Orleans, December, 1858.
Summers v. U.S. Life Insurance Co., No. 5423, 13 La. Ann. 504. New Orleans, December, 1858.
Walker v. Sanchez, No. 4485, 13 La. Ann. 505. New Orleans, December, 1858.
Wright v. Railey, No. 5731, 13 La. Ann. 536. New Orleans, December, 1858.
Pope v. Anderson, No. 4891, 13 La. Ann. 538. New Orleans, December, 1858.
Marshall v. Watrigant, No. 5220, 13 La. Ann. 619. New Orleans, December, 1858.
Jamison v. Bridges, No. 5522, 14 La. Ann. 31. New Orleans, January, 1859.
Brown v. Raby, No. 5797, 14 La. Ann. 41. New Orleans, January, 1859.
McCutcheon v. Angelo, No. 5425, 14 La. Ann. 34. New Orleans, January, 1859.
Roquest v. Boutin, No. 5446, 14 La. Ann. 44. New Orleans, January, 1859.
Underwood v. Lacapère, No. 5348, 14 La. Ann. 276. New Orleans, January, 1859.
Perkins v. Shelton, not reported No. 5654. New Orleans, February, 1859.
Kessee v. Mayfield and Cage, No. 6022, 14 La. Ann. 90. New Orleans, February, 1859.
Bisland v. Provosty, No. 6030, 14 La. Ann. 169. New Orleans, February, 1859.
Levy v. Petrovic, not reported No. 6031. New Orleans, February, 1859.
Metoyer v. Caretta, not reported No. 5644. New Orleans, March, 1859.
George v. Demouy, No. 5969, 14 La. Ann. 145. New Orleans, March, 1859.
Pauline, f.w.c., v. Hubert, No. 6012, 14 La. Ann. 161. New Orleans, March, 1859.
King v. Neely, Nos. 6056, 6074, 14 La. Ann. 165. New Orleans, March, May, 1859.
Jackson v. Van Pelt and Moore, No. 6062, 14 La. Ann. 213. New Orleans, March, 1859.
Succession of Woodruff, No. 5699, 14 La. Ann. 295. New Orleans, April, 1859.

Logan v. Hickman, No. 5736, 14 La. Ann. 300. New Orleans, April, 1859.
McDermott v. Cannon, No. 5706, 14 La. Ann. 313. New Orleans, April, 1859.
Dohan v. Wilson, No. 5368, 14 La. Ann. 353. New Orleans, May, 1859.
Vienne v. Harris, No. 5823, 14 La. Ann. 382. New Orleans, May, 1859.
State v. Slave Jack, No. 5926, 14 La. Ann. 385. New Orleans, May, 1859.
Lewis v. Morgan, No. 6131, 14 La. Ann. 401. New Orleans, May, 1859.
Matta v. Henderson, No. 5286, 14 La. Ann. 473. New Orleans, May, 1859.
Gaiennie v. Freret, No. 5710, 14 La. Ann. 488. New Orleans, May, 1859.
Poree v. Cannon, No. 6006, 14 La. Ann. 501. New Orleans, May, 1859.
Bowman v. McKleroy, Bradford, and Sheriff, No. 5545, 14 La. Ann. 587. New Orleans, May, 1859.
Hickman v. Judge, No. 6353, 14 La. Ann. 504. New Orleans, June, 1859.
State v. Peter, a Slave, No. 6175, 14 La. Ann. 521. New Orleans, June, 1859.
State v. Mullen, No. 6146, 14 La. Ann. 570. New Orleans, June, 1859.
State v. Adams, No. 321, 14 La. Ann. 620. Alexandria, August, 1859.
State v. Charles, 14 La. Ann. 649. Monroe, July, 1859.
State v. Bennett, 14 La. Ann. 651. Monroe, July, 1859.
Faulk v. Hough, 14 La. Ann. 659. Monroe, July, 1859.
Deloach v. Elder, 14 La. Ann. 662. Monroe, July, 1859.
Smith v. Taylor, 14 La. Ann. 663. Monroe, July, 1859.
State v. Fuller [Marion], 14 La. Ann. 667. Monroe, July, 1859.
State v. Davis, 14 La. Ann. 678. Monroe, July, 1859.
Eager v. Brown, 14 La. Ann. 684. Monroe, July, 1859.
Boatner v. Wade, 14 La. Ann. 695. Monroe, July, 1859.
Price v. Ray, 14 La. Ann. 697. Monroe, July, 1859.
McLean v. Fulford, 14 La. Ann. 711. Monroe, July, 1859.
State v. Fuller [Robert], 14 La. Ann. 720, 726. Monroe, July, 1859.
Dyson v. Phelps, 14 La. Ann. 722. Monroe, July, 1859.
Alford v. Hughes and Randolph, 14 La. Ann. 727. Monroe, July, 1859.
Gardner v. Thibodeau, 14 La. Ann. 732. Opelousas, August, 1859.
Deshotels v. Soileau, 14 La. Ann. 745. Opelousas, August, 1859.
Hardy v. Voorhies, 14 La. Ann. 776. Opelousas, August, 1859.
Satterfield v. Keller, No. 315, 14 La. Ann. 606. Alexandria, August, 1859.
State v. Adams, No. 321, 14 La. Ann. 620. Alexandria, August, 1859.
Crawford v. Puckett, No. 306, 14 La. Ann. 693. Alexandria, August, 1859.
State v. Swift, No. 6318, 14 La. Ann. 651. New Orleans, December, 1859.

State v. Swift, No. 6318, 14 La. Ann. 827. New Orleans, December, 1859.
Interdiction of Rochon, f.w.c., No. 6532, 15 La. Ann. 6. New Orleans, January, 1860.
Levy v. Wise, No. 5962, 15 La. Ann. 38. New Orleans, January, 1860.
Tom v. Ernest, No. 6009, 15 La. Ann. 44. New Orleans, January, 1860.
Bateman v. Frisby and Kendig, No. 6242, 15 La. Ann. 58. New Orleans, January, 1860.
Caretta v. Lopez, No. 6028, 15 La. Ann. 64. New Orleans, February, 1860.
Bloom v. Beebe, No. 5921, 15 La. Ann. 65. New Orleans, February, 1860.
State v. Gore, No. 6507, 15 La. Ann. 79. New Orleans, February, 1860.
Pousargas v. *Natchez,* No. 6250, 15 La. Ann. 80. New Orleans, February, 1860.
Maille v. Blas, No. 5975, 15 La. Ann. 100. New Orleans, February, 1860.
State v. Slave Bill, No. 6560, 15 La. Ann. 114. New Orleans, February, 1860.
State v. Joshua, No. 6530, 15 La. Ann. 118. New Orleans, February, 1860.
Perrine, f.w.c., v. Planchard, No. 6031, 15 La. Ann. 133. New Orleans, March, 1860.
State v. George, No. 6501, 15 La. Ann. 145. New Orleans, March, 1860.
State v. Henry, No. 6239, 15 La. Ann. 297. New Orleans, March, 1860.
State v. Gutierrez, No. 6360, 15 La. Ann. 190. New Orleans, April, 1860.
Foster v. Mish, No. 6344, 15 La. Ann. 199. New Orleans, April, 1860.
Folse v. Kittridge, No. 6580, 15 La. Ann. 222. New Orleans, April, 1860.
Crawford v. Graves, No. 6706, 15 La. Ann. 243. New Orleans, April, 1860.
Palmes v. Kendig, No. 6279, 15 La. Ann. 264. New Orleans, April, 1860.
Rost and Montgomery v. Doyal, No. 6564, 15 La. Ann. 265. New Orleans, April, 1860.
Nouret v. Bollinger, No. 6313, 15 La. Ann. 293. New Orleans, April, 1860.
State v. Henry, No. 6239, 15 La. Ann. 297. New Orleans, May, 1860.
England v. Gripon, No. 6316, 15 La. Ann. 304. New Orleans, May, 1860.
Succession of Taylor, No. 6090, 15 La. Ann. 313. New Orleans, May, 1860.
Howes v. *Red Chief,* Nos. 5944, 6487, 15 La. Ann. 321. New Orleans, May, 1860.
Succession of Minville, No. 6447, 15 La. Ann. 342. New Orleans, May, 1860.
Freeman v. His Creditors, No. 6473, 15 La. Ann. 397. New Orleans, June, 1860.
Henderson v. Rost, No. 6726, 15 La. Ann. 405. New Orleans, June, 1860.

State v. Recorder (Miciesis), No. 6800, 15 La. Ann. 406. New Orleans, June, 1860.
Simons v. Jacobs, No. 6498, 15 La. Ann. 425. New Orleans, June, 1860.
Beverley v. *Empire,* No. 6323, 15 La. Ann. 432. New Orleans, June, 1860.
Buie v. Kendig, No. 6356, 15 La. Ann. 440. New Orleans, June, 1860.
A.M.E. Church v. City of New Orleans, No. 6291, 15 La. Ann. 441. New Orleans, June, 1860.
Pagett v. Curtis, No. 811, 15 La. Ann. 451. Monroe, July, 1860.
Andrews v. Kemp, not reported No. 812. Monroe, July, 1860.
State v. Solomon, 15 La. Ann. 463. Monroe, July, 1860.
Callaway v. Bobo, Sheriff, 15 La. Ann. 467. Monroe, July, 1860.
Brainard v. Sheriff, 15 La. Ann. 489. Monroe, July, 1860.
Atkinson v. Atkinson, 15 La. Ann. 591. Monroe, July, 1860.
Wood v. January, 15 La. Ann. 516. Monroe, July, 1860.
Burnham v. Hart, 15 La. Ann. 517. Monroe, July, 1860.
Virgin v. Dawson, 15 La. Ann. 532. Monroe, July, 1860.
Barbin v. Gaspard, No. 347, 15 La. Ann. 539. Alexandria, August, 1860.
Maillon v. Lynch, No. 359, 15 La. Ann. 547. Alexandria, August, 1860.
Louisiana, f.w.c., v. Estate of Baillio, No. 362, 15 La. Ann. 555. Alexandria, August, 1860.
Hyman v. Bailey, No. 360, 15 La. Ann. 560. Alexandria, August, 1860.
Décuir v. Lejeune, No. 353, 15 La. Ann. 569. Alexandria, August, 1860.
State v. Simon, 15 La. Ann. 568. New Orleans, December, 1860.
Décuir v. Levy and Bondy, No. 317, 15 La. Ann. 573. Alexandria, August, 1860.
Lazare v. Jacques, 15 La. Ann. 599. Opelousas, August, 1860.
Ney v. Richard, 15 La. Ann. 603. Opelousas, August, 1860.
Cahn v. Costa, No. 6252, 15 La. Ann. 612. New Orleans, November, 1860.
Broxton v. Bloom, No. 6665, 15 La. Ann. 618. New Orleans, November, 1860.
Paty v. Martin, No. 6368, 15 La. Ann. 620. New Orleans, November, 1860.
Walker v. Hays, No. 6606, 15 La. Ann. 640. New Orleans, December, 1860.
Syndic of Courcelle v. Vitry, f.w.c., No. 6544, 15 La. Ann. 653. New Orleans, December, 1860.
Boulin v. Maynard, No. 6396, 15 La. Ann. 658. New Orleans, December, 1860.

Harper v. Pierce, No. 6502, 15 La. Ann. 666. New Orleans, December, 1860.
Blair v. Collins, No. 6449, 15 La. Ann. 683. New Orleans, December, 1860.
Girault v. Zuntz, No. 6445, 15 La. Ann. 684. New Orleans, December, 1860.
State v. Howard, not reported No. 6798. New Orleans, [?], 1860.
Bill (Slave) v. Lacy and Co., not reported No. 6560. New Orleans, [?], 1860.
Euphrémie, f.w.c., v. Maran, f.w.c., and Noble, alias Jourdan, not reported No. 6740. New Orleans, filed 1860, decided 1865.
Abeilard v. Morel, not reported No. 6867. New Orleans, [?], 1860.
Mehle v. Lapeyrollerie, No. 6546, 16 La. Ann. 4. New Orleans, January, 1861.
Bell v. Lacy, No. 6563, 16 La. Ann. 51. New Orleans, January, 1861.
Pelham v. *Messenger,* No. 6629, 16 La. Ann. 99. New Orleans, February, 1861.
Morrison v. White, No. 442, 16 La. Ann. 100. New Orleans, February, 1861.
Gause v. Bullard, No. 6533, 16 La. Ann. 107. New Orleans, February, 1861.
Ford v. Danks, No. 18, 16 La. Ann. 119. New Orleans, February, 1861.
Ranson v. Labranche, No. 6526, 16 La. Ann. 121. New Orleans, February, 1861.
State v. Moses, not reported. New Orleans, February, 1861.
State v. Karn, No. 177, 16 La. Ann. 183. New Orleans, March, 1861.
Carmena v. Blaney, No. 116, 16 La. Ann. 245. New Orleans, April, 1861.
McCaleb v. Douglas, No. 97, 16 La. Ann. 327. New Orleans, May, 1861.
State v. Mulholland, 16 La. Ann. 376. New Orleans, December, 1861.
State v. Brown, No. 317, 16 La. Ann. 384. New Orleans, December, 1861.
State v. Walters, No. 294, 16 La. Ann. 400. New Orleans, January, 1862.
State v. David, slave of Drake, not reported No. 312. New Orleans, January, 1862.
State v. Miciesis, not reported No. 1-6902. New Orleans, January, 1862.
Jones and Daugharty v. Goza, No. 90, 16 La. Ann. 428. New Orleans, February, 1862.
State v. Peyton, not reported No. 388. New Orleans, February, 1862.

State v. Slave Leonidas, not reported No. 429. New Orleans, filed March, 1862.
Euphrémie, f.w.c., v. Maran, f.w.c., and Noble, alias Jourdan, not reported No. 6741, New Orleans, May, 1865.
Hull v. McLauren, No. 6812, 17 La. Ann. 35. New Orleans, May, 1865.
Huntington v. Brown, No. 15, 17 La. Ann. 48. New Orleans, May, 1865.
Mouras v. *A. C. Brewer,* No. 6856, 17 La. Ann. 82. New Orleans, May, 1865.
Coulon v. Semmes, No. 141, 17 La. Ann. 119. New Orleans, June, 1865.
Succession of Chappel: Hannah, f.w.c., v. Eggleston, No. 198, 17 La. Ann. 174. New Orleans, June, 1865.
Murphy v. Guiterez, No. 506, 17 La. Ann. 269. New Orleans, December, 1865.
Dejona, f.w.c., v. Steamboat, No. 6781, 17 La. Ann. 277. New Orleans, December, 1865.
Gatlin v. Kendig, No. 6894, 18 La. Ann. 118. New Orleans, February, 1866.
Chapman v. Matthews, No. 438, 18 La. Ann. 118. New Orleans, February, 1866.
Morphy v. Blanchin, No. 573, 18 La. Ann. 133. New Orleans, February, 1866.
Henderson v. Montgomery, No. 388, 18 La. Ann. 211. New Orleans, March, 1866.
Walker v. Cucullu, No. 326, 18 La. Ann. 246. New Orleans, March, 1866.
Succession of Olivier, 18 La. Ann. 594. Opelousas, September, 1866.
Lynch v. Wieman and McRee, No. 270, 18 La. Ann. 640. New Orleans, November, 1866.
Succession of Poindexter, No. 805, 19 La. Ann. 22. New Orleans, January, 1867.
Fenn v. Carr, No. 884, 19 La. Ann. 106. New Orleans, March, 1867.
Folse v. New Orleans Coast and Lafourche Transportation Co., No. 301, 19 La. Ann. 199. New Orleans, April, 1867.
Wainwright v. Bridges, No. 1305, 19 La. Ann. 234. New Orleans, May, 1867.
Austin v. Sandell, No. 1317, 19 La. Ann. 309. New Orleans, June, 1867.
Addison v. Seltoon, No. 1263, 19 La. Ann. 352. New Orleans, June, 1867.
Tate v. Fletcher, No. 1299, 19 La. Ann. 371. New Orleans, June, 1867.

Gremillon v. Crousillac, No. 1204, 19 La. Ann. 377. New Orleans, June, 1867.
Courtney v. Shelton, No. 1271, 19 La. Ann. 380. New Orleans, June, 1867.
Posey v. Martingley, No. 1265, 19 La. Ann. 384. New Orleans, June, 1867.
Martin v. Kelly, No. 48, 19 La. Ann. 444. Natchitoches, August, 1867.
Halley v. Hoeffner, No. 1071, 19 La. Ann. 518. New Orleans, December, 1867.
Dickinson v. Maynard, No. 6760, 20 La. Ann. 66. New Orleans, December, 1867.
Delaporte v. Bourg, No. 1173, 20 La. Ann. 152. New Orleans, February, 1868.
Bourgeois v. Billin and Perkins, No. 1560, 20 La. Ann. 153. New Orleans, February, 1868.
Armstrong v. Bach, No. 1683, 20 La. Ann. 190. New Orleans, March, 1868.
Posey v. Driggs, No. 1266, 20 La. Ann. 199. New Orleans, March, 1868.
Levee Commissioners v. Harris, No. 102, 20 La. Ann. 201. New Orleans, March, 1868.
McAlister v. Burton, No. 405, 20 La. Ann. 205. New Orleans, March, 1868.
Jennings v. Gosselin, No. 1644, 20 La. Ann. 214. New Orleans, March, 1868.
Lapice v. Bowman, No. 1658, 20 La. Ann. 234. New Orleans, March, 1868.
Murphy v. Guiterez, No. 506, 20 La. Ann. 407. New Orleans, June, 1868.
Joffrion v. Wilson, No. 1334, 20 La. Ann. 412. New Orleans, June, 1868.
Fisk v. Bergerot, No. 6814, 21 La. Ann. 111. New Orleans, February, 1869.
Thomas v. Hacket, No. 2068, 21 La. Ann. 164. New Orleans, March, 1869.
Lytle v. Whicher and Henshaw, No. 430, 21 La. Ann. 182. New Orleans, March, 1869.
Gosselin v. Womack and Thompson, No. 2129, 21 La. Ann. 193. New Orleans, March, 1869.
Kleinpeter v. Harrigan, No. 2088, 21 La. Ann. 196. New Orleans, March, 1869.
Casanave v. Bingaman, No. 1639, 21 La. Ann. 435. New Orleans, May, 1869.
Haden v. Phillips and Foster, No. 163, 21 La. Ann. 517. Natchitoches, August, 1869.

Armstrong v. Lecomte, No. 129, 21 La. Ann. 527. Natchitoches, August, 1869.

Porter v. Brown, No. 137, 21 La. Ann. 532. Natchitoches, August, 1869.

Dranguet v. Rost, No. 174, 21 La. Ann. 538. Natchitoches, August, 1869.

Groves v. Clark and Carnal, No. 139, 21 La. Ann. 567. Natchitoches, August, 1869.

Succession of Rice, No. 705, 21 La. Ann. 614. Opelousas, September, 1869.

Levy v. Gremillion, No. 687, 21 La. Ann. 635. Opelousas, September, 1869.

Heirs of Bedell v. Hayes, No. 703, 21 La. Ann. 643. Opelousas, September, 1869.

Succession of Patin, No. 723, 21 La. Ann. 661. Opelousas, September, 1869.

Nunez v. Winston, No. 706, 21 La. Ann. 666. Opelousas, September, 1869.

Sandidge v. Sanderson, No. 2473, 21 La. Ann. 757. New Orleans, December, 1869.

Satterfield v. Spurlock, No. 2495, 21 La. Ann. 771. New Orleans, December, 1869.

Hebert v. Chastant, No. 2590, 22 La. Ann. 152. New Orleans, March, 1870.

Barrow v. Heirs of Bird, No. 2706, 22 La. Ann. 407. New Orleans, March, 1870.

Walker v. Ducros, No. 1804, 22 La. Ann. 214. New Orleans, April, 1870.

Merritt v. Merle, No. 1379, 22 La. Ann. 257. New Orleans, April, 1870.

Rodriguez v. Bienvenu, No. 2829, 22 La. Ann. 300. New Orleans, April, 1870.

Seely v. Blanchard, No. 2581, 22 La. Ann. 409. New Orleans, April, 1870.

Succession of Woodward, No. 1649, 22 La. Ann. 305. New Orleans, May, 1870.

Allen v. Tarleton, No. 697, 22 La. Ann. 427. Opelousas, June, 1870.

Conrad v. Callery, No. 710, 22 La. Ann. 428. Opelousas, June, 1870.

Castille v. Offut, No. 676, 22 La. Ann. 430. Opelousas, June, 1870.

Smith v. McWaters, No. 708, 22 La. Ann. 431. Opelousas, June, 1870.

Thompson v. Simmons, No. 91, 22 La. Ann. 451. Monroe, July, 1870.

Wise v. Hill, No. 65, 22 La. Ann. 469. Monroe, July, 1870.

Succession of Ross, No. 173, 22 La. Ann. 480. Monroe, July, 1870.

Powell v. Daniell, No. 3186, 23 La. Ann. 289. New Orleans, April, 1871.

Osborn v. Osborn, No. 2534, 23 La. Ann. 496. New Orleans, May, 1871.

Smith v. Henderson, No. 197, 23 La. Ann. 649. Monroe, July, 1871.
Rabun v. Pierson, No. 205, 23 La. Ann. 696. Monroe, July, 1871.
Heirs of Hoover v. York, No. 3776, 24 La. Ann. 375. New Orleans, May, 1872.
Heirs of Brown v. Jacob, No. 170, 24 La. Ann. 526. Monroe, July, 1872.
Succession of Caballero, No. 2255, 24 La. Ann. 573. New Orleans, November, 1872.
Bruin v. Sasser, No. 3210, 25 La. Ann. 224. New Orleans, March, 1873.
Consolidated Association v. Blanc, No. 2676, 25 La. Ann. 226. New Orleans, March, 1873.
DeLaLande v. Poydras, No. 3228, 25 La. Ann. 405. New Orleans, May, 1873.
Dupérier v. Darby, No. 771, 25 La. Ann. 477. Opelousas, June, 1873.
Dejean v. Arnaud, No. 601, 25 La. Ann. 521. Opelousas, June, 1873.
Winter v. Tournoir, No. 4584, 25 La. Ann. 611. New Orleans, November, 1873.
Pierre v. Fontenette, No. 4757, 25 La. Ann. 617. New Orleans, November, 1873.
Brusle v. Hamilton, No. 5081, 26 La. Ann. 144. New Orleans, March, 1874.
Succession of Randall, No. 5057, 26 La. Ann. 163. New Orleans, March, 1874.
Succession of Hebert, No. 5674, 27 La. Ann. 300. New Orleans, April, 1875.
Neel v. Hibard, No. 6737, 30 La. Ann. 808. New Orleans, April, 1878.
Succession of Pearce, No. 801, 30 La. Ann. 1168. New Orleans, April, 1878.
Succession of Hebert, No. 1116, 33 La. Ann. 1099. Opelousas, July, 1881.
Succession of Colwell, No. 8511, 34 La. Ann. 265. New Orleans, March, 1882.
Succession of Fortier, No. 13,094, 51 La. Ann. 1562. New Orleans, April, 1899.
Sterrett v. Samuel, No. 14,155, 108 La. Ann. 346 (32 So. 428). New Orleans, May, 1902.
Johnson's Heirs v. Raphael, No. 16,241, 117 La. 967 (42 So. 470). New Orleans, November, 1906.
Briggs v. McLaughlin, No. 19,587, 134 La. 133 (63 So. 851). New Orleans, December, 1913.

Succession of Ransom, No. 6325, 12 Orleans App. 246. New Orleans, March, 1915.
Marzette v. Cronk, No. 20,880, 141 La. 437 (75 So. 107). New Orleans, April, 1917.
Wiley v. Bowman, No. 22,761, 144 La. 181 (80 So. 243). New Orleans, June, 1918.
Succession of Blackburn, No. 25,485, 154 La. 618 (98 So. 43). New Orleans, October, 1923.
Succession of Young, No. 28,403, 166 La. 285 (117 So. 150). New Orleans, April, 1928.
Anderson v. Thomas, No. 31,645, 174 La. 721 (141 So. 441). New Orleans, April, 1932.

Court of Errors and Appeals in Criminal Matters

State v. Seaborne, alias Moore, 8 Rob. 518. New Orleans, July, 1843.
State v. Bill, 8 Rob. 527. New Orleans, February, 1844.
State v. George, 8 Rob. 535. New Orleans, July, 1844.
State v. Lennon, 8 Rob. 543. Opelousas, September, 1844.
State v. McCoy, 8 Rob. 545. New Orleans, February, 1844.
State v. Hornsby, No. 19, 8 Rob. 554. Opelousas, September, 1844.
State v. Kennedy, No. 18, 8 Rob. 590. Opelousas, September, 1844.

First District Court of New Orleans

Cruzat v. State (Slave Victoire, alias Mamzelle), No. 10,723. New Orleans, November, 1855.
Elizabeth v. State (Slave Annie, alias Amelia), No. 10,737. New Orleans, November, 1855.
Fortier v. State (Slave Menos, alias Aimée), No. 10,736. New Orleans, November, 1855.
Fortin v. State (Slave Adeline), No. 10,734. New Orleans, November, 1855.
Murphy v. State (Slave Martha), No. 10,680. New Orleans, November, 1855.
Perret v. State (Slave Ellen), No. 10,686. New Orleans, November, 1855.
Widow Bourg v. State (Slave Gaston Delille), No. 10,735. New Orleans, November, 1855.
Widow Clay v. State (Slave Justine), No. 10,764. New Orleans, November, 1855.

United States Supreme Court

Amiable Lucy v. U.S., 6 Cranch (U.S.) 330. February, 1810.
Alerta v. Moran, 9 Cranch (U.S.) 359. March, 1815.
The *Joseph Segunda,* 5 Wheat (U.S.) 338. February, 1820.
The *Mary Ann,* 8 Wheat (U.S.) 380. February, 1823.
The *Joseph Segunda,* 10 Wheat (U.S.) 312. February, 1825.
U.S. v. Preston (*Joseph Segunda*), 3 Pet. (U.S.) 57. January, 1830.
U.S. v. *Garonne, Fortune,* 11 Pet. (U.S.) 73. January, 1837.
Heirs of Emerson v. Hall, 13 Pet. (U.S.) 409. January, 1839.
Groves and Graham v. Slaughter, 15 Pet. (U.S.) 449. January, 1841.
Gaines v. Chew, 2 Howard (U.S.) 619. January, 1844.
Michoud v. Howard, 4 Howard (U.S.) 503. January, 1846.
Waring v. Clarke, 5 Howard (U.S.) 441. January, 1847.
Erwin v. Lowry, 7 Howard (U.S.) 172. January, 1849.
Norris v. Crocker, 13 Howard (54 U.S.) 429. January, 1852.
Executor of McDonogh v. Murdock, 15 Howard (U.S.) 367. December, 1853.
Dred Scott v. Sandford, 19 Howard (U.S.) 393. December, 1857.
Adams v. Preston, 22 Howard (U.S.) 473. December, 1859.
Generes v. Campbell, 11 Wallace (U.S.) 193. December, 1870.
Handlin v. Wickliffe, 12 Wallace (U.S.) 173. December, 1870.
White v. Hart, 13 Wallace (U.S.) 646. December, 1871.
Palmer v. Marston, 14 Wallace (U.S.) 10. December, 1871.
Slaughterhouse Cases, 16 Wallace (U.S.) 36. December, 1872.
Boyce v. Tabb, 18 Wallace (U.S.) 546. October, 1873.

Cases from Other States and Great Britain

Alabama

State v. Clarissa, a Slave, 11 Ala. 57 (1847).
Wyatt, a Slave, v. State, 25 Ala. 9 (1854).
Mangham v. Cox and Waring, 29 Ala. 81 (1856).
Massey v. Cole, 29 Ala. 364 (1856).
Bob, a Slave, v. State, 32 Ala. 497 (1858).
Dinah, a Slave, v. State, 39 Ala. 359 (1864).
William, a Slave, v. State, 39 Ala. 532 (1865).

Delaware

Page v. Vandegrift, 5 Harrington 176 (Del. 1849).

Florida

Simon, a Slave, v. State, 5 Fla. 285 (1853).

Georgia

Barry v. State, 10 Ga. 511 (1851).
Jim, a Slave, v. State, 15 Ga. 535 (1854).

Kentucky

Edwards v. Vail, 3 J.J. Marsh 595 (Ken. 1836).
Bracken v. Steamboat *Gulnare,* 16 B. Mon. 444 (Ken. 1855).
Meekin v. Thomas, 17 B. Mon. 710 (Ken. 1857).

Maryland

Steam Navigation Co. v. Hungerford, 6 Gil and John. 291 (Md. 1834).
State v. Baltimore and Susquehanna Steam Co., 13 Md. 181 (1859).

Massachusetts

Commonwealth v. Aves, 18 Pick. 193 (Mass. 1836).

Mississippi

Isham, a Slave, v. State, 6 How. Miss. 35 (1841).
Peter, a Slave, v. State, 4 S. and M. 31 (Miss. 1844).
Van Buren, a Slave, v. State, 24 Miss. 512 (1852).
Jordan, a Slave, v. State, 32 Miss. 288 (1858).
Simon, a Slave, v. State, 37 Miss. 288 (1858).
Mitchell v. Wells, 37 Miss. 235 (1859).

Missouri

Eaton v. Vaughan, 9 Mo. 743 (1846).
Calvert v. Rider, 20 Mo. 146 (1854).
Phelps v. Evans, 38 Mo. 305 (1866).

New Jersey

Gibbons v. Morse, 2 Halsted 253 (N.J. 1821).
Cutter v. Moore, 3 Halsted 219 (N.J. 1825).
Gibbs v. Mennard, 6 Paige 258 (N.J. 1837).

North Carolina

State v. Hale, 2 Hawks 582 (N.C. 1823).
State v. Mann, 2 Devereux 263 (N.C. 1829).
State v. Charity, 2 Devereux 543 (N.C. 1830).
State v. George, a Slave, 5 Jones N.C. 233 (1858).

South Carolina

Witsell v. Earnest, 1 N. and McCord 161 (S.C. 1818).
State v. Raines, 3 McCord 538 (S.C. 1826).
Richardson v. Dukes, 4 McCord 156 (S.C. 1827).
Jennings v. Fundeburg, 4 McCord 161 (S.C. 1827).
Ellis v. Walsh, 4 Richardson 468 (S.C. 1851).

Tennessee

Elijah, a Slave, v. State, 20 Tenn. 102 (1839).
Duncan v. State, 7 Humphreys 148 (Tenn. 1846).
Ann v. State, 11 Humphreys 159 (Tenn. 1850).
Scruggs v. Davis, 5 Sneed 261 (Tenn. 1857).

Virginia

Case v. Woolley, 6 Dana 17 (Va. 1837).
Bailey v. Poindexter, 14 Grattan 132 (Va. 1858).

Great Britain

Somerset v. Stewart, Left 1 (1772); 20 Howell St. Tr. 1.
The Slave, Grace, 2 Haggard Admiralty 94 (1827).

OFFICIAL DOCUMENTS

Acts . . . of the Legislative Council of the Territory of Orleans. New Orleans, 1805–1811. Cited by year as *Orleans Territory Acts*.

Acts . . . of the Legislature of the State of Louisiana. New Orleans, 1812–1859; Baton Rouge, 1859. Cited by year as *Louisiana Acts*.

Civil Code of the State of Louisiana. New Orleans, 1825.

Civil Code of the State of Louisiana. Edited by Thomas Gibson Morgan. New Orleans, 1853.

Civil Code of the State of Louisiana. New Orleans, 1867.

Code of Practice in Civil Cases for the State of Louisiana. New Orleans, 1824.

Code of Practice in Civil Cases for the State of Louisiana. New Orleans, 1830.

Code of Practice in Civil Cases for the State of Louisiana. New Orleans, 1839.

Collections of Regulations, Edicts, Declarations, and Decrees Concerning the Commerce, Administration of Justice, and the Policy of the French Colonies of America. Paris, 1765.

Benjamin Wall Dart, ed. *Constitutions of the State of Louisiana and Selected Federal Laws*. Indianapolis, 1932.

A Digest of the Civil Laws Now in Force in the Territory of Orleans. New Orleans, 1808; rpr. Baton Rouge, 1971.

A Digest of the Decisions of the Supreme Court of the United States in Louisiana Cases. Edited by John Edwards Leonard. New Orleans, 1875.

A Digest of the Statute Laws of Kentucky. 6 vols. Frankfort, 1834.

First District Court of New Orleans. *Minute Book, 1855–1856*.

Gales, Joseph. *Annals of Congress*. 2 vols. Washington, D.C., 1834.

Historical Records Survey, Works Progress Administration. *Case Papers Synopsis, United States District Court of Louisiana, Nos. 1,806–3,000*. 1940–1941.

———. *Conspicuous Cases in the United States District Court of Louisiana*. 10 vols. 1940–1941.

———. *Inventory of the State Archives of Louisiana, Series II, the Judiciary: No. 2, the Supreme Court of Louisiana*, 1939.

———. *Judicial and Congressional District Boundary Law in Louisiana*. New Orleans, 1939.

Kerr, Lewis. *An Exposition of the Criminal Laws of the Territory of Orleans. . . .* New Orleans, 1806.

Laws of the Territory of Louisiana Passed by the Governor and Judges Assembled in Legislature. St. Louis, 1810.

The Laws of Las Siete Partidas Which Are Still in Force in the State of Louisiana. 2 vols. L. Moreau Lislet and Henry Carleton, trans. New Orleans, 1820.

Louisiana Digest: 1809 to Date. 20 vols. St. Paul, Minn., 1959.

Louisiana Supreme Court, Minute Book, Western District, 1813–1843.

Morehead, C. Z., and Mason Brown, comps. *A Digest of the Statute Laws of Kentucky of a Public and Permanent Nature*. Frankfort, 1834.

Reports of Cases Argued and Determined in the Supreme Court of Louisiana and the Superior Court of the Territory of Orleans. 30 vols. St. Paul, Minn., 1913.

United States Census (Louisiana), 1810–1860.

NEWSPAPERS

Louisiana Courier (New Orleans)
New Orleans *Bee*
New Orleans *Daily Picayune*

ARTICLES AND ESSAYS

Batiza Rodolfo. "The Influence of Spanish Law in Louisiana." *Tulane Law Review,* XXIII (December, 1958), 29–34.

———. "The Louisiana Civil Code of 1808: Its Actual Sources and Present Relevance." *Tulane Law Review,* XLVI (September, 1971), 4–166.

———. "Sources of the Civil Code of 1808, Facts and Speculation: A Rejoinder." *Tulane Law Review,* XLVI (April, 1972), 628–52.

Baudouin, Louis. "The Influence of the Code Napoleon." *Tulane Law Review,* XXIII (December, 1958), 21–28.

Benjamin, Judah P. "Negroes as Property." In *The Louisiana Book: Selections from the Literature of the State,* edited by Thomas McCaleb. New Orleans, 1894.

Billings, Warren M. "The Legal Treatment of Slavery in Early America." *Plantation Society,* I (June, 1979), 265–71.

———. Review of *A History of the Louisiana Civil Code: The Formative Years, 1803–1839,* by Richard Holcomb Kilbourne, Jr. *Louisiana History,* XXX (Summer, 1989), 325.

Brown, Elizabeth Gaspar. "Legal Systems in Conflict: Orleans Territory, 1804–1812." *American Journal of Legal History,* I (January, 1957), 35–75.

Burns, Francis P. "Stephen Henderson." New Orleans *Times-Picayune Dixie Roto,* September 24, 1950.

Cable, George Washington. "The Dance in Place Congo." *Century,* XXXI (February, 1886), 517–32.

Cross, Thomas Jones. "The Eclecticism of the Law of Louisiana." *American Law Review,* LV (May–June, 1921), 405–25.

Darkis, Fred R., Jr. "Madame Lalaurie of New Orleans." *Louisiana History,* XXIII (Fall, 1982), 383–99.

Dart, Henry Plauché. "History of the Supreme Court of Louisiana." In *The Celebration of the Centenary of the Supreme Court of Louisiana.* New Orleans, 1913.

———. "The Influence of the Ancient Laws of Spain on the Jurisprudence of Louisiana." *Tulane Law Review,* VI (December, 1931), 83–93.

———. "The Law in Louisiana." *Loyola Law Journal,* II (June, 1921), 1–17, and III (January, 1922), 1–22.

———. "The Legal Institutions of Louisiana." *Southern Law Quarterly,* III (1918), 247–80.

———. "The Place of the Civil Law in Louisiana." *Tulane Law Review,* IV (February, 1930), 163–77.

Dart, William Kernan. "Justices of the Supreme Court." *Louisiana Reports,* CXXXIII (1913), lxxiv–xc.

———. "The Louisiana Judicial System." *Louisiana Digest Annotated,* I (1917), 1–61.

Ellis, T. C. W. "The Louisiana Bar, 1813–1913." *Louisiana Reports,* CXXXIII (1913), lxvi–lxxx.

Everett, Donald Edward. "Emigrés and Militiamen: Free Persons of Color in New Orleans, 1803–1815." *Journal of Negro History,* XXXVIII (October, 1953), 377–402.

Fede, Andrew. "Legal Protection for Slave Buyers in the U.S. South: A Caveat Concerning *Caveat Emptor.*" *American Journal of Legal History,* XXXI (October, 1987), 322–58.

———. "Legitimized Violent Slave Abuse in the American South, 1619–1865: A Case Study of Laws and Social Change in Six Southern States." *American Journal of Legal History,* XXIX (April, 1985), 93–150.

———. "Toward the Solution of the Slave Law Dilemma: A Critique of Tushnet's *The American Law of Slavery.*" *Law and History Review,* II (October, 1984), 301–11.

Fenner, C. P. "Jurisprudence of the Supreme Court of Louisiana." *Louisiana Reports,* CXXXIII (1913), lxi–lxvi.

Fernandez, Mark. "From Chaos to Continuity: Early Reforms of the Supreme Court of Louisiana, 1845–1852." *Louisiana History,* XXVIII (Winter, 1987), 19–36.

Finkelman, Paul. "Exploring Southern Legal History." *North Carolina Law Review,* LXIV (November, 1985), 77–116.

———. "Slavery and the Constitutional Convention: Making a Covenant with Death." In *Beyond Confederation: Origins of the Constitution and American National Identity,* edited by Richard Beeman, Stephen Botein, and Edward C. Carter II. Chapel Hill, 1987.

———. "Slaves as Fellow Servants: Ideology, Law, and Industrialization." *American Journal of Legal History,* XXXI (October, 1987), 269–305.

Flanigan, Daniel J. "Criminal Procedure in Slave Trials in the Antebellum South." *Journal of Southern History,* XL (November, 1974), 537–64.

Franklin, Mitchell. "The Eighteenth *Brumaire* in Louisiana: Talleyrand and the Spanish Medieval Legal System of 1806." *Tulane Law Review,* XVI (April, 1942), 514–61.

———. "Equity in Louisiana: The Role of Article 21." *Tulane Law Review,* IX (June, 1935), 485–516.

———. "The Place of Thomas Jefferson in the Expulsion of Spanish Medieval Law from Louisiana." *Tulane Law Review,* XVI (April, 1942), 319–38.

Gayarré, Charles. "The New Orleans Bench and Bar in 1823." In *The Louisiana Book: Selections from the Literature of the State,* edited by Thomas McCaleb. New Orleans, 1894.

Genovese, Eugene D. "The Medical and Insurance Costs of Slaveholding in the Cotton Belt." *Journal of Negro History,* XLV (July, 1960), 144–55.

———. "Slavery in the Legal History of the South and the Nation." *Texas Law Review,* LIX (May, 1981), 969–98.

Groner, Samuel B. "Louisiana Law: Its Development in the First Quarter-Century of American Rule." *Louisiana Law Review,* VIII (January, 1948), 350–82.

Helis, Thomas W. "Of Generals and Jurists: The Judicial System of New Orleans Under Union Occupation, May, 1862–April, 1865." *Louisiana History,* XXIX (Spring, 1988), 143–62.

Hendrix, James Paisley, Jr. "The Efforts to Reopen the African Slave Trade in Louisiana." *Louisiana History,* X (Spring, 1969), 97–124.

Hindus, Michael Stephen. "Black Justice Under White Law: Criminal Prosecutions of Blacks in Antebellum South Carolina." *Journal of American History,* LXIII (December, 1976), 575–99.

Hood, John T., Jr. "The History and Development of the Louisiana Civil Code." *Tulane Law Review,* XXIII (December, 1958), 7–20.

Horowitz, Harold W. "Choice-of-Law Decisions Involving Slavery: 'Interest Analysis' in the Early Nineteenth Century." *UCLA Law Review,* XVII (February, 1970), 587–601.

Howe, William Wirt. "Memoir of François-Xavier Martin." In *The History of Louisiana, from the Earliest Period,* by François-Xavier Martin. New Orleans, 1882.

———. "Roman and Civil Law in America." *Harvard Law Review,* XVI (March, 1903), 342–58.

Howington, Arthur F. "Not in the Condition of a Horse or an Ox." *Tennessee Historical Quarterly,* XXXIV (Fall, 1975), 249–63.

Ingersoll, Thomas N. "Free Blacks in a Slave Society: New Orleans, 1718–1812." *William and Mary Quarterly,* XLVIII (April, 1991), 173–200.

Ireland, Gordon. "Louisiana's Legal System Appraised." *Tulane Law Review,* XI (June, 1837), 585–98.

Johnson, Michael P. "Planters and Patriarchy: Charleston, 1800–1860." *Journal of Southern History,* XLVI (February, 1980), 45–72.

Jones, Howard. "The Peculiar Institution and National Honor: The Case of the *Creole* Slave Revolt." *Civil War History,* XXI (March, 1975), 28–50.

Kendall, John Smith. "The Huntsmen of Black Ivory." *Louisiana Historical Quarterly,* XXIV (January–October, 1941), 9–34.

———. "New Orleans' Peculiar Institution." *Louisiana Historical Quarterly,* XXIII (July, 1940), 864–86.

———. "Shadow over the City." *Louisiana Historical Quarterly,* XXII (January, 1939), 142–65.

Kiple, Virginia H. "Black Tongue and Black Men: Pellagra and Slavery in the Antebellum South." *Journal of Southern History,* XLIII (August, 1977), 411–28.

Kotlikoff, Lawrence J., and Anton J. Rupert. "The Manumission of Slaves in New Orleans, 1827–1846." *Southern Studies,* XIX (Summer, 1980), 172–81.

Kunkel, Paul A. "Modifications in Louisiana Negro Legal Status Under Louisiana Constitutions, 1812–1957." *Journal of Negro History,* XLIV (January, 1959), 3–25.

LaChance, Paul F. "The 1809 Immigration of Saint-Domingue Refugees to New Orleans: Reception, Integration, and Impact." *Louisiana History,* XXIX (Spring, 1988), 109–41.

———. "The Politics of Fear: French Louisianians and the Slave Trade, 1786–1800." *Plantation Society,* I (June, 1979), 162–200.

Lang, James O. "Gloom Envelops New Orleans, April 24 to May 2, 1862." *Louisiana History,* I (Fall, 1960), 281–89.

Lyons, Grant. "Louisiana and the Livingston Criminal Codes." *Louisiana History,* XV (Summer, 1974), 243–72.

McLoughlin, James J. "The Black Code." *Louisiana Historical Quarterly,* VIII (1914–15), 28–35.

Miller, Ben Robertson. "Judicial Reorganization." *Tulane Law Review,* VII (February, 1933), 235–51.

Mills, Gary B. "Miscegenation and the Free Negro in Antebellum 'Anglo' Alabama: A Reexamination of Southern Race Relations." *Journal of American History,* LXVIII (June, 1981), 16–34.

Moody, V. Alton. "Slavery on Louisiana Sugar Plantations." *Louisiana Historical Quarterly,* VII (April, 1924), 191–301.

Moore, Wilbert E. "Slave Law and the Social Structure." *Journal of Negro History,* XXVII (April, 1941), 171–202.

Morris, Thomas D. "'As If the Injury Was Effected by the Natural Elements of Air, or Fire': Slave Wrongs and the Liability of Masters." *Law and Society Review,* XVI (1981–82), 569–99.

———. "'Villeinage . . . as it Existed in England, reflects but little light on our subject': The Problem of the 'Sources' of Southern Slave Law." *American Journal of Legal History,* XXXII (April, 1988), 95–137.

Nash, A. E. Keir. "Fairness and Formalism in the Trials of Blacks in the State Supreme Courts of the Old South." *Virginia Law Review,* LVI (February, 1970), 64–99.

———. "A More Equitable Past? Southern Supreme Courts and the Protection of the Antebellum Negro." *North Carolina Law Review,* XLVIII (February, 1970), 197–242.

———. "Reason of Slavery: Understanding the Judicial Role in the Peculiar Institution of Slavery." *Vanderbilt Law Review,* XXXII (January, 1979), 7–218.

———. "Texas Justice in the Age of Slavery: Appeals Concerning Blacks and the Antebellum State Supreme Court." *Houston Law Review,* VIII (January, 1971), 438–56.

———. "The Texas Supreme Court and the Trial Rights of Blacks, 1845–1860." *Journal of American History,* LVIII (December, 1971), 622–42.

Nelson, Alice Dunbar. "People of Color in Louisiana." *Journal of Negro History,* I (October, 1916), 361–76.

"Northern and Southern Negro Laws." *De Bow's Review,* XXIII (December, 1857), 561–70.

Nott, G. William. "How Louisiana Escaped the Inquisition." New Orleans *Item Magazine,* May 11, 1924, p. 3.

Oppenheim, Leonard. "The Law of Slaves: A Comparative Study of the

Roman and Louisiana Systems." *Tulane Law Review,* XIV (April, 1940), 384–406.

———. "The Revocation of a Testamentary Disinherison." *Tulane Law Review,* XVI (December, 1941), 97–110.

Palmer, Vernon V. "The Death of a Code—The Birth of a Digest." *Tulane Law Review,* LXIII (December, 1988), 221–64.

Pascal, Robert A. "Sources of the *Digest of 1808:* A Reply to Professor Batiza." *Tulane Law Review,* XLVI (April, 1972), 603–27.

Rankin, David C. "Black Slaveholders: The Case of Andrew Durnford." *Southern Studies,* XXI (Fall, 1982), 343–47.

———. "The Impact of the Civil War on the Free Colored Community of New Orleans." *Perspectives in American History,* XI (1977–78), 379–416.

———. "The Origins of Black Leadership in New Orleans During Reconstruction." *Journal of Southern History,* XL (August, 1974), 417–40.

———. "The Tannenbaum Thesis Reconsidered: Slavery and Race Relations in Antebellum Louisiana." *Southern Studies,* XVIII (Spring, 1979), 5–31.

Reinders, Robert C. "Slavery in New Orleans in the Decade Before the Civil War." *Mid-America,* XLIV (October, 1962), 211–21.

Richter, William L. "Slavery in Baton Rouge, 1820–1860." *Louisiana History,* X (Spring, 1969), 125–46.

Ridell, William R. "Le Code Noir." *Journal of Negro History,* X (July, 1925), 322–28.

Savitt, Todd L. "Slave Life Insurance in Virginia and North Carolina." *Journal of Southern History,* XLIII (November, 1977), 583–600.

Schafer, Judith Kelleher. "'Guaranteed Against the Vices and Maladies Prescribed by Law': Consumer Protection, the Law of Slave Sales, and the Supreme Court in Antebellum Louisiana." *American Journal of Legal History,* XXXI (October, 1987), 306–21.

———. "The Immediate Impact of Nat Turner's Insurrection in New Orleans." *Louisiana History,* XXI (Fall, 1980), 361–76.

———. "The Long Arm of the Law: Slave Criminals and the Supreme Court in Antebellum Louisiana." *Tulane Law Review,* LX (June, 1987), 1247–68.

———. "New Orleans Slavery in 1850 as Seen in Advertisements." *Journal of Southern History,* XLVII (February, 1981), 33–56.

———. "'Open and Notorious Concubinage': The Emancipation of Slave

Mistresses by Will and the Supreme Court in Antebellum Louisiana." *Louisiana History,* XXVII (Spring, 1987), 165–82.

Seip, Terry L. "Slaves and Free Negroes in Alexandria 1850–1860." *Louisiana History,* X (Spring, 1969), 147–65.

"Slave Marriages." *De Bow's Review,* XIX (July, 1855), 130.

Smith, J. Denson. "The Louisiana Criminal Code." *Louisiana Law Review,* V (1942–44), 1–82.

Stahl, Annie Lee West. "The Free Negro in Ante-Bellum Louisiana." *Louisiana Historical Quarterly,* XXV (1942), 301–96.

Stone, Ferdinand. "The Civil Code of 1808 for the Territory of Orleans." *Tulane Law Review,* XXIII (December, 1958), 1–6.

Sweig, Donald M. "Reassessing the Human Dimension of the Interstate Slave Trade." *Prologue,* XII (Spring, 1980), 5–27.

Sydnor, Charles. "The Southerner and the Laws." *Journal of Southern History,* VI (February, 1940), 3–23.

Tansey, Richard. "Bernard Kendig and the New Orleans Slave Trade." *Louisiana History,* XXIII (Spring, 1982), 159–78.

Taylor, Joe Gray. "The Foreign Slave Trade in Louisiana After 1808." *Louisiana History,* I (Winter, 1960), 36–45.

———. "New Orleans and Reconstruction." *Louisiana History,* IX (Summer, 1968), 189–208.

———. "Slavery in Louisiana During the Civil War." *Louisiana History,* VII (Winter, 1967), 27–33.

Touchstone, Blake D. "Voodoo in New Orleans." *Louisiana History,* XIII (Fall, 1972), 371–87.

Tregle, Joseph J. "Early New Orleans Society: A Reappraisal." *Journal of Southern History,* XVIII (February, 1952), 20–36.

Tushnet, Mark. "The American Law of Slavery, 1810–1860: A Study in the Persistence of Legal Autonomy." *Law and Society Review,* X (Fall, 1975), 119–84.

Voss, Louis. "Sally Miller, the German Slave." *Louisiana Historical Quarterly,* XII (July, 1929), 447–60.

Wall, Bennett H. "An Epitaph for Slavery." *Louisiana History,* XVI (Summer, 1975), 229–56.

Webre, Stephen. "The Problem of Indian Slavery in Spanish Louisiana, 1769–1803." *Louisiana History,* XXV (Spring, 1984), 117–35.

Wells, Tom Henderson. "Moving a Plantation to Louisiana." *Louisiana Studies,* VI (Fall, 1967), 279–89.

Wiecek, William M. "*Somerset:* Lord Mansfield and the Legitimacy of Slavery in the Anglo-American World." *University of Chicago Law Review,* XLII (Fall, 1974), 86–146.

Wiethoff, William E. "The Logic and Rhetoric of Slavery in Early Louisiana Civil Law Reports." *Legal Studies Forum,* XII (1988), 441–57.

Wigmore, John J. "Louisiana: The Story of Its Legal System." *Southern Law Quarterly,* I (January, 1916), 1–15.

Williams, E. Russ, ed. "Slave Patrol Ordinances of St. Tammany Parish, Louisiana, 1835–1838." *Louisiana History,* XIII (Fall, 1972), 399–412.

Wish, Harvey. "The Slave Insurrection Panic of 1856." *Journal of Southern History,* V (May, 1939), 206–22.

Witten, David O. "Medical Care of Slaves: Louisiana Sugar Region and South Carolina Rice District." *Southern Studies,* XVI (Summer, 1977), 153–80.

Wooster, Ralph A. "The Structure of Government in Late Antebellum Louisiana." *Louisiana Studies,* XIV (Winter, 1975), 361–78.

DISSERTATIONS AND THESES

Bringier, Gladys Stella. "Transition from Slave to Free Labor in Louisiana After the Civil War." M.A. thesis, Tulane University, 1977.

Coulon, Earl C. "Attitude of New Orleans Newspapers Toward Slavery and Secession." M.A. thesis, Tulane University, 1939.

Dubroca, Isabelle. "A Study of Negro Emancipation in Louisiana." M.A. thesis, Tulane University, 1924.

Everett, Donald Edward. "Free Persons of Color in New Orleans, 1803–1865." Ph.D. dissertation, Tulane University, 1954.

———. "Legislation Concerning Free People of Color in Orleans Parish, 1840–1860." M.A. thesis, Tulane University, 1952.

Foote, L. B. "Bibliography of the Official Publications of Louisiana, 1803–1934." M.A. thesis, University of Illinois, 1938.

Hepler, Morris K. "Negroes and Crime in New Orleans, 1850–1861." M.A. thesis, Tulane University, 1960.

Highsmith, William Edward. "Louisiana During Reconstruction." Ph.D. dissertation, Louisiana State University, 1953.

Howington, Arthur Fletcher. "The Treatment of Slaves and Free Blacks in the State and Local Courts of Tennessee." Ph.D. dissertation, Vanderbilt University, 1982.

Kerr, Derek. "Petty Felony, Slave Defiance, and Frontier Villainy: Crime and Criminal Justice in Spanish Louisiana, 1770–1803." Ph.D. dissertation, Tulane University, 1984.

Kramer, Ethel Elizabeth. "Slavery Legislation in Antebellum Louisiana, 1803–1860." M.A. thesis, Louisiana State University, 1944.

Luke, Josephine. "From Slavery to Freedom in Louisiana." M.A. thesis, Tulane University, 1939.

McDowan, Emma Weaver. "Free People of Color in New Orleans, 1803–1860." M.A. thesis, Tulane University, 1939.

Martin, Jerrye Louise Baehr. "New Orleans Slavery, 1840–1860: Testing the Wade Theory." M.A. thesis, Tulane University, 1972.

Miceli, Mary Veronica. "The Influence of the Roman Catholic Church on Slavery in Colonial Louisiana Under French Domination, 1718–1763." Ph.D. dissertation, Tulane University, 1979.

Mills, Wynona Gillmore. "James Govan Taliaferro (1798–1876): Louisiana Unionist and Scalawag." M.A. thesis, Louisana State University, 1968.

Nuhrah, Arthur G. "John McDonogh: Liberal Slaveholder." M.A. thesis, Tulane University, 1947.

Poole, William J., Jr. "The *Creole* Case." M.A. thesis, University of New Orleans, 1970.

Puckett, Erastus Paul. "The Free Negro in New Orleans in 1860." M.A. thesis, Tulane University, 1907.

Rankin, David C. "The Forgotten People: Free People of Color in New Orleans, 1850–1870." Ph.D. dissertation, Johns Hopkins University, 1976.

Reddick, Lawrence D. "The Negro in the New Orleans Press, 1850–1860: A Study of Attitudes and Propaganda." Ph.D. dissertation, University of Chicago, 1939.

Robert, Mary Elizabeth Phillips. "The Background of Negro Disenfranchisement in Louisiana." M.A. thesis, Tulane University, 1932.

Russell, Mary F. P. "The Life of Julien Poydras." M.A. thesis, Louisiana State University, 1940.

Schafer, Judith Kelleher. "The Long Arm of the Law: Slavery and the Supreme Court in Antebellum Louisiana, 1809–1862." Ph.D. dissertation, Tulane University, 1985.

Scott, Sterling Charles. "Aspects of the Liberian Colonization Movement in Louisiana." M.A. thesis, Tulane University, 1953.

Sherman, Honorine Ann. "The Freedmen's Bureau in Louisiana." M.A. thesis, Tulane University, 1936.

Stahl, Annie Lee West. "The Free Negro in Antebellum Louisiana."M.A. thesis, Louisiana State University, 1934.

Tregle, Joseph G., Jr. "Louisiana in the Age of Jackson: A Study in Ego-Politics." Ph.D. dissertation, University of Pennsylvania, 1954.

Wegener, Vernon A. "Negro Slavery in New Orleans." M.A. thesis, Tulane University, 1935.

Wetta, Francis Joseph. "The Louisiana Scalawags." Ph.D. dissertation, Louisiana State University, 1977.

White, Howard Ashley. "The Freedmen's Bureau in New Orleans." Ph.D. dissertation, Tulane University, 1956.

———. "The Freedmen's Bureau in New Orleans." M.A. thesis, Tulane University, 1950.

Woessner, Herman C. III. "New Orleans, 1840–1860: A Study in Urban Slavery." M.A. thesis, Louisiana State University, 1967.

BOOKS

Aptheker, Herbert. *American Slave Revolts*. New York, 1943.

Arnold, Morris S. *Unequal Laws unto a Savage Race: European Legal Traditions in Arkansas, 1686–1836*. Fayetteville, 1985.

Bancroft, Frederic. *Slave Trading in the Old South*. Baltimore, 1931.

Bartlett, Vernon. *Struggle for Africa*. New York, 1953.

Baudier, Roger. *The Catholic Church in Louisiana*. New Orleans, 1939.

Benjamin, Judah P. "Negroes as Property." In *The Louisiana Book: Selections from the Literature of the State,* edited by Thomas McCaleb. New Orleans, 1894.

Berlin, Ira. *Slaves Without Masters: The Free Negro in the Antebellum South*. New York, 1974.

Berry, Mary Frances, and John W. Blassingame. *Long Memory: The Black Experience in America*. New York, 1982.

Bibb, Henry. *Narrative of the Life and Adventures of Henry Bibb, an American Slave*. New York, 1849.

Billings, Edward C. *The Struggle Between the Civilization of Slavery and That of Freedom, Recently and Now Going On in Louisiana*. Northampton, Mass., 1873.

Billings, Warren M., ed. *The Historic Rules of the Supreme Court of Louisiana, 1813–1879*. Lafayette, La., 1985.

Blassingame, John W. *Black New Orleans, 1860–1880*. Chicago, 1973.

———. *The Slave Community: Plantation Life in the Antebellum South*. New York, 1979.

Bodenhamer, David J., and James W. Ely, Jr., eds. *Ambivalent Legacy: A Legal History of the South*. Jackson, Miss., 1984.

Boles, John B. *Black Southerners, 1619–1869*. Lexington, Ky., 1983.

Buckland, W. W. *The Roman Law of Slavery: The Condition of the Slave in Private Law from Augustus to Justinian*. Cambridge, Eng., 1908.

Bullard, Henry A. *Discourse on the Life and Character of the Honorable François-Xavier Martin, Late Senior Judge of the Supreme Court*. New Orleans, 1847.

Campbell, Randolph B. *An Empire for Slavery: The Peculiar Institution in Texas*. Baton Rouge, 1989.

Campbell, Stanley W. *The Slave Catchers: Enforcement of the Fugitive Slave Law, 1850–1860*. Chapel Hill, 1968.

Carleton, R. L. *Local Government and Administration in Louisiana*. Baton Rouge, 1935.

Carter, Hodding, ed. *The Past as Prelude: New Orleans, 1718–1968*. New Orleans, 1968.

Castellanos, Henry C. *New Orleans as It Was*. New Orleans, 1895.

Catterall, Helen T. *Judicial Cases Concerning American Slavery and the Negro*. 5 vols. 1926; rpr. New York, 1968.

Chamier, Daniel. *A Manual of Roman Law*. New York, 1893.

Chase, John Churchill. *Frenchmen, Desire, Good Children, and Other Streets of New Orleans*. New Orleans, 1949.

Clark, John G. *New Orleans, 1718–1812: An Economic History*. Baton Rouge, 1970.

Cobb, Thomas. *An Inquiry into the Law of Negro Slavery in the United States of America*. Philadelphia, 1858.

Cover, Robert. *Justice Accused*. New Haven, 1976.

Crete, Lillian. *Daily Life in Louisiana, 1815–1830*. Translated by Patrick Gregory. Baton Rouge, 1981.

Cross, K. A. *Pleading in Courts of Ordinary Jurisdiction*. New Orleans, 1885.

Cummins, Light Townsend, and Glen Jeansonne, eds. *A Guide to the History of Louisiana*. Westport, Conn., 1982.

Dargo, George. *Jefferson's Louisiana: Politics and the Clash of Legal Traditions*. Cambridge, Mass., 1975.

Dart, Henry Plauché. *The Colonial Legal Systems of Arkansas, Louisiana, and Texas*. New Orleans, 1926.

———. *The Legal Institution of Louisiana*. Baton Rouge, 1919.

———. *The Sources of the Civil Code in Louisiana*. New Orleans, 1911.

Davis, David Brion. *The Problem of Slavery in the Age of Revolution, 1770–1823*. Ithaca, N.Y., 1975.

———. *The Problem of Slavery in Western Culture*. Ithaca, N.Y., 1966.

———. *Slavery and Human Progress*. New York, 1984.

Davis, Edwin Adams, ed. *Plantation Life in the Florida Parishes of Louisiana, 1836–1846*. New York, 1967.

Davis, Ronald L. F. *Good and Faithful Labor: From Slavery to Sharecropping in the Natchez District, 1860–1890*. New York, 1982.

De Conde, Alexander. *This Affair of Louisiana*. Baton Rouge, 1976.

Degler, Carl N. *Neither Black nor White: Slavery and Race Relations in Brazil and the United States*. New York, 1971.

———. *The Other South: Southern Dissenters in the Nineteenth Century*. New York, 1973.

Domat, Jean. *Les Lois civiles dans leur ordre naturel*. 5 vols. Paris, 1689–97.

Du Bois, W. E. B. *The Suppression of the African Slave Trade to the United States of America, 1638–1870*. New York, 1896.

Eaton, Clement. *The Growth of Southern Civilization, 1790–1860*. New York, 1961.

Elkins, Stanley M. *Slavery: A Problem in American Institutional and Intellectual Life*. Chicago, 1976.

Esmein, A. *A History of Continental Criminal Procedure*. New York, 1968.

Faust, Drew Gilpin, ed. *The Ideology of Slavery: Proslavery Thought in the Antebellum South, 1830–1860*. Baton Rouge, 1981.

Fearn, Francis, ed. *Diary of a Refugee*. New York, 1910.

Fehrenbacher, Don E. *Slavery, Law, and Politics: The Dred Scott Case in Historical Perspective*, New York, 1981.

Ficklen, John Rose. *History and Civil Government of Louisiana*. Chicago, 1901.

———. *History of Reconstruction in Louisiana (Through 1868)*. Baltimore, 1910.

Finkelman, Paul. *An Imperfect Union: Slavery, Federalism, and Comity*. Chapel Hill, 1981.

———. *The Law of Freedom and Bondage: A Casebook*. New York, 1986.

Fogel, Robert W., and Stanley L. Engerman. *Time on the Cross: The Economics of American Negro Slavery*. Boston, 1974.

Foner, Laura, and Eugene D. Genovese, eds. *Slavery in the New World: A Reader in Comparative History*. Englewood Cliffs, N.J., 1969.

Fortier, Alcée. *A History of Louisiana*. 4 vols. New York, 1904.
Fortier, James J. A., ed. *Carpet-Bag Misrule in Louisiana; The Tragedy of the Reconstruction Era Following the War Between the States: Louisiana's Part in Maintaining White Supremacy in the South*. New Orleans, 1938.
Fossier, Albert A. *New Orleans, the Glamour Period, 1800–1840*. New Orleans, 1957.
Franklin, John Hope. *From Slavery to Freedom: A History of Negro Americans*. New York, 1980.
Friedman, Lawrence M. *American Law*. New York, 1984.
———. *A History of American Law*. New York, 1973.
Garraty, John A. *The American Nation: A History of the United States to 1877*. New York, 1983.
Gayarré, Charles. *History of Louisiana*. 4 vols. New Orleans, 1903.
Genovese, Eugene D. *Roll, Jordan, Roll: The World the Slaves Made*. New York, 1976.
Goodell, William. *The American Slave Code in Theory and Practice*. New York, 1853.
Grace, Albert L. *The Heart of the Sugar Bowl: The Story of Iberville*. Plaquemine, La., 1946.
Greenleaf, Simon. *Treatise on the Law of Evidence*. Boston, 1842.
Gutman, Herbert G. *The Black Family in Slavery and Freedom, 1750–1925*. New York, 1976.
Haas, Edward F., Jr., ed. *Louisiana's Legal Heritage*. Pensacola, Fla., 1983.
Hart, W. O. *Fragments of Louisiana Jurisprudence: Twelve Lectures Delivered to the Students of the Law Department of Louisiana State University*. Baton Rouge, 1908.
Herman, Shael, David Combe, and Thomas E. Carbonneau. *The Louisiana Civil Code: A Humanistic Appraisal*. New Orleans, 1981.
Hindus, Michael Stephen. *Prison and Plantation: Crime, Justice, and Authority in Massachusetts and South Carolina, 1767–1878*. Chapel Hill, 1980.
Hollander, Barnett. *Slavery in America: Its Legal History*. New York, 1964.
Horwitz, Morton. *The Transformation of American Law, 1780–1860*. Cambridge, Mass., 1977.
Howard, Warren S. *American Slavers and the Federal Law, 1837–1862*. Berkeley, 1963.
Hurd, John C. *The Law of Freedom and Bondage in the United States*. 2 vols. Boston, 1858; New York, 1862.
Hyman, Harold M., and William M. Wiecek. *Equal Justice Under Law: Constitutional Development, 1835–1875*. New York, 1982.

Johnson, Michael P., and James L. Roark. *Black Masters: A Free Family of Color in the Old South*. New York, 1984.

Johnston, James. *Race Relations in Virginia and Miscegenation in the South, 1776–1860*. Amherst, 1970.

Jordan, Winthrop. *White over Black: American Attitudes Toward the Negro, 1550–1812*. Chapel Hill, 1968.

Kendall, John Smith. *History of New Orleans*. 3 vols. Chicago, 1922.

Kilbourne, Richard Holcomb, Jr. *A History of the Louisiana Civil Code: The Formative Years, 1803–1839*. Baton Rouge, 1987.

Klein, Herbert S. *Slavery in the Americas: A Comparative Study of Virginia and Cuba*. Chicago, 1967.

Lane, Ann J. *The Debate over Slavery: Stanley Elkins and His Critics*. Urbana, Ill., 1971.

Lang, Meredith. *Defenders of the Faith: The High Court of Mississippi, 1817–1875*. Jackson, Miss., 1977.

Latrobe, Benjamin H. *Impressions Respecting New Orleans: Diary and Sketches, 1818–1820*. Edited by Samuel Wilson, Jr. New York, 1951.

Laussat, Pierre Clément de. *Memoirs of My Life*. Edited by Robert D. Bush. Translated by Agnes-Josephine Pastwa. Baton Rouge, 1978.

Leonard, John Edwards. *A Digest of the Decisions of the Supreme Court of the United States in Louisiana*. New Orleans, 1875.

Levine, Lawrence W. *Black Culture and Black Consciousness: Afro-American Folk Thought from Slavery to Freedom*. New York, 1977.

Lieber, Francis. *Legal and Political Hermeneutics; or, Principles of Interpretation and Construction in Law and Politics with Remarks on Precedents and Authorities*. Boston, 1838.

Livermore, Samuel. *Dissertations of the Questions Which Arise from the Contrariety of the Positive Laws of Different States and Nations*. New Orleans, 1828.

Lloyd, Christopher. *The Navy and the Slave Trade: The Suppression of the African Slave Trade in the Nineteenth Century*. New York, 1949.

Lonn, Ella. *Reconstruction in Louisiana After 1868*. New York, 1918.

McCrary, Peyton. *Abraham Lincoln and Reconstruction: The Louisiana Experiment*. Princeton, 1978.

MacDonald, Robert R., John R. Kemp, and Edward F. Haas, eds. *Louisiana's Black Heritage*. New Orleans, 1979.

McKitrick, Eric L., ed. *Slavery Defended: The Views of the Old South*. Englewood Cliffs, N.J., 1963.

Martin, François-Xavier. *The History of Louisiana, from the Earliest Period.* 2 vols. New Orleans, 1827–29.

Martin, Gilbert E., Sr. *Creoles: A Shattered Nation.* Detroit, 1981.

Menn, John Karl. *Large Slaveholders of Louisiana in 1860.* New Orleans, 1964.

Miller, Ben Robertson. *The Louisiana Judiciary.* Baton Rouge, 1932.

Mills, Gary B. *The Forgotten People: Cane River's Creoles of Color.* Baton Rouge, 1977.

Morgan, Edmund S. *American Slavery, American Freedom: The Ordeal of Colonial Virginia.* New York, 1975.

Mullin, Gerald W. *Flight and Rebellion: Slave Resistance in Eighteenth-Century Virginia.* New York, 1972.

Nicholas, Barry. *An Introduction to Roman Law.* New York, 1962.

Northup, Solomon. *Twelve Years a Slave.* Edited by Sue Eakin and Joseph Logsdon. Baton Rouge, 1968.

Oakes, James. *The Ruling Race: A History of American Slaveholders.* New York, 1982.

Olmsted, Frederick Law. *The Cotton Kingdom: A Traveller's Observations on Cotton and Slavery in the American Slave States.* Edited by Arthur M. Schlesinger. New York, 1953.

O'Neill, Charles Edwards, *et al. Louisiana: A History.* Edited by Bennett H. Wall. Arlington Heights, Ill., 1984.

Owens, Leslie Howard. *This Species of Property: Slave Life and Culture in the Old South.* New York, 1976.

Phillips, Ulrich B. *American Negro Slavery: A Survey of the Supply, Employment, and Control of Negro Labor as Determined by the Plantation Regime.* Baton Rouge, 1966.

Planiol, Marcel. *Treatise on the Civil Law.* 2 vols. Baton Rouge, 1939.

Pothier, Robert Joseph. *Oeuvres de Poithier.* 28 vols. Paris, 1773–78.

Postell, William D. *The Health of Slaves on Southern Plantations.* Baton Rouge, 1951.

Reinders, Robert C. *End of an Era: New Orleans, 1850–1860.* New Orleans, 1964.

Rightor, Henry. *Standard History of New Orleans.* Chicago, 1900.

Ripley, C. Peter. *Slaves and Freedmen in Civil War Louisiana.* Baton Rouge, 1976.

Robertson, James A., ed. *Louisiana Under the Rule of France, Spain, and the United States, 1785–1807.* 2 vols. Cleveland, 1911.

Rousseve, Charles Barthelemy. *The Negro in Louisiana: Aspects of His History and His Literature*. New Orleans, 1937.

Saunders, Eugene D. *Lectures on the Civil Code of Louisiana*. Edited by Alfred J. Bonomo. New Orleans, 1925.

Savitt, Todd L. *Medicine and Slavery: The Diseases and Health Care of Blacks in Antebellum Virginia*. Urbana, Ill., 1978.

Scarborough, William Kaufman. *The Overseer: Plantation Management in the Old South*. Baton Rouge, 1966.

Sellers, James Benson. *Slavery in Alabama*. University, Ala., 1950.

Semmes, Thomas J. *The Civil Law as Transplanted in Louisiana*. Philadelphia, 1883.

Sitterson, J. Carlyle. *Sugar Country: The Sugar Cane Industry in the South, 1753–1950*. Lexington, Ky., 1953.

Stampp, Kenneth M. *The Peculiar Institution: Slavery in the Antebellum South*. New York, 1956.

Starobin, Robert S. *Industrial Slavery in the Old South*. New York, 1970.

Sterkx, Henry E. *The Free Negro in Antebellum Louisiana*. Rutherford, N.J., 1972.

Story, Joseph. *Commentaries on the Conflict of Laws*. Boston, 1834.

Stroud, George McDowell. *A Sketch of the Laws Relating to Slavery in the Several States of the United States of America*. Philadelphia, 1856.

Sydnor, Charles S. *Slavery in Mississippi*. New York, 1933.

Tannenbaum, Frank. *Slave and Citizen: The Negro in the Americas*. New York, 1946.

Taylor, Joe Gray. *Louisiana: A History*. New York, 1976.

———. *Louisiana Reconstructed, 1863–1877*. Baton Rouge, 1974.

———. *Negro Slavery in Louisiana*. Baton Rouge, 1963.

Tinker, Edward Larocque. *Creole City: Its Past and Its People*. New York, 1953.

Tunnell, Ted. *Crucible of Reconstruction: War, Radicalism, and Race in Louisiana, 1862–1877*. Baton Rouge, 1984.

Tushnet, Mark V. *The American Law of Slavery, 1810–1860: Considerations of Humanity and Interest*. Princeton, N.J., 1981.

Voorhies, Albert. *A Treatise on the Criminal Jurisprudence of Louisiana*. New Orleans, 1860.

Wade, Richard C. *Slavery in the Cities: The South, 1820–1860*. New York, 1964.

Wallach, Kate. *Research in Louisiana Law*. Baton Rouge, 1958, No. 6.

Warmoth, Henry Clay. *War, Politics, and Reconstruction: Stormy Days in Louisiana.* New York, 1930.
Watson, Alan. *Roman Slave Law.* Baltimore, 1987.
———. *Slave Law in the Americas.* Athens, Ga., 1989.
Wigmore, John Henry. *A Treatise on the System of Evidence in Trials at Common Law.* Boston, 1904.
Woods, Frances Jerome. *Marginality and Identity: A Colored Creole Family Through Ten Generations.* Baton Rouge, 1972.
Zainaldin, Jamil S. *Law in Antebellum Society.* New York, 1981.

INDEX